ALSO BY NIKHIL GOYAL

Schools on Trial: How Freedom and Creativity Can
Fix Our Educational Malpractice

LIVE TO SEE
THE DAY

LIVE TO SEE
THE DAY

. . .

COMING OF AGE IN
AMERICAN POVERTY

NIKHIL GOYAL

METROPOLITAN BOOKS

HENRY HOLT AND COMPANY   NEW YORK

Metropolitan Books
Henry Holt and Company
Publishers since 1866
120 Broadway
New York, New York 10271
www.henryholt.com

Metropolitan Books® and m® are registered trademarks of
Macmillan Publishing Group, LLC.

Copyright © 2023 by Nikhil Goyal
All rights reserved.
Distributed in Canada by Raincoast Book Distribution Limited

Library of Congress Cataloging-in-Publication data is available.

ISBN: 9781250850065

Our books may be purchased in bulk for promotional, educational, or business use. Please contact your local bookseller or the Macmillan Corporate and Premium Sales Department at (800) 221-7945, extension 5442, or by e-mail at MacmillanSpecialMarkets@macmillan.com.

First Edition 2023

Designed by Kelly S. Too

Map by Jeffrey L. Ward

Printed in the United States of America

1 3 5 7 9 10 8 6 4 2

To Ryan, Corem, and Giancarlos

Never say never whenever I thought my life was stable
I came home to doors boarded and my life on the doorstep
yet still I said Amen.

—Corem Coreano

CONTENTS

CAST OF MAIN CHARACTERS

RYAN RIVERA
Rayni: mother
Ildefonso: father
George: stepfather
Avry: brother
Julia: half sister
Tino: half brother
Armando: half brother
Bianca: girlfriend and mother of his first son
Yamilet: girlfriend and mother of his second son
Marc: first son
Emilio: grandfather
Laura: grandmother

EMMANUEL/COREM COREANO
Ivette: mother
Ivan: father
Michael: brother
Joaquin: brother
Freddie: boyfriend of Ivette

GIANCARLOS RODRIGUEZ
Marta: mother
Wilfredo: father
Frank: brother
Isabelesse: sister
Luna: grandmother
Vincente: grandfather
Leo: uncle
Jennifer: girlfriend and mother of his son

Note: Some names and identifying details have been changed to protect the individuals' privacy.

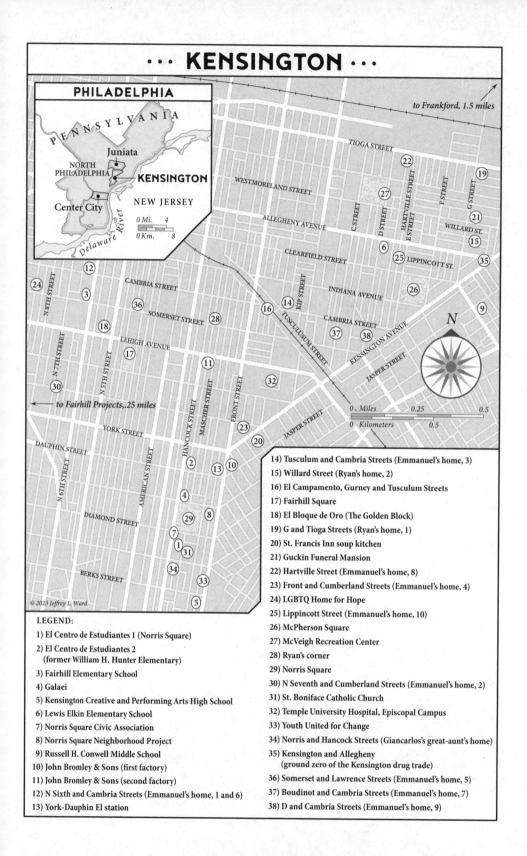

··· KENSINGTON ···

PHILADELPHIA

PENNSYLVANIA

Juniata

NORTH PHILADELPHIA — KENSINGTON

Center City

NEW JERSEY

Delaware River

0 Mi. 4
0 Km. 8

to Frankford, 1.5 miles

TIOGA STREET
WESTMORELAND STREET
ALLEGHENY AVENUE
CLEARFIELD STREET
LIPPINCOTT ST.
INDIANA AVENUE
CAMBRIA STREET
SOMERSET STREET
LEHIGH AVENUE
CAMBRIA STREET
KENSINGTON AVENUE
JASPER STREET
TUSCULUM STREET
KIP STREET
C STREET
D STREET
HARTVILLE STREET
E STREET
F STREET
G STREET
WILLARD ST.

N 8TH STREET
N 7TH STREET
N 5TH STREET
N 6TH STREET
HANCOCK STREET
MASCHER STREET
FRONT STREET
AMERICAN STREET

to Fairhill Projects, .25 miles

YORK STREET
DAUPHIN STREET
DIAMOND STREET
BERKS STREET
JASPER STREET

0 Miles 0.25 0.5
0 Kilometers 0.5

N

© 2023 Jeffrey L. Ward

14) Tusculum and Cambria Streets (Emmanuel's home, 3)
15) Willard Street (Ryan's home, 2)
16) El Campamento, Gurney and Tusculum Streets
17) Fairhill Square
18) El Bloque de Oro (The Golden Block)
19) G and Tioga Streets (Ryan's home, 1)
20) St. Francis Inn soup kitchen
21) Guckin Funeral Mansion
22) Hartville Street (Emmanuel's home, 8)
23) Front and Cumberland Streets (Emmanuel's home, 4)
24) LGBTQ Home for Hope
25) Lippincott Street (Emmanuel's home, 10)
26) McPherson Square
27) McVeigh Recreation Center
28) Ryan's corner
29) Norris Square
30) N Seventh and Cumberland Streets (Emmanuel's home, 2)
31) St. Boniface Catholic Church
32) Temple University Hospital, Episcopal Campus
33) Youth United for Change
34) Norris and Hancock Streets (Giancarlos's great-aunt's home)
35) Kensington and Allegheny
  (ground zero of the Kensington drug trade)
36) Somerset and Lawrence Streets (Emmanuel's home, 5)
37) Boudinot and Cambria Streets (Emmanuel's home, 7)
38) D and Cambria Streets (Emmanuel's home, 9)

LEGEND:
1) El Centro de Estudiantes 1 (Norris Square)
2) El Centro de Estudiantes 2
  (former William H. Hunter Elementary)
3) Fairhill Elementary School
4) Galaei
5) Kensington Creative and Performing Arts High School
6) Lewis Elkin Elementary School
7) Norris Square Civic Association
8) Norris Square Neighborhood Project
9) Russell H. Conwell Middle School
10) John Bromley & Sons (first factory)
11) John Bromley & Sons (second factory)
12) N Sixth and Cambria Streets (Emmanuel's home, 1 and 6)
13) York-Dauphin El station

LIVE TO SEE
THE DAY

Introduction

Ryan almost made it to spring break without a hitch. On the Friday before the break, Ryan and his friend Andres decided to ditch class and hang out in the hallways on the third floor of Grover Washington Jr., an underachieving public middle school, named after the famed jazz saxophonist, in Olney, a working-class neighborhood in North Philadelphia. Built less than a decade earlier, the building had a baby blue exterior with sunny yellow accents; it was in better condition than many of the decrepit school buildings in the city.[1] Ryan was twelve years old, a month shy of becoming a teenager. As the two seventh graders zoomed down the stairs, they collided with three boys who were also cutting class. This chance meeting provided the perfect opportunity for Caleb, Luis, and Javier to derive some pleasure from intimidating the two denizens of the bottom of the social food chain. Caleb had spied Andres getting high before school and prodded him for his lighter. Andres dug it out of his pocket, expecting to light a cigarette or give the lighter up. But Caleb challenged him to set some paper on fire. Andres immediately complied, ripping a few sheets from his notebook and setting them alight. When the pages, curling with flame, landed on the floor, Andres snuffed them out with his sneaker. Then Caleb upped the ante, proposing they light a trash can on fire.

Now down on the first floor near the atrium, Andres tore another sheet of paper from his notebook, lit it, and then tossed it into the can, where it quickly ignited. Ryan threw in a second burning sheet. The boys were riled up with their amateur pyrotechnics until Ryan had a sudden change of heart. He lowered his arm into the can and put out the flame with the garbage bag lining the can. His conscience had temporarily kicked in. He knew that fire was no laughing matter. Nearly seven years earlier, Ryan, his twin brother, Avry, and their mother had nearly perished when their row home caught fire. When Ryan and Andres caught up with the other boys, who had wandered away from the trash can, they were roundly mocked: "Why y'all do that?" "You scared?" Today was not the day that Ryan could muster the courage to stand up to the bullies, even as he understood the danger of the fire spreading. So he let Andres light another paper and leave it burning.

* * *

As the bustling 47 uptown bus leaves Society Hill, tree-lined cobble-stone streets give way to Kensington's blocks of aging row homes broken up by derelict shells of factories, copious needle-strewn lots, and papi stores. Babies born in North Philadelphia's Kensington neighborhood are expected to live to seventy-one, seventeen years less than the babies no more than four miles away in Society Hill—a life span on par with countries such as Egypt, Bhutan, and Uzbekistan.[2] Philadelphia is the poorest large city in the nation, a hypersegregated metropolis where one third of children are "smother[ed] in an airtight cage of poverty" in the most affluent land on the planet, as Martin Luther King Jr. once put it.[3] These conditions may not be what come to mind when people think of Philadelphia, known as the birthplace of the American democratic experiment, as the stage of the classic *Rocky* films, and the home of mouth-melting cheesesteaks at Reading Terminal Market.

Kensington is poor and working-class, predominantly Latino and African American, and suffers from toxic pollution while housing a billion-dollar open-air drug market; Society Hill is rich, mostly white, leafy, with eye-popping real estate values.[4] In one neighborhood, children attend underfunded, overcrowded schools where they drink from lead-laced water fountains, play in gymnasiums caked with asbestos, and fall ill in classrooms with no heating. In the other, the children study in modern, safe schools that prepare them for the Ivy League with small class sizes, well-paid teachers, counselors, psychologists, and librarians. In Kensington, children live in broken-down housing with mold and mice droppings but without hot water and endure sudden evictions with less than twenty-four hours to pack up their clothes, toys, and belongings and move into a homeless shelter or a relative's dwelling. In Society Hill, they live in decent, secure housing with running water, heat, air-conditioning, and high-speed broadband.

Live to See the Day follows three Puerto Rican children growing up in North Philadelphia, a city that embodies the awesome inequalities at the heart of the American body politic. Across the nation, too many are "denied the greater part of what the very lowest standards of today call the necessities of life," as President Franklin Delano Roosevelt described economic deprivation in his second inaugural address.[5] Today nearly forty million languish in poverty, more than half of the population lives paycheck to paycheck, tens of thousands die prematurely due to lack of health care each year, and millions are housing insecure.[6]

This was not our destiny. Amid the wreckage of the Great Depression, Roosevelt's New Deal put starving and jobless Americans to work building roads, parks, schools, libraries, post offices, and other infrastructure, established social insurance for the elderly, unemployed, and single mothers, and provided collective bargaining rights to workers. He restored their faith in the power of democratic government to relieve suffering and protect against the accidents of life. A few decades later, Lyndon B. Johnson's Great Society renewed this vision when he razed the Jim Crow caste system, guaranteed health care to seniors and the poor, and expanded social security. Wages were climbing, trade unions were formidable, and income and wealth inequality had sunk to historic lows. Straggling decades behind their Western European allies, Americans were finally laying the planks of a multiracial social democracy. But over the past half century, the New Deal order ruptured, and the country reversed course with the gutting of public goods and the social safety net, the hegemony of market fundamentalism, and the rise of hyper-incarceration. One of the seminal moments in this shift was the passage of welfare reform legislation in 1996; for the first time in decades, low-income families were no longer entitled to cash assistance to stave off hardship.[7] Today, the level of American child poverty is one of the highest in the industrialized world. In 2019, a fifth of children in the United States were poor compared to a mere 4 to 5 percent of children in Finland and Denmark.[8]

Ryan Rivera, Emmanuel Coreano, and Giancarlos Rodriguez—the three children at the heart of *Live to See the Day*—came of age in the new neoliberal era. With everything stacked against them, they strive to do the impossible: to jettison the scarlet letter of "dropout" and become high school graduates. Each would enroll in an alternative "last chance" high school called El Centro de Estudiantes. Although they overlapped at times, they didn't cross paths or know each other well. The book also follows their mothers, Rayni, Ivette, and Marta, in the process tracing the history of Puerto Rican migration, deindustrialization, the war on drugs, and the end of welfare as we know it, revealing how American society punishes low-income single parents and makes it almost impossible to raise children with their self-worth intact. Together, they chronicle a tale of a metropolis and the nation from the bottom up.

The landscape for these children is one of cash-starved public schools that blunt curiosity with humdrum pedagogies and criminalize and push out students through the use of metal detectors, school resource officers, repressive discipline, and rigid administrators. Their families struggle for dignity amid crushing economic insecurity, chronic joblessness, crime, hunger, an opioid epidemic, domestic violence, and the habitual peril of incarceration. Their story is one of survival, where eighteenth-birthday celebrations are not rites of passage but miracles. It is a story of a social contract in tatters.

* * *

Before long, a cafeteria worker discovered the burning trash can and extinguished the blaze. A crowd of curious students had quickly formed, but by then, the boys had fled the scene. Everyone thought the surveillance cameras were busted, but Ryan wasn't taking any chances. He bolted to his locker and put on a blue button-down to make himself harder to identify. It was the kind of move he'd picked up from his obsession with crime shows and movies such as *The Wire*, *The Sopranos*, and *Scarface*.

Food fights had a habit of flaring up in the cafeteria, so at lunchtime, the students had to wait in the adjacent auditorium in rows, each row escorted in at staggered intervals. Ryan's row was called up, but before he could enter the cafeteria, he saw Javier and another student accompanied by the principal, the dean, and the school resource officer. The dean approached him. "Mr. Rivera, can you come with us?" He thought, *Oh shit. They got me.* It was a familiar feeling. A wrecking ball in the classroom, he had racked up more than twenty disciplinary slips at Grover Washington, so he knew the drill. A call home followed by his vexed mother picking him up, capped with some punishment. Only this time would be much worse.

The Fireman

Ryan, Javier, and two African American boys who had played no part in the fire incident were hauled into an office, where two resource officers, who were assigned to the school by law enforcement, were watching the security monitors. They were seated around a conference table. The principal, Jordan Thompson, directed Officer Taylor Bailey to roll a videotape. The boys were shown some grainy surveillance footage of the minutes before the fire. As the tape progressed, Ryan's lean five-foot frame slumped in his chair. *As soon as I get home*, he thought, *my mom's going to beat my ass.*

Thompson asked to pause the tape. "Who's this kid with the white shirt?" Silence. Ryan's and Andres's faces weren't recognizable on the tape, but the administrators matched their complexions and hauled in Ryan and Javier. They were among the few Puerto Ricans in the school and were considered troublemakers by the administration.

Bailey and the dean, Christopher Anderson, towered over the four boys. Thompson, fatherly at first, now turned threatening: "I hope you guys know that we already called the police, and y'all are going to jail." The prospect of getting locked up had never crossed Ryan's mind. It was just a stupid prank. But Thompson kept hounding them, and after fifteen minutes Ryan was trembling and on the verge of tears. He had grown claustrophobic in the cramped room. As a boy, he had been locked in bedroom closets by an older cousin when they visited their grandmother's house. He still had nightmares of dying in his sleep and awakening in a tightly shut coffin from which he couldn't escape.

Desperate to conclude the ordeal, he finally stood up and pushed his chair back. "I'm the kid with the white T-shirt. I'm right here." He unbuttoned his blue shirt to show them. He was sure Thompson was bluffing about calling the police.

"Who is the kid next to you?" Thompson asked. Ryan kept mum for a while but eventually caved to repeated interrogation. "It was Andres!" he blurted out. The other boys shot him dirty looks. He had violated the most basic rule: never snitch. Andres wasn't on the administration's radar. He was a mostly rule-abiding student and had kept a low profile at Grover Washington. Now Anderson brought him in.

Up until two officers from the Philadelphia Police Department walked in the door, Ryan still had hope that he would worm his way out of this mess with no more than the usual consequences. The school officials showed the police the tape, and Ryan and Andres admitted their part in the fire. Javier was suspended for three days for his presence at the scene while the two African American boys were dismissed. Had it really been necessary to involve the police? No one had been hurt. Surely the school administrators could have handled the situation internally? But they had made their fateful decision, and there was no turning back. They had washed their hands of the problem, even as they knew what the criminal justice system did to boys who looked like Ryan and Andres.

Anderson scanned Ryan's socks—purple with Tinker Bell patterns, borrowed from his mother. "They're going to love those socks in the Youth Study Center," he taunted, referring to the city's juvenile detention center. Reality finally started to sink in. Ryan's mother had warned him once that if he ever got arrested, she wouldn't come to pick him up. He knew his mother didn't make idle threats, so when the officers said his mother could retrieve him at the station, he started spiraling. "Y'all don't get it; my mom already told me that she's not coming to get me," he protested. The officers weren't interested. They handcuffed Andres and Ryan and paraded them through the building to their lockers. When Ryan started showing signs of resistance, one of the police, Officer James King, grabbed fistfuls of his collar and pants to keep him in line.

Kids pressed their faces to the narrow windows in the classroom doors to catch a glimpse of the duo's walk of shame. A few of them darted into the hallway only for their teachers to corral them inside. "Ryan's getting locked up," they singsonged. *He was the man.* But a cocky swagger masked the fact that he was actually scared witless. He had watched countless arrests in his neighborhood, but this was the first time he was on the other end. This was real. With no playbook to ease his panic, a torrent of questions filled his mind, each escalating in severity: *Will I be allowed to return to Grover Washington? How long will they keep me in custody? When am I going to see my mom again? Will someone try to rape me in jail?* Ryan no longer felt autonomy over his body.

On the way downstairs, they passed the stairwell where Andres had first lit up the scraps of paper. Ryan stopped and spun around to glare at Anderson. "Can you stop dragging my fucking hoodie on the floor?"

"Watch your mouth," Officer King countered. "Don't talk to him like that."

"Can't you see he's dragging my shit on the floor?" Ryan snapped.

Anderson told him to shut it and keep walking. Only days earlier, Ryan had written in a short essay, "Next week will be spring break I really hope it is fun for me and my family This is so because we haven't done anything fun in a long time." Near the front entrance, Ryan's gym teacher, who was fond of him, witnessed the grim scene as he was heading out of the gymnasium. He shook his head in disappointment.

* * *

SINCE ELEMENTARY SCHOOL, Ryan's teachers had repeatedly called his mother to complain about his antics. Ryan interrupted instruction, refused to do work or obey rules, constantly got out of his seat, threw chairs, flipped tables, took ill-timed naps, kicked walls, slammed doors, and ridiculed other students. He had endless energy and desired only to run around, play, and dish out wisecracks. Rayni, a Puerto Rican–Nicaraguan woman with long straight black hair and light skin, couldn't believe the shenanigans Ryan got up to at school. At home, he was largely well behaved. He said his prayers. He washed the dishes. He went to bed on time. She thought he was two-faced: Dr. Jekyll at home and Mr. Hyde at school. Suspensions piled up. His disciplinary woes came at the expense of his academic performance. He scored in the lowest brackets on the annual state standardized tests and chalked up dozens of absences.

School administrators initially ignored Rayni's attempts to obtain a psychological evaluation for Ryan. Developing an Individualized Education Program and providing high-quality special education was not cheap, requiring sums of money that the federal government consistently failed to appropriate. The lack of funds for special education created a decades-long crisis that persisted in chronically money-starved school districts like Philadelphia.[1]

Frustrated by the runaround, Rayni had confronted the principal at James R. Lowell Elementary School. "Do you think I'm here because I want to collect a check for my son? Do you really think I want to label my child?" Her request was finally granted. If Ryan hadn't had a mother who was savvy enough to soldier through a byzantine bureaucracy until she was satisfied, would anyone have looked out for him? Ryan was given a diagnosis of Attention Deficit/Hyperactivity Disorder and Oppositional Defiant Disorder. Further testing placed his verbal and nonverbal reasoning skills in the average range. It wasn't easy getting him through the arduous examination. "He proved to be impulsive, manipulative, oppositional, and even somewhat sassy, mimicking the examiner," noted the report. "However, he sat for almost three hours and with firm but kind redirection, completed the testing."

The antidote was Ritalin—the typical treatment for restive boys in the city. Rayni was happy to report that the medication helped to check some of his impulsive behavior, but Ryan wasn't on the same page. The drug gave him heart palpitations and made him feel lethargic. Some mornings he would lodge the pill in his cheek and spit it into the trash when his mother wasn't looking.

This was the simple and convenient solution: to drug Ryan in order to fix his apparent psychological defects. Perhaps it wasn't that Ryan was ill-suited for school but that school was ill-suited for him; repressive schooling had suppressed and punished his natural proclivity for play and exploration by forcing him to sit at a desk, shut up, and raise his hand for permission to speak and use the bathroom.[2] Submitting to a rigid authority for seven hours a day was an affront to Ryan's very being, and Ritalin was unable to resolve that.

A few blocks from their one-bedroom apartment on Fifth Street in Olney, Lowell was Ryan and Avry's fifth school in less than three years—economic and housing instability forced the family to move often. As Philadelphia's population swelled during the early twentieth century, architect Henry deCourcy Richards designed dozens of public schools in the city, including Lowell, which was named after the poet and abolitionist. Built between 1913 and 1914, it was a three-story concrete edifice designed in the Classical Revival style with brick walls, terra-cotta and granite trimmings, and seventeen classrooms.[3] The rooms were old and dreary. Students screamed and jumped on their desks at the sighting of rats and mice. The water in the fountains tasted awful, especially during the warm months of the year. Building reports indicated lead in the drinking water and the presence of lead paint, asbestos, and an assortment of asthma triggers.[4]

The best parts of Ryan's day were gym and recess. Like most elementary schools in the city, Lowell didn't have a playground, so the kids chased each other and played dodgeball on the cracked concrete parking lot.[5] Ryan and Avry talked in the hallways and ate lunch together. They found school meals less than appealing: packaged mini-pancakes and French toast sticks for breakfast and lukewarm pizza, mac and cheese, chicken nuggets, and tater tots in plastic boxes for lunch.

Ryan's teachers at Lowell talked up Grover Washington as he and his classmates prepared to transition to middle school. Unlike Lowell's decaying carcass, the middle school's building was only a few years old. They would make new friends and have new teachers. They were moving into the next phase of their lives. But when the fourth-grade class toured Grover Washington, Ryan was not allowed to attend. In what was his final suspension, he sat in a narrow, dim room next to the classmate he had earlier smacked with a book. Lowell was finished with him. When he went back there years later, his old gym teacher recalled, "When he was here, he *ran* this school."

In Ryan's mind, Grover Washington would be his fresh start. He would leave his old larks behind and buckle down on his education. Fifth grade initially proceeded according to plan. He loved having a locker and transitioning from class to class. He felt grown up. He also developed a passion for the drums, something he had wanted to learn for years. At Lowell, he had attended a performance of the school band and was awed by its talents. When he asked the music teacher if he could try an instrument, he curtly replied, "No. You don't have what it takes." The teacher had heard of Ryan's less-than-stellar reputation.

The new school year started well, but as time went on, the monotony of the traditional academic classes paled in comparison to the thrill of roaming the hallways, and it became too tempting for Ryan to resist. "Hallways all days," as he described it. Ryan and some other students would press up against the windows in the classroom doors and urge their friends to join their escapades. One of their favorite activities was drawing graffiti using fat Sharpie markers they stole from the art room. To build up his stature in the graffiti crew, Ryan's artwork needed to be visible around the school. Inspired by *Marc Eckō's Getting Up: Contents Under Pressure* video game, he started defacing walls and doors with "SAVE was here," "SAVE the World," "SAVE Your Ass," and "SAVE 2008."

He made sure to throw out the markers when he was finished and meticulously scrub smudges from his hands to wipe away the evidence. But he got in trouble for violating other rules, particularly the "Prohibition of Disruption of School" and "Prohibition of Fighting." Some comments on his numerous disciplinary slips read: "Out of seat and left classroom. Refused to take textbook—waiting for security to come and get him." "Ryan was punching and hitting Alex in the lunchroom." "Did not come up with class from lunch. Received no permission to go somewhere. Stopped by Mrs. Evans so they could get a pass at 11:53 but lunch ended at 11:30."[6]

Like many underfunded urban schools, Grover Washington had adopted the broken-windows theory of policing in its disciplinary practices, which holds that tolerating minor quality-of-life violations will allow serious crime to fester. Based on that approach, low-level infractions, such as disorderly conduct, willful defiance, and truancy were penalized and sometimes criminalized, causing suspensions to surge and fueling the criminal justice system.[7] Studies showed that students who were suspended or expelled were much more likely to drop out of school altogether.[8]

In the 1990s, amid a tough-on-crime political agenda and panic over juvenile "superpredators," hysteria over school discipline erupted. Political scientist John J. Dilulio coined the term to refer to savage, murderous juvenile criminals who "pack guns instead of lunches" and "have absolutely no respect for human life." It was later invoked by First Lady Hillary Clinton while on the trail stumping for her husband's reelection: superpredators have "no conscience, no empathy . . . first we have to bring them to heel." In 1994, the year juvenile arrests for violent crime peaked, President Bill Clinton signed the Gun-Free Schools Act, which effectively mandated states to enact legislation that would impose a minimum yearlong expulsion on any student who brings a firearm to school or else risk losing federal funds. Although juvenile and school crime fell as the decade progressed, zero-tolerance policies for violence, weapons, and firearms became ubiquitous in schools.[9]

Five years after the enactment of the GFSA, two Columbine High School seniors perpetrated a grisly massacre at their school, leaving thirteen people dead and more than twenty wounded. The Columbine shooting altered the American imagination and galvanized sweeping political change that transformed school security measures. Schools installed thousands of resource officers along with metal detectors and security cameras, especially in poor urban schools disproportionately attended by African American and Latino students.[10]

From time to time, racial drama erupted between students at Grover Washington, the majority of whom were African American. As Puerto Rican kids, Ryan and his brother Avry were sometimes targeted and beat up. Both were slim and had close-cropped black hair. Their pale gringo skin made some think they were white. Kids called them racist slurs such as "spic" and "wetback." Ryan wasn't the type to brush it off and walk away. When challenged or threatened, Ryan would fight, but he wasn't usually an instigator, more a joiner than a leader. Yet he would always defend himself, heeding the macho code of the streets and standing his ground. Nobody was calling him a *pussy* without facing retribution. Avry, however, was a model student who almost never fought or got into trouble.

Ryan's school career became an eternal cycle of headaches for Rayni, composed of seemingly daily phone calls and meetings with the principal. At one point, she requested a transfer for Ryan, but it was denied. The school employed every available disciplinary device short of expulsion to correct his behavior, such as Saturday detentions and out-of-school suspensions. By now, it was obvious that Grover Washington was not going to be the site of transformation that Ryan had anticipated. In fact, his behavior deteriorated.

One afternoon, Ryan was rummaging through boxes at his grandmother's hair salon and came across dozens of pornographic DVDs. "That bastard!" she screamed upon realizing it was her partner's collection. A few moments later, she told Ryan, "You can sell these films." He happily obliged. He had been a veteran hustler since Lowell, where he had sold Juicy Fruit and Doublemint gum for a quarter a stick. One day in math class, he unzipped his backpack and discreetly pulled out a DVD with a nude woman on the cover.

"Yo bro, look at this," he told his friend Adam, whose eyes lit up. "Can I get one?" Adam whispered. Ryan sold his first DVD for $3 and began giving out a few complimentary copies, just like dealers did with drug samples in his neighborhood, so students could vouch for the quality of his product. He never personally watched them, out of allegiance to one of Biggie Smalls's commandments: "Never get high on your own supply."

Demand spiked, and Ryan hiked the price to $7, even $10, and sold some fifteen DVDs. He blew his profits on a new pair of Nikes and snacks like chips, Snickers, and Reese's Peanut Butter Cups. At home, he kept his backpack of bootlegs near his bed and carried it wherever he went, raising his mother's suspicions. She was attentive to the slightest variations in how Ryan and Avry acted, looked, or walked.

Rayni tossed and turned in bed. She wanted to know what was in that backpack. She assumed the worst. What if he was selling drugs? Or worse, using? She saw how her brother's cocaine addiction and drug dealing had destroyed his family. She turned to her fiancé, George, and asked him what to do, but he mumbled that he didn't know and fell back asleep.

Around six in the morning, after staying up most of the night, she went to the door of Ryan's room and got down on her hands and knees. As she contrived how she would punish him if she found drugs, she crawled to the foot of the bed. Ryan sometimes woke up during the night and did push-ups, but he was fast asleep. The edge of the backpack rested on the footboard. Rayni reached for it and opened the zipper.

Her heart thumped as she looked inside. Relieved that he wasn't hoarding drugs, she was now puzzled by the pornos. "What the fuck is this, Ryan?" she yelled, holding up his bag. "Where the fuck did you get this from?" Ryan stirred awake and rubbed his eyes. "They're not for me. I'm selling them," he said.

"Who is giving them to you to sell?" Rayni asked, beginning to calm down.

"I can't tell you," he replied.

"Ryan, I'm going to beat your ass."

Ryan confessed that her mother had said he could hawk them. To his surprise, Rayni said he could sell the last batch of DVDs. And she didn't even demand a cut. The family had so little money, and she trusted that he wasn't watching them.

But just when his buoyant business was about to come to an end, he found a new supplier. One day, Ryan cut school with his friend Samuel, a short, chubby Black kid. At his house, Samuel showed him his father's overflowing box of more than a hundred adult DVDs and let Ryan take an armful. He didn't know about Ryan's business nor did Ryan disclose what he would do with the DVDs, expecting that Samuel would insist on a share of the profits.

With the replenished stock, Ryan revived his side hustle for a few more months. A student got caught with one of the DVDs, but he didn't rat Ryan out.

*   *   *

GROVER WASHINGTON WAS near the SEPTA regional train tracks, a strip mall, Tacony Creek Park, and long stretches of row homes. One day after school, Ryan and his friends were exploring the neighborhood and came across a gate at the bottom of a mound of dirt. They climbed through an open hole, scampered through wild vegetation, and ended up on the train tracks. They began regularly using the route as a shortcut to get to the other side of the neighborhood. Word of their discovery quickly spread among the students.

With rising cases of children being hit by trains, SEPTA workers held an assembly at Ryan's school to discourage the students from going onto the tracks. Ryan ignored their advice. He lived by the credo espoused in the film *Paid in Full*. In one scene, as he munched on chips, the main character Rico told Ace, a fellow drug dealer whose head was bandaged from a gunshot wound, that the shooting shouldn't derail him from the street life: "Niggas get shot everyday, B." The line stuck with Ryan. He had often seen or heard of random shootings and car crashes. Shit happens all the time, he figured. He wasn't going to let that change how he lived. He was invincible.

On a day when Ryan ditched school, he, Samuel, and another friend, Peter, a wiry Asian boy, started wandering south on the curving tracks. When they made it to Olney Station, an employee on the platform began screaming, "Get out of the way!" A northbound train was approaching. Ryan and Samuel jumped off the tracks onto the grassy dirt path, but Peter was stuck, so he had to duck underneath the platform, just in time. Ryan was hyped up as adrenaline coursed through his body. He thought, *How am I still alive?* But flirting with death didn't sour their fascination with the tracks. It had the opposite effect: they kept going back.

On another adventure, Ryan, Avry, and their group of friends discovered an abandoned rusty yellow school bus parked diagonally on a dead-end street. Some of the boys lobbed a barrage of rocks to bust open the windows. Ryan and a few others jumped onto the hood and giddily kicked at the windshield with their sneakers. They didn't have much collective strength and made no more than a dent.

Ryan and Avry then climbed aboard to investigate as stale dust filled their lungs. The seats were tattered, and the bus looked as if it had been retired years ago. As Ryan poked around, a rock sailed through an open window and nailed him in the head.

"Who hit me?" Ryan demanded as he disembarked. Nobody confessed. Suddenly, he felt hot sweat dripping down his neck. But when he touched it, his hand was smeared with blood.

Avry took a closer look at his head. "*Ohhhhh shiiiit*, you're bleeding a lot." Panicked, the brothers ran the few blocks home and prepared a plausible story for their mother. Ryan told Rayni that some unknown kids had thrown rocks at him and his friends. Inspecting his head, Rayni didn't think the injuries were serious enough to warrant a trip to the emergency room. A pro at dressing his wounds, she applied New-Skin liquid bandages and told him to avoid napping for awhile in case he had a concussion.

Ryan spent hours every day engaging in free-wheeling play, expending his restless energy in mostly harmless ways. It could have been worse. He could have joined one of the neighborhood youth gangs, such as TNT, Paper Boys, or Dollar Crew, and gone around sticking up random pedestrians for cash and electronics. But his boyish mischief did not emerge out of a vacuum. Few of the children of North Philadelphia had even an inkling of the enrichment programs, music lessons, and sports teams that their counterparts in wealthier neighborhoods took for granted. They had plenty of time to stir up trouble.

* * *

AT THE 35TH Police District on Broad Street, Ryan pulled out the shoelaces and strings from his pristine white Nike Air Force 1 sneakers, hoodie, and basketball shorts and handed them over. Andres did the same. The boys were plunked in a dingy juvenile cell with a concrete bench that jutted out from the wall. As Ryan entered the room, he felt the oxygen leave his lungs.

The officers told them they'd be out by evening. It was early after-noon, so Ryan began counting down the hours. He felt his life crashing down before his eyes, but he found solidarity with Andres imagining the imminent beatings by their parents. Andres wasn't yet aware that Ryan had ratted him out, and Ryan pushed it from his mind. Two other boys trickled in and squeezed onto the bench of misfit toys. One was around their age. He explained that he was sleeping with an underage girl whose parents had reported him to the police. The other boy was several years older and claimed to have been in a fight outside a train station in North Philadelphia.

In the evening, an officer swung open the cell door. "Who's Ryan Rivera?" Ryan perked up.

"We're getting ready to go."

"I'm supposed to be going home."

"We're taking you to the Youth Study Center."

"You need to stop playin' with me," Ryan said, assuming the offi-cer was joking. He thought he was going home. They said he would be going home.

A little later, the officer returned with his partner holding Ryan's backpack and belongings in a plastic bag. He was handcuffed for the second time that day. Andres was next in line.

Once outside, Ryan began to panic: "Is that a paddy wagon? I don't want to go in that. I get very claustrophobic." An officer scoffed, "Paddy wagon is a racial slur towards Irish people." When the police put him in the rear, in the confined, pitch-black space, he was overcome with terror: *If this van flips over, I'm going to fucking die.* All alone, separated from Andres, he peered out of a tiny square window between him and the driver's seat to stave off his anxiety. It had been many hours since his arrest, and he had yet to talk to his mother or a lawyer.

* * *

THE YOUTH STUDY Center was temporarily housed in a former psychi-atric institute in East Falls while a new building was being erected in West Philadelphia. The asylum shared the air of a prison, and both were part of what French philosopher Michel Foucault famously described as the "carceral continuum," which "diffuse[s] penitentiary techniques into the most innocent disciplines . . . and plac[es] over the slightest illegality, the smallest irregularity, deviation or anomaly, the threat of delinquency."[11] Once inside the old tan-brick building, Ryan sat in an open-air cell with an older Black boy, who disclosed that he had stolen a car. After getting his blood test and tuberculosis test, his vitals checked, and his mug shot taken, Ryan was escorted to the shower room. A slightly overweight male guard instructed him to remove his clothes. When he had stripped down to his boxer shorts and socks, he asked, "Do I have to take off my boxers?" The guard replied in the affirmative.

Ryan protested, "Come on, for real? In front of you?"

"Yeah," said the guard. Just as he began pulling them down, the guard stopped him and handed him a towel. He told Ryan to tie it around his waist and then take off his underwear. After that, he made Ryan pick up each foot and wiggle his toes followed by squatting and coughing so the guard could check him for drugs.

When Ryan finished showering, he examined the clothes the guard had left for him. The white briefs had skid marks. With his towel wrapped around his waist, he opened the door, held up the underwear, and said, "This shit is dirty as shit."

"That's all we got," shouted the guard. Ryan pulled them on with a great sense of shame.

Shortly after, the same officers brought in Andres, who went through the same routine. Unlike Ryan, Andres had spoken to his mother on the phone during processing. Ryan presumed Rayni was refusing his calls and holding out against picking him up to teach him a lesson. It seemed to be working.

It was past midnight when a guard escorted the two boys down a hallway to their cells. Andres's cell was so congested that he couldn't walk without stepping on someone. Ryan was put in a cell with one other boy, who was dozing off on a makeshift bed—a mattress on top of a storage container lid. Ryan's threadbare blanket hardly shielded him from the blasts of the air conditioner. As morning dawned, he lay stiffly on his metal bed, which was bolted to the floor, near his cellmate, who was still asleep. He managed to drift off for a few hours, shocked by what had happened over the past day and terrified by the prospect of being beaten or raped. When his cellmate, an older Black Muslim boy named Rashad, woke up, he introduced himself. He was in for armed robbery. Ryan told him his age and about the fire. "Damn, you're too young to be in here," Rashad said, amazed that he wasn't even a teenager. "You're a young boul!" He gave him a quick rundown of the place and imparted some wisdom: make sure this is the last time you find yourself here. The Youth Study Center was no place for a child. He said it so sincerely that Ryan was taken aback.

Rashad explained that he had ingratiated himself with the guards, who let him keep pencils, notebooks, and books in his cell. He stored them beneath his mattress. Ryan noticed that he was reading one of his favorite books, *The Bully*, a young adult novel in the Bluford series. It was about a Black high school student who moves with his mother from Philadelphia to California and confronts a school bully. Ryan wished he could have been as brave.

Before they were let out for breakfast, Rashad instructed Ryan to make his bed neatly and tuck in the sheets on all sides. A guard inspected their cell and, with a nod to Rashad's stature, said that he would bring him a new black kufi to replace his fraying one in time for his next court date.

Apple Jacks were the first calories to enter Ryan's body in some twenty-four hours. He rejected the carton of whole milk and gave Rashad his powdered jelly doughnut, a carceral delicacy. After breakfast, Ryan, Andres, and another boy were told to line up in the hallway to wait for a meeting with a court official. Ryan put out his arms to be cuffed by two guards. Then he lifted his feet into ankle cuffs. The boys were put into separate holding cells, each with a bench and a door with a window. They could hear but not see each other. Andres was called first, and when he returned, he told Ryan that his parents had arrived and were taking him home.

"Did you see my mom and dad out there?" Ryan asked.

"No, I couldn't tell," Andres replied.

Nobody was coming to rescue him. He didn't know that Rayni had learned of his arrest a few hours after the fact and had called the police district, but she was not allowed to visit or speak with him. A female officer had told her she would get a call with details of how to retrieve her son, but the call never came.

Ryan waited for hours, sinking into deeper despair until a corrections officer informed him that, as one of the youngest children at Youth Study, he was being transferred to VisionQuest, a juvenile residential placement in Pennsylvania for lower-risk offenders. Ryan was relieved, mostly because he was escaping the communal, curtain-free showers at Youth Study.

*   *   *

IN THE VAN on the way to VisionQuest, Ryan sat next to two boys. Their arms were shackled together. On his arrival, dinner was being served: chicken with gravy, a biscuit, and cheese-stuffed baked potatoes, just like his uncle made them, which soothed his nerves. Afterward, he took a quick shower. The showers were grimy and crawling with cockroaches, but at least they had curtains. He rinsed his underwear with soap, a compulsory daily chore, and hung it to dry in his room, a "hut" he shared with nearly a dozen other boys.

In the morning, he was fed a breakfast of eggs and bacon—plus an extra strip for helping to clean up. He fielded questions from his hut mates about why he was there and talked about the fire. They found it weird that his accomplice, Andres, wasn't at VisionQuest with him. They thought it might be because Andres had snitched on him, and Ryan wasn't going to correct the record. He also mentioned that he was from the Badlands, as his neighborhood was known. One stocky, tall kid said he had never seen him in the neighborhood and quickly proceeded to disseminate rumors that Ryan was lying.

On the basketball court, he heard kids whispering about him. Once again, his ideas about how to comport himself came from multiple viewings of *Prison Break* and other shows. He figured that he needed to retaliate so that nobody could prey on him. He picked up a basketball and ambled toward the instigator on the opposite side of the court. His plan was to smash the kid's face with the ball and, when he cowered, finish him off with a punch to the stomach. It wasn't his nature to start fights. Only now, in his mind, he was in prison, and he didn't have to guess what they did to boys who were perceived as weak.

Two older Black boys blocked him as he crossed the court and ushered him to a table in the living area. Ryan sat across from Justin, the boss of the clique, with two of his associates on either side. "What are you about to go do?" Justin asked. "I see you quiet and you got that basketball." He told Ryan that if he went through with this plan, then they'd all get locked down in their rooms. Instead, he extended an offer. "Why don't you join my crew? I run shit around here. If you join me and do things for me, we'll do things for you."

"Yo bro, I'm not gay. I don't know what you want me to do for you, but I'm doing none of that." Justin let out a deep belly chuckle, alarming Ryan.

"What's wrong with this kid?" He looked to an associate and turned back to Ryan. "Ain't no shit like that over here. If you gay, you go to K unit. I'm saying that if I fight or one of the people in my crew fight, then you fight. And if you fight, then we fight with you." Ryan, awash in relief, said he was cool with that arrangement.

More than forty-eight hours after getting arrested, Ryan finally got hold of his mother on Sunday afternoon during daily phone time. A cauldron of rage had built up inside him over the past few days, but hearing her voice diffused his anger. Rayni told him that she had spent the weekend sobbing, shattered by the paranoid scenarios running through her head in which he had been seriously hurt. She felt part of her heart had been ripped out. Her sons were her babies. They were her life. She never would have abandoned Ryan. She wanted him to understand that she had been desperately trying to determine his whereabouts. She vowed to attend his court hearing the next day, the first step to getting him out of incarceration.

In the short time he had been at VisionQuest, Ryan had earned the nickname "The Fireman." A few boys were prodding him to start a fire to distract the guards so they could escape. He promised to set one when he returned from court, secretly banking on being released into his mother's care.

On Monday, a rowdy busload of boys headed to Philadelphia for their court appearances. By this point, Ryan had been in custody for nearly seventy-two hours, during which time he'd been handcuffed numerous times and shepherded from a holding cell to two juvenile facilities, all the while petrified of physical violence at the hands of the guards and the other boys. While he was sitting outside the courtroom, Ryan's fingers started to twitch.

Rayni hadn't slept much the night before. She was teeming with anxiety. She and George arrived to court early. They had been together for the past five years, and had two boys, Tino and Armando. Eight years younger than Rayni, George worked odd construction gigs while she stayed home and took care of the kids; they had relative economic stability—a first for Rayni in a long time. They were devastated to see Ryan in his navy and tan prison scrubs. Inside the courtroom, the first question the old white male judge asked him was: "Are you a gang member?" It wasn't uncommon for gang members to flash signs, and a guard had interpreted Ryan's nervous twitching as a gang signal and reported it up the chain. The judge was satisfied with his explanation and released him to his mother.

When they went to pick up the paperwork, Rayni tried to hug him, but he brushed her off. She tried again a few minutes later. He initially concealed how much he had missed her, but he was then overcome with emotion, accumulated from days of longing for his mother's protection, love, and assurance that everything would be okay. He started bawling and clutched her tightly. But the goodwill was short-lived.

"Put your laces back in your shoes," Rayni ordered him when he stepped out of the building after changing into his own clothes. She didn't want people to see that he had been in custody and judge her as a mother. The comfort of being back in his old clothes quickly dissipated.

"Stop telling me what to do," he screeched. "You ain't come get me when you were supposed to."

Passions were running high. Ryan was torn between the relief of going home and resentment toward his mother for not picking him up earlier. As they walked out of the facility, Rayni lashed out. Ryan lashed back. Rayni could see how broken he felt, and she wondered how she had fallen short in raising him. She had walked through fire—literally—for her boys, raising them as a single mother when they were small and providing for them as far as their welfare checks stretched. George intervened to keep the peace before the row could blow up and attract scrutiny only minutes after Ryan had been freed. They took him to McDonald's for lunch. Usually his mother only let him get one or two things off the dollar menu, but today she let him get a full meal: a Big Mac with large fries, washed down with a Coke. Ryan thought it was the least she could do after all that he had gone through. He didn't understand that his mother had been carrying great pain.

2
...

Little Vietnam

No one had expected Emmanuel. His mother, Ivette, had woken up in the middle of the night in a puddle. She thought she had wet the bed, but in fact her water had broken. Ivan, her husband, declared that he was taking her to the hospital.

It was the early hours of an icy January day in 1997. They deposited their two sons, Joaquin and Michael, who were eight and nine, at their grandmother's house and rushed to Einstein Medical Center in North Philadelphia.

"Ma'am, do you think you're pregnant?" the nurse asked Ivette as she was escorted to a room in a wheelchair.

"I'm married, but I don't think so," she muttered, irritated by the question. "You must be crazy." A doctor examined her and saw a baby's head. He exclaimed, "Oh my God. This lady is about to give birth."

"*Ay, Dios mío,*" moaned Ivan, who had a paunchy body, receding black hair, and a short-cropped beard. Ivette was stunned and ready to strangle him. She weighed nearly four hundred pounds and had had no inkling that she was pregnant. Six months ago, she hadn't been feeling well and had gone to the doctor; he did a pregnancy test, but it came back negative.

On the way to the delivery room, the doctor instructed her, "Lady, be as calm as you can. Please don't sneeze or cough." Within minutes, sans epidural, a baby boy was born. He came out with yellow skin coloring, the result of newborn jaundice. Ivette thought, *Oh my God. This is a miracle.*

She named him Emmanuel, one of God's names in the Bible meaning "God with us." Both mother and son were discharged within a few days. A nurse came to visit their house on Sixth and Cambria Streets to check on Emmanuel because he had developed eczema. Ivette lathered his body with Aveeno cream and dressed him in long-sleeved shirts.

Emmanuel was a quiet baby. He slept soundly through the night and was easy to manage. His parents hoped that he would develop differently than his brothers. Early in childhood, Michael could not sit still, threw erasers, and had temper tantrums at school. He was once suspended for throwing a rock at another classmate, hitting him square in the temple. Joaquin had trouble speaking and remembering colors and numbers. After special education evaluations, Michael had been diagnosed with ADHD and Joaquin with intellectual disability. Ivan was worried that his history with schizophrenia had played a role in his sons' conditions. Both boys had Individualized Education Programs and were prescribed Ritalin, with one dose taken in the morning and the second at school. Michael and Joaquin complained that the medication made them drowsy.

With no advance notice of Emmanuel's arrival, Ivan and Ivette relied on family members to pitch in with diapers, clothes, a Moses basket, and other necessities. They fished out Joaquin's old crib from storage. Another mouth to feed strained their already negligible budget. Ivan received a monthly Supplemental Security Income check for his schizophrenia. When SSI was established in 1972, Congress assured that "the Nation's aged, blind, and disabled people would no longer have to subsist on below-poverty-level incomes." But for decades, SSI benefit levels fell short of the federal poverty line. And with strict income ($85 a month) and asset limits ($2,000 for individuals or $3,000 for couples), beneficiaries—about eight million today—were trapped in destitution and risked losing eligibility upon minor boosts to their finances.[1] To make ends meet and keep their SSI payments, Ivan and Ivette were forced to work under the table, both as salespeople. Ivan worked at a retail store, and Ivette hawked Avon products to her friends and people in the neighborhood. The family made do with the little they had.

Although he made economic contributions to the family, Ivan had a darker side. As the boys grew older, he began drifting apart from the family, and Ivette became their primary caregiver. Their marriage fractured. He spent most of his free time at his mother's house. Ivette would lace into him, "You're no mommy's boy no more. You have a family."

Then he started becoming violent toward her. She had bruises on her arm to prove it. He was most belligerent when he had been drinking. Ivette noticed that his family was, by nature, hot-tempered, and she felt that he was envious of her popularity, especially at church, where the members would shower her with attention and pay no heed to him. He would get furious when she invited her friends over to the house.

Following Emmanuel's birth, Ivette couldn't stand or sit for extended periods of time, so she leaned on her husband for basic functions. She had recently fallen down the stairs to the basement in her Kensington home and frequently felt fierce pain in her legs. The least painful position for her was lying flat on the floor. When she visited the doctor for her lower back pain, she was prescribed a suite of pain medications—Percocet, codeine, and tramadol—on and off since the narcotics were highly addictive. They slightly eased her suffering, but over the following year, her condition became chronic, and the doctor recommended that she, too, apply for SSI. She had to produce documentation that she was physically incapable of engaging in full-time employment, so she went for a diagnostic test, an electromyography, which examined the electrical activity of nerves and muscles.[2]

"This is an ABNORMAL study," the report read. "The electrodiagnostic findings are most likely indicative of acute irritation of the root at the S1 level on the left side." Her doctor ordered magnetic resonance imaging to pinpoint the problem around her lumbar spine and advised that losing weight "will be of great benefit in reducing the mechanical stress of the spine and risk for continuing degenerative joint disease and disk compression." Ivette had a long history of morbid obesity and hypertension, which exacerbated her lower back pain and caused swelling and pain in her left knee and tingling in her left foot.

The next step was a disability determination. "On observing this woman," wrote Dr. Jeffrey Erinoff, "it was quite obvious that she was having difficulty getting on and off the examination table." He listed her conditions: back pain, left knee pain, morbid obesity, hypertension, and depression. He stated that she was able to stand or walk only three to four hours a day and should refrain from "bending, balancing, and climbing." A month later, another physician concluded that Ivette met the Social Security Administration's obesity criteria to qualify as disabled.[3]

The several hundred dollars a month in additional SSI benefits wasn't a significant sum, but the sense of relief that it brought to the family was boundless. It helped cover utility bills, clothing, books, toys, and other goods that the family had forgone for years. It made Ivette and Ivan feel much less insecure.

* * *

JOAQUIN AND EMMANUEL were in the living room watching Scooby-Doo while Ivette was in the kitchen making French toast. Emmanuel, who was now four, was attending preschool at John F. Hartranft school. The family had recently moved to a house on Seventh and Cumberland Streets, exchanging their home with Pastor Diego and his wife, Ora, who moved into their old house on Sixth Street. Ivette ran through her mental checklist: feed the kids and get them dressed for Sunday school and Ivan would drive them to church. Ivette brought the boys to a Pentecostal church almost every day for a few hours; there were activities for the children while she sat through the service. Ivan would occasionally join them. This time, though, he abruptly changed his plans and announced he was going to his mother's house.

Ivette yelled out, "What? You ain't going to drive us to church?" Ivan raced downstairs to the kitchen and grabbed a knife. As he put it to her throat, an episode of *Felix the Cat* was about to begin on the television. *Oh my God. Give me strength*, she thought. She managed to twist Ivan's arm, grab at his neck, and seize the knife from his weak hand. She held the tip to his throat.

Amid the commotion, the boys turned their attention away from the TV and stared at their parents in bewilderment. Suddenly, Ivan broke loose of Ivette's grip and ran upstairs. She went after him, saying she was going to walk to church with the kids. Then she called Diego and narrated the sequence of events. Diego reprimanded Ivette for threatening Ivan's life and handed down a punishment: no preaching in church for a year. Ivette did not demur.

She opted against reporting the knife attack to the police for fear that he might follow through and kill her next time.

A few months later, on a chilly November day, the boys were playing in their parents' bedroom before breakfast. Joaquin, who had recently turned thirteen, was working on a puzzle when Michael, who was a year older, started jumping on the bed, sending the pieces flying. Emmanuel slid to the edge of the bed and tumbled into the narrow gap next to the wall. Joaquin reached over to pick him up. His father later claimed he thought Joaquin was hurting Emmanuel. He grabbed the boy aggressively, biting his arm and hitting other parts of his body as Ivette and the children screamed at him to stop. The assault left severe bruising. It turned out that Ivan had been refusing to follow his mental health treatment plan, not taking prescribed antipsychotic medications for his schizophrenia.

At this point, Michael and Joaquin were receiving intensive services for their behavioral and mental health conditions through a social service agency. The family was attending therapy sessions with a psychologist, Peter Goldman. Ivette had forgotten that Goldman was due to swing by the house for a visit. When he knocked on the door, Ivette panicked and ordered Joaquin to go upstairs; she feared that the Department of Human Services might take him away if anyone saw his injuries. But Goldman had overheard her command and asked why the boy had been sent upstairs. In tears, she had no choice but to recount what had transpired. Goldman examined Joaquin and reported an allegation of child abuse to the DHS.

At St. Christopher's Hospital for Children in North Philadelphia,

Joaquin's injuries were considered acute and he was given a tetanus shot and pain medication. Two DHS social workers met with the family. They made three essential points: the house was unsafe for the children, Joaquin had to be removed from the home immediately, and Ivette was to find someone to care for him or else he would be placed in foster care. Pastor Diego's wife, Ora, agreed to look after him. Michael, who was boarding at Devereux Pennsylvania Children's Intellectual and Developmental Disabilities Services, happened to be home on a visiting pass, so he would return to the facility later that day.

As for four-year-old Emmanuel, DHS would remove him from her custody unless Ivette found a safe place to live. Ivette had stayed with Ivan despite the violence out of a belief that matrimony should prevail through the highs and lows, but this was the breaking point. She couldn't risk losing Emmanuel, too. Ora owned a house in Kensington, which became vacant a few months into Ivette's search. Ora fixed the windows and cleaned up the yard and rented it to Ivette.

Ivette had solved the housing crisis, but she was worried about the disastrous economic effect of her new situation as a single, disabled mother. DHS did not extend emergency aid. The housing authority provided no rental assistance or temporary housing. Surviving as a single parent solely on her SSI benefits and food stamps and Emmanuel's child-only Temporary Assistance for Needy Families aid, she would not be able to cover her expenses.[4] How would she support herself and Emmanuel all on her own?

On the day Ivette was preparing to leave, Ivan taunted her. "I know you are going to come back. You love me."

"I don't think so," she said, bidding him farewell.

Emmanuel was too young to understand why his parents had split up. The turmoil also inflicted lasting damage on his relationship with his brothers. "They were sent away," he said, years later. "I stayed."

For Ivette, the abuse, housing precarity, and despair were all too familiar. It felt as if she were reliving the worst moments of her childhood.

*   *   *

As IVETTE'S MOTHER, Valentina, walked her children to school in Jersey City, she put on dark-tinted sunglasses to hide her newly minted black eye, a casualty of her partner Liam's latest fit of rage. The night before, after attending their cousin's birthday party, Valentina, Ivette, and her brother, Pedro, had come home to Liam chugging beer. From her bedroom, Ivette could hear her parents hurling and smashing objects. Liam was furious Valentina had disobeyed him by going to the party. He feared she had disclosed details of their dimming relationship to her sister, Rosario.

This battering was one too many. Valentina left Liam and brought the children to her mother's house in Brooklyn, where they finished the rest of the school year. It was the late 1960s. That summer, the family moved to Valentina's stepmother Beatriz's house near the beach in Naguabo, a village on the eastern coast of Puerto Rico. Beatriz lived with her son and two other daughters on a small farm, where they tended pigs and grew plantains and bananas. It was a homecoming of sorts for Ivette and Pedro. A baby of the sixties, Ivette had been born in Aibonito, a bucolic town known as *la ciudad de las flores,* set in the mountains with the highest elevation on the island. When Valentina went into labor with Ivette, Liam, a towering, slightly chubby baseball player with short black hair, was competing in the playoffs and had to race to the hospital. Pedro arrived a year and a half later, and the family moved to a poor New Jersey neighborhood in Jersey City, just across the Hudson River from Manhattan, where Valentina's sisters lived.

Now Valentina enrolled the children in school in Naguabo—first grade for Ivette, kindergarten for Pedro. They learned in both Spanish and English, so the transition wasn't too difficult. Valentina picked up shifts as a waitress and went to night school to get her high school diploma, which she managed to finish in less than a year.

The holiday season soon rolled around. On Thanksgiving, the family celebrated Puerto Rican–style with turkey, *arroz con gandules*, *pasteles*, *arroz con dulce*, *tembleque*, *dulce de coco*, and *dulce de lechoza*. Then for Christmas, Liam flew in from Jersey City to reunite with his children, bearing gifts: a doll house for Ivette and a red remote-controlled car for Pedro. He was only in town a few days. Even though her father had rarely been around before her parents' split, Ivette didn't understand why he had become abruptly absent from their lives. *Maybe he doesn't love us anymore*, she thought.

One afternoon, Beatriz was at the market picking up yams to make *pasteles*, which she would sell. Ivette was at home on her lunch break from school when her uncle, a pastor, came out of the bathroom with a towel fastened around his waist. He grabbed her and covered her mouth with his hand to muffle her screams. She kicked him and tried to break free of his grip, but he was too strong. He threw her on his bed and raped her. She was eight years old. Drowning in shame, she told no one. Who would have believed her? It would be her word against that of a man who preached the Lord's gospel. She knew how that would turn out.

The trauma of the rape and then repeated encounters with her uncle caused Ivette to lose focus in school, and her grades plummeted. Valentina met with the school principal. "Is there any problem at the house?" she was asked. "No," Valentina answered. "Maybe it's that we travel time to time, and that's what's affecting her." Valentina closely monitored Ivette's schoolwork, and she was able to catch up and progress to the next grade.

The next summer, Valentina returned to Jersey City with the children and moved into an apartment near Rosario. Ivette didn't like the lunch at school in New Jersey, so when the bell rang for lunch, Ivette and Pedro would meet up and walk over to their aunt's house. Rosario fed them a spread of meatball sandwiches, hot dogs, pork and beans, ham and cheese sandwiches, and *pastelillos*. In between bites, Ivette felt like a child again, relieved to be away from her uncle.

Now Valentina split her time between training to be a missionary and working as a youth counselor at the family's church. The Pentecostal Christian faith, which adhered to a literal interpretation of the Bible, was seminal to Ivette's childhood. The church was a second home, where the family went nearly every day of the week. When her mother gave her a Bible for Christmas, Ivette treated it as a milestone in her life. She thought she had never felt a greater affinity to God.

Shortly before Ivette was due to begin sixth grade, Valentina unexpectedly decided to move back to Naguabo. The moves were so frequent that Ivette had stopped asking why. Once back in Puerto Rico, Valentina got a new job at a cosmetics factory. She quickly fell into a routine: getting Ivette and Pedro ready for school in the morning and then heading out. In the evenings, she moonlighted as a waitress. Liam periodically reappeared in their lives only to quickly disappear. He was trying to win back Valentina, who did not share his interest. Ivette saw him as a friend who came and departed as he pleased with little care for his children.

During the holiday season that year, Pedro and Ivette visited Liam's mother in the town of Cayey. One day, their grandmother was at the store when out of the blue, their cousin started striking and suffocating Pedro with a pillow. He tied Pedro to a pillar of the canopy bed with a rope. Ivette kicked her cousin, but that brought his attention to her. He pummeled and strangled her and then threw her on the bed and raped her. Pedro could only watch helplessly.

When their grandmother came home and saw her crying, Ivette lied that she had fallen down the stairs, which had caused the bruises all over her body. Her parents were called, and they rushed to Cayey and took her to see a psychologist. But Ivette would not deviate from her original story. Valentina brought her and Pedro back to Naguabo. After the rape, Ivette developed a blood infection; she was prescribed some medicine and stayed home from school.

As she rested, Ivette obsessed why this kept happening to her. She arrived at an explanation: this was a man's world, run for and by men. Young as she was, she realized that men would act as if they had an inalienable right to violate her body, with impunity, for as long as she lived. She had little recourse. She had never felt more alone.

* * *

THE FAMILY WAS living at Ivette's uncle Marcos and aunt Sophia's home in Fajardo, a seaside town on the eastern edge of the island, when Valentina met Kevin, a friend of theirs. Valentina and Kevin married in a private ceremony and moved back to Jersey City with the children. Ivette felt that her mother kept her in the dark about familial developments, but over time she began to see Kevin as a father figure.

Ivette and Pedro entered eighth grade, the final year before high school. Kevin found a job at Caldor department store in shipping and receiving, and Valentina started cleaning rooms at the Meadowlands Plaza Hotel in Secaucus. Before long, she became pregnant, giving birth to Carolina when Ivette was fifteen. Now a high school student, she started skipping classes to take care of Carolina—feeding, bathing, and watching over her. She adored her baby sister.

One day, two police officers paid a visit to the house and asked why Ivette was not attending school. Valentina promised them she would go the next day. Ivette went for a couple of months, but she failed the tenth grade and dropped out. She understood that getting a high school diploma would be necessary if she wanted to do well in life, but she found the classes, especially math, to be quite difficult and preferred caring for Carolina and hanging out with her friends.

A few days after Ivette's seventeenth birthday, Valentina gave birth to another girl, named Jessica, not long after Kevin had confessed he had been having an affair. He promised never to cheat again, and Valentina decided to give him another chance. She began looking for a bigger home for the growing family and filled out an application for Jersey City's Curries Woods public housing project. The family was accepted.

Curries Woods was constructed during the postwar public housing boom when high-rise towers such as the Pruitt–Igoe in St. Louis and the Robert Taylor Homes in Chicago shot up in cities around the country. Completed in 1959, it had 712 units across seven twelve- and thirteen-story buildings.[5] Ivette and the family (without Pedro, who had left to join the air force) took up occupancy in a three-bedroom, one-bathroom apartment on the first floor of the 5 Heckman Drive tower, which had mostly African American tenants. They were the only Puerto Ricans on their floor. The walls of the tower were plastered with graffiti, and the unreliable elevators were coated with urine and feces and used for selling drugs. Still, the apartment was spacious and well kept with the added perk of a washer and dryer. Their only quibble was that Carolina and Jessica's bedroom sat above the boiler room, so the floor tiles rattled, and the fan had to be on at all times to keep them cool. The home was almost an oasis in a nightmare.

In one of a series of dispatches called "American Industries" for *Scientific American* in 1879, Hamilton S. Wicks described Jersey City as "a workshop of the metropolis of no little importance. Its shipping industries are large, and it is the site of such extensive manufacturing industries . . ." But like many other cities in the nation, it had endured a postwar industrial collapse. Tens of thousands of manufacturing jobs disappeared throughout Hudson County, in which Jersey City was the largest city.[6] A product of disinvestment combined with hypersegregation, the crack epidemic, and the war on drugs, Curries Woods of the 1980s was marked by economic pain and criminalization, or as sociologist Loïc Wacquant put it, was a living embodiment of the state's "simultaneous retraction of its social bosom and expansion of its penal fist."[7] There was the never-ending police presence, arrests, raids, and mostly young men shuffling in and out of correctional facilities for committing all shades of crime.

As crack became a bonanza, drug dealers staked their claim to individual buildings in the project, which led to factions declaring war on each other. Ivette referred to the buildings as "a little Vietnam." Gunshots cut through the air at all hours. Homicides were abundant. "You think we're going to let you come in front of our building to sell?" said James, a former resident of Curries Woods and a drug dealer, describing the warfare over turf. "We were willing to kill you. A lot of my childhood friends are dead. Prison saved me."

Some drug dealers kept pit bulls as pets and used them for protection and to rob people. They trotted around the grounds of the project, which was blanketed with tampons, empty green- and yellow-capped crack vials, and "so very much glass, as though some urban gardener has mulched the detritus of a million beer and soda bottles," exclaimed the *Washington Post.*[8] The smell of urine was so pungent and constant it was an ordinary part of the air the residents breathed. Carolina and Jessica liked to play on the rusty merry-go-rounds, but they had to scatter for safety when shootings erupted. During the summers, they attended a camp with other children who lived in the project, which included a complimentary lunch. The fire hydrants were often cracked open to blunt the zealous heat.

In Curries Woods, Ivette found herself stuck in the center of the new American political economy, in conditions that would determine her life and Emmanuel's over the next two decades.

3

...

Don't Nobody Leave This School

"Ryan will not be able to survive @ CEP, I fear for his safety," Rayni wrote in a frantic letter sent to Jackie Atkinson, a student intervention specialist and hearing officer, a few weeks after Ryan came home. Following his return from lockup and a five-day suspension, Rayni had received notice that he had been recommended for a transfer to Community Education Partners, an alternative disciplinary school for sixth through twelfth grade in the Hunting Park neighborhood. "The regular educational environment with supplementary aids and services was considered as an option," the notice read. But that option was rejected. "It is proposed that Ryan receives learning support services in an alternative educational setting as determined by the discipline policy in concert with the student code of conduct." The IEP team had concluded that his actions were not the byproduct of his ADHD and ODD.

Rayni had heard all about CEP's morbid stature as a vessel for the children nobody wanted to deal with, and there were rumors that the staff assaulted students. She was sure the transfer would be disastrous for Ryan.

CEP, a for-profit company, was established in 1996 by men with ties to the Republican Party, with an early investment from Thomas W. Beasley, co-founder of the world's first private prison enterprise. CEP quickly landed a $17.9 million contract with the Houston Independent School District, led by superintendent Rod Paige, who was eventually tapped by President George W. Bush to serve as his first education secretary. CEP's pitch to districts was simple: treat our schools as a destination for your least obedient and educable students. In city after city and state after state, CEP employed lobbyists, proffered campaign donations to lawmakers, and drew on connections to key players in the GOP orbit to approve legislation allowing CEP and other companies to siphon public dollars and procure district contracts.[1]

In 1997, the Pennsylvania General Assembly approved alternative private disciplinary programs, which were afforded millions of dollars in state grants. Three years later, CEP opened a disciplinary school in Philadelphia, becoming the first for-profit company to be granted a contract by the city's school district. More such institutions opened over time, with student bodies that were disproportionately male, poor, and African American or Latino. The city also adopted a new zero-tolerance discipline policy, and juvenile offenders returning to the city from detention were now placed in alternative schools like CEP, building a pipeline of hundreds of new customers each year.[2]

For the moment, Ryan was back at Grover Washington. After a few days, the principal phoned Rayni to pick him up in light of ongoing threats. Targeted by his classmates for tattling on Andres, he now found himself at the bottom of the school's pecking order. The following week, a student hit Ryan in the face as he was walking out of school in what was certain to be just the beginning of a full-on onslaught. He never knew whether Andres had found out that he had given his name to the authorities, but Andres wasn't someone who would have tried to even the score. The beef was with the town criers, Javier and the two other boys, who had gotten off with a slap on the wrist but felt perfectly fine smearing him. There had been unspoken tension between Ryan and Javier since sixth grade, when Javier fought a kid named Nathan and thought Ryan was taking his side. Ryan didn't even know the boy.

A few days after Ryan turned thirteen, he was scheduled to attend a disciplinary hearing at the school district headquarters on Broad Street. Rayni went with him and presented letters of support for Ryan from his counselor at school and the pastor of their church. Rev. Isaac Harris listed Rayni's activities at church: collecting and distributing food and clothing, running social events, and advising youth in their religious education. "Ryan, her son, has been raised by such a very competent, committed, and concerned mother," he wrote. He noted that Ryan often helped with these activities and catalogued some of his hobbies: Civil Air Patrol's cadet program, accompanying his grandmother to flea markets, watching movies, and selling drinks and bottled water outside his house in the summer. "From my experience, Ryan has lots of potential to continue to do great things," he concluded. "With the right direction, he can take advantage of his opportunities and avoid costly mistakes."

But at the hearing, school district officials argued that his escalating pattern of misbehavior warranted a proportionate response with a transfer to CEP, despite Rayni's pleading letter. Rayni mentioned the house fire the family had narrowly escaped when Ryan was younger to show that they both understood the severity of his actions. When it was Ryan's turn to speak, he said he had been involved with starting the fire because he thought it might help him fit in at school. But he had also tried to put it out, he added. He deeply regretted his actions.

The hearing was merely a technicality. The decision had already been made. In spite of Rayni's vehement objection, Ryan was ordered to report to CEP, as was Andres. Rayni was deflated by the decision. Instead of prompting an intervention to better address his learning disability, the arson event had turned into a convenient pretext for the school administrators to give Ryan a shove out the door.

* * *

GEORGE DIDN'T HAVE much wisdom to offer to help with Ryan's predicament. He had been in a similar situation in 1993, when he had been one of the few Puerto Ricans in his majority-Black high school. His classmates called him "pretty boy"—he had light skin and long black hair that the girls liked to braid.

One frigid January morning, sixteen-year-old George was walking to school with his friend Anthony and came upon a Nissan car key abandoned on the sidewalk. He didn't know what a Nissan was until he noticed the same emblem on a dark-gray vehicle parked nearby. When he stuck the key in, the door cracked open. George didn't have a license, but he and Anthony took off, picked up two friends, and drove around the city.

Later in the day, he pulled down the sun visor and found a police officer's license. "Oh shit!" George yelled. "We took a cop car." That evening, he stored and covered the car with a tarp in a friend's backyard. After two weeks of doing this, he planned to bring the car to a chop shop for cash. But as he reached the intersection of Broad Street and Cecil B. Moore Avenue, some cops noticed him and his friends.

George and Anthony took off running, but they were quickly nabbed by the cops. Their friends, Tim and Jacob, were still locked in the back of the car. At the police district, George was separated from his friends and ordered to stand on a bench with his arms spread out like a scarecrow so he could be monitored.

"What happened to him?" someone asked.

"He likes to steal cars," a cop replied dryly.

His mother picked him up, beat his ass, and phoned his father, Rafael. George was standing on the corner with a few friends when Rafael rolled down the block in his Cadillac. The others bolted as Rafael threw George in the car. His yelling put such a scare in him that an ass-whooping would have been a pile-on.

When George went to court at the old Youth Study Center, he told the judge, smiling, "Next time, I'm going to steal your car." The comment earned George detention in the facility. He, too, had learned about jail from the movies and was scared stiff of getting raped. In fact, his weeklong stay there was quite uneventful—hanging out, playing cards, and watching television. Then George learned he was being transferred to Glen Mills, a youth detention facility in Delaware County, and he was terrified. This would be a *real* prison. His hands were shackled to the boys sitting with him in the van. Upon arrival, the facility was on lockdown because of a fight. It was stricter than the Youth Study Center, but it was still nothing like the movies. After a few mundane days passed, his mother picked him up. "Next time, I'll leave you in there," she warned.

George was put on probation for nine months with conditions: an attendance sheet at school to be signed by all his teachers, an evening curfew, and mentorship by a Big Brother, whom George's neighbors thought was a drug dealer because his license plate read SMACK. But the car theft marked the end of George's ephemeral high school career. Skipping days here and there turned into skipping weeks and months until, in tenth grade, he formally dropped out.

*　*　*

RYAN'S DISCIPLINARY HEARING was followed by a juvenile case hearing in Family Court. Rayni, George, and Ryan—dressed in a white-and-blue-striped button-down shirt and navy pants—headed downtown. Ryan knew this hearing was the ultimate test. If the proceedings went awry, he feared being taken back into custody and reliving the abyss of juvenile detention, so he was determined to be on his best behavior and honestly answer whatever questions came his way. In advance, Rayni had written a letter to the judge: "I am concerned about his academics. Seventh grade is a very important year I would like for him to finish these last seven weeks, and then teach him for eighth grade through homeschooling. I have a lot of support because I don't want Ryan in the system . . . If I am allowed to teach him academically and get him ready for high school. And also to teach him the law of behavior I guarantee that my son will be a model citizen. Please pardon my son Ryan he is a very good boy."

Judge Lori Dumas-Brooks opened the proceedings with a critical disclosure: "I did inform Commonwealth that Principal Thompson I do know personally and professionally. He's also been in this room as a witness before . . . I don't know if that's going to be a big deal, but I did want to let you know so that you can be placed on notice."[3] As the judge revealed her relationship with Ryan's principal, Rayni's body went numb. She had worked in a lawyer's office, and this seemed like a clear conflict of interest. She wanted to speak up, but something stopped her. It was her inner spirit, which told her that transferring to a different judge wouldn't bring the best outcome for Ryan. Sticking with Dumas-Brooks was their best bet.

"I think that's fine, Your Honor," said William Bachman, Ryan's public defender.

"So the admission is to . . . this is—really isn't against Mr. Thompson . . . It's against the school."

"Yes, correct," said Bachman. He outlined the incident. "There was a fire lit in a trash can at school. The trash can was taken outside. The fire was doused. The plastic liner melted. The fire marshal came out to inspect, and everything was done." Assistant District Attorney Christen Tuttle announced the charges: failure to prevent catastrophe, possession of an instrument of crime, and conspiracy. "Ryan Rivera along with Andres did light a fire in a trash can within that school. After lighting the fire, they ran away. The fire was put out by school staff," she added.

Bachman explained that Ryan's mother had applied to homeschool him, but in the meantime, he would attend CEP. "The problem has always been Ryan with other kids who are more . . . advanced than him, and he's taken advantage of," he continued. "And so she wants to get him out of that aspect of the situation and into the homeschool. So to the extent—and we're obviously asking for a deferred. I've asked him to go to CEP for as long as it takes to resolve the homeschool situation, at most six weeks. I'm not enamored of that as a possibility, but I still want him to do well obviously, in hopes of getting a deferred adjudication."

"Counsel?" asked Dumas-Brooks.

"Your Honor, this is a first contact, and the Commonwealth does realize that," said Tuttle. "But my one concern is that this isn't just from someone just sort of lighting paper. This is lighting in a trash can and running away and leaving it there in the middle of a school day. So I would request that he participate in a fire starters program, have the necessary evaluations, and see what's going on."

Dumas-Brooks agreed. "This is a deferred adjudication. Place on interim probation with mandatory school, no unexcused absences, lateness, or class cuts." She also ordered him to attend the fire starters program. "I do understand that Mom thinks that this was child's play, but this is very dangerous child's play. And I need you to understand that I don't know what your reasoning was for doing it or participating in it, but you could have cost people their lives."

Ryan replied, "Yes, ma'am."

Dumas-Brooks had misinterpreted Rayni's letter, in which she earnestly acknowledged the gravity of the situation. "What Ryan did," she wrote, "was very serious. There is nothing that I can take away from it . . . Please pardon my son for this dangerous way of playing around."

Instead, Dumas-Brooks continued her finger-wagging. "And that is the reason why the fire starters program is ordered so that you can understand the significance of your actions and hopefully learn not to do it again. You're putting people's lives in danger including your own. Understand?"

"Yes, ma'am," Ryan replied obediently.

He was also ordered to obey a 7 p.m. nightly curfew, participate in random drug tests, and meet with a social worker. Coming out of court, Ryan felt that the judge had already made up her mind, and it was only a matter of time before he was sent to a juvenile facility for the long haul. Dumas-Brooks hadn't given him the chance to tell his side of the story. He had uttered only a handful of words in the hearing. The judge had papered over the fundamental issue: Had he really been trying to harm his classmates, or was this an act of stupidity? Had she asked, Ryan would have insisted that he'd just been thoughtless.

Rayni and Ryan worried that Principal Thompson wanted to get him kicked out of Grover Washington. The judge's admission that she had ties to Thompson only increased their concern. But Rayni continued to listen to her spirit and did not bring up her concerns with Bachman. For now, at least, the ball was in Ryan's court. He had the chance to prove he was reforming his ways.

* * *

RYAN'S LIFE HAD changed utterly in the course of one month. From the moment he had watched the flames leap up from the garbage can, he had gone from being an underachieving wise guy on the cusp of adolescence to a delinquent, condemned by the state and plunged into a labyrinth of curfews, court appearances, and social workers, with the threat of incarceration stalking his every move.

The night before his first day at CEP, Ryan was on edge. He, too, had heard rumors about the wild students, belligerent guards, and uncaring teachers. Everyone had. CEP was a storied institution in North Philly. He wondered if this was the payback for his years of shenanigans. Rayni told him not to dwell on that thought. The only thing that mattered now was that he adjust to his new surroundings if he was going to survive this chapter of his childhood.

As he would every day for the next two months, Ryan entered CEP that first morning through the boys' entrance on Front Street, across the street from Greenmount Cemetery, a tidy postbellum burial ground that stretches across a seventy-five-acre green expanse, ringed by gritty factories, warehouses, and row homes. Civil War veterans, Major League Baseball players, and generations of German, Polish, Irish, Latino, and Asian immigrants are buried side by side, earning the cemetery the distinct title of the most integrated place in the city. Only in the afterlife did the Jericho walls of segregation finally come crashing down.

There were two airport-style metal detectors and four security guards at the male entrance to CEP. Dressed in burgundy shirts and tan pants, the boys were directed through the metal detectors, with shoes and belts off. Then they were patted down and lined up against the hallway wall with their hands behind their backs. No backpacks, school supplies, or cell phones were permitted beyond that point.

Many of CEP's schools across the country similarly resembled prisons, with draconian disciplinary methods, dragnet surveillance, and restricted freedom of movement. CEP's motto served to demonstrate the order of priorities: "Be Here, Behave, and Be Learning." There were several grade-specific, gender-segregated classrooms, which were called "communities." Each community had four rooms, where desks were arranged in rows, and which were reached through a single doorway. Students entered their community in the morning and remained there until the close of the day.

Ryan's community was filled with Black and Latino students and a largely Black teaching staff. He quickly scoped out the classroom culture and was surprised to see that there was no apparent hierarchy, not of race, height, or looks. It seemed that your presence spoke for itself.

You had to have gotten into some serious trouble to have been booked into this dungeon.

As Ryan sat in class, he watched a short, skinny boy masterfully exploit a disturbance that diverted the teacher's attention. The small window allowed the boy to break into the storeroom, swipe some items, and put them in his pocket. His kleptomania was one of innumerable distractions. Ryan feared that the room would erupt in fighting at any moment. He was right: he witnessed two fights just before lunch. The teachers took a laissez-faire approach and let it go on for some minutes before intervening. As for the lessons, they often involved the students copying sentences from the board into their notebooks. There was rarely a lesson plan or program of activities and goals. Were they actually learning anything?

Philadelphia school district officials were unfazed by mounting evidence of falling test scores and negligible graduation rates at CEP-run schools. The city was not an outlier. Dallas schools had severed its contract with CEP two years early after an internal evaluation showed poor results. In Houston, one study found that students performed worse on reading and math standardized tests and had a lower passing rate after a year at CEP compared to their level when they first enrolled. The *Houston Press* reported on allegations of fabricated grades on student records at CEP's Ferndale campus: "If a student had a failing grade or 'incomplete' written on the card, the grade was crossed out and replaced by a flat 70—just enough to pass." The article also quoted a former employee who declared, "That school needs to be closed down. Ain't a damn thing being learned in that school. Nothing." Years later, another study found that 90 percent of students enrolled in a CEP school in Houston in 2004 had dropped out or transferred to another district; only 1 percent had graduated.[4]

When it was time for lunch, staff delivered to the classrooms on trays. Wrapped in aluminum foil, the main dish was hot dogs. On his first day, the students forfeited their allotted cartons of milk for poor behavior. Ryan bit into his hot dog and found it cold and stale, almost as if someone had just taken it out of the fridge after leaving it there overnight. This was a far cry from what he was used to at Grover Washington: hot buffet-style lunches with turkey burgers, macaroni and cheese, and Ellio's rectangular pizza slices. He never ate lunch at CEP again. He had developed a knack at suppressing his hunger over extended stretches. It had certainly come in handy during his incarceration.

On his second day at CEP, Ryan walked to the public bus stop with his mother. A student warned him that as a new kid, he should be prepared to fight if he got on the bus. Rayni was shocked, and they agreed that he should make the forty-five-minute journey to school by foot instead. Once there, he overheard students rehearsing a plot to break into the room where the cell phones, SEPTA passes, and tokens were stored in a safe—if only they could get hold of a screwdriver. Students found quirky ways to entertain themselves amid mass ennui. Some attempted to smuggle candy and phones past the metal detectors and sharp-eyed guards and their thorough pat-downs. It seemed impossible until someone conceived of a novel method: a few students were dispensing Starbursts that reeked, and it turned out they had jammed the candy between their buttocks, the one bodily crevice beyond the reach of the surveillance complex. Ryan never accepted another piece of candy at school.

Twenty minutes before dismissal, a fight broke out. Ryan always reacted to violence in the same way (although he wouldn't understand this about himself until years later): fight or flight. He had almost gotten through the second day without incident, when the classroom instantly became the site of physical combat between clusters of boys. Ryan fled before he could become collateral damage. As he left, his teacher, Ms. Lewis, stopped him. He had two choices: "Leave the school and come back with a parent, or get back in the classroom." Ryan left. Rayni called the teacher and explained that Ryan didn't want to get caught in the crosshairs of the scrum. Ms. Lewis corrected her: it wasn't a brawl. It was just one fight. Boys will be boys. Still, Rayni wanted Ms. Lewis to understand that Ryan didn't fit the traditional CEP mold. He was antsy around violence. The best Ms. Lewis could do, she said, was isolate him in the classroom, but the next day, the teacher failed to follow through.

From the moment he set foot in the school, Ryan had to face a near constant barrage of physical and verbal threats. And instead of deterring fights, the staff at CEP adopted a hands-off approach. There was a class bully named Miles, who, with a crew of friends to back him up, liked to play-fight, put kids in headlocks, and volley insults. One morning, Ryan whispered to a classmate within Miles's earshot: "Ain't this shit funny? He ain't talking to nobody. He ain't saying nothing about nobody. He is quiet as shit. When his friends are around, he wants to mouth off." The classmate spread the word about Ryan trash-talking Miles. Later, when Miles's friends finally showed up at school, he approached Ryan.

"What's all that shit you've been talking all day?" Miles wanted to go at it.

"I'm not trying to fight you," Ryan said. "I'm trying to get out of here."

Miles smirked. "Don't *nobody* leave this school." Then he put up his fists. After dodging Miles's swing, Ryan punched him square in the face. Before he could get in another, Miles's crew of friends boxed him in, and Ryan knew it was over. Still standing, he lowered his head near his legs and covered his face with his hands.

A teacher looked on, lagging by the door, and only after Ryan had taken five punches did he and another staff member intervene, claiming they thought the boys were playing. One had put Ryan in a headlock. Although they were slow to break up fights, it was common practice for teachers to restrain students physically. Ryan sometimes even saw staff punching and hitting students for talking back or resisting an order.

As punishment for the fight with Miles, Ryan was simply sent home. Detention, suspension, or expulsion would have been futile—after all, CEP was the last resort. Not that going home was a walk in the park. Ryan's CEP uniform, a mark of the worst kids in the city, made him a target on the streets. Sometimes the SEPTA buses wouldn't stop for CEP students, so he had to walk home. On his way home with Andres one day, a few Olney High School students jumped Andres and stole his boots. One of them knew Ryan, so they left him unscathed.

In many ways, he felt as if he were still at VisionQuest. And while at CEP, Ryan frequently had nightmares in which he was alone, back in his hut at VisionQuest and overcome by the scent of the outdoors. He would abruptly wake up in a cold sweat and leap out of bed to make sure he was home. He couldn't shake off the fear of juvenile detention for months, and to him, CEP seemed like more of the same.

Ryan had also been assigned a youth advocate. Imani had come of age in a segregated public housing project and had persevered to graduate college. She was less a mentor than an auntie who gave him a taste of middle-class pleasures. Several times a month, she met Ryan and a few other boys to take them to the movies, Red Lobster, an arcade, or bowling. They even did some cooking classes, making pies, macaroni and cheese, and rotisserie chicken.

One time, Imani took him to her old neighborhood, where her family still lived: the Fairhill Apartments, which was made up of two eighteen-story brown brick buildings overlooking low-rise units. Built in 1961, it housed predominantly poor Black tenants. Many waited years for an opening, and when their patience paid off, they were met with slum conditions from decades of negligence—elevators covered in feces and urine and filled with trash, open-air drug sales, flooded apartments, and structural damage that was left unaddressed. The state had deposited the residents behind these walls and rendered them invisible. Imani tried to explain to Ryan that if she could make it out of the projects, he could overcome his predicament, too.

As per the judge's order, Ryan also attended a fire safety program at the Philadelphia Fire Department. There were three other kids around the same age: two boys and a white girl named Amy. They watched dull, corny videos covering the risks of playing with fire and completed worksheets. But he liked going to the program so he could hang out with Amy. They often excused themselves to use the bathroom and instead made out and felt each other up in the stairwell. Ryan didn't learn anything about fire, but he made a profound discovery: white girls were way easier to hook up with than the girls in his neighborhood.

He had been at CEP for less than two months when the school year wrapped up, but it felt like an eternity. The daily struggle to dodge violence at school and on the way home, evade abuse by the staff, submit to pat-downs and surveillance, show up for drug tests and probation, be home by curfew—it had all taken its toll.

* * *

NATIONWIDE, CEP FACED growing scrutiny for its educational methods. In the summer of 2009, the Atlanta Independent School System in Georgia axed its $7 million annual contract with CEP, the only alternative disciplinary school in the district.[5] The decision followed a class action lawsuit filed by the American Civil Liberties Union charging that the school, Forrest Hills, denied students their right to an adequate public education. In the complaint, the ACLU accused the school, which had about four hundred middle and high school students, nearly all Black, of producing an environment "so violent and intimidating that learning is all but impossible" and submitting their students to unjustified "daily invasive, humiliating and dehumanizing searches." As with a standard police stop and frisk, some students were ordered to put their hands on the wall and spread their arms and legs in preparation to be searched. Female students were put through a daily regimen of searches where they were directed to "grab the sides of their bras, extend them out, shake them, and snap them back in," sometimes while a male faculty member observed. One of the plaintiffs endured this practice when she was pregnant.

The ACLU described classrooms in which students filled out worksheets much of the time, with almost none achieving basic proficiency. "Teachers (and at least one administrator) routinely hit students, throw books at them, and throw students against walls or to the floor," it noted, while school resource officers sometimes put students in chokeholds. Not surprisingly, the school posted high suspension, juvenile court referral, and dropout rates. Among those who didn't get pushed out, few returned to traditional schools.

In 2008, on the first day of state testing season, the school took in eighteen new students. Dozens of students had also been transferred to Forrest Hills the month before. This "accomplished the purpose they wanted," CEP's CEO Randle Richardson revealed, referring to Atlanta district administrators. "It got disruptive kids out. It got the low performers out"—out of the traditional public schools to massage their student achievement figures. When the district canceled its contract with CEP, the ACLU dropped the lawsuit.[6]

* * *

RYAN HAD TWO more court hearings over the summer. The first was pro forma, just to check the status of the case. The second would decide his fate. Ryan and Rayni arrived at the court building on a hot August day. William Bachman, Ryan's public defender, had told Rayni that he should accept time at Saint Gabriel's Hall, an Archdiocese-run residential program in a suburb of Pennsylvania for court-adjudicated male youth, so he could turn his life around. Rayni was indecisive about the best course of action. The trauma and blemish of residential placement would follow Ryan for years, but maybe it would turn him into an upstanding adult. As they waited to be called in, she decided to leave it in the hands of God. "If I send him to this school, he's going to learn how to be bad. I may lose him to the system. But if you think it's going to help him," she prayed, "then take him." It was better for Ryan's sanity that she didn't fill him in on her thought process. Residential placement was the last place he wanted to go.

Hours passed. Bachman said something was up; the doors of the courtroom were locked. He went to inquire, and when he returned, he handed Ryan a letter saying that his case was dismissed. Just like that. On the brink of being locked up in juvenile placement, he was free to go. No more peeing in a cup. No more curfews. No more fear or recurring nightmares. How was it possible? Rayni reread the letter. Mother and son embraced. They would never learn why the case had been dismissed; they were just grateful for the stay.

Then something even more remarkable happened. Ryan's CEP school was shut down. It was a harbinger of further trouble for the company in Philadelphia. Later, Philadelphia axed its contract with the rest of the CEP schools following a review of disciplinary providers. The decision had come amid lawsuits against CEP and public relations fiascos in multiple cities.[7]

Before long, John Perzel, CEP's most powerful political ally in the state and a thirty-two-year Republican incumbent in the Pennsylvania

House of Representatives, was unseated by a Democrat. The following year, in a scandal dubbed "Computergate," Perzel pled guilty to illegally routing $10 million in public money into technology and software to aid his and other Republican legislative campaigns. He served less than two years in prison.[8]

4

...

Hamburger Helper

.

It was a few weeks before Christmas 1985, and Ivette was preparing lunch for her sisters. Her mother, Valentina, was hospitalized with advanced breast cancer, and Ivette had become their primary caretaker. As she was about to leave to pick her sisters up from school, Kevin grabbed her and dragged her to his room. Then he raped her. Three men, three strikes. Ivette's first reaction was guilt and the thought that she had disrespected her mother. In the next moment she asked, *Why me? Why me? What did I do to deserve this?*

She decided not to tell Valentina, who was too sick for such news. And she waited until the next day to call the police, which she realized was a crucial mistake. An officer came to the apartment when nobody else was home and heard her account of the rape. He told her that she had reported it too late for a thorough investigation. Ivette told nobody else. She was sure the family would accuse her of lying.

Valentina remained in the hospital as her health continued to decline. When Ivette visited, she was in excruciating pain and could hardly mutter more than a few words. Ivette came home and locked herself in her room and cried. What would happen to her and her sisters if Valentina died? The prospect of living with Kevin without at least the veneer of protection from her mother was terrifying, but how could she leave? Who would take care of her sisters?

Then life at home became even more intolerable. Kevin introduced them to Eva, a woman he had been seeing secretly. She would look after them while their mother was sick, he said. Ivette tore into him. "You have no respect for your wife," she cried. But Eva stayed.

* * *

MEMBERS OF VALENTINA'S church surrounded her hospital bed and prayed. Kevin held Carolina's and Jessica's hands as they stood at the foot of their mother's bed and watched her eyes widen as she gasped for air. Kevin called Ivette to leave the Sunday church service she was attending and come to the hospital. But by the time she arrived, Valentina had gone. She was forty-one. She died in the dark about the sexual violence her daughter had suffered at the hands of men in her family.

Pedro, Ivette, their father, Liam, and the rest of the family traveled to Jersey City for the funeral. When Carolina went up to her mother's casket, Valentina was in a wig, and her face felt cold to the touch. Noticing that Ivette was not crying, one of her aunts asked, "You didn't love your mom?"

"I loved my mom," she replied. "I know she is in a better place. Someday I'm going to see her again."

Eva and her two sons quickly moved into the apartment at Curries Woods. One evening, Ivette put Carolina and Jessica to bed and went to sleep in her room. She woke up, feeling something moving next to her and saw Kevin, who had climbed into the bed. He covered her mouth, and although she kicked, scratched, and pulled his hair, he raped her a second time. He denied both incidents. This new attack didn't distress Ivette as much as the previous assaults; the violence had almost become normalized. But this time, she called the police within hours— when the rest of the family had left. Two officers stopped by and took notes, brought her to the hospital to collect DNA evidence, and said they would be in touch. But no one followed up. Nor did she. Ivette figured it was a lost cause. She had lost her trust in the criminal justice system, which she had assumed would help her at a time like this, even more than her own family. Kevin would get away with it, just as the men before him had.

Ivette was at her friend's house some weeks later when she suddenly felt dizzy. She went to the bathroom and threw up. After she recovered, she called her pastor to bring her to church. Once there, she began to pray. "What is happening to me? I never felt this way. What is the cause of this? Tell me, please. Hear my prayer."

She found the answer at the health clinic, where she did a pregnancy test that came back positive. The family would blame her and accuse her of provoking Kevin, so she only opened up about the rape to her father, Liam, and her aunt Rosario. Liam was irate and advised her to have an abortion. But she could not take the "life of an unborn child." It would be a grievous breach of her faith, and Rosario agreed, saying, "It's a living soul inside of you."

So that spring Ivette made the agonizing decision to leave the apartment in Curries Woods and her sisters. It would be unwise to be around Kevin while she was expecting, and Eva was now openly hostile toward her. Ivette had complained to the building management about Eva moving into an apartment that was under her mother's name. In response, Eva had held a small pocket knife to Ivette's throat for a few moments.

Ivette moved out without saying goodbye to her sisters, who were in school. She didn't want to risk a violent reaction from Eva. Nobody told Carolina and Jessica where she had gone or why. Carolina only learned about the pregnancy from a girl in her class. Meanwhile, the girls were stranded with Eva. For years, they endured her callous abuse. Carolina nicknamed her "Little Chihuahua," a tiny woman who couldn't express herself without yelling or hitting. After Ivette left, she began shuffling from house to house of friends and relatives in the tristate area before finally settling with her aunt Nydia and uncle Luis in Stamford, Connecticut. Kevin was no longer a threat, but she was reminded of him every time the baby kicked.

* * *

IVETTE NEVER WANTED to become a mother so young, at the age of twenty-two. Her baby, Michael, had been conceived in violence. Worse, her mother had taught her that a child conceived out of wedlock could not be granted God's blessing.

She was thirty-eight weeks pregnant when she attended her first prenatal appointment. Her blood pressure was high, and her immune system was rejecting the fetus. The doctor wanted to deliver the baby immediately to avoid a high-risk birth. By the end of the day, the baby was born via cesarean section. The sight of her son washed away her despair; becoming a mother turned out to be one of the happiest moments of Ivette's life. Michael's lungs weren't fully developed, so he had to be intubated and remain in the hospital with Ivette for a few weeks.

Kevin, his father, made no attempt to be in contact—at that time or ever. Nor did Ivette or Michael, when he was older, try to be in touch. *It was for the best*, she thought. No need to take him to court for child support or custody, no distractions, no harm. She tried to call her sisters with the news, but no one picked up or returned her messages. To move on with her life, she had to act as if her family in Jersey City no longer existed.

Ivette was determined to raise Michael as she had been raised. She felt God would give her strength and wisdom and held on to Psalm 23: "The Lord is my shepherd; I shall not want. He makes me lie down in green pastures. He leads me beside still waters. He restores my soul. He leads me in paths of righteousness for his name's sake." She started receiving Women, Infants, and Children benefits, which went toward essentials like formula, milk, and cereal. She also received federal Aid to Families with Dependent Children, an unconditional monthly sum of over $200, which largely went to poor single mothers; Connecticut was one of the most generous states in the country for welfare recipients.[1]

At home, Nydia's husband, Luis, started bringing gifts for Michael: a crib and clothing. He had always wanted a boy, but he and Nydia had a girl. Nydia began to grow jealous of Ivette, suspecting something romantic brewing between her and Luis, even though that was not the case.

So almost as quickly as she arrived, Ivette explored the idea of moving out. One day, a missionary and former nurse named Roselyn paid a visit to Nydia's house. Roselyn had occasionally led services at their church. They became friends, spending July Fourth together at Roselyn's home in Waterbury, an hour's drive northeast, where they grilled hamburgers and had a picnic in the backyard.

After talking it over with Roselyn, Ivette, who was now twenty-three, decided to move to Waterbury and live with her, the most convenient escape from the mounting family drama. As Ivette settled into her new home, in a low-rise estate with greenery and wide plots of land separating the buildings, her life began to seem simpler, organized around caring for Michael, WIC appointments, and church services. But she longed for her family back in Jersey City, wondering whether she would ever see or speak to her sisters or aunt Rosario and whether they ever thought about her. She had done nothing wrong, she told herself. She was the victim. Yet she had been forced to pick up and leave. How was that fair? If her mother were alive, none of this would have happened.

*　*　*

ROSELYN WAS PLANNING to visit her sister Mercedes in Philadelphia and invited Ivette to join her. On a September morning, they set out from Waterbury, reaching Philadelphia in the late afternoon. Mercedes had a red brick house with a gated porch on Sixth Street in Kensington. Ivette was introduced to her enormous family, including her many sons. One was Ivan, who was playing the guitar and crooning Christian tunes.

As Ivette sat at the dining table, Ivan remarked to Roselyn, "She truly is a missionary of God." Ivette blushed. *Who is this man?* she thought. *I don't even know him. Do I have to deal with this for three days straight?* She learned that Ivan was a salesman at a local retail store and in-house guitarist at the church around the corner, where Roselyn had been invited to preach the next evening. After dinner and feeding Michael a bottle of milk, Ivette slipped into her pajamas and dozed off in the upstairs bedroom.

The next morning, Ivan greeted her as she ate some sausage and scrambled eggs. Roselyn was going to visit her other sister and asked if Ivette wanted to come. She yelped, "Yes, please!" to get away from Ivan. She figured that he, like many of the men she had encountered, had ulterior motives.

For the evening church service, Ivette dressed herself and Michael elegantly. Ivan began ogling her, making her uncomfortable. After a light meal, she walked over to the church with Roselyn so they could pray privately before the others arrived. During the service, Roselyn introduced Ivette as a missionary, a flattering gesture.

Ivette was relieved to leave the next day and drop Ivan from her sight and mind.

* * *

WITHIN A WEEK of returning to Waterbury, Roselyn told Ivette that her sister had called, saying that Ivan urgently needed to speak with her. Ivette didn't want to associate with any men, still reeling from her past traumas, but Ivan wouldn't let up, so eventually she relented and took his call. He asked if she was coming with Roselyn on her next trip to Philadelphia.

"I don't know yet," she said. "Maybe, maybe not. Why the question?"

"Nothing. Just wanted to know. That's all."

When they spoke again, he revealed that she hadn't left his mind since her visit.

"Why are you saying this to me?" she replied. "I hardly know you."

Ivan asked if he could call her every so often. She wasn't sure why she agreed, but after that, she took his calls. During one of their chats, he declared that they would be married and have a child together. She was shaken by his gall. How was this possible? No mutual affection had been expressed.

Roselyn advised her to pray about it. "I'm not searching for nobody," Ivette responded. "I don't want to be with nobody. Why should I pray for something that I really don't want?"

"Love can come in many different ways," Roselyn said.

* * *

Around Thanksgiving, Roselyn was going back to Philadelphia. Ivette tagged along because she still wasn't in touch with her family in New Jersey and she didn't want to be alone.

Ivan greeted her with a bouquet of red roses. Thanksgiving dinner featured a Puerto Rican twist with *arroz con dulce*. As they gorged on the feast, Ivan started strumming "Kumbaya" on his guitar. All of a sudden, he kneeled in front of Ivette. On cue, his mother, Mercedes, handed him a jewelry box. At the sight of the gold ring, Ivette almost choked on her turkey. *Oh my God. Lord, please have mercy*, she thought.

Ivan met her eyes. "Will you marry me? I'm going to be your best friend, your companion, a father for your child. I will give him my last name. I will always be there for both of you." As the rest of the family were fixed on Ivette in anticipation, she felt cornered. She said nothing but accepted the ring, and the family broke into celebration. They pulled out a medley of musical instruments—snare drum, maracas, and tambourine—and launched into a performance.

At that moment, Ivette realized the proposal had been carefully orchestrated, and she had been the only one out of the loop. She stopped eating and held back tears. Later, she put the ring back in the box and gave it to Roselyn. Ivette told her that she wouldn't have come, had she known of the plan. She spent the rest of the trip steering clear of Ivan. Marriage—and to Ivan no less—was unthinkable.

Ivan called Ivette in Waterbury and told her that God had spoken to him, saying his wife would be named Ivette with a son named Michael. She opened up to him about the sexual assaults, but he didn't care about her past and accepted her regardless. He was a churchgoing man, and she took that as a sign of God's approval. How could she, a God-loving woman, reject God's plans?

As she prayed and mulled it over, she decided to go through with the engagement in spite of having no romantic feelings for Ivan. At least Michael would have a father, she reckoned. He wouldn't be stigmatized or treated differently for being raised by a single mother. Ivan proposed that they get married in Philadelphia the following month, and Ivette agreed.

* * *

AFTER THE WEDDING, Ivette and Michael lived with Ivan at Mercedes's house for a month before returning with Roselyn to Connecticut to pack up their belongings and transfer her welfare records. As they were driving on Interstate 95, Ivette turned pale and began feeling dizzy. They stopped at a McDonald's. As soon as Roselyn parked, Ivette hurled.

"Oh my God," Roselyn exclaimed. "I think you're expecting." Joaquin was born in Hahnemann University Hospital on November 4, 1988, and his younger brother, Emmanuel, arrived nine years later.

* * *

HAD GOD INTENDED an abusive marriage in his plans for Ivette? What had she done to deserve such a fate? After more than a dozen years with Ivan, the intervention of DHS and the threat of losing her youngest son finally compelled Ivette to leave him. Once she made the move, she wanted a clean slate. She wanted to shed the toxic memories of their old house and the volatile relationship with her husband. So she left all the furniture behind when she and Emmanuel moved into the two-bedroom house owned by Ora, the pastor's wife. It was just over the A Street bridge, near the intersection of East Tusculum and Cambria Streets and not far from El Campamento, a notorious open-air heroin camp where people shot up drugs and took refuge on mattresses and in tents.

Over the months, Ivette slowly assembled what she needed in the living and dining rooms. The final piece was a bed for Emmanuel's room. DHS did not allow him to sleep in her room, but Emmanuel had developed extreme separation anxiety. Even when he had his own bed, he clung to his mother and nestled in her arms until he fell asleep.

The school year was well underway when they moved, so Emmanuel remained in kindergarten near his old address. This forced him and Ivette to trudge more than a mile to and from school through the rain, sleet, and snow. When she dropped him off each morning, the sight of her walking away was the worst feeling in the world for him.

Emmanuel and Ivette saw Joaquin, who was living with Pastor Diego and Ora, most days of the week at church. They tried to maintain some normalcy by holding joint family outings to swimming pools, movies, and Nockamixon State Park for picnics and BBQs. Ivette's DHS social worker was surprised at how close the two families had become. They would become closer: after a year, Emmanuel and Ivette moved a few blocks away to an apartment above Diego's church on Front Street; Diego did not ask for rent. At the same time, Joaquin was admitted into Don Guanella, a residential facility in the suburbs for people with intellectual disabilities.

Meanwhile, Michael left Devereux, the behavioral health treatment center, and was placed with African American foster parents in Cheltenham, a lush, quiet suburb just outside the city. Two months into foster care, he and his foster father got into an argument. Michael threatened him, "You don't know me. I could really hurt you." He then ran away to a friend's house for two weeks, returning to a monthlong punishment of no PlayStation, Sega Dreamcast, or playing outside. That was the only time he ran away, before he realized how caring his new family was.

Emmanuel once visited their two-story home, which had three bedrooms, two bathrooms, a basement with a pool table, television, and wood shop, a basketball hoop in the driveway, and a backyard. "Wow, this house is big!" he exclaimed to Michael as they toured the expansive rooms, taking in the well-stocked fridge. It was like a house in his favorite film, *High School Musical*. Getting a glimpse of how the other half lived, Emmanuel was jealous of Michael. How much better his life could be if his family had money. He dreamed of having a closet full of new clothes, a pantry crammed with unlimited snacks, and cable. *Here I am living in the hood*, he thought. *I wish DHS had taken me, too.*

For her part, Ivette made a last-ditch effort to save her marriage. While visiting Ivan in the hospital as he was being treated for an injury, she said she was willing to give it another chance if he would agree to participate in family therapy. He refused, and she declined to beg. That was the final time she saw him, although without the means to engage a lawyer, they were unable to divorce. So Ivan became the latest man she pushed out of her mind. Then her DHS social worker stopped making visits to her home now that it was clear that Emmanuel was in a safe environment. She had come to the end of a torturous ordeal, but the fear of the authorities snatching her baby never left her.

Emmanuel's elementary school years were spent bouncing about the housing market of North Philadelphia. Within a few months, he and Ivette moved from Pastor Diego's apartment into a room in a shared house in Kensington, living with a couple, Pablo and Yesenia. Pablo viciously abused and beat Yesenia, and Ivette would intervene to defend her. Occasionally, Ivette would leave Emmanuel in their care. He would bawl his eyes out, and they would lock him in the basement to shut him up.

Fortunately for Emmanuel, staying in the house became untenable. Pablo had a crush on Ivette, although the feeling wasn't mutual. Yesenia felt jealous of her, and one day the situation turned violent. Ivette had met a man, Freddie, who hung out at the house. He and Pablo ended up dueling it out on the block with a sword and a broomstick. A crowd formed. The local drug dealers thought it wasn't a fair fight, so they took the weapons away and made the two men spar old-school. Pablo took a licking. By the end, his face was busted up, and he could barely open his eyes.

That was the end of Pablo and Yesenia. Ivette and Emmanuel slept at her friend Eve's place for a few days, before moving to a room in a house on Sixth and Cambria Streets followed by a stint in another place nearby. Freddie began shacking up with them and chipped in from his job at a landscaping company to help cover the bills. Brawny with a pudgy face, a trimmed black beard, and dark brown skin bronzed by days spent under the beating sun of his homeland, Puerto Rico, he had a rattail hairstyle with a short braid at the back.

The instability caused Emmanuel to fail and repeat first grade at two different elementary schools, Lewis Elkin and Henry A. Brown. He grasped early on that at any moment he and his mother could get kicked to the curb for no reason other than the fact that they were dirt poor. "Why can't we have our own crib?" he pestered Ivette. She had no good answers—she, too, felt the weight of their economic insecurity and the absence of a safety net. Finances were a frequent subject of her therapy sessions; the therapist took note of her crippling anxiety and lack of self-esteem.

Headed by a disabled single mother, the family of two largely survived on roughly $10,000 a year in SSI and TANF benefits plus food stamps.[2] With this, Ivette had to cover housing, utilities, food, clothing, furniture, transportation, laundry, household goods, and other basic needs. She did so by pinching pennies, skipping meals, struggling to afford birthday and Christmas presents, and counting the days until the end of the month only to start the process again. She swallowed the humiliation of wearing tattered clothing, turning to food pantries, living in squalid housing, and moving again and again. She endured this under the weight of repeated physical and sexual violence and the abandonment of the people she thought loved and cared for her.

Had Emmanuel and Ivette lived in a European nation like Sweden, Finland, or the Netherlands, the government would have sent the family the equivalent of hundreds of dollars each month in the form of a child allowance to help defray the costs of raising a child and sustain them above the line of immiseration.[3] But this was America, the land of rugged individualism, a credo yoked to the myth of meritocracy. Where cash welfare has been all but eliminated, leaving families at the mercy of the vagaries of the market.

At Elkin, Emmanuel started playing the violin. He was constantly worried about being judged for sounding terrible. One time he was practicing in the schoolyard and a boy came over, snatched the instrument, and punched him in the stomach. Emmanuel lost his breath for some thirty seconds. He was often picked on at school, and with the running barb that he was gay. "Why do you sound like a girl?" kids asked him. His voice was gentler than theirs, higher pitched, and he liked to wear bright colors. He heard it from his mother, too. When he played with Barbies with his cousin, Ivette would reprimand him. "That's gay. You can't do that." He didn't understand what gay meant, but at this early age, he already felt the pressure to toe the normative line and suppress his inner spirit, which plunged him into anxiety.

Unlike his brothers, he was a studious learner who didn't need cajoling from his mother. When he got home from school, he would eat a snack—usually Ritz cheese crackers or string cheese, capped with a Capri Sun—and dive into his homework. With no cable or Internet access at home, Ivette would walk him to McPherson Square Library, a nineteenth-century Carnegie-funded branch. The library was a sanctuary for the children, seniors, job seekers, and unhoused people of the neighborhood and one of the few public institutions still functioning after decades of austerity. For hours, Emmanuel would play computer games on sites such as CoolMath4Kids and borrow books and movies. His favorite books were the Diary of a Wimpy Kid series. He related to Greg, the depressed protagonist, and his dysfunctional family. Ivette made sure to save a few dollars so he could purchase a book at the Scholastic Book Fair in school to satisfy his literary itch.

* * *

WHEN EMMANUEL WAS nine and in third grade, Ivette and Freddie moved into a dilapidated house on Hartville Street. The floors and drywall were broken. Paint was peeling off the walls. The kitchen had mold, roaches, and soot buildup in the stove. Emmanuel slept on a worn box spring in a room without a door.

Michael, who had graduated from high school and aged out of foster care, moved in with them and took the couch in the living room (Joaquin remained in the long-term residential care facility). Michael quickly developed serious reservations about Freddie and his mother's relationship with him. "He's no good for you," Michael warned her. He saw how Freddie drank at all hours of the day, reeking of Budweiser, Heineken, and Hurricane High Gravity. He drank when he woke up. He drank on work breaks and at home. He drove drunk. He was rarely sober.

Ivette suffered a miscarriage only a few weeks after learning she was pregnant. Her doctor suspected that her cocktail of hypertension medications likely contributed, but Freddie blamed Michael—he and Ivette had been jumping around and playing on the bed. That's when the abuse began. Freddie told Ivette she was worthless, she should have stayed with the father of her children. And he attacked her physically. Michael saw Freddie's rage and jealousy swell with each gulp—he was like Ivan, cut from the same cloth. He wouldn't even let Michael bring friends over, convinced that Ivette would cheat on him with one of them. She was still broken from her failed marriage to Ivan and could not bear the prospect of being alone, so she put up with it.

It was on Hartville where Emmanuel had his first real feelings for a boy (not counting Zac Efron in *High School Musical*). Within a few weeks of moving in, he found any excuse to be out of the house to hang out with Mario, a skinny Puerto Rican boy with short dark-brown hair and a light-brown complexion who lived on the same block. He thought Mario was cute. At the nearby McVeigh Recreation Center, they played Manhunt and went on the swings, and Michael and his new girlfriend, Aida, took them swimming when the weather got warm. Aida, a high school student, was living on Hartville with her aunt.

Emmanuel and Mario pretended they had superpowers: telekinesis and superspeed. But mostly, they made out. Emmanuel knew he fancied boys. Being with Mario felt right, more than anything else. *But I can't be gay, right?* he thought. When he was younger, he had prayed when he woke up in the morning and before falling asleep. The Pentecostal sermons he heard at church had drilled into him that homosexuality was a grave sin against God—Adam and Eve, not Adam and Steve. Worried about how his relationship with Mario could be perceived by God, he asked his mother, "Is it bad to like boys if you're a boy?"

"God doesn't like that," she said.

For months, he and Mario role-played being each other's boyfriend. Emmanuel thought that if they called it a game, they could pretend their attraction wasn't genuine and stay within the bounds of acceptable moral conduct. This involved experimenting sexually in Emmanuel's house, which was especially risky since Ivette could just walk into his doorless room and he didn't have to imagine how she would react. Emmanuel comfortably explored his body with Mario, finally moving past a lingering trauma. He had been splashing in the pool a few summers ago when his friend pulled down his swimming trunks and started performing oral sex on him without his consent.

One afternoon, Emmanuel came home from school to find his mother crying in Freddie's green Chevy Trailblazer. The house had been boarded up, and the car was loaded with their belongings. Ivette explained that she had been sleeping when a man appeared in the bedroom. She thought he was there to rob them, but he said he was from the real estate office and had come to tell her to leave by the end of day.

"Why?" she replied, startled. "I paid my rent."

"Somebody purchased the house," he said.

"You didn't send me a notice," she said, but it didn't make a difference.

Ivette had little attachment to the crumbling house, but it was *their* crumbling house—at least for the past few months. Where were they supposed to go on a dime? Who would take them in? In shock and desperation, she called one friend after another, trying to find a place to sleep. She would *not* go to a homeless shelter. Finally, Freddie's brother's ex-wife, who was also a friend, said they could stay with her.

They had to abandon their furniture and mattresses and even Emmanuel's toys since there was no room in their new place. Ivette insisted to Emmanuel that this wasn't her doing; she had indeed paid the rent on time. By now Emmanuel had mastered the art of starting over in a new neighborhood, but the eviction was especially brutal. He was leaving Mario, his best friend and first love, and hadn't had a chance to say goodbye properly. Emmanuel saw that it took as little as the whim of a landlord to lose his home and upend his friendships, his schooling, his entire world, and neither he nor his mother had the power to do anything to stop it.

They weren't the only family in Philadelphia to endure this violence; more than one out of fourteen households faced evictions annually between 2010 and 2015. Worse, in some neighborhoods of North Philadelphia, such as Kensington, that figure topped 15 percent of households.[4] "Losing a home sends families to shelters, abandoned houses, and the street," wrote sociologist Matthew Desmond. "It invites depression and illness, compels families to move into degrading housing in dangerous neighborhoods, uproots communities, and harms children. Eviction reveals people's vulnerability and desperation, as well as their ingenuity and guts."[5]

In their new home in Frankford, Emmanuel, Michael, and his girlfriend, Aida, were relegated to sleeping on couches. It was the middle of the school year, and Ivette wasn't able to transfer Emmanuel to a school nearby, so he had to set out every morning before daybreak with the hope of arriving while the cafeteria still served breakfast. He loathed the hour-and-a-half journey to Elkin, which he did with his chaperone Michael on foot because they couldn't afford the fare. Sometimes he had to walk home alone. Once he desperately had to urinate but was too afraid to go into a store and ask to use the restroom, so he soaked his pants. *Why is my life such shit?* he muttered to himself.

Ivette was eventually able to get Emmanuel a TransPass for the bus, and he started to make new friends in the neighborhood, spending afternoons playing Double Dutch with a few girls. Then he met two boys, Dylan and Will. One afternoon, after toying around with a pogo stick, the three walked to Dylan's house to play *Halo* on Xbox. His mother made them some Hamburger Helper and left them alone. It was too watery for Emmanuel, so he didn't touch it. Suddenly, unprovoked, Will, who had seemed annoyed by Emmanuel all day, burst out: "You're a faggot! You're a faggot! You're a faggot!" Will was irritated by Emmanuel's feminine-sounding voice. Emmanuel had heard this on countless occasions, but the slur landed differently this time. He was fresh off his gay encounters with Mario. It felt personal, like a violent assault on his existence, and Will's repeated shouting triggered a visceral reaction.

"Are you going to keep calling me a fucking faggot?" Emmanuel roared as he inched closer to Will. "Stop calling me a faggot!" He picked up his styrofoam bowl of Hamburger Helper and hurled it at Will. "You're not going to keep calling me a fucking faggot!" Flying meat and cheese landed on Will's face and clothes. He kicked Emmanuel, but Emmanuel got in a few punches before Dylan, who had been staring in astonishment, made him go home.

Emmanuel couldn't believe that he might be gay, but at least he felt that Mario would have been proud of him.

5

. . .

All Weed and No Seed

Shortly after half past eight on a late July evening in 1979, a seventh alarm, which indicated the severity of a fire, was issued by Fire Commissioner Joseph A. Rizzo less than two hours after the fire was first reported. The colossal Bromley & Sons textile mill was ablaze, sending columns of thick smoke billowing across the shell of the industrial ghetto. Built in 1889 and now defunct, it had six buildings ranging from one to five stories each, plus a seven-story office tower. Hailed as the "largest of the kind in the world," the mill took up an entire city block. In its heyday, it had 2,300 workers spread across eleven acres of floor space, making rugs, chenille and lace curtains, and table covers. With its 750 Smyrna looms, Bromley & Sons was the biggest employer of handweavers in the United States at the time.[1]

As firefighters hurried to salvage the complex, thousands of people came to watch. The fire expanded rapidly, and sparks rose two hundred feet in the air. One resident claimed that her screen doors began to melt from the intensity of the heat. At 9:11 p.m. the fire was declared under control. Only two buildings emerged unscathed, and one was partially burned out. The rest had perished, but no injuries had been reported.[2]

The Bromley fire sounded the final death knell of Philadelphia's repute as the "Workshop of the World"—the world's greatest and most diverse textile enterprise at the turn of the twentieth century.[3] "Phila-delphia is the godmother of the world's republics," crowed Nathan T. Folwell, president of the city's Manufacturers Club, "the Mecca toward which the faces of all who love liberty are turned." He was comment-ing in 1917 on the world dominance of Philadelphia's manufacturing base, adorning the people of Valparaiso with its hats, transporting the denizens of Siberia and Egypt on its locomotives, and healing soldiers in Europe with its medicines.[4] Of the 264 industry classifications in the 1910 Census, 211 were represented in Philadelphia, among them textiles, locomotives, carpets and rugs, hats, leathers, cigars, glass, pharmaceu-ticals, iron, steel, and shipbuilding.[5]

At the time, Philadelphia's total annual production output was remarkable, including 28 million yards of woolen goods, "enough to make uniforms for all the armies of Europe now in active service"; 12 million "dozen hose and half hose, enough to allow 2 pairs for each man, woman, and child in the United States"; 34 million yards of worsted goods, "enough to make a suit of clothes for every man over 19 years of age now resident in the New England and Mid-Atlantic states"; 2,663 locomotives; and 45 million yards of carpet, "enough to put a belt around the earth and leave a remnant long enough to reach Cincinnati."[6]

Three British immigrant families commanded the city's industrial economy: the Bromleys for carpets, the Disstons for sawmaking, and the Widdicombs for furniture.[7] John Bromley was born and raised in the village of Hanging Heaton in West Yorkshire, England. The fam-ily had been in the wool weaving business for generations; his father sold blankets, coats, and other army goods, and John Bromley became a handloom weaver. After some two dozen ventures failed, he made the decision in 1837 to move across the Atlantic Ocean with his wife and children. For a few years, Bromley toiled in a northern New Jersey woolen spinning mill. During this time, his wife and son died and he later remarried.[8]

In 1845, after the New Jersey mill flopped, Bromley relocated to Philadelphia, where he learned carpet handweaving and began plying the craft on a handloom in a rented space. His three oldest sons pitched in. Bromley fathered children well into his early sixties and had ten living sons and daughters. In 1860, he bought an idle dyehouse in Kensington, which housed his thirty-seven handlooms.[9]

Kensington buzzed with textile production, the largest industrial sector in the city. When Bromley purchased his factory, there were 464 textile firms employing 18,521 workers, with more than 40 percent based in Kensington.[10] The industry was bolstered by the deluge of tens of millions of European immigrants.

In the following decades, Bromley's sons began taking over their father's business and spun off to establish their own firms. During the 1880s, strife was in the air as capital and labor butted heads. The Knights of Labor organized the textile mill workers in Philadelphia while management like the Bromleys retaliated against strikers by sacking them, coercing them to "renounce" the Knights, and drawing up a "blacklist" of workers for other carpet bosses.[11]

As Bromley's sons grew older, married, and raised their own families, they passed the baton to successive generations, who adapted to changing times. Carpeting was ebbing, and curtains and upholsteries were on the upswing. According to historian Philip Scranton, "By 1913, the Bromley group employed over 4,000 workers, operated more than half the Nottingham lace machines in the United States (251 of 487), and enjoyed annual sales nearing $10 million."[12] However, by the 1920s, there were signs that the textile industry was flagging. It began to succumb "to large-scale producers of standardized threads and fabrics (and clothes) operating in increasingly modernized facilities in low-wage areas of the country, namely the South," observed historian Walter Licht. "Had a market for specialized goods maintained its strength, the city's mill owners might have survived."[13] The Bromley family's three companies— Quaker Lace, North American Lace, and Bromley & Sons—sputtered along for a few more decades until they folded.[14]

Still, in 1953, the manufacturing workforce boasted 359,000 Philadelphians strong, encompassing nearly half the city's private labor force. Resident Iris Brown said, "You could quit one day, and you were working again tomorrow." By 1985, this was no longer true. Two-thirds of those jobs had ceased to exist and less than a fifth of city residents were employed in manufacturing.[15]

Northeast and Midwestern cities and towns and some regions of the South had hemorrhaged factories and jobs, shifting operations to low-wage, nonunionized areas of the Sunbelt and foreign countries. Some also relocated to the suburbs. The labor-capital contract that had underpinned decades of booming economic growth—in which workers squeezed concessions from management via stronger unions in the form of higher wages, better working conditions, health care, and pensions as profits flowed like champagne—unraveled in the face of falling profits, stagflation, oil shocks, the breakdown of fixed currency exchange rates, and increased international competition. Deindustrialization, which one historian deemed "antiseptic terminology for social devastation," was estimated to have cost as many as thirty-eight million jobs nationwide.[16]

"Kensington's air is polluted, its streets and sidewalks are filthy, its juvenile crime rate is rising, its industry is languishing," bemoaned journalist Peter Binzen. "No more than a handful of new homes have been built there in the last third of a century. Its schools are among the oldest in the city. Its playgrounds—the few that it has—are overrun with young toughs. Industry is moving out. Social workers and clergymen often give up in despair." And as Kensington lost manufacturing jobs, fires in old factories, some the result of arson, became a familiar sight. The neighborhood had devolved into an industrial wasteland pocked by blight and economic misery.[17]

"None of our sons is interested in coming into the business," lamented Jean Seder, a veteran of the neighborhood in which her family ran a textile mill. "Our building is surrounded by shells of old factories. Our watchmen wage an endless battle with the children of the neighborhood who harass them and vandalize the building. Rolls of tapestry are stolen. The neighbors surrounding us now seem hostile. They refuse to be responsible for their children."[18]

White flight sped up. Hundreds of thousands of white residents decamped for the middle-class neighborhoods of Northeast Philadelphia or to the suburbs, leaving behind a metropolis that had become poorer and more Black and Latino.[19] Puerto Rican migration to the mainland had exploded, beginning with nearly half a million coming over in the 1950s. Philadelphia was the third most popular destination after New York and Chicago. Puerto Ricans, who numbered less than two thousand in 1950, hit nearly seventy thousand in the city four decades later.[20]

Up until World War II, the Puerto Rican economy had been powered by agriculture, particularly the production of sugar, tobacco, and coffee. That changed in 1947 with "Operation Bootstrap," an industrial development program to "modernize" the agrarian economy into a manufacturing one. The government lured foreign investment and corporations to set up shop on the island with a decade-long tax holiday. It also facilitated contracting out Puerto Ricans as laborers for U.S. agricultural and manufacturing companies, at a time when the local sugar and home needlework industries were degenerating.[21]

The migrants who came to sell their labor power in the Philadelphia metropolitan area mostly hailed from the tobacco- and sugar-rich regions of San Lorenzo and Salinas rather than urban centers like San Juan. Displaced from their rural lives, they arrived in an unfamiliar city, the most prosperous days of which were over, and they were relegated to the rock-bottom rungs of the economic order—not too distant from African Americans.[22]

The conditions in Kensington were set for a race war. As the North Philadelphia ghetto creeped eastward, Front Street had become the cordon sanitaire, as former Kensington resident Ronald Whitehorne put it. East of Front Street was rigidly all white, an epicenter of white poverty and a sundry of social ills. The population preferred to stay or couldn't afford to leave. Black and Latino families who tried to break the color barrier were met with vandalism, violent protests, and vicious attacks. Commission on Human Relations staff spoke with local residents, who proclaimed that "somebody was trying to 'break' their neighborhood"—in other words, integrate. "We will burn these houses down before we will let Negroes move in," one of them said.[23] A nonwhite phenotype was all that was required to trigger a racist mob. Racial unrest boiled between the youth as well, involving Kensington and Penn Treaty High Schools. When Puerto Rican students at Penn Treaty missed the bus or stayed late for detention, they were met with whites who threw bricks and bottles and chased them with bats and knives.[24]

As manufacturing slumped to new lows, white-collar service jobs became the leading industry, soon to employ nearly half of the city's workforce.[25] Those positions were inaccessible to the many African Americans and Latinos without the necessary credentials and social capital. But the fledgling drug economy imposed no such requirements. "It was a nightmare," said Iris Brown. "You couldn't walk the streets. There was a lot of desperation, dead people . . . It was like you were in a war."

*   *   *

PRESIDENT RICHARD NIXON declared the "war on drugs" in a June 1971 press conference. "America's public enemy number one in the United States is drug abuse," he said. "In order to fight and defeat this enemy, it is necessary to wage a new, all-out offensive." Reports of alarming numbers of Vietnam War veterans returning home addicted to heroin had prompted his administration to act. He told Congress that addiction should be addressed by investing in rehabilitation. "I will ask for additional funds to increase our enforcement efforts to further tighten the noose around the necks of drug peddlers, and thereby loosen the noose around the necks of drug users," he added.[26]

Although more federal dollars were doled out for treatment and prevention than law enforcement between 1970 and 1978, the Nixon administration pioneered a number of innovative and brutal tools to fight crime and the drug war: "no knock" raids (nearly 1,500 conducted between April 1972 and May 1973), preventive detention before trial, wiretapping powers, and advanced weaponry. The administration established the Drug Enforcement Administration in 1973 to house all federal drug-related enforcement activities under one roof.[27]

John Ehrlichman, a domestic policy advisor to Nixon, later confessed that this was aimed at quashing the anti–Vietnam War movement and uppity Black communities who were demanding equal civil and economic rights. "We knew we couldn't make it illegal to be either against the war or black, but by getting the public to associate the hippies with marijuana and blacks with heroin, and then criminalizing both heavily, we could disrupt those communities," he told journalist

Dan Baum. "We could arrest their leaders, raid their homes, break up their meetings, and vilify them night after night on the evening news. Did we know we were lying about the drugs? Of course we did."[28]

At the time, cocaine was expensive and limited to rich whites. "No hangover," trumpeted *Time* magazine. "No physical addiction. No lung cancer. No holes in the arms or burned-out cells in the brain. Instead, drive, sparkle, energy."[29] By the 1980s, an excess supply of cocaine powder led to prices tumbling up to 80 percent.[30] Dealers began refashioning it into crack, dissolving the cocaine in water, mixing in baking soda, boiling the substance down to crystals, and cutting them up.[31] The resulting product was cheap and highly addictive, drawing a new stream of customers.[32]

President Ronald Reagan doubled down on Nixon's crusade to rid the country of drugs, invoking the seven hundred thousand casualties in the Battle of Verdun in World War I to illustrate the severity of the task.[33] It was the death of Leonard Bias that catapulted the issue to a fever pitch. "He would become the Archduke Ferdinand of the Total War on Drugs," as Baum put it.[34] On June 19, 1986, forty hours after he was selected by the defending champion, the Boston Celtics, in the National Basketball Association draft, Bias was pronounced dead at Leland Memorial Hospital after suffering seizures and cardiac arrest. The diagnosis was cocaine intoxication. At six foot eight with a chiseled 210-pound frame, Bias was an all-American forward at the University of Maryland, expected to hail among the greatest stars in the sport. The previous night, he had overdosed snorting powder cocaine.[35] But in the month after his death, many of the news reports confused crack and powder cocaine, often attributing crack as the cause of death, as Baum noted.[36] It didn't help that the assistant medical examiner concluded from the level of concentration of cocaine in his blood that he had smoked crack, conflicting with the original diagnosis.[37]

On Capitol Hill, chatter was dominated by the death of Bias. Conscious of the looming midterm elections, Democratic House Speaker Tip O'Neill led the charge for punitive antidrug legislation.[38] In September, President Reagan and First Lady Nancy Reagan appeared in a joint address at the White House to launch a "national crusade" against "this cancer of drugs." The president called for strengthening drug laws and ratcheting up federal spending on antidrug measures to three billion dollars. "When we all come together, united, striving for this cause," he declared, "then those who are killing America and terrorizing it with slow but sure chemical destruction will see that they are up against the mightiest force for good that we know." Nancy Reagan made her famous plea to the public: "Say yes to your life. And when it comes to alcohol and drugs, just say no."[39]

By the time the war on drugs went into full swing, drug use was in fact falling. But data was no match for the zeal of the political and media class to rev up the war and stoke the crack epidemic scare in a bid for votes and ratings.[40] Days before the election and without holding a single committee hearing, Congress radically reshaped the criminal justice system with the passage of the Anti-Drug Abuse Act of 1986. The law authorized $1.7 billion to wage the drug war, with most of the funding going to law enforcement and corrections, leaving little for treatment and prevention. It also enacted a five-year mandatory minimum sentence for drug offenses that involved five grams of crack cocaine, five hundred grams of powder cocaine, one hundred grams of heroin, and one hundred thousand grams of marijuana. The 100:1 crack versus powder cocaine sentencing disparity inevitably meant that the brunt of punishment came down hardest on African Americans and Latinos, who were more likely to be crack offenders than whites, who were more likely to use powder cocaine.[41] When Nixon announced his war on drugs in 1971, the combined state and federal prison population was just shy of two hundred thousand. By 1989, with the changes in criminal justice policies, that figure had grown more than threefold.[42]

* * *

BEFORE RAYNI MOVED in with George, before she gave birth to Ryan and Avry, she was with Ildefonso. She first saw him one spring day in the nineties when she drove her friend Leah to see her boyfriend in Kensington. As Rayni waited in the car, she saw a gorgeous man race by on a motorcycle. His skin radiated with "a drug dealer tan," she said. Tattoos of hearts, a panther, Jesus, and other designs covered his body. She thought, *I want him to be my baby daddy*. When her friend returned, she told Rayni that the man's name was Ildefonso, but everyone called him June.

Soon after, Rayni spotted him on the drug corner he oversaw. There was a glamour associated with dealing drugs. You had money. You had power. You were the shit. This time, she introduced herself and asked if he was single. Ildefonso said no. "That's a shame." She drooped. "When you're single, let me know." A few years would pass before that happened.

Ildefonso was a drug kingpin who ran a mini-empire in Kensington. His turf was part of a three-square-mile tract that the police and media called the Badlands. With some of the highest poverty, unemployment, dropout, crime, murder, and housing vacancy rates in the city, it was where 70 percent of the drugs in Philadelphia were sold. When crack landed on the streets of urban America, it engulfed impoverished, ex-industrial communities like Kensington as collateral damage, sending the homicide rates soaring. Some of this was due to the gang violence prompted by the struggle to maintain and defend turf. Most customers traveled in from the suburbs of Pennsylvania, New Jersey, Delaware, and Maryland to buy the dirt-cheap dope. The glut of deserted houses was prime real estate for the drug factions, which turned them into shooting galleries and crack houses.[43]

Ildefonso's success put a target on his back, and several years earlier, at 3 a.m. one morning, Julia, his five-year-old daughter, was woken by a commotion in the house. She tiptoed out of her bedroom into the hallway when a man gripped her and pointed a gun at her face. Her mother, Gabriela, also came into the hallway and screamed, "That's my daughter!"

"Tell her to shut up or I'll shoot her," the man commanded. Julia stood frozen. He let Gabriela approach to take her downstairs to the living room, where Ildefonso, five foot nine with brown eyes and a round, gentle face, was handcuffed and sitting on a mattress on the floor with his two-year-old son, Hector. Julia and Gabriela, who was also holding her infant daughter, Alexis, crouched behind the sofa in terror. Five men toting AK-47s towered over them.

Over the next hour, as his accomplices were ransacking the rooms upstairs, one of the men pricked the side of Ildefonso's forehead with a box cutter each time he refused to reveal where he was stowing the stash of drugs and cash. Tiny beads of blood welled on his flesh. "Don't kill me, don't kill me," he pleaded.

His attackers couldn't find the narcotics or money (which had been stealthily stored inside the barstool cushions) and were running out of patience. Suddenly the police barged through the door. They were able to nab one of the men, but the others escaped through the back. The call had come from Ildefonso's mother, who lived across the street. He had instructed her that if she ever saw his curtains closed, it meant something terrible was happening, and she should call the police.

Ildefonso, who was born in Salinas, on Puerto Rico's southern coast, and Gabriela were childhood friends from the neighborhood. When their friendship turned romantic and Gabriela became pregnant, she dropped out of high school. Their first daughter, Julia, was a daddy's girl. He called her baby, and she was the object of her father's many hugs and kisses. Then Ildefonso joined the military and severed almost all contact with the family. When he came home, he was in the suffocating grip of crack addiction, unable to curb his anger or impatience. The drug crippled him, but you couldn't tell unless you knew him; he was a functioning addict. He began operating on both sides of the narcotics economy, as a consumer and a supplier.

Before long, Ildefonso hooked Gabriela on crack, too. Julia would wake up in the night and see her parents getting high together downstairs. In the mornings, they were asleep, so she dressed for school on her own. School was her escape. Her teachers could see that she was dealing with havoc at home, and she was not alone. Virtually every household was touched by the wretched state of Kensington. But the state did not launch an urban Marshall Plan to invest in jobs, housing, education, and health care to eliminate poverty and other causes of crime. The state did not provide methadone maintenance treatment or supervised injection sites. Rather, it doubled down on handcuffs, armed police, prison cells, and austerity measures on the assumption that poor

African Americans and Latinos were undeserving and predisposed to a malady of waywardness and criminality.[44]

At Julia's home, domestic abuse followed addiction. Ildefonso took out his anger from the strife of the streets on Gabriela. He would thrash her with such intensity that her injuries left her nearly unrecognizable. Once Julia woke up to the sound of ghastly screeching. Ildefonso had thrown hot oil on Gabriela's leg. Julia applied toothpaste to her burns, but it didn't help, and the assault left permanent scars.

A little over a year after the home invasion, Gabriela called it quits. She was pregnant again, this time with their son Ricardo, and feared that Ildefonso would kill her if she stayed any longer. She promptly located a new apartment in Kensington and moved with all three children. They found temporary stability, but addiction and poverty were too formidable. Gabriela couldn't take care of the children and had to give them up. Julia went to live with her aunt in New Jersey, and the two boys were placed in foster care. For Julia, the trauma of the hostage episode never dissipated. She could not forget the feeling that she could have died at any moment. She rarely crossed paths with her father, but when she did, she would not let him forget his failings. "You don't do anything for me. You are never there for us."

* * *

IN THE WAKE of the Los Angeles riots following the acquittal of the four police officers who beat Rodney King, President George H. W. Bush embarked on a whistle-stop tour of Philadelphia to drum up support for his urban agenda. It was May 1992, months ahead of the presidential contest, and he was vying for a second term. Bush began with a visit to a police mini-station, and in the late afternoon, he rolled up in his black Lincoln Town Car limousine to St. Boniface Catholic Church at Norris Square in Kensington, which had acquired the name Needle Park. The ever-present drug dealers, who worked in the heroin and crack trade, had been evacuated. He was greeted by a sea of protesters chanting, "We want jobs! We want jobs!"[45]

Now inside the church's gymnasium, Bush sat at a table with Police

Commissioner Willie L. Williams, United States attorney for the Eastern District of Pennsylvania Michael M. Baylson, and more than a dozen community organizers and residents. He spoke briefly about the Weed and Seed program and listened to various testimonies.[46] Operation Weed and Seed was a pilot program administered by the U.S. Department of Justice. Nineteen cities were each given a minuscule $1.1 million to weed "out gang leaders, drug dealers, and career criminals" and seed "communities with expanded employment, educational, and social services," as Bush put it. In Philadelphia, the vast majority of the federal grant went into "weeding," leaving chump change for "seeding."[47]

At the forum, neighborhood activists requested more funding for the community. Similarly, Florence Richardson, a member of the local Weed and Seed Steering Committee and community activist in Hunting Park, a neighborhood north of Kensington, asked the president, "What I need to know from you is that since we're talking about a multimillion-dollar business as far as drugs are concerned, exactly how are we supposed to fight this kind of problem, especially talking about agencies, community agencies, that deal with housing with limited funds?" Bush replied, "Well, I'm not sure that funds is the entire answer." He later said that producing jobs in the private sector was critical.[48]

Other speakers hammered home the same plea for investment in education, jobs, housing, and youth recreational activities, to muted responses by Bush.[49] Recognizing that many families depended on the drug trade for economic security, Wilfredo Rojas, founder of the Norris Square Civic Association, explained, "We wanted them to eradicate drugs from the top and provide jobs at the bottom for the masses."

For his final stop of the day, Bush headlined a $1,000-a-plate Republican fundraiser five miles south at the Bellevue Hotel in Center City, where fat-cat donors devoured chicken with tarragon sauce and white wine. The gig raked in a cool half million dollars.[50]

My Baby Daddy

Like Ildefonso, Rayni had grown up in Philadelphia and had familial roots in Puerto Rico. As the story went, her parents, Emilio and Laura, met at the port of Corinto in Nicaragua, where Emilio was unloading supplies from a ship. "You see that woman down there?" Emilio exclaimed to his fellow merchant marines, pointing to a stunning woman in a well-fitting dress with fair skin, hazel eyes, and flowing blond hair. "That's going to be the mother of my children."

His colleagues razzed him, "Skinny dog dreaming of a steak." Laura was nineteen, twenty-four years younger than Emilio, and had a son, Hugo. One of thirteen children, she lived in deep poverty, roaming the streets, peddling tortillas, eggs, lemons, and chicha, a sweet corn-based beverage she served in sandwich bags. When Emilio saw and wooed her, it was a sign that God had answered her prayers for a man who could take care of her and Hugo.

After the birth of a daughter, Maritza, and a short stint in Emilio's hometown in Puerto Rico, the family flew to the U.S. mainland and settled in North Philadelphia. Rayni, the second daughter, was born in 1968. Laura opened a hair salon in a bustling business district on Fifth Street that became known as El Bloque de Oro, "the golden block," with cafés and furniture, clothing, hardware, music, and barber shops.

Her salon quickly became one of the most popular in the area. The family lived in a flat on the second floor. Often when Rayni woke up, she would peek out of her window and see a line of Latina and older white women snaking out the door. Every summer, Laura closed the salon for a few months, and the family trekked to Nicaragua by car. At the border, customs would check their suitcases and swipe items, so Laura started bribing them with money and small gifts. To her family, she was Santa Claus. She brought them clothing, appliances, perfume, makeup, and jewelry. She was the only one to have made it out of poverty.

Early on, Rayni and her sisters were tasked with sweeping and cleaning the brushes and other tools at the salon. Her mother kept the girls secluded and issued a constant stream of injunctions: Don't talk like that. Don't sit like that. Don't laugh like that. They were expected to meet her towering standards and her exacting nature. Laura was determined never to return to the shame and poverty of her youth. She had worked too hard. She made sure Rayni and her sisters understood that, too.

Rayni went to Catholic school for most of her childhood until her younger sister Brandy convinced her to transfer to a vocational school because it would be less strict and have boys. But she and Brandy attracted unwelcome attention for their flowing hair, immaculate makeup, and glowing porcelain skin. Students stuck gum to Rayni's hair, and she was once punched in the back. It was the price of being a hairdresser's daughter.

Once she graduated, Rayni went to Temple University with the goal of becoming a psychologist, but she was ill prepared for the rigors of college, finding it difficult to sit through lectures and take notes. Her classmates appeared to manage, but she was lost. She could have attended office hours to talk to her professors, but she didn't know what office hours were. Although Rayni had grown up less than two miles from campus, Temple operated in such a different universe that it may as well have been a foreign land. There were white professional codes, rituals, and etiquettes that would have to be mastered for her to succeed in higher education, but Rayni was a first-generation college student without the necessary support.

During the second semester, Rayni's mother suddenly declared that she would provide not another penny for her college education. Her grand career ambitions to become a psychologist went up in smoke. Her mother expected her to marry, breed, and run the salon. She hadn't thought it was even necessary for Rayni to finish high school. So she dropped out. Nobody from Temple contacted her, and she had no inkling that she could apply for student loans.

What followed was a daze of boyfriends, clubbing, and miscellaneous jobs. At one point, Rayni lived in a series of hotels with a drug-dealer boyfriend who was on the run from the cops. She started bartending to spite her mother, helped run a salon that Brandy opened in North Philadelphia, and discovered the thrill of emancipation from Laura's demands.

A few months after her first brush with Ildefonso, Rayni was driving to her mother's salon and passed through his block. Ildefonso crept up to the window of her beige Honda Civic. "I'm single," he announced.

"That's nice," she cooed.

"Do you want to go to Wildwood this weekend?" he asked. They ended up driving to Wildwood Beach on the Jersey Shore in his convertible along with a brown paper bag of beers. Rayni lusted for him—he was very handsome and generous with money—but she held back. He had recently left a relationship, and she didn't want to get played. She knew nothing about his abusive past or the neglect of his children.

Ildefonso moved into her apartment within a few weeks of them dating. One evening, he came home after a grueling day on the corner and said he wasn't sure they were going to work out. Rayni interpreted his doubt as a rebuke of her desire to take things slowly. So that night, they made love for the first time. He left the next morning and didn't return. She was shattered to learn that he had resumed his relationship with his ex-girlfriend, Amanda. *This is what happens when I trust a man*, she thought.

She was at Brandy's hair salon when she realized that she might be pregnant. She had been feeling a strange quivering sensation in her stomach. Then she missed her period, all but confirming her intuition. Rayni was excited about becoming a mother. Ildefonso heard that she was pregnant through the grapevine and wanted them to work things out. But she had promised herself that if she were ever in this position, she wouldn't be with her baby daddy just for the sake of it. *I'm twenty-five years old*, she thought. *I'm independent, and I don't need nobody.*

The two were talking on the phone when Ildefonso announced once again that he was single. But Rayni felt she couldn't trust him. Who could? *I'm not going to be with someone if I have to worry about what time he's coming home or even whether he's going to come home*, she told herself. She wasn't convinced that he wasn't off sleeping with Amanda or some other woman, so she tried to pry out the truth.

"I'm not with nobody," he insisted. After a few more denials, annoyed by her persistence, he finally admitted that he was seeing a new woman.

Rayni hung up. Her temper flaring, she left the salon and drove to his corner.

"What did you just say to me on the phone?" she bellowed, attracting the attention of his boys selling across the street. "You said you're with somebody?" Ildefonso kept mum, peering off into the distance with his hands stowed in the pockets of his baseball jacket. She moved closer and slapped him on each cheek. His face snapped sideways.

He grabbed her. His dealers, primed for a fight, rushed over. "She's pregnant," someone called out. Rayni pushed him away and left. Over the following weeks, she tried to purge her mind of Ildefonso, but her desire got the better of her.

*   *   *

"Did you know that June has been coming around?" Rayni's friend Leah asked her. After their fallout, she and Ildefonso hadn't spoken much apart from the time she hustled $400 out of him for new clothes. She had lied that she needed money for an abortion.

"What do you mean?"

"Oh, yeah—in the middle of the night. He was drinking. He did it again last night."

After the clubs let out in the wee hours of the morning, Ildefonso twice stopped by Leah's house, where Rayni was now living. "Rayni! I love you!" he howled. "I want my family back!" Her room was in the back, so she couldn't hear him.

Although he was now dating another friend, Elena, Rayni couldn't shake off the attraction. They started chatting on the phone again and hanging out.

Just before Valentine's Day when Rayni was six months pregnant, Ildefonso said he'd be tied up on the corner until late, but he promised to come over by 1 a.m. She stayed up, staring at the clock until dawn, telling herself he had reformed, and this time would be different. But he didn't show. She had never felt more crushed, but it wasn't entirely his fault. The law had finally caught up with him. Ildefonso had been arrested with five baggies of cocaine, 32.2 grams, and was charged with the offense of having "unlawfully manufactured, delivered, or possessed with intent to deliver a controlled substance."

* * *

ON THE LAST morning of April, Rayni's water broke. It was two weeks before her due date, and she was now expecting twins.

She knew it wasn't going to be easy raising them, but she hoped that these children could perhaps fill the void in her life and grant her the purpose that she had been longing for.

Brandy brought her to Parkview Hospital, but the doctor told her to take walks and come back when her contractions were five minutes apart. Rayni expected to return that evening. Brandy drove her to the Cherry Hill Mall over the border in New Jersey, where she paced among the shops. Shoppers stared at her belly and remarked, "Wow! You're so big."

By 9 p.m., Rayni had been admitted to the hospital, and in the early wet hours of May 1, she gave birth to Avry and Ryan, six minutes apart. She had told herself that she needed to be calm so the boys wouldn't come out hyper, but now she felt numb. She pushed away the pain of Ildefonso's absence. *Why did I have to get pregnant by a guy who's not going to be here?* she thought. They hadn't spoken since his arrest on Valentine's Day, and she saw no point in reaching out to him.

It took him five weeks to come and see the babies. Rayni was walking to Brandy's salon with a friend, pushing the stroller, when a motorcycle began tailing them. The rider was wearing a full-face helmet so she couldn't tell that it was Ildefonso. *Whoever he is, I hope he's cute,* she thought.

Ildefonso parked and walked over. "Well, it's about time," Rayni said. He knelt in front of the stroller and touched his sons' tiny hands.

"I see you're doing a good job," he said. Rayni took this to mean, *You don't need me.*

Ildefonso pled not guilty to his drug offense, but the court wasn't swayed and handed down a guilty verdict. By the end of the year, he had been sentenced to three to six years in prison. Rayni hadn't heard from him, assuming he had forgotten about the boys until she learned that he was locked up.

* * *

RAYNI'S HOUSING SITUATION fluctuated month to month. After the birth of the twins, she lived with Brandy for a few months, then stayed with a friend, finally moving in with her sister Maritza. Most days were spent studying toward a cosmetology license from Baron's Castle Beauty Academy in Northeast Philadelphia. After she got the license, she went to work at Hair Cuttery, but that didn't last more than a few months. Eventually, Rayni fought with Maritza because her sister was bringing home lots of men. Rayni and the babies were kicked out and left scrambling for a place to stay.

In late summer, Rayni, reluctant to bother her friends and lacking savings, swallowed her pride and brought Ryan and Avry to a downtown homeless shelter. As she waited to get a spot, the others in line struck terror into her heart. They taunted her, saying that people would touch her sons and steal her belongings while they slept. Two hours passed before she decided to ditch the shelter and make the long walk up to North Philadelphia, where a new boyfriend let them crash with him.

Through talking to friends, she learned that as a low-income single mother, she could apply for Temporary Assistance for Needy Families. TANF, signed into law in 1996 by President Bill Clinton, fulfilled a campaign promise to "end welfare as we know it."[1] TANF replaced Aid to Families with Dependent Children, generally known as welfare, which had been established as part of President Franklin Delano Roosevelt's

New Deal in 1935. For decades, AFDC had been a punching bag for Republican and right-wing Democratic lawmakers, who lambasted the program for giving rise to welfare dependency, out-of-wedlock births, and lazy Black "welfare queens" milking hardworking white taxpayers.[2]

Debunking these racist, anti-poor tropes, scholars found that families joined the welfare rolls for temporary relief during economic distress, and the average recipient received benefits for less than two years (a minority lingered for a longer period).[3] States with higher benefits in fact had lower out-of-wedlock birth rates than those with low benefits.[4] And Black families never made up a majority of those receiving assistance.[5] At its peak, for more than 14 million people, including nearly 10 million children, AFDC benefits were a lifeline, covering basic necessities.[6] Anthropologist Carol Stack documented that welfare, in addition to a network of family and friends, made it possible for parents to survive. But, she found, public assistance programs "systematically tend to reduce the possibility of social mobility" by preventing the formation of nuclear families through rules penalizing the presence of a "man in the house" and setting low asset limits.[7]

In contrast to AFDC, Clinton's TANF had several declared aims beyond providing assistance to needy families: to "end the dependence of needy parents on government benefits by promoting job preparation, work, and marriage; prevent and reduce the incidence of out-of-wedlock pregnancies . . . and encourage the formation and maintenance of two-parent families." The new legislation imposed a five-year lifetime benefit limit for recipients (with some hardship extensions) and required people to start looking for work immediately and secure a job within two years. And unlike AFDC, which was a federal entitlement program, funding for TANF was distributed to states in fixed block grants, and they were allowed to set their own eligibility criteria, benefit amounts, work requirements, and sanctions.[8]

Democratic senator Daniel Patrick Moynihan of New York was the most fervent opponent of the bill (an ironic twist since he had authored the watershed eponymous 1965 report that had pathologized poor Black families for their economic and social failings and railed against AFDC receipt as "a measure of the steady disintegration of the Negro family structure").[9] Decrying it in Congress, he said, "If, in 10 years time, we find children sleeping on grates, picked up in the morning frozen, and ask, Why are they here, scavenging, awful to themselves, awful to one another, will anyone remember how it began?"[10] Gutting welfare, he said, would "surely be the most brutal act of social policy since Reconstruction," and its chief architects "will take this disgrace to their graves. The children alone are innocent."[11] Several Clinton administration officials also resigned in protest, among them Peter Edelman, who warned that the law would "hurt millions of poor children by the time it is fully implemented" and lead to growing homelessness, malnutrition, crime, and other social ills.[12]

These predictions were soon realized. Millions were thrown off welfare rolls, in large part due to the punitive work requirements and time limits of benefits. In 2008–9, for every 100 Pennsylvania families in poverty, only 41 participated in TANF, down from 85 who received AFDC in 1994–95.[13] Moreover, the purchasing power of TANF benefits fell sharply in dozens of states, including Pennsylvania, where amounts remained frozen.[14] Studies found that since the law's passage, the deep poverty rate, measured as 50 percent of the poverty line, grew for children, especially those being raised by single mothers, and extreme poverty, defined as households with children living on less than $2 per person per day, more than doubled.[15]

* * *

As RAYNI WAS walking to catch the bus to the welfare office to apply for TANF, Brian, a Puerto Rican man, approached her, asking, "Do you know how much apartments rent for around here?" Around $300 to $350, she told him. Brian explained that he had just purchased a roomy one-bedroom flat nearby, on G and Tioga Streets. Rayni told him about her financial woes and intention to apply for welfare, and on the spot he agreed to rent her the property. It was obvious he had the hots for her, and Rayni was quick and clever enough to capitalize on it. He said he would call her after the apartment renovations were finished.

More than a week went by without a word from Brian. Rayni, who had been approved for $403 per month in TANF benefits, began selling marijuana with a friend for some extra cash. She was bagging the chopped marijuana when the phone rang. It was Brian with the news that the apartment was ready for her to move in. But he consistently and brazenly flirted with her from the start. Even as she batted away his advances, he constantly pestered her. "Why don't you want to be with me?" he asked. She would have preferred a less horny landlord and a safer neighborhood, but the $350 monthly rent was affordable. The TANF check plus under-the-table income plus food stamps helped cover the rest of her expenses. At least she and her boys had a home, Rayni reminded herself, and they didn't have to go to a shelter.

Fresh off his reelection victory, President Clinton delivered a rousing State of the Union address to Congress in February 1997. "We must make the 13th and 14th years of education, at least 2 years of college, just as universal in America by the 21st century as a high school education is today, and we must open the doors of college to all Americans," he said. He proposed a new tax credit for two years of college tuition and an expansion of the Pell Grant program. "In the 21st century, we must expand the frontiers of learning across a lifetime," Clinton added. "All our people, of whatever age, must have the chance to learn new skills."[16] Rayni had dreamed of a college degree, but she felt she had missed the window of opportunity. Hearing the president speak about age not being a barrier gave her the confidence to consider returning to school.

Shortly after moving into the new apartment, she came across a newspaper ad for the PJA School, a for-profit institution in Upper Darby, Pennsylvania. With the encouragement of friends, she enrolled in PJA's business and accounting program, taking hour-long bus rides north to the suburbs. She received some aid and took out loans to cover the rest of the tuition.

In Philadelphia, as soon as they received benefits, TANF recipients were required to participate in at least twenty weekly hours of allowable activities, which included employment, job training, or a job search. Otherwise, they risked being sanctioned, with their benefits cut or eliminated.[17] When Rayni went to the welfare office, the caseworkers sometimes harassed her and threatened that if she didn't participate in the job search classes, her TANF benefits would be cut off (her studies did not grant her an exemption). That wasn't true, not for the moment; penalties wouldn't begin to kick in for at least another year.

But Rayni was sufficiently terrified that she dragged herself to the classes. Sitting with the other women, she felt stupid as the staff told them how to create a résumé, dress professionally, and use appropriate manners and etiquette in the workplace. *What the hell am I doing here?* she thought. *I got things to do. I got kids.* She couldn't leave until the class was dismissed. After a few sessions, she complained that she already knew what they were teaching. So she was ordered to visit businesses in her neighborhood, fill out job applications, and pick up business cards. But she didn't want to work at a corner or retail store. She wanted to be a white-collar professional who carried a briefcase. That's why she was going to PJA.

Rayni felt a wave of mental anguish each time she had an appointment at the welfare office, knowing that no matter how kind and patient she was, the TANF caseworkers would hound, mock, and belittle her. She was at their mercy, for they had the unilateral power to rescind her benefits and put her and her two boys on the street. It was as if the cash assistance was coming out of their own pockets, she felt. "Why you been on TANF so long?" they would ask. "You can get a job." "Why are you doing nothing with your life?"

* * *

RAYNI HAD A few boyfriends after Ildefonso, but nobody else matched up, and she could never seem to quash her love for him. She wrote to him in jail, but he did not respond; she never knew whether he received her letter. During his sentence, he was shuttled between several correctional institutions in Pennsylvania: Camp Hill, Waynesburg, and Philadelphia Community Corrections Center.

The twins were three and a half when he was finally paroled. For the next three years, he had to take drug tests, avoid alcohol, support his dependents, keep away from people who sell or use drugs, maintain employment or search for a job, stay in touch with his parole officer, and pay a stack of fees. Few could comply with such burdensome restrictions. He was set up to fail.

Rayni's wait was over. She wanted to get back with her children's father, thinking he must have matured behind bars. Soon enough, Ildefonso paid a visit. Rayni was no less attracted than the first time she had laid eyes on him, zooming past on his motorcycle. He still looked delicious, as she put it, his sexy manner and smooth, golden-brown skin unchanged by incarceration. He apologized for abandoning her during the pregnancy. "You're the only woman who never took my shit." He took Avry to his house for a few hours. Ryan threw a fit and didn't want to go.

But when Rayni asked Ildefonso to pitch in with some cash, he declined. Regrettably, he couldn't help his mother, either. Then she heard through the grapevine that he had bought two new cars, a Ford Explorer and a Chevrolet Blazer. Now she came to her senses and let go of her fantasies of romance: he hadn't changed one bit. She tracked him down at his girlfriend's business and called him outside. "You don't support your kids," Rayni barked. "You can't even give me thirty dollars a week." She gripped him by his white undershirt, slightly tearing it. "You're going to take care of your kids even if you die trying."

Rayni took him to Family Court to negotiate child support, and he requested a DNA paternity test to stall for time. The test results surprised nobody: Ildefonso was their father. Meanwhile, Rayni and the boys might pass him on the street and he wouldn't acknowledge them. She felt he was acting like they weren't his children.

Rayni had begun to harbor doubts about raising them as a single mother. During the pregnancy, she had become an avid reader of *Parents* magazine, which offered statistics indicating the benefits of children growing up in two-parent households. She became so worried that she weighed giving the boys up for adoption. Her mother was off the table—her house was unsuitable for children, dirty, filled with empty beer cans and chewed-up chicken bones. Then she thought of giving the twins to her friend Carmen, and they did a trial run at her house. Carmen's husband was watching a football game when Ryan turned off a switch that connected to the television. The husband smacked Ryan, and Rayni realized there was nobody she could trust to raise them well. The adoption plans were scrapped.

* * *

RAYNI LOST TOUCH with Ildefonso after the child support case, and she came to feel that he belonged to her past. Then she heard from her mother that he was dying of cancer. Less than two years after his release, he had violated the conditions of his parole by consuming illicit drugs and was shipped back to prison. A stint in two halfway houses followed, before Ildefonso landed in the hospital. At this point, Rayni had graduated from the PJA school with an associate's degree and a 3.58 GPA. She went on and off welfare amid irregular employment in accounting jobs at a property management company and the Internal Revenue Service.

She had left the apartment on G and Tioga after Brian's harassment escalated. One day, on the drive back from withdrawing cash at an ATM, Brian placed his hand on her bare thigh. On instinct, she bit him. He waved it off as a bit of a joke. The next time she saw him, he tried to enter the apartment, so she fetched a can of air freshener and sprayed him with it. Now he was annoyed. "Stop that!" he yelled at her. "Stop coming near me!" she yelled back. "Just leave!" Brian finally had enough and left. Worried that he might physically harm her, Rayni quickly devised an exit strategy.

Rayni and the boys, who had recently turned six, moved into a room in a house on Kip Street, a hot drug-trafficking block. At around this time, she called a friend of Ildefonso's to arrange a hospital visit. "He just died this morning—an hour ago," he said. Ildefonso was thirty-four years old, and according to his death certificate, he was a laborer in the manufacturing industry—a diplomatic term for drug dealer.

The funeral was held at Escamillio D. Jones Funeral Home. Rayni wore a long gray patterned dress, put Ryan and Avry in suits, and brought along a friend for moral support. She only went so her children could see their father for the final time. As she walked in, she saw many of Ildefonso's ex-lovers, there to pay their respects. On the way to the open casket, Ryan started crying and pulling on her leg. She picked him up, and he rested his head on her shoulder. "Don't you want to see your father?" she asked gently, as people turned their heads in her direction. Only a few friends and relatives had seen the twins in the flesh.

Ildefonso was unrecognizable. The cancer had devoured him from the inside out. Rayni felt no sorrow or rage as she looked at his swollen face, his skin a melange of black and blue. She was numb. Her steadfast belief in God trumped her desire to detest him. Ryan and Avry knew that he was their father, but they, too, seemed to feel nothing and asked no questions. They never knew him. He amounted to no more than a sperm donor.

* * *

As Ryan and Avry neared the completion of first grade at Lewis Elkin School, the family left Kip Street and moved to a ramshackle dwelling in North Philadelphia. It was littered with trash, and the charcoal-dark walls were punctured with holes. Stale urine sloshed in the toilet like a cold stew. The place was uninhabitable, but Rayni didn't know where else to go. It was the only house she could afford on her budget.

One evening, she gave the boys a bath, and they fell asleep with Rayni and a friend in an upstairs bedroom. In the predawn hours, her friend, roused from sleep, saw a blaze in the hallway ripping toward them. He shut the bedroom door and frantically woke everyone up. Rayni tried to pry the window open, but it was nailed shut. Just as Rayni thought this was the end, her friend punched through the glass window, bloodying his hand. Down below, firefighters had quickly arrived on the scene, but they were hesitant to raise a ladder to the roof because they thought it was about to collapse.

"Pass me the kids!" shouted the woman who lived next door. Their houses were physically attached. One by one, they were able to escape through the window and into her house. Ryan noticed wisps of smoke coming through the holes in the wall where picture frames had once been nailed. The four were whisked away to Temple University Hospital, where they were treated for smoke inhalation. Rayni's friend needed stitches in his hand. They later learned that the cause of the fire was the house's faulty electrical wiring. It took a few hours for it to hit Ryan that they could have died. He was barely awake when they fled.

The upshot of the fire was that Rayni moved into her sister Brandy's apartment above the hair salon. Ryan and Avry didn't return to school for the rest of that year, which caused them to be held back. In Ryan's report card, his teacher, Mrs. Walsh, observed, "Ryan lacks the motivation to complete task[s]. He is unwilling to put forth much effort to gain progress. Ryan is below basic in all subject areas. He must adjust his behavior and attitude for achievement."

In September, Ryan and Avry moved to a new school, where they repeated first grade. They knew it was only a matter of time before they would have to pick up and move again, and it was tough for them to pay attention in class or form lasting friendships. Rayni, sapped by years of uprooting her family, noticed the pernicious effect it was having on the boys and their schooling, and she longed for a lasting home. By the spring of that year, Brandy decided to put the hair salon and apartment on the market, but she located an affordable one-bedroom apartment above an insurance agency for Rayni and the boys. The rent started out at $400 for the first six months and then increased to $450. Rayni converted the vast living room into a bedroom for Ryan and Avry, who were enrolled in yet another new school.

Some time after Ildefonso's death, the boys started receiving Social Security survivors benefits, and Ryan, who had been diagnosed with a learning disability, also qualified for a monthly SSI check. By then, Rayni no longer received TANF, and her only paid job was to help out with the food bank at a local church. Until she met George the following year, she struggled to make ends meet. She struggled as well with conflicting feelings: peace that came from the comfort of her new home, but a sense that she was living to die, just waiting for her life to pass.

* * *

HE SPORTED A fresh cut and a slim-fitting white T-shirt that accentuated his strapping build and copious tattoos. Less than twelve hours earlier, George, who was in his late twenties, had been released after a year-long confinement at Philadelphia's House of Corrections, a century-old overflowing city jail shaped like an asterisk. Two years ago, he had shattered a car window and tried to steal a radio. He was given six months of probation but soon violated the sentence when he and his friends broke more car windows with a spark plug while inebriated and high on cocaine and Xanax.

George was a familiar face in the criminal justice system. After dropping out of high school, he started managing a high-stakes drug corner when his friend Chris insisted that he fill the spot of Chris's brother, who had been killed. Shootings, stickups, and fights were so common that George carried a .380 handgun without a license for protection. He caught a few illegal weapon and drug charges, which led to multiple tours of the archipelago of city jails. There were six of them clumped together on a campus on State Road, Philadelphia's "gray wastes," as journalist Ta-Nehisi Coates put it, "a sprawling netherworld of . . . jails."[18]

The House of Corrections lacked a sprinkler system and modern security. In the cell George shared with another inmate, spiders scampered alongside fat flying cockroaches. For amusement, he would take a thread from his blanket, tie it to his cereal, and dangle it for the resident mouse to crawl out of the vent and snatch before dashing back to its den. The heating system didn't work. Air-conditioning didn't exist. When he took showers in the throes of summer, he would be drenched in sweat by the time he returned to his cell.[19] George spent his days pumping iron, playing cards, and watching television.

After getting a shape-up haircut on this steaming July day, George walked over to his brother's house for a ride home. On the way, they took a detour and stopped by their sister Zoe's place. She was friends with Rayni. They were all lounging in chairs on the sidewalk, while nine-year-old Ryan and Avry played with Zoe's daughter upstairs. George started gloating about all the places he would stick up and the women he would impregnate now that he was free. He was joking, or so he claimed. Rayni didn't find his ranting funny, but her heart thumped as she fixed her eyes on him. So when he started chatting to her, she didn't turn away.

"Where can I get a beer around here?" he asked. She knew he was playing dumb so that she'd escort him to the corner store. He asked if she wanted one, too, but she declined. She was craving an icy Budweiser, but if she accepted, he would presume that she owed him something.

This game went on for a while. On his third trip to the store, Rayni asked George to pick up a six-pack of Coors Light for Zoe, but she did her part to deplete the stock. The two kept up some flirty banter and spent the rest of the day together, well after the sun set. She took him home the following evening, and before long, Ryan noticed George was staying over almost every night. He was a mother's boy and would run into her room as soon as George left.

Two weeks into the fling, George confessed that he was in love with Rayni. She broke into a grin but said nothing. She had dated enough men to have learned some healthy cynicism—too many times she'd been reeled in by their charm and crushed when they cheated or the romance fizzled out. She wanted a man who would be faithful, street savvy, and hold a stable job. *If George is the man for me,* she thought, *he'll have a job within the month.*

When George tried to leave the streets for a legitimate job, he saw that his criminal record made him a pariah. There were only a handful of industries open to formerly incarcerated people. By mid-August, through his friend James, he had nonetheless secured a construction job to remodel condos. Just as long as he worked, Rayni told herself. She'd rather he made $9 an hour than sell drugs and do nine years in jail. For his part, George was ready to settle down, tired of playing games and running around. He officially moved into the apartment above the insurance agency, bringing his CD collections of Tupac Shakur and Wu-Tang Clan and introducing the boys to hardcore rap. Ryan didn't like him at first, taken aback by how quickly he had moved in and suspicious that he would report his mischief to Rayni. George had once snitched after catching him red-handed scooping out food from the pot with his hands, and Ryan bore a grudge.

George brought Rayni joy and critical economic support, becoming the family's primary breadwinner. He taught her patience, and she taught him vulnerability. Beneath his iron-willed, macho veneer was a tender man who wanted to love and be loved. By the end of their first year together, Rayni was pregnant with their first son. George already had two daughters, so he was excited to have a boy. In July, Tino was born, followed by Armando a year and a half later. In less than three years, the family had doubled in size.

7
...

Our Pyromaniac

It wasn't until the mid-1990s that David Bromley realized how oblivious he had been to the struggles of people living on the margins. That was when he took a job teaching social studies at Jefferson High School, a mammoth low-performing, nearly all-Latino school in South Los Angeles. Describing the school in *Education Week,* journalist David Hill wrote, "It is like an oasis in the desert, a desert made up of tired-looking bungalows and graffiti-covered walls." Some blocks away, "on a small commercial strip, you can still see the burned-out reminders of the 1992 riots."[1]

A few years earlier, Bromley had picked up a copy of Jonathan Kozol's 1991 book *Savage Inequalities: Children in America's Schools,* an illuminating indictment of the grossly unequal American public education system and an exploration of the appalling conditions of segregated, underfunded urban schools. "One searches for some way to understand why a society as rich and, frequently, as generous as ours would leave these children in their penury and squalor for so long—and with so little public indignation," said Kozol of the poorest children. "Why do we reduce them to this beggary—and why, particularly, in public education? Why not spend on children here at least what we would be investing in their education if they lived within a wealthy district like Winnetka, Illinois, or Cherry Hill, New Jersey, or Manhasset, Rye, or Great Neck in New York?" The culprit was the way public schools had been financed: in large part by local property taxes with minimal investment from the federal government, a model that inherently discriminates against poor communities with a low tax base.[2]

Bromley had grown up in Bryn Mawr, a wealthy suburb of Philadelphia with idyllic homes and manicured lawns. After attending public elementary and middle schools in the amply funded Lower Merion district, he was enrolled in the Haverford School, a pricey all-boys private college prep school. Both systems had all the resources that the Philadelphia public schools, only a few miles away, were denied. Bromley continued his education at Pepperdine University in Malibu with the dream of becoming an actor. However, tutoring students in writing in Los Angeles stirred him to ditch his Hollywood plans and formally enter urban education.

For five years, Bromley, a handsome, tall man with a mop of black hair, taught in the Humanitas program at Jefferson High, an interdisciplinary theme- and team-based school-within-a-school that aimed to produce "critical thinkers, responsible problem solvers, intelligent articulators, and socially conscious community members." More than half the high schools in Los Angeles had adopted the model with financial support from foundations. Courses included "Women, Race, and Social Protest" and "The Protestant Ethic and the Spirit of Capitalism." Bromley designed a yearlong curriculum about world history based on Jared Diamond's book *Guns, Germs, and Steel*. According to a study of Humanitas and non-Humanitas students in several schools, which drew on performance-based assessments and school records, those in the Humanitas program made gains in writing skills, content knowledge, and conceptual understanding. They also had better attendance and lower dropout rates (although there may have been some selection bias with more engaged students seeking out the program). At Jefferson, students had to apply for the program, but grades were not a factor in admission.[3]

Working with youth who were poor, Latino, first-generation, and sometimes undocumented gave Bromley a foundation to ask why he had been given so much while others had so little. On a trip back home, he met up with one of his favorite high school teachers. Ashamed of his ignorance of poverty and inequality, he posed him a question that had been gnawing at him: "Why did you guys choose books and conversation topics that in hindsight seemed to avoid the difficult questions of privilege, equity, and race?"

His teacher looked away and answered, "You couldn't handle it. You guys would squirm and not deal with anything that challenged your privilege." Bromley was not satisfied. *That's your job as a teacher*, he thought. To interrogate, reflect upon, provoke uncomfortable, essential debates. It was a reminder of why he was in urban education. He committed to doing better for his students.

In 2000, his Jefferson colleague Matthew Spengler invited him to visit the Metropolitan Regional Career and Technical Center in Providence, the first school set up by the nonprofit organization Big Picture Learning. With the backing of the Bill and Melinda Gates Foundation, Spengler envisioned launching a Big Picture–model school in Oakland and asked Bromley to be a teacher there (called advisors). Listening to the students in Providence talk about taking ownership over their education and observing the relationships between students and their advisors, Bromley was dazzled by the MET's progressive philosophy, which featured a real-world learning approach based on student interests, a democratic process, and student exhibitions. He thought it made Humanitas look amateurish. After his first day at the school, he called his wife and asked if she wanted to move to Oakland.

Pioneered by John Dewey, Maria Montessori, Rudolf Steiner, A. S. Neill, Paulo Freire, and Ivan Illich, progressive education champions the dignities and rights of the child. It is based on principles such as educating the whole child—attending to their socio-emotional, physical, and cognitive development—learning by doing, holistic rather than high-stakes assessment, and democratic citizen-making. The school, as Dewey argued, becomes "a miniature community, an embryonic society," rather than "being only a place to learn lessons having an abstract and remote reference to some possible living to be done in the future."[4]

Bromley and Spengler ended up as co-principals and co-advisors at MetWest High School in Oakland with an inaugural class of thirty-four ninth graders. Most were low-income, half were Latino, and the rest were Black, Southeast Asian, and white. The public school was housed in two classrooms at Laney community college. As in Providence, project-based learning was the central pedagogy and was connected to internships in the community at health clinics, museums, businesses, and schools. Mathematics instruction was outsourced to the college, the only subject that was taught in a traditional way.

Rather than relying solely on grades, students put together portfolios of their work and were assessed through oral exhibitions. At the end of tenth grade, they were required to write a twenty-page research paper. The process of accepting feedback and cycling through innumerable drafts taught them how to conduct research and write. Because the class sizes were so small, Bromley was able to go deep with each student and identify their strengths, weaknesses, and passions. He observed that they really loved coming to school, so attendance rates were nearly perfect, and that translated to outstanding scores on state standardized tests.

Each successive year brought a new ninth-grade class and more staff, and eventually the district invested in a permanent building for the school. After four years, Bromley decided to move home to the Philadelphia area, where he began fashioning plans to open a Big Picture–model alternative high school in the city.

* * *

IN ITS MAY 1960 issue, *Life* ran a feature profiling a motley collection of male school dropouts accompanied by their dour portraits. Some of the captions read, "Average Student, Fatherless, and Floundering," "Tough and Truant," and "Lost in Large Family." The "youngsters portrayed around these pages make up a woebegone gallery of dropouts, and the causes for their failure represent the causes for many dropouts," wrote *Life*. "Long before such youngsters quit school physically, they have dropped out in spirit . . . Retarded in reading since elementary school, many cannot learn from books, cannot use words to express ideas." Together the scourge of dropouts resulted in "a national waste"—soaring rates of job-lessness and a dearth of qualified candidates to fill skilled jobs.[5]

Once mass schooling became the norm, it was followed in the first half of the 1960s by an expectation that students would achieve a high school diploma. Leading political and education officials grappled with the Gordian knot of high school dropouts.[6] In what was his final State of the Union address in 1963, President John F. Kennedy said, "The future of any country which is dependent upon the will and wisdom of its citizens is damaged, and irreparably damaged, whenever any of its children is not educated to the full extent of his talent, from grade school through graduate school. Today, an estimated 4 out of every 10 students in the 5th grade will not even finish high school—and that is a waste we cannot afford." Later in the year, he launched a nationwide summer dropout campaign that identified, contacted, and encouraged tens of thousands of dropouts to return to school.[7]

That same decade, Lucius Cervantes conducted a famous study of three hundred youth, half of whom were high school graduates and half were dropouts. The participants lived in cities, including New Orleans, Boston, St. Louis, Omaha, Los Angeles, and Denver. Cervantes wrote, "We find that six out of ten dropouts (62 percent) report their school experiences to have been either 'very unfavorable' or 'unfavorable'; while three out of four graduates (76 percent) found their educational experiences to have been either 'favorable' or 'very favorable.'"

The matched pairs of dropouts and graduates showed similar family socioeconomic conditions, which led Cervantes to conclude that "poverty is the milieu but not the cause of premature withdrawal from high school" and considered another explanation: "'the deficiency orientation' of the dropout." Based on the results from the psychological test, Cervantes suggested there were "psychological tendencies" of the dropout compared with the graduate. Some of his dropouts compared to graduates were "troubled–calm," "radical–conservative," "proletarian–capitalistic," "anti-authority–pro-authority," and sought "immediate gratification–deferred gratification." He believed he had unearthed a "variant breed of teen-agers." "It is from this hard core of dropouts," he warned, "that a high proportion of the gangsters, hoodlums, drug addicted, government-dependent-prone, irresponsible and illegitimate parents of tomorrow will be predictably recruited."[8]

The common thread in historical studies of "the dropout" is that failing to finish school is the fault of dropouts themselves, hinging on such characteristics as poor attitude, lack of self-motivation, flawed character, and disobedient, lazy, and mischievous behavior, along with their membership in dysfunctional families—single-parent or father-less households, parents who are jobless, drug-addicted, or welfare-dependent. This "blame the victim" narrative was pervasive in a range of policy debates, among them the culture-of-poverty thesis, which posited that cultural deficiencies caused poverty. Daniel Patrick Moynihan's hotly contested 1965 report *The Negro Family: The Case for National Action* chastised the weak Black family structure as a "tangle of pathology" that impaired the advancement of African Americans. Political, economic, and social structures and institutions emerged unsullied and irrelevant in this analysis.[9]

Since the 1960s, the dropout crisis has continued to be the subject of much hand-wringing among the media, politicians, policymakers, and school administrators. It was given new life with the publication of *Time*'s April 2006 cover story, "Dropout Nation." In "today's data-happy era of accountability, testing and No Child Left Behind, here is the most astonishing statistic in the whole field of education: an increasing number of researchers are saying that nearly 1 out of 3 public high school students won't graduate," reported journalist Nathan Thornburgh. "For Latinos and African Americans, the rate approaches an alarming 50%. Virtually no community, small or large, rural or urban, has escaped the problem."[10]

Since then, high school graduation rates have markedly improved across the country, but the problem remains concentrated in districts in high-poverty areas. One is the Philadelphia schools.[11] Research found that the four-year graduation rate for the classes of 2000 to 2005 hovered around 50 percent.[12] In 2004, Philadelphia Schools CEO Paul Vallas created the Office of Multiple Pathways to Graduation and called for proposals for alternative accelerated schools to help overaged and undercredited youth obtain a high school diploma. It was part of the city's efforts to tackle the dropout crisis. The first contracts were issued to One Bright Ray and Career and Academic Development Institute, two nonprofits, and the for-profit Camelot Education.[13] The Project U-Turn campaign, launched in 2006, also aimed at reengaging out-of-school youth. When Mayor Michael Nutter was elected two years later, he pledged to slash the high school dropout rate in half and double the rate of residents with bachelor's degrees.[14] Accordingly, enrollment in the city's alternative schools, which included accelerated and disciplinary programs, mushroomed 436 percent from 2002 to 2009.[15]

Alternative education is a big tent that encompasses several models. The earliest alternative schools, known as free schools, were organized during the political and social unrest of the 1960s. Hundreds of free schools aimed to develop critical consciousness, clashing with the technocratic capitalist order. They featured open-ended curriculum, free play, experiential learning, and democratic governance.[16] In 1965, the Elementary and Secondary Education Act boosted funding for alternative education.[17] Many of the free schools had died out, but there was an emergence of alternative schools for students who had disciplinary issues, dropped out, or were in need of academic or social remediation.

In her study of alternative high schools in California, Deirdre Kelly argued that they operated as a safety valve, "provid[ing] a mechanism to rid mainstream schools of failures and misfits without holding school administrators fully accountable for the consequences, a mechanism that reinforces students' disengagement from school."[18] As concerns about violence in schools went mainstream, companies like Community Education Partners brandishing new district contracts crowded the disciplinary school market. By the 2014–15 school year, nearly half a million students were enrolled in 5,449 alternative schools in the United States (less than 1 percent of the public school population).[19] One study found that students were transferred to alternative schools and programs for a variety of reasons: engaging in physical attacks or fighting; possession, sale, and use of alcohol and drugs; disruptive verbal behavior; failing academic performance; chronic truancy; and possession and use of a weapon.[20]

*　*　*

GROWING UP, DAVID Bromley had often heard his aunts and uncles speaking of their immense pride in the family's historic textile business, and he knew he was a beneficiary of the great wealth it had generated. But he had never done research on the companies or where they had operated until he began looking for real estate for the new school. In Kensington, he stumbled across some of the defunct Bromley factories and started reading about the history of industry in the neighborhood. At this point in his life, he knew all about the role that racist housing policies, deindustrialization, hostility to organized labor, and capital accumulation had played in the shaping of cities. Now he connected the dots between the economic riches into which he was born and Kensington's demise. It was a sad irony to be starting a school in the neighborhood that had been historically denied its share of his family's wealth.

As it happened, the new school's location, in the former St. Boniface Catholic School building on Norris Square, was in walking distance of the old Bromley mills. The site was freighted with historical significance: Isaac Norris was a wealthy Quaker merchant, slaveowner, and friend of William Penn. Norris had purchased hundreds of acres of land on which he built the Fair Hill country estate in the eighteenth century. Following the death of his descendant, Joseph Parker Norris, in 1841, the Norris heirs deeded it to the District of Kensington, and its land was sold for building lots. But they stipulated that two designated plots, Fairhill Square and Norris Square, be "held for public use as a public green and walk forever," for "light, air and recreation forever."[21]

Over the next few decades, Norris Square became home to several venerable institutions, St. Boniface Catholic Church and Kensington Hospital for Women, the city's first women-only hospital, which was still in operation.[22] In a fitting coincidence, it had also been home to members of Bromley's own family, who had taken up residence in the square's opulent brownstones.[23] But by the aughts, Norris Square had gone from being what the *Philadelphia Inquirer* called "an uptown equivalent of Rittenhouse Square" during its industrial apex to Needle Park, an urban archetype of the crack epidemic and war on drugs, to a gentrifying section of Kensington marked by the encroachment of white yuppies and the displacement of Puerto Rican residents.[24]

In the crucible of the dropout crisis, El Centro de Estudiantes opened its doors in September 2009, one of more than a dozen accelerated high schools in the city. Research had found that more than a quarter of Philadelphia youth aged eighteen to twenty-four were "disconnected"—unemployed and out of school. The figures were highest in the neighborhoods surrounding the new school: nearly 40 percent were disconnected there, compared to one in ten in downtown Center City.[25]

Progressive education was a proven success for wealthy white children, but the jury was still out on its suitability for the poor and working class. Could this approach, derided by its critics as "loosey-goosey," work for the most disengaged urban youth who were living in deep poverty?[26]

* * *

"OH LOOK, OUR pyromaniac is back," one teacher in the hallway at Grover Washington muttered to another. Ryan had finished his tour of Community Education Partners and had returned to his old middle school for eighth grade, the final year before high school. He was on his way to the special education resource room when he heard the comment. He was the only student nearby, so he knew the teacher was talking about him. When he looked up the word in the dictionary, he was outraged: a pyromaniac is an individual who has an "irresistible impulse to start fires."

Grover Washington's administrators were dismayed to see Ryan, Andres, and some of their fellow CEP cohort shipped back to their school. Only a fifth of students at CEP schools had reentered the traditional system, underscoring the purpose of CEP: warehousing the educational untouchables.[27] Ryan's classmates now thought he was a badass. The bullying was over—he had finally climbed out of the bowels of the school hierarchy.

At the prodding of the coach, Ryan decided to try out for the basketball team. He couldn't dribble. He couldn't shoot. He had no expectation of making the team. But the coach—the last person who had seen Ryan when he was escorted from the school by the police—thought basketball might shield him from trouble, so he put him on the roster.

Ryan was thrilled. His behavior in school improved, and afterschool hours were dedicated to basketball. He loved traveling with the team to away games in other parts of the city. But he rarely shot the ball because he was afraid of missing and setting back the team.

As soon as the season concluded, he went into a downward spiral. Ryan and his friends Peter and Samuel were walking to school one morning and collectively decided to play hooky. They were walking down Rising Sun Avenue, about a mile from school, when Ryan suggested that they go to the Gallery. The problem was that they didn't have transit passes and were more than six miles from the shopping mall, which was in Center City.

The three got tired of walking and stopped near Olney High School football field to rest on a stoop. Ryan spotted a police car parked a few blocks away, and the officer was looking their way. Ryan knew they could get picked up for truancy. "There's a cop down the block," he told his friends. "Relax. Don't run. Get up and walk slowly. We'll walk up the Boulevard." But they ignored his instructions and tore down the street. The police car pulled out from the curb into traffic and sped toward them. The boys made a sharp left onto a side street and squeezed between a long van and a garage. They heard the slam of a car door.

Ryan hissed at Peter and Samuel to stay put. But before the officer could reach the van, the two once again took off, and Ryan followed. The officer yelled at them to stop, got back in her car, and switched on her siren.

Halfway down the block, Samuel, who was on the plump side, was chugging along well behind the others before doubling over from exhaustion. Ryan and Peter decided to abandon him. As they cut through a grassy opening between the houses that led to a parallel block, two older Black men who had heard the wail of the sirens, yelled, "Get your little badasses to school!"

The officer caught up to Samuel and cuffed him. Ryan might have been watching a slow-motion car crash: *You know it's inevitable, and there's nothing you can do about it.*

Ryan and Peter ran back to school, planning to act as though they'd just arrived late. But the police officer had called ahead about the truant trio, and the two were taken to Principal Thompson's office. He wasn't pleased. He'd be calling their parents to pick them up. Turning to Ryan, he advised him to quit playing games and putting his mother through these hassles. It felt genuine, as if the principal were being a caring educator. But Ryan wasn't buying it. Where was the empathy and concern last year, when Ryan really needed it, when he was escorted from the building in cuffs? Thompson was too late.

Ryan was lucky the school didn't call the police. When he got home, Rayni didn't even raise her hand or her voice. She had given up on reforming his ways. *He belongs to the streets now*, she thought. For the rest of the year, he mostly stayed in school but cut classes and zoomed around the building, attracting rebuke from teachers and resource officers.

What was he thinking? Not a year had passed since he was in juvenile detention and CEP. He seemed to have learned no lessons. By the final month of school, Rayni kept him home much of the time—she was afraid he'd get jumped by some kids after he got embroiled in a dumb fight in the park across the street. Ryan's time at Grover Washington ended on a fitting note: he missed the graduation ceremony.

Not My Government Name

Rayni began browsing Craigslist looking for a new home. When Tino and Armando were toddlers, they could manage to squeeze the six of them into their spacious one-bedroom apartment, with the boys sleeping on bunk and twin beds in the living room. But now they were growing.

Ryan was supposed to start ninth grade at Samuel Fels High, a failing and notoriously violent neighborhood school, while Avry had been admitted to Charter High School for Architecture and Design. Rayni didn't want to send Ryan to Fels, given its infamous reputation and the fact that he would be mingling with the same kids who had instigated mayhem at Grover Washington. She figured that if they moved to a different neighborhood, the local high school would be obligated to enroll him.

She came across an affordable row home on East Willard Street, near Kensington and Allegheny, the city's preeminent market for narcotics. The rent was $675 a month, and it had three bedrooms and one bathroom. The house was on a slim one-way block where the cars were parked on the sidewalk. When the family took a tour, they noticed that the block seemed quiet, empty of dealers and drugs. It was an oddity in Kensington, but they didn't think much of it.

Just before the start of the school year, the family rented a U-Haul truck and moved in. Avry now shared a room with Tino and Armando while Ryan took the smallest room in the back of the house, thrilled to have some privacy. But he had no peace. The block that had seemed so sterile on their first visit was crackling with vitality: casual shootings, dealers milling on the corner near the papi store day and night, people injecting in public, the air thick with the waft of marijuana, crack cocaine, and PCP. Ryan heard the dealers yelling, "J. Reid!" which puzzled him until he discovered it was the alias of an undercover cop who poses as a dealer in the movie *In Too Deep*, and the locals used the name to warn of approaching police. To evade arrest, they would zigzag through two parallel blocks south of Willard—Madison and Hilton— and stop at the houses asking people to stow them away until the danger passed.

The ring of gunshots became so normal that Ryan often slept soundly through it. In their first week in the new house, he and Avry were throwing a football around with the dealers when a shooting broke out. They had to duck between cars to dodge the bullets.

George was hired to mop the floors and clean the offices at the Liberty Coca-Cola Beverages bottling plant in Juniata for $10 an hour. He also started doing tattoos at home. During a stint at the House of Corrections, an inmate had left him his tattoo machine, and George began practicing the craft on his cellmates. When he left jail, he bought his own equipment and built up a client roster.

Rayni told herself that she lived in the house, not the streets, and God would protect her from evil. She soon learned that this was a wild delusion. She tried to keep to herself and avoided eye contact with the dealers and neighbors on the block. But her tactics made people think she considered herself too good for them. One girl spread the word that Rayni was racist because she wouldn't let George do tattoos for the Black dealers in their house. It almost led to a fight with the dealers. Rayni's attitude changed. "Either be humble and walk by, or be a warrior," she now said. "If they tell you something, punch them in the mouth."

To avoid Fels, she tried to enroll Ryan at Kensington Business High School but was told that he had to report to his designated place. Rayni appealed to the district, which said the same thing. They were exhausted by the runaround, so she signed him up for Penn Foster, a for-profit online high school diploma program. Ryan was subjected to a sequence of boring lessons and exams. After a week, he refused to log on, and Rayni ended up completing many of his assignments. To avoid encounters with the police over truancy, he burned his days sitting around at home. He lost touch with Peter, Samuel, and other friends. The monotony of home quarantine made him want to be in school.

It was his half sister, Julia, who first told him about El Centro de Estudiantes and gave him an application. He had to explain why he wanted to go to the school, which he liked. It made the place sound more like an exclusive club than a compulsory exercise. It would be a quick ride southbound on the El train. And it had to be more fun than moldering at home.

* * *

No searches or metal detectors. A pleasant female resource officer who greeted him at the front desk. As Ryan entered El Centro de Estudiantes on his first day of orientation, he knew this school would be very different from Grover Washington or CEP.

With a child care center on the first floor, the school took up the second and third stories of the archaic building. Heating was inconsistent. One student would bring a thermometer to check the temperature and poll his classmates whether they should stay or leave. The basement flooded whenever it rained or snowed. The sewage frequently backed up. There was one time when students smelled something burning near the water fountain, and it turned out to be an electrical fire.

Ryan had not yet been in high school, but his classmates generally fit the profile of dropouts. They came from a hodgepodge of institutions— traditional neighborhood public schools, charter schools, cyber charters, and alternative schools, with many having gone to two, three, four, or more before coming to El Centro de Estudiantes. There were students who showed up with ankle bracelets because they were on probation and mandated to attend school. Some of them talked about the failings of their past schools to accommodate the way they preferred to learn and acknowledge their struggles as juvenile offenders, pregnant teenagers, and young mothers, fathers, and caretakers.

As scholars and activists have noted, the term "dropout" effectively faults the student for failing to complete school, absolving the institutions of their role in producing or failing to address the underlying issues. Instead, they have begun using the word "pushout," putting the onus of responsibility on the array of "institutional policies and practices that enable, obscure, and legitimate this mass exodus" from schools, as social psychologist Michelle Fine put it.[1]

Students often came to El Centro with failing grades (on average, they performed at second-to-fourth-grade levels in reading and mathematics) and countless suspensions and expulsions on their records. They had also skipped enough school to qualify as truant—sometimes having missed as much as half the school year. Issues related to school and life outside of school contributed to the students having been pushed out. They reported overcrowded classes, monotonous and irrelevant curricula, a dearth of extracurricular activities, strict discipline, and fighting and chaos brewing on the daily. "They would throw packets at us," one student put it, which summed up the educational approach in many of their old schools. The dominant pedagogy frequently involved teachers handing out textbooks and worksheets. "I wasn't engaged at all. The classrooms—you couldn't learn," another student, Mia, explained. "What's the point of you going to school?" As a result, students deserted their classrooms and hung out in the hallways, which "were more interesting than my classes," said Victoria.

The youth reserved their harshest criticism for their teachers: They "were just there to get a paycheck," "They didn't care if you learned what they taught or if you passed," "They'd curse at us," "They wouldn't take our opinions seriously," "They didn't get to know you," "The teachers didn't care if there was something going on with you," "The teacher wouldn't know how to control the kids," and "A teacher told me I was going to be homeless if I didn't listen." It was rare for them to talk about a teacher who was engaging, responsive, and paid heed to their specific needs. Dehumanizing school experiences were compounded by all the problems outside of school. The students were also regularly funneled to the next grade level regardless of low performance. Overall, school felt like a huge waste of time.

In a school of about 150 students, the rooms were set up in a U formation, rather than in rows of desks. Each class, or "advisory," had fifteen to twenty students, headed by an advisor. Apart from subject-based seminars, internships, and other experiential learning opportunities, students stayed with their advisory most of the day, working on interdisciplinary projects that emerged from their interests and level of knowledge and skills, a centerpiece of the Big Picture Learning approach. They were evaluated through grades, low-stakes formative assessments, and end-of-term exhibitions, when their mentors and family were invited to take part in the evaluation and offer constructive feedback.

Ryan had enrolled in the middle of the school's second year. The first year had been a maelstrom of chaos. A lack of remedial academic instruction stymied the students' independent projects. Without existing relationships with local businesses, schools, museums, and community organizations, the internship opportunities were minimal. And among the staff, there were disparities of experience in teaching, urban education, and working with youth who had been educationally disengaged. In the absence of an established culture, the disorder that had characterized the students' past experiences was replicated in fighting and truancy. The advisors were often demoralized to find that more than half of their students hadn't shown up.

One March morning during the first year, JuDonn DeShields, a biracial man in his midtwenties, visited the school to give a demo lesson. "Attendance is light because there was a snowstorm and students haven't come back," the principal warned. JuDonn, a special education English teacher, had been working at a charter school in Washington, D.C. Discouraged by its formulaic and test-driven approach, he came across Big Picture Learning and applied for an advisor position. Touring the school, he found it jarring to see children wander freely around the building. He described the scene as "controlled chaos." He went to his appointed advisory, and Tristan, the advisor, told the students to get into a circle so that their guest could do his demo. At that, one boy named Raymond got out of his seat and darted into the hallway. "Probably going to start another trash can fire," a student snarked.

Tristan shot JuDonn a glance that seemed to mean this was a typical day. JuDonn watched out the classroom door as Tristan stalked Raymond, who had recently set a fire in the bathroom. "Raymond, we're trying to have a new day compared with yesterday," Tristan said. "I would appreciate if you can rejoin the advisory and give feedback on the candidate if he makes a good advisor."

"Tristan! Not my government name! I told you, it's Felix." Like many students, Raymond preferred to be called by his nickname. He went to the bathroom and returned to the advisory a few minutes later. In the circle, JuDonn shared photos of his family as a way to open a discussion about the people who mattered to the students. They grilled him with questions about his background, interests, and teaching style, gauging whether he would be a good fit in the quirky place. Raymond, who had been cracking jokes, chimed in, "We're not traditional students. A lot of these kids are *badasses*. How are you prepared to deal with that?"

"Nobody is only defined by their actions," JuDonn said. "There's time to change, grow, and develop. I'd like to see the root of the issue or problem."

In any other city high school, Raymond would probably have been treated as Ryan had been: as an educational untouchable, funneled through juvenile detention, expulsion hearings, transfer to a disciplinary school, and multiple trips to court. After that day's behavior, he would have been barred from school for a while. Instead, El Centro staff had a conversation with him and his mother, making it clear that his actions were unacceptable, and if it happened again, he would not be welcome in the school. Raymond acknowledged the harm he had caused and appreciated that he was being treated as a young adult, not suspended or expelled. This was what restorative justice looked like. Carting Raymond off to carceral institutions would have been anathema to El Centro's ethos. But by involving him in the critical decision of whether to hire an advisor, the school wanted him to know that his opinions and intelligence were respected, and that he was still an essential member of the community.

* * *

AT THE END of Ryan's first week at El Centro de Estudiantes, on Friday evening, he greeted hundreds of guests for a school art show, "El Centro State of Mind," at a Fishtown art gallery. Each student had work showing—graffiti, paintings, fabric prints, drawings, and self-portraits. One student, Christian, had set up a table to sell his graffiti. Another, Liam, had his class put on a hip-hop performance. The show was the culmination of months of work in Ryan's advisor Andrew Christman's class, which was rooted in the museum-based learning pedagogy he had honed during his career: observing, synthesizing, and presenting.

Andrew was first introduced to art education during his undergraduate years at the Pratt Institute in New York City. He began working as a teaching artist in a Brooklyn gallery and conducting residencies in public schools before co-teaching world civilizations and religions, American history, and science at an innovative school devoted to museum collaborations.

After picking up a master's degree in Asian art history, Andrew moved to Philadelphia. He struggled to find work and felt pigeonholed as either a teacher or an artist. When a position opened up at El Centro de Estudiantes, he was lured by the prospect of having autonomy over the curriculum and instruction. His demo lesson focused on the geography of Haiti at the time of its cataclysmic earthquake. He showed maps and work by Haitian artists depicting the nation's landscape.

As Ryan discovered, the mornings began with a circle in the advisories. In circles, he began to open up about his family, schooling, passions, goals, and challenges. His advisory quickly seemed like a close-knit familial unit where he felt safe to be goofy and playful but also affectionate and sensitive. Ryan had never sought out male role models, and he didn't know his biological father well enough to serve as a reference point for what he was missing, but Andrew—who was stocky, wore fedoras and scarves, and had a thick black goatee and copious patience—became a father figure. Until meeting Andrew, Ryan had never had a teacher with whom he felt comfortable sharing his raw inner feelings.

Not long after Ryan joined the school, he, Andrew, and a few students in their advisory went to the burial of a classmate's mother, who had been ill for a while. The service was in Greenmount Cemetery, across the street from the former CEP building. Just as they were about to leave, Ryan motioned to Andrew and the others. "My dad's buried here. I could show you." He had talked about his complicated relationship with Ildefonso during the circles.

Ildefonso's tombstone said simply, "We Love You," with the dates of his birth and death, along with a photo of him grinning and a space left for his mother to join him. Ryan spoke to him directly. "Hey, June, let me introduce you to my friends." One of the boys asked him how Ildefonso died, and Ryan described his illness. The visit felt completely natural. To Ryan, the advisory was an intimate group where the student could reveal their full self without judgment or stigma. He could drop the front when he walked into school.

The advisors took the students into the city as much as they could, and it was through these field trips that Ryan began to understand what the French sociologist Pierre Bourdieu termed the "habitus" of affluent white people.[2] Ryan had lived in Philadelphia virtually all his life but had rarely ventured downtown or into the prosperous white neighborhoods except to attend a court hearing or visit his probation officer. The students often found it unnerving to be in "white spaces," to draw on sociologist Elijah Anderson, where they would most likely be seen as trespassers, truants, or criminals if they weren't in a school group.[3] In JuDonn's journalism class, he brought the students downtown and assigned them to take photos with disposable cameras and interview people on the street. Afterward they talked about their discomfort being in an area with fancy restaurants and so many white people, a lot of them dressed in suits. One student said that to him, suits signaled lawyers, district attorneys, and court officials.

When Andrew's advisory toured the Philadelphia Museum of Art, the students ran amok in the exhibitions. They were boisterous and cursing, and Ryan noticed some white people gawking at them. Reflecting on the trip, Ryan said, "To go to a different section of the city, we were having so much fun we didn't know how to control our behavior." The experience taught him that they couldn't "act like little ghetto kids" in public. "That scares white people. They start touching their bags and shit. I feel their sense of safety is rattled."

Another day, the advisories took them on a historical scavenger hunt on the University of Pennsylvania campus. Strolling down Locust Walk, a tree-lined pedestrian street, Ryan felt as if he were in a scene of *American Pie*, as students and faculty hustled past him to get to class or their dorms. The outing was designed to plant the idea of college in their minds, but Andrew lamented that it was mostly a false hope, since the students would get their SAT or ACT scores and lose confidence. Their reading comprehension and mathematics skills were significantly below high school level.

For Ryan, college was hardly a thought. His only dream was to become a police officer and serve his community in more humane and respectful ways than the officers he had run into. The job only required a high school diploma or GED.

* * *

RYAN HADN'T FINISHED his first full year at El Centro de Estudiantes when Philadelphia's school district announced that its thirteen contracts with the city's accelerated alternative schools, serving 1,800 students, were to be terminated. The disciplinary schools would also see their budgets cut. The district planned to move the accelerated programs to five regional centers that had "small class sizes, individualized learning plans, strong social supports, and project-based learning," claiming the move would save tens of millions. It also intended to open ten evening "twilight" programs at high schools with steep dropout rates. These moves would help the city plug a $629-million budget deficit.[4]

When the staff at El Centro de Estudiantes broke the news to the students, there was little surprise. *This is what they do to kids who look like us*, they thought. Ryan was extremely upset. He had heard rumors about the schools shutting down but brushed them off as speculation. After the madness of Lowell, Grover Washington, and CEP, he had finally found a school where he was engaged and learning and loved going to every day, and he couldn't believe they would take this community away from him. There was no backup plan, and based on his struggles to find an appropriate high school, he was sure the search for another one would be grueling.

Laura Shubilla, president and founder of the Philadelphia Youth Network, brought the heads of the schools together to build a strategy to stop the closures. With the help of Youth United for Change, an educational justice organization, students made posters and signs for the rallies and wrote letters. Ryan took an active role. He felt the school was worth defending with his time and sweat. He didn't want to be forced to settle for a GED program or worse, drop out.

A moving letter by Matthew Prochnow, an advisor, described the school as a "place full of a familial type of love," although a conflicted one, like any family. "It is a place where we have had to strive for love, and on some days we have had to fight, to claw and to scratch and to gnash our teeth for something even resembling love," he wrote. "And even then, sometimes we have failed." His students had long felt disempowered in their education and had rarely fought for better conditions in their previous schools. "They were accustomed to leaving and looking for something new," he said.

* * *

THEY HAD SAT through more than five hours of testimony on the proposed reduction of full-day kindergarten to half day and on cuts to afterschool, summer, and other programs, and the El Centro de Estudiantes students were growing restless. As the crowd thinned, they moved from the mezzanine to the main level. It was a Wednesday evening in late May, and they were waiting to testify before the Philadelphia City Council in the hope of saving their school.[5] The council chambers, built in the French Second Empire style, had a dazzling ornamental golden ceiling, a striking array of light fixtures, mahogany desks, and red carpeting.[6]

When David Bromley, who was overseeing operations at the school as well as Big Picture Learning's work in the city, finally stood up to testify, he framed the proposed elimination of the alternative schools through the lens of the families' relationship with the district. "So what will happen if this proposal stands? One can only speculate but most likely many of these students, despite our best efforts, will not attend the proposed District-run learning centers and will drop out once more. There is a fundamental lack of trust between these students and families and the School District." He was followed by more than a dozen students, staff, and parents.

The mic was eventually passed to Ryan. Baby-faced with short-cropped black hair, he was dressed up in a white-and-navy plaid button-down shirt. He was anxious. It was his first time speaking in public and on such a momentous occasion, no less. He was there of his own volition, to fight for the first school he ever felt proud to belong to.

Ryan related the journey that had brought him to El Centro de Estudiantes. He talked about his experiences in the art class and his internship at a motorcycle shop. "Now I know for a fact that the alternative schools the school district runs do not have classes like this," he said, reading from his notes. "I've had my experiences. I went to CEP and it wasn't fun . . . It had packed classes filled with disruptive kids, no learning happening there, and I felt as though they were always violating my space by searching us whenever they wanted to. Even when I would go in the morning, they would make us walk through metal detectors, but that wasn't enough, because they would still search us by hand."

El Centro was different. "There are no metal detectors. We don't get searched. It's just way better. I can't even call El Centro an alternative school. To me, an alternative school feels like a prison, but El Centro feels like home. Don't take away my home." He ended by thanking his teacher for helping him with the speech. "Our teachers from El Centro are still here up until seven, seven I don't know, seven something, but they still here fighting with us to keep our school open. We don't want our school closed."

For many of the students, it felt like no high school wanted them. El Centro de Estudiantes was the first institution to accept them unconditionally *because* of their blotchy academic and disciplinary records.

Closing the school would mean forfeiting small class sizes, progressive teaching methods, and internships for the same old humdrum, violent schools they were pushed out of. One student, Stella, wrote, "We came from a school where we were not learning anything and now that we have the opportunity of learning. We never want to lose that." Another, Carter, said he learned more in three months at El Centro de Estudiantes than in three years at his old school, Kensington Creative and Performing Arts.

To the students, the planned closure was a personal affront and an act of injustice, tantamount to denying them the chance of graduating and becoming somebody in life. "Taking away my school is taking away my life," said Gabriel. "It's taking away my future . . . It's taking away who I am."

At a rally a few weeks later, more than a hundred students marched around city hall, chanting, "No education, no life!" and "Save our schools!" Some wore T-shirts with the slogan "I'm worth 25 cents," referring to a proposed soda tax, which, if approved, would help fund public education. Mayor Michael Nutter stepped out to speak, saying he was on their side. "You deserve better than what we've been able to do. You really have to have high quality schools and we shouldn't have to trade the swimming pools. These are the things that adults are supposed to do to support children. So it's time for the adults to stand up." He invited the students inside to plead their case directly to city council members.[7]

Bromley noticed that the fight was the "perfect medicine" to improve the school's culture. Some of the kids who were making trouble at city hall barely showed up to school. He was outside city hall one day. *When was the last time we had this many kids in our building?* he thought. Ryan witnessed the massive enthusiasm and turnout and figured that the city had no choice but to listen and come up with a plan to keep the schools open.

He was right. A few days later, the city council shot down Nutter's soda tax proposal but voted to increase property taxes and street meter parking rates. When supplemented with other funds, the measure would raise $53 million, a portion of which would help bail out the alternative schools.[8] Direct action got the goods, and El Centro de Estudiantes was spared.

Ryan was relieved but wondered whether the anguish could have been avoided. Why did they have to beg the people in power for public schools that respected and helped their students? Why wasn't that a basic right for all?

9
. . .

Pray the Gay Away

The housing merry-go-round had become a constant integral feature of Emmanuel's life. Emmanuel, Ivette, and Freddie were now
living in Freddie's mother's house in the upper stretch of Kensington.
Michael, who now received SSI checks, had moved out, having enough
income to rent a place with his girlfriend, Aida. The three slept on mattresses on the concrete floor of an unfinished basement with nothing
but space heaters and an industrial lamp. When it rained or snowed, the
basement flooded and mud seeped in. There were no windows and no
exit, so they would be trapped in the event of a fire.

Emmanuel's excellent academic performance had earned him
admission to Russell H. Conwell Middle Magnet School, named for the
founder of Temple University. The three-story, brick building with stone
trim had been built in the Late Gothic Revival style in the mid-1920s.[1]
The school was somewhat diverse, with a few white and Asian students among the mostly Black and Latino population, "the young prod-
igies of the hood," as he put it. A few weeks into fifth grade, Emmanuel
was bumped up to sixth, where he got into English and music, playing
the keyboard and perfecting the theme song to the film *Halloween*.

After school, Emmanuel would plop himself on the couch in the living room upstairs and watch *America's Next Top Model* and *The Ellen Show*. He was twelve and hitting puberty, and his attraction to boys hadn't gone away. He found solace watching Ellen, a gay woman—he thought she was hilarious, and her guests seemed to have fun on the show. He wished she would pluck him from obscurity and move his family to a majestic house.

Freddie's mother's shabby home on East Tioga and Jasper fit the pattern of Emmanuel's childhood: he abhorred his living conditions and spent most of his free time out of the house. He would beg Freddie's mother for money to buy ice cream, and she would say either "I haven't got any. Leave me alone," or "Here, take it," dipping into her black fanny pack to pull out a dollar. He would get two generous scoops of butter pecan or cookies and cream at the corner store and sit on the swings in the park across the street.

It was an escape from Ivette and Freddie's fighting, which was, as usual, at its most raucous when Freddie had been drinking. Finances were the most common bone of contention—the family was getting by on Ivette's skimpy SSI and TANF checks. Freddie was barely contributing, instead blowing most of the money from his landscaping, construction, and scrap metal and recycling gigs on pot and booze. When he couldn't be bothered to lumber upstairs to the bathroom, he urinated in beer bottles or in a corner of the basement, adding an ammoniac scent to the aroma of mildew. The intensity and frequency of his abuse accelerated to a point that Emmanuel thought Ivette was finally going to leave him, but that remained a mirage.

When Freddie landed in the hospital with alcohol poisoning, his mother's landlord discovered their illegitimate living quarters. The family had to move yet again and find somewhere else to live. They were fortunate to land in a small but cozy two-bedroom, one-bath house on D Street in another section of Kensington. Emmanuel was overjoyed to have his own room, with a bed and a door—finally a space where he could shut out Ivette and Freddie's affairs and personalize with his style. He plastered the walls with *J-14* teen magazine covers and Pokémon posters. His first few nights were sleepless—he was used to being near his mother—but he eventually overcame that. He often stayed up late practicing the local Philly D-Mac dance or dancing to the New Boyz's hit song "You're a Jerk."

In his spare time, Emmanuel sold bootleg mixtape CDs for $5 a pop to drug dealers on the block. He bought bundles of blank CDs, invited customers to give him a list of songs, downloaded them from YouTube, and burned the CDs on his rented HP laptop, cribbing Wi-Fi from a neighbor who didn't password-protect his network. His entrepreneurial venture quickly caught on. From his bedroom window, Emmanuel could hear his customers blasting songs by artists like Soulja Boy and Daddy Yankee. With his profits, he bought junk food and Day's Blue Pop soda, reinvesting what remained into buying more blank CDs. The business flourished for a few months until his free Wi-Fi access got cut off.

One afternoon, Emmanuel came home to find Freddie smoking marijuana with a guy named Joel, who was in his twenties, tall and brawny, with long curly black hair in a ponytail. A former member of a gang, he continued sporting his affiliation by incorporating their color in his outfit. On Cambria Street in Kensington, he worked with a small drug faction as a caseworker—the person who deals with the block boss, stores and restocks the drugs, and takes a small cut. Mature for his age, having been forced to grow up quickly, Emmanuel found it easy to make friends with older guys and started chatting with Joel. He had all the latest gaming systems and offered to let Emmanuel game using his PlayStation. Before long, Emmanuel was going to Joel's house straight from school and began to see him and his girlfriend, Destiny, as a big brother and sister. They played video games, went laser-tagging, and ran errands together. Whenever he ran out of food at home or needed someone to talk to, Joel's house was the go-to spot.

Emmanuel didn't mind that Joel sold drugs. In North Philadelphia, drug dealers were as common a sight as row homes, and many of them were Emmanuel's friends, people hustling to make money and put food on the table, as he saw it. It was just a job. His mother sometimes worried that he might be influenced to go down the same path, but Joel was adamant. "This isn't a life for you," he said. "It's not what you want."

He didn't say much about his work and shielded Emmanuel from the minutiae of the business; he wasn't even allowed in the house when Joel's colleagues came by. Both Joel and Destiny encouraged Emmanuel to devote himself to his education.

Emmanuel was working on his homework at the table one day while Joel's stepdaughter Grace and infant daughter, Claudia, ate mac and cheese. Joel was lounging on the couch playing *Call of Duty: Black Ops—Zombies*. Suddenly, the front door was smashed in. Several cops in SWAT gear barged in, shouting, "Everybody up! Hands on the wall!" It was a textbook no-knock drug raid. They grabbed Joel and cuffed him, demanding that he reveal where he was hiding the drugs. He pleaded the fifth.

Grace and Claudia started weeping. Joel tried to console them. "It's okay. They're just going to look through the house," he said. Emmanuel was petrified, too. With his hands on the wall, he was frisked and patted down while an officer combed through his backpack. He knew there was only one thing to do: keep his mouth shut. Say nothing that could rat Joel out.

But when Emmanuel was under pressure, his mind sometimes produced strange images. The officer pulled out an Elmer's glue stick from his backpack, but Emmanuel saw a pill bottle. "That's not mine," he blurted out.

"This glue stick?" the officer asked.

They ransacked every room in the house. They pulled out drawers, emptied cabinets, and flipped couch cushions and mattresses. It looked like the aftermath of an earthquake. But Joel had hidden the drugs so that the police couldn't find them. Still, they took him anyway. Emmanuel teared up at the sight of his friend getting hauled away, but he knew nothing had been found, so Joel probably wouldn't be gone for long.

It wasn't Joel's first rodeo with the authorities. He calmly told Emmanuel what to do next. "Watch the kids for me. Destiny is on her way." Aida and Michael, who was selling crack nearby, came over to help.

Destiny came home a few hours later, and Emmanuel filled her in, giving her Joel's cell phone and password. Joel was released soon after, less shaken by the raid than by the fact that Emmanuel had freely given up his password. Destiny had combed through his texts and saw he was flirting with another woman. Fortunately, things hadn't escalated beyond that.

* * *

AFTER MORE THAN a year, Ivette, Emmanuel, and Freddie were evicted and on the move again. Freddie found their new home through a friend: a brown row home on a rail-thin block—Lippincott Street near McPherson Square in Kensington—surrounded by abandoned lots invaded by wild vegetation. Ivette didn't have a chance to tour it before they moved, and if she had, she might have preferred going to a home-less shelter. The neighborhood was fizzing with traffic, brawls, drug transactions, an orchestra of gunshots, and police patrols.

The house violated nearly every basic housing code. Cockroaches, spiders, and plump rats with long tails scurried about, finding their way into the beds and cupboards. The floors were caked with dirt. The drywall was damaged. Mold festered in all the rooms. There was no electricity, so Freddie took it from his nephew next door, the orange extension cords snaking through an upstairs window to power the tele-vision, radio, and space heater. The bathroom was smeared with urine and feces, and the tub threatened to fall through the cracked ceiling to the kitchen. They took scary, chilly baths using buckets of water boiled on the stove, the tub shifting slightly when they stepped in it. For Emmanuel, it was maddening to watch his mother stay committed to an alcoholic who let them live in such squalor.

He also had to adjust to yet another new school. His grades had sagged during eighth grade, so his options were limited to two. He opted for Esperanza Academy Charter High School because his friend Omar, a heavy, pale-skinned Puerto Rican boy, would be attending, so he would know at least one person. On the first day of ninth grade, after catching two buses, Emmanuel walked into Esperanza sporting a freshly dyed burgundy Afro that he hoped would help him seem cool. But the school was populated by a near-homogenous Latino student population with a religious conservative upbringing. With his squeaky voice, long, curly hair, and L'Oréal Paris black eyeliner, Emmanuel looked androgynous and out of place. Other students ridiculed his hairstyle and bullied him for being overweight. One time he was chewing some gum in class, and the teacher told him to spit it out. "You're chewing like a cow," a student remarked. "Oh wait—you are a cow." This was unlike anything he had experienced at Conwell, where he had a tight circle of caring friends.

Emmanuel tried to zone out the cruelty. When it came to his weight, there was not much he could do. His neighborhood was a food desert with little access to affordable, nutritious meals, and it was in the second "hungriest" congressional district in the nation, where half the households with children went short.[2] Ivette often used up her monthly food stamps in a single trip to the store, forcing the family to ration the final week or two of the month or buy on credit. Emmanuel was always anxious about where his next meal would come from, so when he did have food, he feasted.

Michael Harrington's description of people "fat with hunger," fat from cheap food, fit Emmanuel's family.[3] Their carb diet featured helpings of rice, beans, and chicken, and endless servings of fast food from establishments such as Kentucky Fried Chicken, Burger King, McDonald's, and the nearby Chinese store, where they ordered pork fried rice, lo mein, chicken wings, and egg rolls. Emmanuel and Ivette loved their delicious homemade lemonade. The sugary drink calmed her hot temper.

Affording the school uniform was another issue. The dress code at Esperanza was a light-blue collared shirt, navy sweater vest, navy tie with yellow stripes, navy slacks, and black dress shoes, all of which had to be purchased from a designated vendor; the bill came to more than a hundred dollars with no financial aid from the school. Emmanuel alternated between two sets. He outgrew his shirts quickly, so Ivette would buy cheap ones from the discount store and sew on the logo herself. The house did not have a washer or dryer, so she had to wash the uniform by hand and dry it by double fisting an iron and a hair dryer. But sometimes it wouldn't dry in time, and Emmanuel would get teased by his classmates because his shirt was stained or smelled of sweat.

Classes were a struggle, too. At Conwell, his teachers had given individual attention and extra guidance; at Esperanza, they scolded him for not paying attention and missing classes, which involved packets and textbooks with little formal teaching. In English, instead of writing his own stories, he had to fill out worksheets. The only class he enjoyed was music, where he played the trumpet. After settling into the school, he dipped into a few of the low-status cliques: the nerds, the *Minecraft* players, the heavy-metal enthusiasts. Listening to grating, aggressive music was unusually consoling and helped alleviate his anxiety. At home, he taught himself how to play the guitar. He hoped to be a musician one day.

Emmanuel maintained straight As during the first half of the year, but he grew more and more withdrawn as he began finally to confront his sexuality. He had hoped being attracted to boys was a phase that would pass, especially if he acted straight. He flirted with girls he thought he had crushes on and asked a few out (they always said no), but he couldn't deny that his feelings for them were just platonic and his attraction to boys was not a fluke. But homosexuality was anathema to his family's Pentecostal faith. He thought a wicked force had taken hold of him, and he wrestled not to surrender to it.

More and more often, he lay in bed, depressed, snacking on Nutty Buddy peanut butter and fudge wafers. He ended up missing so much schoolwork that he would have to repeat the ninth grade. Ivette chided him. "You need to go to school. You need to stop being a bum." She didn't see depression as a serious condition that required treatment. She thought Emmanuel was afflicted by a demon that could be prayed away. She knew nothing about Emmanuel's struggle with his sexual orientation—or that he had begun to harm himself to help manage his emotions, hiding the scars under long sleeves.

In the bathroom at Joel's house, Emmanuel cut himself more deeply than he had before. It was not pretty. Joel came to his rescue, helping him apply butterfly strips to the lacerations. Emmanuel knew that Joel wouldn't snitch on him to his mother, but he couldn't rely on Destiny, so he decided to tell her himself. "I'm tired of everything," he confessed to Ivette. "I don't want to live. I'd like everything to end." Freddie drove him and Ivette to a psychiatric hospital in the city, but Emmanuel refused to be admitted, scared of being separated from his mother. Had he stayed, he would likely have been diagnosed with clinical depression and given medication. But he insisted on leaving, and the worst part was that Freddie had left, so the two had to walk an hour in the cold to get home.

* * *

EMMANUEL TOOK TO his Facebook feed without revealing the precise source of his trouble:

> I have such a broken home but yet still I try to smile even though the pain is so unbearable as I watch us slowly drift away the memories just fading away without remembering the past. I don't even know who to call family anymore I guess i'm alone slowly fighting but being strong isn't as easy as in the movies holding back tears may be the hardest thing I have to do ~but stay true live life~ things happen for a reason.

He tried praying to God, pleading, "Please don't make me gay. Please don't make me gay. Please don't make me gay." He hoped he could pray the gay away. His worst nightmare was of God taking vengeance and depositing him at the gates of hell. Esperanza didn't help: during a makeup test, as he doodled zigzags on a Scantron sheet, he overheard the two proctors talking about the upcoming presidential election. The men agreed that they wouldn't vote for President Barack Obama because he had endorsed legalizing same-sex marriage. *I will never be somebody in life,* Emmanuel thought. And he would never feel safe or accepted at Esperanza.

Eventually, following exhaustive searches online—Googling phrases such as "how to know if you're gay" and "how to be gay and Christian," as well as reading blogs and articles—Emmanuel came to believe that homosexuality and Christianity weren't necessarily mutually exclusive. He could be spared the wrath of God. He had already hinted about it to Omar, and now, a day before his sixteenth birthday, he called his friend Angelina from Conwell and came out as bisexual. He didn't close the door on the possibility that he might like girls, and this was easier than accepting that he only liked boys. "Now we can fawn over guys together!" she exclaimed. He had a low-key birthday party with her and Omar, comforted that his friends treated him no differently.

A week later, Angelina suggested that he tell his mother. Coming out to his friends had been relatively painless, but Ivette was a wholly different breed—a card-carrying evangelist of Pentecostal Christianity. At best, she wouldn't care; at worst, she would disown him and excommunicate him from the household, and he had no way of knowing where her reaction would land on the spectrum. But he realized that he didn't want to hide it from her forever and knew she would find out eventually. It would be better coming from him than from rumor and gossip.

To prepare, Emmanuel binge-watched dozens of coming-out videos on YouTube and tried to craft the simplest way of breaking the news. He woke up that morning with a feeling in his stomach he described as a paper cut that wouldn't stop bleeding, but "this time I was bleeding out my truth." He called softly to his mother. "I want to tell you something," he said. "Mom, I think I'm bisexual."

"What, so you like boys, too?" Ivette said. "You know God destroyed two cities because of that, Sodom and Gomorrah?" She teared up. "I need time to process this."

Emmanuel tried to put on a show of strength. "Cool," he said. "There's nothing you can do about it. I'm bisexual." She disappeared into her bedroom. He imagined her thinking that her youngest child was her biggest disgrace.

Eventually Ivette came out and gave him a hug. "No matter what you feel at this moment," she said, "I am there to support you. I love you no matter what you are. I'm going to love you always." But in the next breath, she worried that he would catch AIDS. Emmanuel explained that that was a hurtful stigma attached to the LGBTQ community.

Despite his mother's vow of solidarity, Emmanuel didn't truly feel relieved or liberated. He didn't think she would fully accept who he was, and she was the entirety of his family. He had no one else to turn to. His father had disappeared. Joaquin was in residential care. And Emmanuel and Michael weren't talking much since Michael had moved out of the city. But when Emmanuel finally opened up to his brother, Michael didn't judge or look at him differently and said that he shouldn't feel inadequate.

Over the next several weeks, Emmanuel saw that his mother became increasingly distant. He stopped going to school. He'd cry and take freezing baths to remind himself that he was still alive. At night, he stared at the broken drywall above his head imagining painless ways to end his life and pay for his misdeeds. In his misery, he went back to YouTube and discovered Davey Wavey's channel, which covered coming out, dating, sex, and other LGBTQ issues. He was reminded that he was not alone, that there was nothing immoral about his attraction, and his suffering would not be eternal. This pain and turmoil were not uncommon for people coming out in conservative, religious families, and his mother's reaction could have been much worse. Being persistently miserable was not the life he envisioned. With the help of the Internet, he slowly, day by day, began to accept all his multitudes.

10

...

How Do You Feel Bout Me Being Prego?

Just as Ryan was about to turn seventeen, his ex-girlfriend Bianca called with news: she was pregnant, and he was the most likely father. Ryan's first reaction was exhilaration: the two had recently broken up, but he still imagined them raising their child together. Bianca was a year younger than Ryan, still in high school, a petite, light-skinned Puerto Rican girl. They had met during the summer of 2011 the same way Ryan connected with most girls, through Facebook. He was often chatting to so many different girls simultaneously that he would get confused and mix them up.

At El Centro de Estudiantes, he had taken to keeping a journal and found it therapeutic—he could write anything under the sun. But he thought doing it together with Bianca might strengthen their relationship. Their black composition notebook featured the staples of teenage melodrama: regrets, jubilations, irritation, accusations of infidelity, swinging from bliss to rage and back again. "I'm real fucking mad rite now and I just came at you on the phone," Ryan wrote. "But it's we like for real you always catching a fucking attitude." That was on Friday. "Yesterday nite was the fucking best I really had fun with you," he wrote three days later. "Just laying with you playing with you and also fucking . . . You my Baby, Baby mom, wife. I will really marry you even thoe you wouldn't marry me." The pages were scattered with musings about their vivacious sex life. "The fucking best yo!" Bianca riffed. "I don't ever want it to stop. And I know I ain't gonna find something better." One time they were almost caught by her family flagrantly having sex on the couch.

The subject of pregnancy made an appearance in their journal. Bianca wrote, "We are made for each other. I don't want this to ever end ♡. I know we argue and I say some mean shit to you but I know I can change that, I know I can . . . I think we gonna last more then 3 years. And if I am prego than we might last more than 6 years!" She asked Ryan, "How do you feel bout me being prego?"

Ryan wrote back four days later. "So how do I feel about you being prego I kinda feel happy and I kinda do want you to be cause it's with the girl of my dream no matter how much shit you say that's mean I still want you and no other girl to have my baby." They hadn't intended to have a child, but they regularly had unprotected sex.

Avry thought the news was hilarious and inevitable. "Ryan's always *fuckin'* somebody," he commented. Ryan had the reputation of being a player. In the summer after seventh grade, he had lost his virginity to a newly arrived Puerto Rican girl who only spoke Spanish. For a few days, he flirted in broken Spanish, and then as they were dropping into a friend's barber shop, she pulled him into the bathroom. He grabbed a condom that he knew was in a drawer and let her handle the rest.

He met another girl, Kiara, on MySpace, who was a few years older. He saw her once or twice a week, and they made love at her aunt's house. Like a sugar mama, she would treat him with a wad of twenty-dollar bills to get a haircut or buy some new Nikes. At the same time, he was exchanging sexually charged messages, also on MySpace, with a girl named Andrea. Ryan told Kiara he was heading out of town with his family for a bit so she shouldn't expect to hear from him. Without telling his mother, he used his savings to buy a Greyhound bus ticket to Reading to meet Andrea. She and her aunt picked him up from the bus station and brought him home for the weekend, where Ryan and Andrea hung out and got laid in various rooms. The risks of hooking up with a stranger on the Internet didn't occur to Ryan, who was just looking for some action.

Rayni was furious when she found out about the pregnancy. She thought the pair were incompatible and bound to split up. Bianca was feisty and combative, and Ryan was too controlling. Rayni had forbidden Bianca from coming over, but that made Ryan want to see her more; even bribing him with an MP3 player and a PlayStation hadn't worked. Sometimes Ryan would go to great lengths to see Bianca. Since Bianca's mother had also banned him from their house, he would scale the fence and gutter along the side of her house and sneak in through her bedroom window. Rayni knew Ryan wasn't ready to be a father. Any prospect of him finishing the final two years of high school and maybe even going to college would be torpedoed by the responsibility of raising a child.

Reality hit Ryan a few days after he got the news, once the initial excitement wore off. He asked Rayni what he was supposed to do; he was only a teenager. Rayni called him back: "I'm here for you. I'm not going to let you down. I'm not going to be angry." Bianca's mother, Hermosa, wanted her to get an abortion, but Bianca and Ryan never considered that option. Ryan was prepared to deal with the consequences of not wearing a condom and heeded to the lyrics of Tupac, one of his favorite rappers. "And since a man can't make one, He has no right to tell a woman when and where to create one."

As summer approached, he fought with Rayni over her continued refusal to let Bianca visit him at the house. She laid down the law: my house, my rules. So Ryan found another place to live, moving in with his cousin Anna at Bartram Village in Southwest Philadelphia, a withering low-rise public housing complex built for defense workers during World War II that had fallen into decay, the hallways permeated with the smell of marijuana, urine, and burnt food.

Through El Centro de Estudiantes, Ryan had gained a mentor, Edwin Desamour. His first internship through the school had been with Desamour's organization, Men in Motion in the Community. Desamour served nearly nine years in prison after being convicted at sixteen of third-degree murder for involvement in killing a Philadelphia police officer's son. After his release, he set up MIMIC, which led workshops in schools bringing together formerly incarcerated men and teenage boys at risk of entering the criminal justice system. When Edwin met Ryan, he thought he looked familiar. He had been pals with Ildefonso, who used to come into Desamour's barber shop. For his internship, Ryan would accompany him to the workshops, and he showed Ryan how to code-switch: how to speak and dress professionally to negotiate and fit into white spaces.

That summer, Desamour helped Ryan get a job. For $15 an hour, he spent all day at PECO energy company, inputting data into spreadsheets. Mostly, he learned that he never wanted to work in an office. After work, he'd hang out in North Philadelphia, trying to avoid going back to Bartram Village. When he'd return in the late evening, the residents fastened their eyes on the incongruous pale teen as if he had violated some racial quarantine. "This dude live here?" he heard somebody scoff. Apart from periodic visits by Bianca, he presumed he was the only Puerto Rican in the project, which was predominantly Black.

* * *

RYAN CAME HOME to multiple crises. George was out of work, having broken his hand in a fight at his mother's wedding. Avry was running in the streets with his friends. Ryan himself had a baby on the way. Then Rayni was diagnosed with Stage II breast cancer. Her last mammogram and ultrasound had revealed no abnormalities, but she had skipped a few annual checkups, feeling that her doctor had been rude to her. Now she was terrified.

Her older sister Maritza had died from breast cancer at forty-five, leaving behind a young son. Rayni was fixated on the grim prospect of following in her footsteps, with her four sons, especially Tino and Armando, growing up without a mother. It was Medicaid, one of the signature programs of President Lyndon B. Johnson's Great Society project, that saved her life, giving her access to health care that she wouldn't have otherwise been able to afford. Rayni underwent a lumpectomy, followed by six months of chemotherapy. She was advised to root out sources of stress and anxiety, so she did guided meditations almost every day. And she hid her illness, going to chemotherapy alone and never letting the children see her throwing up.

While Rayni was receiving treatment, George was sinking into a disease of his own, an intensifying addiction to crack. His sister Zoe told Rayni that she noticed his face was turning gray from use of the drug. At first, Rayni didn't believe her, but she began to notice that he would disappear for hours every day. Dark rings appeared around his eyes. He lost weight and developed insomnia. There were times where he would stay awake for two days straight.

George had been introduced to crack as a teenager, when his friends would mix it with marijuana. In his twenties, he had worked at the Center City nightclub Eden Roc, rising from dishwasher to sous chef to night manager, and had taken drugs almost every night, pounding drinks and dabbling with cocaine, marijuana, ecstasy, and acid. It sowed the seeds of his addiction. Now that crack was omnipresent on their block, he could step out of the house and find a momentary wave of euphoria almost at his doorstep. He began blowing the money he earned from inking tattoos and dealing drugs. Avry found out independently, from a friend who was one of George's customers, but Ryan was kept in the dark.

Things came to a head a few days after Thanksgiving. Rayni was running late on her way back from chemotherapy. She stopped at the corner to pick up cash from George and learned that he had just been arrested. She hadn't wanted him to work on the corner, but he'd been doing it for a few weeks against her wishes.

Earlier that day, George and his partner Yaniel had received their supply and stashed the crack and powdered cocaine inside a cinderblock beneath a fence. George noticed a suspicious-looking black car parked nearby. "How long has that car been there?" he asked Yaniel. As a precaution, he decided to retrieve the drugs and take off. He managed to store some bundles under a pile of leaves and dirt in an alleyway, but as soon as he lifted his head, he saw the police had found him. The officers frisked him and confiscated one packet of crack and three packets of powdered cocaine along with $145 in cash. Yaniel was also arrested, with eleven packets of powdered cocaine and $100 in cash.

In the cop car, George found himself sitting next to one of his customers, who had been picked up with two packets of crack cocaine. George still had some crack up his sleeve and in his mouth. It was too late to spit it out, which left him with only one option. As his customer stared at him, George chewed and swallowed several pieces of crack. He was able to discreetly wedge the rest of it under the seat belt. At the district, he knew he would be thoroughly searched, and his fate would be worse if they found drugs on him.

George was released on bail, after being charged with three counts:

1. Manufacture, Delivery, or Possession with Intent to Manufacture or Deliver
2. Intentional Possession of a Controlled Substance by Person Not Registered
3. Conspiracy to Manufacture, Delivery, or Possession with Intent to Manufacture or Deliver

At home, Ryan found himself in charge of the kitchen. Rayni was often receiving treatment, and George was missing in action, after getting bailed out of jail. To Rayni's displeasure, Bianca had moved in after her mother kicked her out, and Ryan had to provide for her and the entire family. Using what he had gleaned from watching his mother and George and reading recipes, he made bacon, egg, and cheese sandwiches for breakfast. For dinner, he whipped up macaroni and cheese sprinkled with breadcrumbs, butter noodles, mashed potatoes, chicken strips, or chicken noodle soup. He also had a part-time job at McDonald's, handing out meals at the drive-through window, preparing food, and taking orders. He had to be on his feet for most of the grueling shifts for just $7.25 an hour. His mother was battling cancer; George was facing jail time. He felt he was carrying the weight of a household in disarray.

Ryan came home after a shift at McDonald's with a cheeseburger for Rayni. As she rose, Ryan saw that her hair was disheveled and went to straighten it when clumps came out in his hands. His eyes welled with tears. "Don't worry," she said, hugging him. "That's supposed to happen. It's going to grow back."

* * *

EL CENTRO DE Estudiantes had moved from its Norris Square location a few blocks north, to a low-key drug block. The school took over a three-story brownstone fortress that had been built in 1909. It had originally been the home of William H. Hunter Elementary School and was in an advanced state of disrepair. The windows, doors, walls, plumbing, ventilation, and other systems all needed work to the tune of at least $9 million, but the district did not have the money to pony up for the renovations.[1] The school moved in regardless. The oil-fired boiler didn't work, so school was sometimes canceled in winter because the classrooms were freezing. A building inspection report suggested that there was asbestos in the pipe insulation in the cafeteria, in the flooring and window glazing in classrooms, offices, and bathrooms, and in the plaster ceiling in the third-floor hallway.[2]

A few blocks to the west was American Street, a thoroughfare that had once accommodated the Reading Railroad's freight line as well as coal and lumber yards, stove and cast-iron manufacturing firms, ice factories, and a Philadelphia Electric Company substation. Now it was effectively an industrial cemetery. East of the school, past the row homes, Puerto Rican restaurants serving tacos, *mofongo*, *camarones*, and *arañitas*, and the Kensington branch of the Free Library of Philadelphia, stood the York-Dauphin El station. Incoming trains rumbled into Front Street's shopping district, where shuttered storefronts sat next to sporting goods and apparel stores, dollar stores, pawn shops, pharmacies, and fast food joints, before heading to Center City or turning onto Kensington Avenue, overlooking the rugged topography of North Philadelphia. A boarded-up building towered over the northbound platform. Once the home of the John Bromley & Sons mill, it was being converted into residential and commercial units.[3] A block south of the station was the site of two landmarks featured in the *Rocky* films: Mighty Mick's boxing gym and J&M Tropical Fish, where Rocky Balboa met his wife Adrian and dog Butkus.

David Bromley took over as principal and adopted a tough love approach with the aim of instilling in the students a solid work ethic, improving attendance rates, and checking the trend of kids coming to school only a few times a month and skipping their internships while still accruing credits. Now students who consistently arrived late and missed more than eight days of school or failed to have an internship by the cutoff date could be removed from the rolls. The new policy got results: average daily attendance for the school's two hundred students soared above 80 percent.

Ryan felt that the new policy was squarely aimed at him. With all the stress at home, he had been coming late or leaving early, sometimes not going at all. Ryan noticed that his friends were being pushed out one after another: Xavier, Josue, Edwin, Alex. He wondered if he'd be next. Avry had joined him at El Centro de Estudiantes, which didn't make Ryan happy. He thought Avry was taking a slot from a student who actually needed it, and he preferred being there by himself. They quarreled at school. One day they shoved each other and started to wrestle. "Y'all don't belong here," Ryan sneered at Avry. The advisors intervened and split them up.

Ryan was in turmoil. He was set off easily and had tantrums. Out of frustration, he punched a hole in a wall. But he was guarded about what was happening at home. He didn't realize that talking about his struggles might have helped him. Shortly before Bianca was due to give birth, Ryan got into an argument with Andrew, his advisor, who was ordering him to sit down and do his work. Ryan lost his temper. "Fuck you," he said. "I ain't doing that shit. Get out of my face."

The next morning, Bromley, Andrew, and a counselor, Celeste, sat with Ryan and suggested he take a trimester off from school. With his poor behavior and deteriorating attendance, his clash with Andrew was the final straw. "This isn't us kicking you out," Celeste told him. "You can come back." To Ryan it felt exactly as if they were kicking him out. He didn't want to take time off. El Centro de Estudiantes was his home. He was committed to staying in school even after his baby was born. All he was asking was for them to take note of his circumstances and cut him some slack.

As he walked to the El, he muttered that he was never going back. Greater than his anger was his sense of betrayal. He had been trying to manage school on top of feeding his family, caring for his mother, toiling at McDonald's, and ferrying his pregnant girlfriend to her appointments.

He was overstretched and exhausted. Who could blame him for putting school at the bottom of his list?

He had given a lot to the school, too, he thought. When El Centro de Estudiantes was on its last legs, who'd fought like hell to keep it open? Who'd rallied the troops and gone to city council? *They gonna do Ryan like that. Fuck 'em.*

Save Our Schools

Members of the Philadelphia Student Union caked in green and red makeup and paint performed a zombie-themed dance to Michael Jackson's "Thriller" and chanted, "No education, no life," outside the Philadelphia School District building on Broad Street, the busy central artery through downtown. Behind them, students held coffin-shaped black signs emblazoned with "RIP Philly Schools." One student was suited up and played the role of the school superintendent, William R. Hite Jr: "I have a plan to improve our public schools by closing thirty-seven of them!"[1]

It was January 2013, and Hite, who had held the job for barely two months, had announced a proposal to close thirty-seven public schools, about one in six, and relocate several more, displacing about 17,000 students. (El Centro de Estudiantes was not on the list.) African American students would account for 79 percent of the displaced population, twenty points higher than their overall representation in the district.

"It is a plan," he wrote, "that focuses on better harnessing our resources to provide safer, stronger schools for all our families." He chalked up the closures to the 53,000 unfilled seats in the district, leaving many schools sparsely occupied. The move was also designed to address the district's more than a billion dollar shortfall over the next five years, in light of major retractions in state funding.[2]

The zombie PSU protesters hoped to drive home the message that the closures risked "creating more 'brainless' students being shuffled through a system that isn't working with them or for them." They drew attention to a report by the Philadelphia Coalition Advocating for Public Schools, which outlined an alternative agenda to the district's proposal: ending state cuts to education; putting a moratorium on closures; halting charter expansion; providing equitable funding through measures such as closing corporate tax loopholes and taxing natural gas production; investing in community schools; a culturally relevant and engaging curriculum; and performance- and portfolio-based assessments. The coalition also called for an end to the School Reform Commission—which had been established during the state takeover of the district in 2001 and had privatized more than forty schools—and a return to a city-run school board. It also offered polling that indicated the public rejected—about seven to one—charter expansion, school closures, budget cuts to district-run schools, high-stakes testing, and hiring uncertified teachers.[3]

"If they destroy our education, they can destroy us too," said Raquanda Rivers, one of the zombies. "They should spend less money on the metal detectors, cops, and cameras and pay more on computers, textbooks, and supplies."[4]

* * *

"OUR ANALYSIS OF current utilization levels . . . showed that to increase utilization from the current level of approximately 72 percent to 85–95 percent, the District would need to close anywhere from 29 to 57 schools depending on key assumptions," the Boston Consulting Group concluded in its blockbuster 2012 report on Philadelphia's public schools. The SRC had awarded the firm a $4.4 million contract to evaluate the district's finances and educational strategy and assemble a restructuring plan, which was funded by the William Penn Foundation, the pro-charter Philadelphia School Partnership, and other groups and unnamed donors. The firm's business school jargon obscured the magnitude of the earthquake it wanted to foist on hundreds of thousands of students, educators, and their families. Recommendations such as mass school closures, contracting with charter operators, school choice, gutting the district's central office, and laying off more than half the staff came straight from the market-based school reform playbook. It prescribed nothing less than a right-wing revolution for public schooling.[5]

The Philadelphia chapter of the National Association for the Advancement of Colored People, Black churches, public education groups, and labor unions denounced BCG's scheme. Reporting revealed a close sphere of influence that included governor-appointed SRC chairman Pedro Ramos, William Penn Foundation president Jeremy Nowak, and the school district's chief recovery officer Thomas Knudsen, who was tasked with managing its finances. They were believed to have been intimately involved in bringing BCG on board and peddling its manifesto and corporate version of school reform, to the point of enlisting public relations firms. They had also reportedly exerted influence over the choice of Hite as superintendent, a graduate of the Broad Superintendents Academy, a one-stop grooming shop bankrolled by billionaire philanthropist Eli Broad for future leaders of urban school districts.[6]

* * *

WHEN PRINCIPAL DARLENE Lomax was notified that her school, Fairhill Elementary, made the district's final cut of closures, her eyes filled with tears.[7] The news came in an e-mail from Hite during a morning school leadership meeting. She read the email to the staff, and they collectively cried. Still, they managed to put on a smile to greet the students. "It was the toughest day of my school life," said Lomax. The school had just completed renovations, installing a new heating system, outside lights, and an accessibility ramp. Over the summer break, she had painted every door on the three floors herself. The K–8 school was struggling academically, with more than three-quarters of students scoring below proficient on the math and English state tests.[8] It was also functioning well under capacity, but this meant their class sizes were not far off from white suburban classrooms—a reprieve compared with North Philadelphia's overcrowded classrooms.

Established in 1887 during the industrial zenith to educate the off-spring of the immigrant workers from Germany, England, Ireland, Italy, Poland, and Ukraine, the Fairhill School was in a very poor neighborhood next to Kensington. The area was once the site of the Norris family's Fair Hill estate in the eighteenth century and well before that, inhabited by the Lenape Native American tribe. The Fairhill Mansion, which had stood where Seventh and York Streets are located, was torched by the British during the Revolutionary War and later rebuilt.[9]

Lomax had come of age in North Philadelphia. She remembered sitting in her parents' bedroom and watching the white families on her block hauling their belongings into trucks and moving out. White flight meant no more playdates with her friends. "That was my first hint of racial disharmony," she said. Up until eighth grade, she lived with both her parents, who were African American. After they divorced, her mother met an Italian man more than a decade younger. He drove a school bus, and she was his monitor. The two married, and he moved in with Lomax and her five siblings. They were able to give the children a working-class upbringing in which dinner was always on the table, but they lived paycheck to paycheck.

By the time she arrived at Germantown High School in the 1970s, which was also on the closures list in 2013, white flight and deindustrialization had transformed the student body into nearly 100 percent African American, with a few white and Asian students. However, the teaching staff was nearly all white. After graduating from Germantown, Lomax enrolled in Rosemont College, a women's Catholic liberal arts college in the suburbs, where she had her first direct brush with racism. While waiting in the lunch line, Lomax heard a student say, "I didn't know they let niggers in here." Lomax turned her head and realized that she was the target of the student's hate. She dashed to her room and called her mother in disbelief. This was the 1980s. She thought such explicit racism had died out twenty years earlier.

Over the next few decades, she took various teaching and principal jobs in public and Catholic schools. In 2010, she assumed the job of principal at Fairhill for a month when the incumbent went on emergency leave. The next year she mentored the new principal. In this position, she identified some thirty sixth-to-eighth-grade students who were regularly disruptive and needed intensive social and emotional support. She put them in a separate classroom and became their primary teacher. Behavioral health specialists from a partner agency were also brought in.

The days began with morning circle to check in on the students: Did you do your homework? How are you feeling right now? What are you going to do differently today? With a marker, they scribbled their goals for the day on their hands: "I'm going to be kinder." "I'm going to compliment my friends more." "I'm going to demonstrate courage." Lomax also set up student government to give them a sense of ownership. "When children are listened to and respected and intimately involved in the decisions that impact their school life," she explained, "they tend to work harder and want to come to school." In general, she added that the students desired "clear, consistent" rules and punishments. She found that the school climate broke down when students felt severed from adults and the larger community.

School maintenance workers noticed that the building was much cleaner because the children weren't littering and vandalizing property. The traditional way to deal with misbehaving students was to suspend them, but Lomax saw that it was futile and yet another punitive measure imposed on children who had endured great trauma. Many of these students were survivors of sexual assault, lived with parents who were abusing drugs and alcohol, or had been placed in foster care. Savage rounds of budget cuts had undermined the resources that could address those challenges. There was only one counselor for the entire student body and two part-time nurses who came in for a few hours on four days of the week. When they weren't on-site, the responsibility of handing out medicine, which included the agony of chasing down students who did not want to take it, often fell to Lomax.

* * *

DARLENE LOMAX AND her staff knew they had to at least try to salvage the school. Over a few wintry weekends, staff members and students knocked on hundreds of doors in the neighborhood asking people to sign a petition to keep Fairhill open. They were bowled over by the sto-ries of people who spoke about how much the school had meant to the multiple generations that passed through its doors. The petition, which amassed more than six hundred signatures, was presented at a School Reform Commission meeting.

District officials also held a parent meeting in the school cafeteria to explain the next steps. Dismayed by the pending closure, the par-ents interrogated them with questions about why they were robbing the children of their nurturing community. The parents were told that their children would be sent to better schools—nearby Julia de Burgos or Potter-Thomas. Lomax overheard one official quip, "This school has outlived its usefulness." She was aghast, and her regional superinten-dent noticed her anger. "Listen, Lomax," he told her. "You have a bright future with the district. This is a done deal. Don't make waves." She interpreted his comments to mean that if she went up against the dis-trict, her job would be on the line.

In response to the outcry, the district revised its original proposal, cutting the number of schools facing closure from thirty-seven to twenty-nine. Hite clarified the rationale behind the change: "We wanted kids at higher performing or the same level—we don't want to move kids in[to] schools with a higher incident of violence."[10] It was a line lifted straight from the Broad Foundation's "School Closure Guide: Closing Schools as a Means for Addressing Budgetary Challenges": "On the list for closure are Schools A, B, and C. The students from these schools will be moving to nearby schools with equal or better academic perfor-mance." The guide suggested selling the plan by emphasizing that the closings would help boost student achievement in the future.[11]

However, an analysis by the Research for Action group found that a majority of the schools on the closure list reported similar reading and math scores on standardized tests as the schools slated to take in the displaced students.[12] While Potter-Thomas posted much higher test scores for reading and mathematics than Fairhill, which was still on the closures list, Julia de Burgos's performance was only marginally better.[13] Lomax argued that she was expected to work miracles with minuscule resources, akin to being "almost set up to fail." She contrasted suburban and urban schooling: "How can you think with the disparity that you're going to have the same outcomes? When you have all the resources from a librarian to a counselor and I have none of those things; when I'm giving out medicines to twenty-five kids every morning and you have a nurse; when my kids are ducking bullets and being shot at and yours are skipping onto the school bus and going to afterschool programs?"

* * *

"PUBLIC EDUCATION HAS been the salvation of this country, and it is at risk in Philadelphia because of your governor and because of this SRC," thundered American Federation of Teachers president Randi Weingarten, towering above a raucous sea of demonstrators outside the district headquarters. "They are saying that public schools that kids go to will be closed, and the charters will stay open." Hours ahead of the School Reform Commission's scheduled vote on the school closings in March, she fired up the crowd, chanting, "Fix our schools, don't close them!" They brandished signs that read "Fund Schools Not Prisons," "Save Our School," and "Don't Punish Our Children For Your Mistakes."[14]

For months, students, educators, parents, and community members had deployed every organizing weapon, staging protests, marches, and sit-ins, launching letter-writing campaigns, and holding up traffic—anything to foil the closures. The city council had voted 14 to 2 for a nonbinding resolution approving a one-year moratorium on the closures, but Mayor Michael Nutter had sided with the district.[15] The final decision rested with the School Reform Commission.

Nineteen people, including Weingarten and youth organizers, were arrested for obstructing the entrance to the auditorium. The meeting proceeded with dozens of speakers, one after another, urging a one-year moratorium on the closures. One outlier, Mark Gleason, executive director of the Philadelphia School Partnership, testified in favor of the plan. But the pleas of the opposition went unheard. The SRC voted to drop the guillotine on Fairhill Elementary School, Germantown High School, and twenty-one other schools, a tenth of the city's public schools—four fewer than the district recommended—and relocate or combine five more. It was one of the largest school closings in U.S. history.[16] Lomax didn't attend the final vote as she figured, based on what the regional superintendent had told her, that the closing was a foregone conclusion.

Next month, after the district removed Dimner Beeber Middle School from the closure list, the SRC considered the final candidate—M. H. Stanton Elementary School in North Philadelphia—and voted to shutter it, bringing the total to an unprecedented twenty-four closures. But this was only the first bout.[17]

* * *

GIANCARLOS KNEW HE wanted to be an activist the moment he climbed up on the rear of a burgundy pickup truck and started chanting, "Na-na-na-na, na-na-na-na, hey, hey, hey, stop closing schools!" It was May 17, and thousands of students from more than two dozen high schools had left their classrooms and walked out in protest of the closings and impending budget cuts.[18] Wiry and wearing a blue T-shirt with the slo-gan "Our city. Our schools. Our vision," Giancarlos was an organizer with Youth United for Change and an eighth grader at Russell H. Con-well Middle Magnet School.

As he protested at the district headquarters, it struck him how differ-ent his life was just a year ago. His mother, Marta, had told Giancarlos and his sister that she couldn't afford to take care of them. Marta and her boyfriend, Nelson, had been drinking in the kitchen. Giancar-los and his sister were starving, and the fridge was bare except for some beer bottles. Nelson was a truck driver and the father of one of Giancarlos's friends. Giancarlos asked him for some money to get something to eat.

"I don't have any money," Nelson replied.

Giancarlos grabbed his bottle of liquor. "You have money for Black Label!" He noticed a wad of cash bulging in Nelson's pocket. He pulled it out and slapped it on the counter.

Nelson tried to grab him, but Giancarlos dashed out of the door without cash or his shoes. He decided to head to his great-aunt Miran-da's house, which was ten minutes away. He knew she would let him spend the night. As he was running there, he heard police sirens and thought his mother had called the police and they were looking for him.

Marta showed up at Miranda's house the next morning and said she was going to call the cops because Giancarlos had run away. Terrified, he went on the run again, this time to his cousin Eric's. Eric suggested he get cash by selling drugs. He was uneasy, scared by the stories of kids getting locked up, but he gave in. Eric introduced him to his girlfriend's family, and Giancarlos moved into their house in Kensington.

He joined two old hands in their syndicate. They had an arrangement with the owner of the nearby corner store, who'd look out for them in exchange for cash. On the first day, Giancarlos slipped on his Conwell uniform—royal blue polo, khakis, and a backpack—thinking it would be a good cover. *Maybe this kid is running late to school or on his way home.* He sold crack cocaine, heroin (sometimes laced with fentanyl), marijuana, and xylazine, an animal tranquilizer known as "tranq dope" and "sleep cut," raking in $350 a day.[19] He bought food and Nike sweatpants and paid his cell phone bill.

He thought this break away from his mother would ease the financial burden on her.

After he spent two weeks standing on the corner, two police officers pulled up to him. "You work here?" one of the cops asked.

"My parents own the store," Giancarlos answered.

"We heard about people coming to buy narcotics off a little kid with a book bag."

They opened his Batman backpack and fished out the drugs. "You know how much you can get for this?" the officer said. "Go wherever you came from and tell the person to get it from this trash can." Giancarlos texted his caseworker that the cops had swung by, and he left the remaining stash in the trash. His days of selling were over.

Giancarlos talked to his mother for the first time in weeks. She was very worried about where he'd been staying. He didn't tell her about dealing drugs but said he wanted to get off the streets and live with his great-aunt permanently. Marta agreed, knowing he would be safe and go to school.

At the end of the school year, his godmother, Andi Perez, the executive director of YUC, suggested that he might like working with the organization. Giancarlos joined in a YUC leadership training, where he talked about how he disliked school—the boring classes, the lunches that tasted of cardboard, and the strict discipline. He was bothered by Conwell's policy of charging students $1 if they wore jeans and suspending them if they failed to wear the correct uniform. The training helped him understand that his gripes weren't irrational.

Fred Ginyard, who joined YUC as a high school student and later became a staff member, explained that the training and education give students the language to make the connection. "You look at your textbooks, and you have a textbook from 1904. You know there's a problem. If you walk through your neighborhood, you know there's a problem. You may not be able to necessarily name it: the racism, the history, and its relation to today. YUC gave us the history and political consciousness and critical thinking to connect these dots that we knew were there but didn't know how they connected to one another."

For Giancarlos, YUC became his sanctuary after school, where he was mentored, fed, and taught about the history of youth-led struggles for social justice, including the historic 1967 student walkout. His mother wasn't a fan of his new activism. "One day, you can get locked up for that," she warned. "It's not worth going to jail." But he knew that the organizing efforts could help transform the conditions of his community.

Outside city hall, Giancarlos and other student protesters hoisted signs. One of them said, "Gov. Corbett: You RUN our schools, you should FUND our schools"; another read, "What will you do about the opportunity gap?" They shouted out creative call-and-response chants: "No ifs! No buts! We don't want no budget cuts!" "S.O.S. Save Our Schools!" and "My people—Yeah—We got a story—Yeah—We tell the whole wide world this is student territory!"

It was at least the third protest organized by students so far that month, but their efforts were to no avail. At the end of May, in a 4–1 vote, the School Reform Commission passed a "doomsday" $2.4 billion budget that stripped schools of counselors, sports coaches, librarians, secretaries, art and music teachers, and support staff, sparing only the principals and essential teachers. To help plug the deficit, some 3,783 employees, including 1,202 noontime aides, 769 support staff, 676 teachers, 307 secretaries, 283 counselors, 127 assistant principals, and others were given pink slips.

"This is not the budget anyone wants," said Hite. "I'm doing everything in my power to prevent this budget from becoming a reality." But, he added, in a nod to the austerity hawks, "To be fiscally responsible, the Philadelphia school district must live within its means." The district responded by requesting emergency relief from the city, state, and teachers union.[20] Parents and community members went further, going on a fifteen-day hunger strike. To prevent more disruption, Republican Pennsylvania governor Tom Corbett announced $127 million in city and state funds for the district, more than $50 million short of the district's request, but it would reverse some of the cuts and layoffs.[21]

* * *

BY AGE FOUR, Giancarlos was singing. At Moffet Elementary School, he participated in music class, where he learned to play the Arabic *doumbek* drum. In his academic classes, however, his teachers found him rambunctious. A psychological evaluation diagnosed him with ADHD and ODD, but his mother refused to medicate him. "He was a boy," Marta said. "He had a lot of energy, and he was very intelligent. They had to find different things for him to be occupied." During elementary school and the early years of middle school, Giancarlos lived with Marta, his older brother, Frank, and younger sister, Isabelesse, in the mostly white but growing Latino neighborhood of Port Richmond. It was calm and largely free of drug activity.

Marta was born in Newark, New Jersey, to a Puerto Rican mother and a Cuban father. Her mother, Luna, married Vincente, her father, at fourteen and had their daughter a year later. Shortly after her birth, Luna and Vincente separated, and Vincente joined the army. He was first stationed in Germany as a tank mechanic, followed by an extended stretch as an air force mechanic at Homestead Air Reserve Base in Florida. He and Luna lost contact for more than three decades.

Luna soon had a son, Ernesto, but quickly broke up with his father and raised the children on her own. When Marta was eight, the family moved to Philadelphia. Many mornings, her grandmother Pilar boarded the Blueberry Bus, which transported her to the picking fields. On the weekends, she tended to her garden, where she grew eggplants, string beans, cherry tomatoes, and watermelons and gave them out to neighbors. Luna would have preferred to work rather than depend on welfare, but she had dreadful asthma and often needed oxygen therapy. She received SSI benefits for herself, and Ernesto did too, due to his disability.

In the 1980s during Marta's teenage years, she briefly attended Kensington High School before moving with the family to Barceloneta, a northern coastal city in Puerto Rico known for its pineapple plantations and pharmaceutical manufacturing, where she earned her high school diploma.[22] She returned to Kensington a few years later and had her first son, Frank, at twenty-one, followed by Giancarlos four years later, with different fathers. Giancarlos's father, Wilfredo, left before their son turned one. He rarely showed up in his life.

Growing up, Giancarlos thought his father was Rodolfo, the man Marta met after Wilfredo left. They had a daughter, Isabelesse, and raised the three kids together in Port Richmond. Giancarlos discovered that Rodolfo was not his biological father when he learned that they had different last names. At some point, Wilfredo stopped by a neighborhood block party and introduced himself to Giancarlos as his father. Giancarlos was shocked, taking the information to Marta. "Yeah, that's your father," she said, "but that's not your dad." The way Giancarlos understood it is that a father is someone who makes a kid. A dad raises and takes care of the kid. A dad is there when his kid pisses himself and needs his diaper changed. A dad is there to make sure the rent is paid. Marta explained that Wilfredo was addicted to drugs; she had caught him coming out of drug dens. Over the years, he had been arrested and incarcerated on drug charges.

Giancarlos's strong academic performance landed him on the honor roll, and Conwell recruited him for middle school. Daily schedules packed with extracurricular activities kept him busy. Conwell didn't offer football, but Giancarlos thought he should prepare for when he could play in high school. He had read that NFL players took ballet lessons to improve their balance and flexibility. He was talking to his friend Ramir, a dancer, and they decided to join the school's dance program. The first year was split into three forms of dance—ballet, jazz, and hip-hop—all capped with public performances. Ramir and Giancarlos were the only two boys, and they figured that the school started them off with ballet to test their resolve. In the beginning, the girls gawked as Giancarlos awkwardly tried the new steps and techniques, but he grew more comfortable over time. Ballet became more than simply conditioning for football.

Giancarlos finished school and raced to either ballet or baseball—in the warmer months. He played for the Port Richmond Tigers and convinced the coach to move him from right field, where he idled waiting for the ball, to the all-important second base. And when he wasn't engaged in ballet or baseball, he was found in church. A friend had introduced him to the Firm Hope Baptist Church, a few blocks from his house. He was there most days of the week for choir practice, Bible study, game nights, music production workshops, and service. Some nights his mother didn't see him until past eight o'clock. Giancarlos felt that spending time in church helped cleanse him of his worst sins: kissing girls and smoking cigarettes.

* * *

FOR DARLENE LOMAX, the final weeks of the 2012–13 school year were draining and painful. She was haunted by the feeling that she had failed her students, that she hadn't done enough to save the school or summoned the courage to confront her superiors. She wasn't alone in blaming herself. "Students said the school closed because they were 'bad,'" Tim Gibbon, an afterschool program coordinator, said—bad test scores, bad attendance, bad behavior. "Teachers felt they were responsible for failing test scores and critical behavior," principals "felt responsible for not being able to turn the school around, and parents also felt a sense of responsibility." But if you looked closely, the school had been "strategically set up to fail," he argued, deprived of "the infrastructure, funding, and energy to make the school thrive and meet students' complex needs."

On the last day, the younger children gathered around Lomax. She gave them a pep talk. "Make sure you know where you're at and what you're doing and who you're hanging with," she said, embracing some of the students. "And when you go to your new school—how many of you are going to de Burgos?" Most raised their hands. "When you go to your new school," she said, "the second thing I'm going to do on the opening day of school is call and see how you guys are doing because I'm going to be at my new school too . . . I want you to make sure that you are showing that you are Fairhill's finest."[23]

It was a day of tears, hugs, and goodbyes. The staff packed up the classrooms and traded memories. Former students stopped by to say farewell. Shortly after three o'clock, Lomax, resigned to the inevitable, made a final announcement: "I'd like to say a final goodbye to some of the best young people in the city of Philadelphia. Have a safe summer and take care of yourselves." On June 21, 2013, Fairhill Elementary School closed its doors, capping a 126-year legacy of serving the children of the working class.[24]

12
...

Protect Your Son

Ryan and Bianca talked about moving into an apartment together after the birth of their son, whom they planned to name Marc. Bianca had dropped out of high school, but she wanted to go back and finish at some point. Same with Ryan. There were a lot of lofty aspirations without much discussion of expenses and logistics or the fact that their relationship was on the ropes.

The truth was that Ryan didn't see much of a future with Bianca. He suspected that she was cheating on him (she denied this), so the baby might not be his. Ryan was planning to break up with her after the birth.

A week before her estimated due date, Bianca returned to her mother's house. Ryan did not accompany her; he was not welcome there. One afternoon in mid-February, Bianca started feeling contractions, so her mother, Hermosa, dropped her at Temple University Hospital. Ryan raced over there and the two watched television in a room they had to themselves, while Bianca, who had gone into labor, sucked on ice chips.

At around midnight, Hermosa and Bianca's father, Oscar, arrived. Only two visitors were allowed in the room with Bianca. To avoid triggering a quarrel, Ryan told Bianca that he would leave and return in an hour. He paced in the waiting area, upset that her parents decided to show up this late, and risk him missing the birth of his son. A nurse told him that once Bianca was ready for delivery, no other visitors would be allowed to be with her.

When Ryan came back to the room, Hermosa said they weren't going to leave. Bianca was only five centimeters dilated, so there was still some time before the birth. Reluctantly, he left again for another hour of pacing. He located a nurse and asked if she could check whether one of Bianca's parents was planning to leave so he could go back in.

"Hey, they said they're not leaving," the nurse reported. "They're going to stay the whole time."

"Oh, really?" Ryan seethed. Returning to the room, he spoke directly to Bianca. "If your parents don't leave there's going to be a problem." Bianca didn't respond. As Oscar scowled, Hermosa stood up and smacked Ryan with such force that he blacked out for a few moments. When his eyes opened, he was standing in the hallway with two nurses in front of him.

"Sir, sir, sir," a nurse reassured him. "We saw everything. We're calling security and Temple police right now. Please come with us."

"I'm about to fuck this nigga up," Ryan said.

"Sir, please no. Come with us. You're not going to be able to see your son being born if you assault this man."

Ryan followed them into the waiting area and was met by hospital security guards and Temple police officers. "This man was assaulted by the woman in the room," the nurse told them.

Ryan called Avry to report that Bianca's mother had hit him and her father was making crazy faces but hadn't tried anything yet. Avry told him to wait there. He was on his way.

A few minutes later, the officers ushered Bianca's parents past Ryan. Oscar, who was short, with a black ponytail, lunged at Ryan, so close their faces almost touched. "I'm going to beat you the fuck up," he growled in Spanish. "You better be scared."

Ryan laughed. "Make sure you ask your wife or your girlfriend, whatever she is to you, about me. You make sure you ask her about me. She knows what's going to happen. I'm going to beat you the fuck up, and I'm going to get someone to beat her the fuck up." Hermosa looked away.

Oscar was amped up now and said he was going to kill Ryan, who grinned and laughed again. "You do what you feel like you want to do. But I guarantee you're going to die before I die, pussy." The police let them squabble for a few moments before pulling Oscar away.

As Bianca's parents were being escorted out of the building, Avry called Ryan to let him know that he'd arrived. Ryan sprinted down to the entrance. Three cars were blocking the exit to the parking garage. Bundled into a dark hoodie, Avry was in the passenger seat of the first car, next to his friend Amir, who had a gun resting in his lap. Ryan hopped in the back seat. "Did you see anybody walk out?"

Avry said no. "So what happened?" Amir asked. This was the first time they had met. Ryan recounted the exchange.

"Oh yeah? We're going to wait right here and see if this mothafucka's gonna kill you like he said he was," said Amir.

As billows of milky-white smoke puffed from their idling engines, the three waited for their target to appear. But Oscar and Hermosa never did. Ryan figured that they must have parked on the street and left through another exit.

He thanked Avry, Amir, and their entourage in the two cars behind theirs. When Ryan returned to Bianca, she was crying. He never wanted it to go down that way, he said. They grew even more stressed when the doctor came to say that Bianca needed an emergency C-section.

Bianca was rolled into the operating room. Ryan washed his hands and threw on some sky-blue scrubs, a face mask, and a cap. He sat next to Bianca, whose legs were covered by a sheet, and held her hand. Shortly after six in the morning, he heard Marc cry before he saw him.

Ryan cradled the baby, studying his face, wondering if he was the father.

* * *

RYAN WAS GROGGY as he went to the vending machine to buy an orange juice and a muffin. On his return to the maternity ward, he passed two security guards. "That's the papi bull that had the parking lot filled up with all his homies last night ready to go looking for the old head," he heard one of them say.

Ryan stopped. "If I would have saw that man, he was going to get the fucking lights stopped out of him."

"You didn't find him?"

"I think he parked on the street."

Bianca's parents were barred from entering the hospital. Bianca spoke to her mother on the phone and said she and the baby were going to live with Ryan. As they were about to be discharged, a social worker came to the room explaining that someone had filed a report with the Department of Human Services alleging that the baby was going to an unsafe house without electricity or running water. They couldn't discharge him until DHS had investigated. Ryan figured this was Hermosa's work. He was outraged. Hermosa was absent until the very end of the pregnancy, and now she wanted to call the shots, Ryan thought.

By the time of the DHS visit to Rayni's house, the family had cleaned every inch of the place. They had a healthy supply of clothes, diapers, wipes, bottles, shampoo, teddy bears, and toys gifted at the baby shower. Rayni's brother had given them a bassinet. Ryan had covered the holes in his bedroom wall with posters.

The DHS employee peered inside the fridge, turned on the cold and hot faucets, and toured Ryan's room, where the baby would stay. The house didn't have gas, but there was a space heater in each room. At the end of the inspection, the employee was indignant at having been called out by a false report. This was a suitable home for a baby, he concluded. The next day, Ryan and Bianca took Marc home.

*   *   *

OVER THE NEXT few weeks, Bianca picked up on signs that Ryan was no longer committed to their relationship. They bickered over what she regarded as his increasingly domineering attitude; her family wanted to meet the baby and he refused to let them visit. The breaking point came when Marc caught the flu and had to be admitted into St. Christopher's Hospital for Children. Despite Ryan advising her to keep him indoors, Bianca had taken him for walks in the dead of winter. It was beyond time for them to break up, and one day, Bianca called her father to pick her up and snuck out of the house with Marc.

Ryan bounced back quickly with a new girlfriend, Maria, a willowy Puerto Rican woman who had a son. They met when she had pulled up to the McDonald's drive-through window and said she thought he was cute. She supported him through the emotional turbulence of being a new father. She helped him make bottles and change diapers and watched Marc so Ryan could sleep on his nights off from work.

One evening, Bianca dropped Marc off at Ryan's house for the night. She told him she was staying with her father temporarily. Ryan didn't say anything, but he was annoyed. Bianca had once told him that she sometimes felt unsafe around her father. Ryan ran through the worst-case scenarios: What if Oscar hurt his son?

Bianca returned in the morning to pick up the baby. "Listen," Ryan told her, "you're not going to take him with you." Bianca stood her ground and refused to leave without Marc. The confrontation developed into a brief physical altercation that involved Rayni and Avry as well. Bianca ran outside, where the police happened to be responding to a nearby situation. An officer explained that she had no authority to act without a custody order.

Hermosa filed an emergency petition on behalf of her daughter for custody of Marc, noting that Ryan had refused to return him and that Bianca was breastfeeding. The petition was granted, giving Hermosa sole physical and legal custody until an upcoming court date. Ryan was jolted from his nap next to the baby by the sound of pounding on the front door. Police officers had descended on the house. When he answered the door, he realized one of the cops was James King, who had arrested him in seventh grade at Grover Washington. They had since made amends and saw each other occasionally since the family lived on a high-crime block.

"This is like family right here," Officer King told the other cops, motioning to them to relax. "I gotta take the baby, but take your time," he said to Ryan, who was surprised that Hermosa had actually gone to court. Rayni had advised him to file his own custody petition, but he hadn't had time or legal counsel.

Ryan handed Marc over to Bianca, who had been waiting by the curb.

* * *

Custody Master James Welkie opened the hearing in a small room in Family Court. He sat at an L-shaped desk in front of Ryan, Bianca, and Hermosa; the couple sat at separate tables a few inches apart. Rayni couldn't make it because she had radiation therapy. Instead, Avry came to offer emotional support and waited outside. Ryan was nervous. He had little knowledge of custody proceedings and hadn't hired a lawyer. But even had he been advised to do so, he didn't have the funds or any idea of how to get one.

Master Welkie explained that the primary dilemma lay with the fact that Ryan was still a minor. But he was less than a month shy of turning eighteen.

"Can I continue this or reschedule this back before me any time after May 1?" Welkie asked.

"Would that mean that they still have temporary custody, and I can't see my son?" Ryan said.

Hermosa jumped in. "I'm sorry, but I never said that he can't see his son because he's his father . . . I just wanna be the grandmother, and I just want . . . the best for my grandson. I never said that he can't see him, but I don't want the baby to stay with him because it's gonna happen— you know, same thing gonna happen. He gonna keep the baby and not gonna return the baby. That's my only fear."

"The order that you have now . . . protects you in that," noted Welkie. He said he would feel more comfortable preparing a formal order once Ryan had turned eighteen and suggested that until then they reach an agreement about the specific days of the week when Ryan would have the baby.

"'Cause I feel as though like I'm scared because that's my son," said Ryan. "I don't want my son taken away from me. I'm scared that if they leave her with temporary custody like if me and her daughter get into a fight or an argument again, she just feels like not letting me see my son, I won't be able to see my son."

"That don't got nothing to do with me," said Hermosa.

"I just want to be with my son," said Ryan. "I only seen him twice since he left."

"I'm never gonna keep you away . . . Because I mean that's not what

I want for my grandson. You know that, Ryan, since day one," said Hermosa.

The two sides came to a temporary agreement. Ryan would have the baby at 10 a.m. every Friday until 6 p.m. on Saturday, with transfers to take place at the 24th/25th Police District. It was as good an outcome as he could have hoped. Welkie encouraged them to hash out matters together before the next month's hearing.

* * *

How many seventeen-year-old boys would have fought for child custody as Ryan did? He was motivated by the fact that he wanted to be a better father than his own father had been. He had always maintained to Bianca that he wanted shared custody split down the middle, no more and no less. From their conversations, he thought Bianca was on the same page.

When they returned to court, the custody transfers had been proceeding smoothly. Now Master Welkie proposed that Ryan, who was still out of school, should have custody of his son on the days he was off from work at McDonald's.

"So that means he's gonna be sleeping over? I don't want him to sleep over," Bianca said.

"Why not?" asked Welkie.

"'Cause I don't want him to."

"Gotta gimme a reason other than you don't want to," said Welkie.

"'Cause she's spiteful," Ryan cut in.

"No, because I don't trust you," said Bianca.

"This is 'cause DHS was involved when my son was first born," Ryan explained, "because the mother didn't want the daughter living with me, and DHS did conclude an investigation, and they finished the investigation. And I live with my mom in the same household that this investigation took place. And this document states that my household and me is suitable for my son to stay in overnight and live in."

Welkie read aloud the DHS letter addressed to Ryan: "This letter is to advise you that my assessment has not found substantial evidence that your family is in need of general protective services."

"And if this is about who my son shouldn't be around," Ryan was now agitated, "my son definitely should not be around her father." He had been told by Bianca that her father abused her and a family member.

"Does your father live with you?" Welkie asked Bianca. She said no.

"But he sees my son," Ryan said. "He stays around my son. She also told me that that wasn't the first time—"

"He never stay around his son," Bianca interrupted.

Welkie brought the discussion back to custody. After a few minutes, the two factions agreed that Ryan would text Hermosa the days he was not working, and he would have his son two or three days weekly. These terms would stay in place until their next court date in August.

The hearing concluded with some fireworks as Hermosa leveled accusations at Ryan. "You kept the baby away from me for one month for no reason," she said, referring to the month after the birth. "That's why she don't wanna bring the baby to the house, because you told her 'I'm gonna take you to court if you bring the baby to her.'"

"But, sir, I was working," Ryan insisted to Welkie. "Sir, I was working. I wasn't home to stop her saying she couldn't go nowhere."

* * *

RYAN WAS RIDING his bicycle around the neighborhood as Avry was cruising on a scooter. They passed Bianca's brother Fernando and a crew of his friends idling on a corner. Fernando, a gangly teenager, yelled out, "Hey, that's Ryan!" A little later, Ryan and Avry foolishly decided to circle back around. This time a dozen guys were with Fernando, and they chased the brothers up the block. Avry stopped to ask what they wanted. He reported back that their beef was exclusively with Ryan, and Fernando was angling to fight: "You gotta fight the nigga. They actin' real crazy."

Ryan and Avry went to see Avry's friend Amir. When he opened the door, he seemed like a zombie. Amir was so strung out that he could barely keep his eyes open. He had a handgun shoved in the waistband of his jeans. "We gotta handle something," Avry told him. "These dudes tryin' to jump my brother. They wanna fight."

Three gun-packing men came out of the house and climbed into a two-door car along with Avry. They sped to the block. Ryan had gone home, but over the phone he agreed to fight Fernando outside the McVeigh Recreation Center. It was muggy and pitch-black. George walked over with Ryan and their neighbor Aaron, who was carrying a pistol and a rifle in his navy Jansport backpack. Two men who knew of George from the neighborhood were standing with Fernando and Oscar, his father. It seemed as if Fernando had invited his whole block. Dozens were in the street, on their motorcycles and bicycles. Ryan took off his T-shirt and tossed it to Amir, revealing his ribbed white undershirt.

Fernando and Ryan had been friends and weren't strongly invested in fighting, but Oscar, who was hostile to Ryan since their spat in the hospital, baited Fernando. "Yeah, he likes to beat your sister," Oscar called out. Then George got in Oscar's face and accused him of abusing his daughter. Oscar went silent. Fernando plunked Ryan once. Then Ryan nailed him a few times, and Fernando fell to the ground. Within minutes, the police pulled up, scattering the fighters and the spectators.

George and Aaron ran home while Ryan walked to Amir's house, hopped on a bike, and zipped over to the 24th/25th Police District. He was worried that someone might have reported the scrap to the cops. He realized that fighting might not have been a good idea. Since the last court hearing, Hermosa had filed a temporary Protection From Abuse order against him after he and Bianca had a physical altercation inside the police district during Marc's handoff. Ryan had been told to refrain from any contact with Bianca, except when it involved their son.

Dripping with sweat, Ryan approached the glass window. "Hypothetically speaking," he said to the officer, "let's say someone has a restraining order out against a person and that person fought their family member. What can happen?"

The officer said the individual would be arrested.

"Did y'all get a call about that?" Ryan asked.

No, replied the officer, who added that he would advise *that person* to lie low for a while. Ryan crashed at Amir's house for a few days, and when nothing happened, he returned home.

* * *

THE HEARING CAME to order at 10:52 a.m. in Judge Peter Rogers's courtroom in Family Court. Ryan answered questions about his job and family. When Rogers asked about his criminal record, Ryan brought up the arson incident from middle school.

"You were adjudicated," said Rogers. "In other words, you were found guilty as a juvenile."

"No, not convicted, dropped, discharged," said Ryan.

"What did you burn?"

"Something in school."

"Did you cease to be a student at that school after that?"

"Yeah."

"Nobody got hurt?"

"No."

"You know, arson is perhaps one of the most serious crimes there is."

"Yeah, I know. The judge told me that."

"Oh, yeah?"

"I ain't do it."

"So was it somebody that you were with who did it?"

"Yeah."

"Okay. Wrong crowd, right?"

"Yeah."

"You still hang with them?"

"No."

Rogers asked if other family members had a criminal record. Ryan said George had been convicted of selling drugs, which set off alarm bells. Rogers explained that because George lived under the same roof, he would be required to complete a professional evaluation to determine whether he was a risk to the child. Ryan said he would ask George.

"What are you seeking in your petition?" Rogers turned to Hermosa.

"Well, the baby to stay with me, but like, he wanted to spend time with the baby," Hermosa said. "I agree for him to spend time with the baby. He—the baby need a daddy—you know, the daddy in his life. But, like I said before—and he knows that I always have concern—the baby being at—in the house—in his house."

"And why did you have a concern?" Rogers asked.

"I just don't want no drama, no problems around the baby because that's—that's not good for him," she replied. "I don't want there to be fighting in front of the baby."

Ryan provided more details about his late father, George, Rayni, and his brothers. Then Rogers addressed the custody arrangements. "We're going to do this gradually. I'm going to tell you how this is going to work, okay? Look, trust me. I want you to have overnights, all right? So, you know how 1801"—the court—"works because you went through that yourself, right?"

"Yeah, yeah," Ryan replied.

"Now I don't know what kind of relationship that you had with your dad while over there. Did he just let you run around, or did he actually talk to you, do things with you?"

"No."

"Would you do the same thing to your son?"

"No."

"You would talk to him?"

"Yeah."

"You would develop a relationship with him?"

"Yeah."

Ryan said he and Hermosa had come to an agreement that he would pick up his son on Friday mornings and drop him off on Sunday.

"I can't do that," said Rogers.

"I understand," replied Ryan.

Rogers asked Bianca: "Did you see any violence over there?"

"No," she answered.

Rogers followed up. "Would you be afraid that your child was over there?"

"Not really because I know his dad's going to protect him," she said. The Protection From Abuse order against Ryan had meanwhile been dropped.

After more back-and-forth, Rogers felt comfortable granting Ryan partial custody the first weekend of every month plus daytime visits at Hermosa's discretion. He also ordered parenting classes for Ryan and an investigation to make sure his house was safe for Marc, but this was later dropped when Ryan brought DHS's favorable assessment from earlier in the year.

"You need to protect that child while that child's with you," Rogers told Ryan. "And what do you say to your child's mother for telling me she's not concerned about harm coming to the child, even though your stepfather has that criminal record? What do you have to say to her?"

Ryan thanked Bianca, and the hearing ended. Rogers asked to see Marc.

"This is Marc," said Bianca as she held him. "Say hi."

"Hi, Marc," said Rogers. "I'd give you some candy, but you're not allowed to have candy." He turned to Ryan, "All right. Raise your son. Protect your son. All right?"

"All right," Ryan said.

13

...

Abombao

After skipping school for several months, Emmanuel's situation at Esperanza was no longer tenable. Two Esperanza administrators came to the house to warn Ivette that if he continued failing to attend school, they would refer him to truancy court, and she could face fines and maybe even jail time.

Terrified, Ivette submitted an urgent application on Emmanuel's behalf to Commonwealth Connections Academy, a free cyber charter school she had heard about through a friend. After Emmanuel was accepted, he was sent a black Lenovo ThinkPad, the most advanced laptop he had ever used. For the first few months, he logged on regularly and completed his assignments. It was easy—he looked up answers to the questions on Google.

Then he stopped logging on and dropped out of Commonwealth as well. Ivette thought this was it: he had squandered his last opportunity to get a diploma—he would be a dropout, like her. But Emmanuel was struggling emotionally. His mood oscillated from day to day—either he was joyful and laughing, or he was deep in despair and barely able to look at himself in the mirror. His mother and Freddie did not understand his mental health crisis; they could neither empathize with him nor alleviate his pain. "Everyday I wake up and everything stays the same," he wrote in his journal. "I can't breathe my life is worthless. I want to die . . . Nobody rawrs me."

He had been able to keep the laptop, so typical days were spent in bed, binge-watching *The Vampire Diaries* and *The Secret Life of the American Teenager* on Netflix. A social media aficionado, he made vlogs about his day on YouTube, blogged on Tumblr, or chatted with online friends he had made through Facebook. One of his online friends was Gerardo, a queer Mexican American high school student in Texas. The two Skyped, played *Minecraft*, talked about boys, depression, school, and life, and bonded over their passion for music, poetry, and Lana Del Rey. They never met in person, but Emmanuel felt as though they had known each other in a past life. There was nobody else he could talk to so frankly. Omar, Angelina, and his cisgender friends couldn't understand how it felt to wrestle with their sexuality, especially since he wondered whether he might be transgender.

Gerardo encouraged him as he was figuring out how to get back into high school, but it was a different friend who provided the key. Emmanuel was chatting with his online friend Gloria, who had dropped out of Philadelphia's Central High, a college-prep magnet school, and she mentioned that she had just enrolled in El Centro de Estudiantes, a school designed for dropouts. Emmanuel was curious and peppered her with questions:

E: Can you wear beanies in class?

G: And yeah. But they don't give you an actual schedule they tell you where to go. Lol. Lol yes.

E: OMGEE OMGEE YUSSS BEANIES IN CLASSSS OH YEAH!!!!

G: The only thing you can't do is smoke in class you can do anything else. xD

E: can you chew gum in class?

G: yes

E: eat??

G: The teacher might even ask you for some food. Xd.

E: lmao can you be on your phone. can you listen to music?

G: Mhm. Not during circle tho.

E: wtf is circle?

G: Like rehab shit.

E: wtf?? lol.

G: In the morning and then at the end of the day. Its just to talk about your goals for the day and how you're feeling.

E: so you can be on your phone in class for real??? I HOPE WE ARE IN THE SAME CLASS OMGEE

E: do they have graduation? Like with robes and caps and gounds

E: do they have picture day?

E: year books?

E: they have music class?

G: Mhm. I told you this.

E: I forgot. Did you join music. Oh did they have writing class?

G: No I rather have Lisa. And you do that In advisory.

E: cooo beans I'm just happy I can wear beanies! Are the teachers homophobic?

The school sounded nothing like Esperanza, and Emmanuel was excited. It felt like a last chance: his old classmates were graduating, and he was almost past the age cutoff for returning to high school. *I'm not going to fuck up this time*, he thought. Omar's mother drove Emmanuel over to pick up an application for the coming year, but when he walked into the 140-year-old building, he saw right away that El Centro de Estudiantes was unlikely to live up to his *High School Musical* fantasy. He'd been naive to expect modern, functioning school facilities for the kids of North Philly.

* * *

EMMANUEL SPENT THE summer on his computer and getting hammered on Four Lokos with his friends Gabriella and Hannah, the three of them dragging their sleepy, drunk bodies to Graffiti Pier to watch the sunrise and stare at the majestic Ben Franklin Bridge in the distance. He was on tenterhooks waiting for news from El Centro de Estudiantes, hoping for an acceptance and a fresh start. The wait was killing him.

"Ugh I still haven't received my orientation letter for my new school," he wrote on Facebook. "I'm shitting bricks . . . and to start it off we haven't gotten mail in days. why am I fbooking this lol." Eleven days after that post, the school called: he had been accepted. The night before his orientation, Emmanuel stayed up Skyping with Gerardo to calm his nerves. "I'm only running on 8 minutes of sleep," he posted in the morning. "And I've eaten one cracker . . . God may you guide me through this day, calmly and ease at mind. Amen."

At orientation, Emmanuel noticed that the students represented the whole constellation of North Philadelphia: Black, Latino, white, poor, gay, straight, queer, transgender. He could see he wasn't the only kid struggling in the hood. When his turn came to introduce himself, he said quietly, "My name is Emmanuel. You can call me Manny. I like to sing and write." The advisors talked about the structure of the program, the daily schedule, and their expectations. Emmanuel would start in an advisory with new students and, after the first trimester, move up to one of the other eight advisories. The accelerated timeline was great news—he could graduate within two years. But he was nervous about maintaining near-perfect attendance and finding an internship. What if he couldn't do it?

A Latina advisor named Adriana told him that she loved his style, which gave a huge boost to Emmanuel's morale. Her praise was important because he tried so hard to dress well despite the limitations of his budget and wardrobe. For one thing, the family's house always smelled awful, an odor that Emmanuel and Ivette described in Puerto Rican slang as *abombao*. Freddie let his dogs defecate indoors and didn't bother to pick up their shit, so Emmanuel stored his clothes in a container, trying to seal them away from the stink. He kept them as clean as he could. The closest laundromat was only a five-minute walk away, but he couldn't always scrape up the cash, so sometimes Ivette washed his clothes by hand and dried them in a room with the window open. But there weren't a lot of options. He was worried that his classmates would notice he kept wearing the same outfits, so he switched up the combinations to keep things fresh. He wrote on Facebook that Adriana's comment had made his day, and he was glad when he was placed in her advisory.

Emmanuel was struck by the school's countercultural vibe: students calling teachers by their first names, going to the bathroom without asking for permission, chewing gum and wearing hats, and the kindness of his advisors, especially Adriana, a spunky Puerto Rican woman who had been an educator for more than a decade. It was a rejection of everything Esperanza stood for. There were no uniforms, and the dress code was radically simple: don't wear anything that would offend your grandmother. Clothing couldn't have references to drugs or guns and had to cover the "four B's": breasts, back, buttocks, and belly. As JuDonn put it, "You go to the corner store in a hoodie, and you won't be served. Why would we treat you the same way your neighborhood treats you? Why would we replicate that?"

Emmanuel's first writing project was an essay: "Who Am I?" "I guess I don't truly know who I am," he wrote. "It's a journey I'm still discovering. Everyday is a new day and new possibilities, I'm slowly creating who I want to be." He put together a personal PowerPoint presentation tracing his life from his unexpected birth to childhood to his mental health troubles.

One of the slides featured a poem he wrote about his life and the violence in his neighborhood of North Philadelphia:

Ode to sleepless nights and overheard fights
The pavements crippled and cracked,
People are even drugged to be exact
The lights come on and the kids come in
The dread parents have of having their phone ring and door ding,
Opening the door as an officer hands them their child's things
Where I am from, the sirens call the drug lords to run

Pointing guns, shooting towards the sky, they say it's just fun,
Yet another innocent kid dies
I am different from the people who reside here
I walk for hours just to get by here
I shed tears though there's no time to
I'm a minority not a majority
I'm a Hispanic male, 5'7, my hair puffy and curly
The richest people would call me to be dirty
I am a beautiful soul,
I have a twinkle in my eye,
I will always be afraid to die,
I am a boy with dreams,
But for now I am only seventeen

In Adriana's class, Emmanuel read *Fist Stick Knife Gun: A Personal History of Violence*, a memoir by Geoffrey Canada, an educator who led the Harlem Children's Zone in New York, about growing up in poverty and violence in the South Bronx. Many passages resonated with his own childhood. The writing assignment was to respond to quotes pulled from the book:

Chapter Seventeen: Quote: "The problem with a used gun was that you didn't know if it had 'bodies' attached to it."

Reflection: This quote is beyond relatable. I grew up in North Philadelphia and around this area there are a lot of drugs, violence due to drugs, and I know that drug lords buy used guns. The whole deal with a used gun is that you never know if somebody killed another human with the gun you hold. When the author wrote, "the problem with a used gun was that you didn't know if it had any bodies attached to it," he was referring to the amount of violence a gun can cause, death will always be a consequence. If you have a used gun and it has been shot to murder another person, if you happen to be caught with that gun, it is more jail time for you. In these violence filled areas, people with guns feel as though they have more power than any other human being. Power over time can bring a person to their knees.

Chapter Nineteen: Quote: "This was a block that people who could afford to had long since fled, a block you could find in any city in America."

Reflection: This quote makes me think about bad blocks in general. My whole life I have lived in "unsafe" neighborhoods due to violence. I remember one night, I was riding my bicycle around with some of my friends, when suddenly we heard loud noises. I turned around to the sight of a man running towards my friends and I in fear. It didn't take long for me to realize that those loud noises were in fact gun shots. The man was running away from someone trying to shoot him. Thank god my friends and I got out alive, the bullets skimmed our bicycles. We could hear the sound of sirens in our ears. A bullet burned my ankle, but luckily it did not penetrate my foot. I spent my days wishing my family had a way out; sadly there was no way we could afford to move. I envied the people who left the bad blocks. I do not want to be a part of the bad blocks anymore.

Chapter Twenty-five: Quote: "The city is cutting youth services again."

Reflection: Are we not important? Are we just a statistic? This is what it feels like to have our schools lose teachers, to lose classes and much more. The people higher up think that we the youth are not entitled to our opinion, after all "let the grown ups talk" is all we hear. We are important. We do deserve a brighter future. Cutting our programs, letting our teachers go, is not helping our economy. Cutting the fundamentals of learning will not further America, it will destroy it with violence and war.

* * *

EL CENTRO DE Estudiantes had a concentration of LGBTQ students who, like Emmanuel, were pushed out of their high schools because of bullying, stringent discipline, an intolerant school climate, a lack of culturally responsive counseling, and homophobia, transphobia, and biphobia and other forms of discrimination. His experience occurs nationwide; according to a study examining the experiences of thousands of LGBTQ students, for many of them, "schools are hostile environments that effectively function to deprive students of the ability to learn, whether by pushing them out, increasing their likelihood of dropping out, or funneling them into the school-to-prison pipeline."[1]

Emmanuel did his internship down the block from the school, at the headquarters of Galaei, an organization founded in 1989 during the HIV and AIDS epidemic to serve queer and Latino people. It ran youth programs and grassroots campaigns and offered counseling for trans individuals and HIV prevention services, including free HIV and STI testing, condoms, and counseling.

Emmanuel worked on Galaei's Positivo campaign, which aimed at erasing the stigma of HIV and promoting positive sexuality and body image in communities of color. One of the target audiences was Latino men who have sex with men. The campaign's website featured six portraits of men with captions such as "I am positive that my status changes lives" and "I am positive that knowing my status makes me beautiful."

Galaei's youth programs manager, Francisco Cortes, worked with Emmanuel to start a Gay Straight Alliance club and offer workshops at the school on gender identity, sexual orientation, and sexual health. The club was later renamed as the more appealing "House of Queers and Allies." Emmanuel learned about the Gender Unicorn graphic, which describes gender identity, gender expression, sex assignment, and physical and emotional attraction. Being surrounded by queer people in safe spaces, Emmanuel no longer felt alone or ashamed of his femininity.

"I am proud to say that I am gender fluid or at least be open enough to have Gender fluidity," he revealed in a Facebook post. "I don't conform to any gender standards, I love boy clothes, girl clothes, makeup. If I feel like walking out the house in heels and makeup so be it. ❤ Always love yourself. This year has been a year of self discovery." For the first time, Emmanuel could unapologetically flaunt his queerness without fear. Galaei and El Centro de Estudiantes had become his refuge.

* * *

Emmanuel had just left home one evening to walk over to Omar's house when an unmarked brown car pulled up in front of him. Two tall white men got out. "Put your hands on the vehicle," they barked. They didn't bother to identify themselves. Emmanuel felt himself freeze as they frisked him, patting his penis and searching his pockets. Then they ordered him into the car. In the back seat, he ran through the possibilities. They looked like plainclothes cops. Was he being framed for a crime? Would he end up in jail? Would his family ever hear from him again? Or worse, perhaps these men intended to sexually assault him or even murder him. Emmanuel pleaded with them. "I've done nothing wrong. Why are you doing this? I was going to my friend's house."

"Shut up!" one of the men yelled.

After five minutes of driving, the car stopped, and a man came over to the window. "Is this her?" the driver asked. "No," the man said. The car traveled a few more blocks before the men kicked Emmanuel out to the curb. He cried on the way to Omar's house, convinced now that they had been undercover police officers. The ordeal cemented his distrust of the police. "I'm watching people get arrested constantly and get treated like shit," he said later. "They think they're above all. They have this complex. Just because I have this uniform and badge makes me think I'm better than you."

"THE COPS JUST THREW ME ON TOP AND IN THEIR CAR!!" he posted on Facebook. In the comments, he explained what happened. "I've never been so scared," he wrote. "I just kept thinking I was gonna get shot."

His friends wrote back quickly. "I'm glad nothing like that happened," said Gabriella.

"That's why I don't like cops," his friend Micah wrote.

* * *

Giancarlos held a sheet of notes and stood before his fellow students and the red Youth United for Change banner outside Philadelphia City Council president Darrell Clarke's office. It was September 2013, a few days before Giancarlos was about to enter the freshman class at Kensington Creative and Performing Arts High School. He wore a YUC T-shirt that matched the banner and sported a fresh buzz cut and bronze tan. Over the summer, he and YUC organizers had canvassed city blocks, collecting more than two thousand responses from residents who were surveyed for their thoughts on that year's doomsday school closings and budget cuts. Now, in his speech, he was furious at Philadelphia's school-funding model, which bilked the city's students, and he demanded that the city council tell the state to institute fair funding.

"When I started hearing about the budget cuts to sports and arts, I was enraged," he said, "because the district's plans were going to kill my dreams. I want to be a professional baseball player and a music producer. How am I going to do that if those resources are taken away from me?" It was unjust for the funding shortfall to be put on the backs of teachers, who had been willing to accept a pay freeze and a stop to contributions to their health care premiums. What if, he asked, Comcast and other large corporations started paying their fair share of taxes instead, and some of that revenue was channeled to the schools?[2]

On September 9, after the city borrowed $50 million to rehire some essential staff, Giancarlos and his peers entered schools bulging at the seams and stripped of basic resources and thousands of staff. The school closures and relocations led to nine thousand students starting at fifty-three new schools.[3]

Opened in 2010, KCAPA had an elegant new building complete with green roofs, rainwater harvesting, geothermal heating and cooling, and dance and art studios.[4] Next to the El tracks on Front Street, the school looked like the area's only beneficiary of public investment in decades, at odds with the sluggish commercial corridor nearby. But the school's modern physical plant could not make up for the general austerity inside its walls. With more than thirty students in his classes, Giancarlos found it impossible to get individual attention from the teachers. For a school of more than four hundred students, there was just one counselor, down from three a year before. Most of the assistants who had monitored the hallways and cafeteria and overseen arrival and dismissal were gone. They had been the glue in the school, rarely acknowledged, as one teacher put it. Theater, drama, and foreign-language programs were shuttered. With no librarian or checkout, the library was just a room of books. KCAPA, known for its creative offerings, was drained of its soul.

Philadelphia's school crisis reached a boiling point one month into the school year when Laporshia Massey, a sixth-grade student at Bryant Elementary, died after an asthma attack at school. There was one nurse on duty just two days a week. Only 179 nurses served more than 200,000 students in 331 public, private, and Catholic schools in the city, a drop of nearly 40 percent from two years earlier.[5] After mounting pressure from civil rights groups, Governor Tom Corbett transferred a one-time $45 million payment—forgiven federal debt—to the city's schools. He had withheld the money as a bargaining chip to compel the school district to heed to fiscal discipline, specifically to extract contract concessions from the teachers union. The injection of aid went to rehiring teachers, administrators, secretaries, and counselors and funding music and athletic programs. But it was still wholly inadequate to address the entrenched inequalities.[6]

Giancarlos joined the Kensington Tigers junior varsity football team just as it was coming off of a winless season. The team was three years old, launched by Fishtown native and KCAPA teacher Ellwood Erb. He had been captain of his high school team, playing fullback and linebacker, and he knew the beneficial effect the sport would have on a community without sufficient activities to occupy the students' time. The blueprint for the new school had included a new athletic field, but it was never built. The designated field had been flattened, with metal, glass, rocks, and other construction debris below the surface, and was covered with a layer of sod that died within weeks. When rain fell, debris reappeared. The lot was uneven, sloping at various points. Any attempt to play on it resulted in twisted ankles, cuts, scrapes, and even femur and pelvic fractures, torn ACLs, and dislocated shoulders were common. So games were forbidden on the Kensington field, and the team was always on the road.[7]

Giancarlos's own football career was short-lived. After the first practice, his face and skin felt itchy. He couldn't stop sneezing, and there was a sharp pain in his lungs. He thought his asthma and allergies were acting up, so he pushed through it. But he didn't feel better, and his doctor diagnosed him with walking pneumonia. Defying the doctor's orders not to play, he was middle linebacker in his first game. Facing the Edison Owls, he picked up a sack, and the Tigers won. Giancarlos was elated, but once Coach Erb heard about his doctor's instructions, he was off the team.

Deflated, Giancarlos put all his energy into music. He played in the school's drum line, learned how to make beats on FL Studio and Garage-Band, joined the school choir, and auditioned for All-City Choir—he was one of the few KCAPA freshmen to land a spot. "Music will forever be my religion and belief if I ever want to have anything I need," he wrote. "Music is not only my belief but it's my God, my savior and happiness."

* * *

It only made sense that Giancarlos found himself at a school that was born out of student struggle, a place where he could apply his organizing skills. KCAPA's predecessor, Kensington High, had been a chronically failing and congested dropout factory. In the early 2000s, YUC students campaigned for it to be broken up into four small schools. The small schools movement had grown out of research that found that smaller schools were associated with better student attendance, a greater sense of belonging, fewer disciplinary issues, stronger student-teacher relationships, and lower dropout rates.[8] YUC had been inspired by their tour of Urban Academy in New York City and the Metropolitan Regional Career and Technical Center in Providence, two stars of the small schools movement.[9]

After years of YUC lobbying, the district created the Kensington Multiplex: three theme-based high schools focusing on business, culinary arts, and creative and performing arts.[10] An early assessment found that daily attendance, test scores, and dropout rates had improved.[11] A fourth school, Kensington Urban Education Academy, was established in 2010.[12] However, as activist Ron Whitehorne pointed out, the vision of student-centered institutions with experiential, project-based learning, relevant curriculum, a healthy school climate, and community engagement was not realized by the district. "Instead, instability and budget austerity have been the rule," he wrote.[13]

One day, Giancarlos led a walkout to educate his classmates about the school-to-prison pipeline. With the support of YUC, he and a few friends gave a workshop outside the building to a few dozen students who answered his call. They, too, were fed up with being criminalized at school and questioned the value of metal detectors. It took as little as bringing in a cell phone or wearing a hoodie to get suspended. Repressive discipline was also an issue at their sister schools. Terrese Thomas, a student at Kensington Culinary Arts, had written, "Why do we have to get patted down like a criminal? We are just coming to school to learn."[14]

Going through metal detectors and being instructed to raise your hands and remove your shoes upon arrival to school each morning soured the rest of the day and seemed like preparation for life in a cage, Giancarlos said. "School puts so much like jail around you that makes you not want to be there anymore." His activism put Giancarlos on the radar of school administrators, some of whom saw him as a nuisance.

"There may be no other large, urban school system that matches the District in its promotion of zero tolerance and in the heavy use of out-of-school suspensions, expulsions, disciplinary transfers," a report by YUC and the Advancement Project concluded. Drawing on public records and hundreds of surveys and interviews with students, the report issued a damning verdict on the city's zero-tolerance discipline, which was first implemented by Philadelphia Schools CEO Paul Vallas. These practices not only failed to make schools safer, they argued, but produced a threatening, alienating, and draconian environment that pushed students into the criminal justice system.

Students gave numerous distressing examples of officers engaging in invasive, inappropriate searches and threatening and physically assaulting them. "When security guards searched me in school for my cell phone the usual routine is for them to pat me on my chest and rub their hand down my cleavage," one girl said. "Then they make us lift and shake our bras out. Also, they would run their hands down from our waist to our ankles. Next they turn us around and pat our back pockets. At the very end they use the wand to search us thoroughly."[15]

For years, a youth-led coalition, including the Philadelphia Student Union and YUC, had been organizing under the Campaign for

Nonviolent Schools to transform the "prison-like" environment and dismantle the school-to-prison pipeline by calling for adequate investment, student voice, classroom engagement, and an end to punitive disciplinary practices.[16] The campaign demanded swapping in restorative methods that address root causes of violence, using measures like suspensions and expulsions as a last resort, and establishing a "graduated discipline matrix" that permits teachers and principals to use discretion.[17]

One of Giancarlos's first actions with YUC was attending a School Reform Commission meeting to address calls for changing the student code of conduct. In the SRC's vote, it adopted many of the group's demands. Under the new policy, low-level infractions such as disrupting class, violating the dress code, truancy, cursing, and failure to carry a hall pass would be handled through an in-school intervention rather than an out-of-school suspension. This might include private discussions with the student, parent/guardian conferences, referrals to counseling, and if none of these options were effective, then an in-school suspension. Had the policy been in place when Ryan was in elementary and middle school, it might have made all the difference to him.

For offenses like fighting, destruction and/or theft of property (less than $1,000), and bullying, out-of-school suspensions were still allowed, but administrators had the option to use in-school interventions. More serious infractions like robbery, assault, fighting that resulted in severe injury, possession of a weapon, drugs, and alcohol, or nonconsensual sexual acts would continue to be punished with out-of-school suspension, disciplinary school transfer, and expulsion. The district later added language letting gender-nonconforming students dress in alignment with their identity, after organizers pushed for the change.[18]

The new rules were a stunning achievement for youth organizing, a crucial defeat for what Jonathan Simon called the "governing through crime" regime. Inevitably, it had been spearheaded by its prime targets: Black and Latino urban youth, who were not willing to quietly tolerate the structures that pathologized and criminalized their bodies.[19]

This Is Some Grown Man Shit

Ryan caught the bus to Front Street and Hunting Park Avenue. He tried to calm his jitters for his first day at Educational Options Program, an alternative education program run by the Philadelphia schools. This was his latest attempt to earn a high school diploma, prompted by a conversation he'd had with a coworker at PECO Energy. The first thing he looked for in an employee, the man said, is whether the person has the diploma. "If you have your GED, what that tells me, at some point in life you quit," he said. "Granted you went back and you got a GED, but you still quit."

Ryan heard about EOP from Carl, a classmate at El Centro de Estudiantes. The program was housed in his old haunt: the tan-brick CEP building. *Fuck, I'm back here*, he thought. Like old times, he walked through the metal detector, albeit no pat-down. And he could bring in his backpack. His anxiety intensified as he passed the classrooms. The vicious fights and staff restraints were lodged in his hippocampus and suddenly surfaced. Nobody had bothered to change the building's layout, which made him mad. Inside the gym were more than a hundred students. Ryan listened as someone gave an overview of the program, which was largely computer-based. It ran from 3 to 6:30 p.m. Monday to Thursday, and he would start the following week.

On the way home, Ryan stopped by the corner of Mutter and West Somerset Streets in Kensington, where his friend Nilsa was selling drugs. Ryan had been fired from his job at McDonald's after he was overheard making disparaging comments about the boss. For some reason, he had been able to collect unemployment benefits for a few months, but they had run out. Now he was desperate for cash for Marc and the rest of the family.

A short, fit Puerto Rican girl with large silver hoop earrings, light-brown bangs, and flower and text tattoos across her right arm, Nilsa was wearing a low-cut white T-shirt, navy pants, and hot-pink-and-white kicks. Like Ryan, she was a 1995 baby, born over a month after him. She walked Ryan over to the trap house, a dilapidated two-story row home. Ryan sat on a seedy couch while Nilsa waited in the kitchen for someone to bring her a replenished supply. The floors were cracked, and the walls had water stains and chipping paint. The house gave off ominous vibes, and he wanted to get the hell out of there. To his relief, they left in under ten minutes. For the rest of Nilsa's shift, Ryan surveilled the block for cops and sold a few of her packets of crack cocaine. She told him to come back the next day ready to sell full bundles.

* * *

"I'M GOING TO go do that," Ryan told Rayni as he was leaving the house in the morning.

"What?" she said.

"You know what."

"You don't have to do that."

"Ain't no money coming up in this house, and I gotta do what I gotta do."

"Listen, don't worry about the bills. Let me worry about them. I see you getting locked up."

"Oh, you don't have to come visit me." Ryan walked out with Avry, who had graduated from El Centro de Estudiantes a few months earlier and agreed to help. With some stubble on his face, Ryan was wearing the same outfit from the day before: navy V-neck, khakis, and black-and-white New Balance sneakers. His left arm was covered by a Jesus and rosary tattoo with his mother's name.

Ryan figured this would be a quick way to haul in some decent money despite the obvious risks. To Rayni, he was following in his father's footsteps. It was his responsibility to break the cycle, she told him, so his children and grandchildren wouldn't grow up to do the same misdeeds. But that wasn't the main thing on his mind this morning.

"You gotta line up," Ryan barked at the gridlock of customers around him and Avry as he wiped off beads of sweat from his forehead. The scene was like the first day of spring at Rita's, when they gave out free Italian ices.

The dozen or so customers made an orderly line in the street. Calmly and methodically, Avry handled the cash, while Nilsa sold heroin and Ryan handed out the crack, which was stored under a white Mustang parked down the block. Ryan heeded the most basic rule: avoid carrying the drugs. He thought about putting the drugs in a crumpled bag of chips and keeping it on the litter-infested sidewalk. Instead, he hid the drugs in a box, attached a magnet, and stuck it underneath a car. Supply was moving briskly. Ryan and Nilsa took turns selling their bundles to the fiends—mostly whites with a handful of African Americans and Latinos. A lot of them had left their suburban enclaves and zoomed along Interstate 95 for their fix of nirvana—the cheapest and purest heroin on the eastern seaboard.[1]

The three were slogging away in the Philly Badlands, which was considered the largest open-air heroin bazaar on the East Coast.[2] When business slowed, two of them surveilled the area for police and thieves. They hopped on a bike and rode around the block, peering into cars with suspiciously tinted windows. Once Ryan and Nilsa exhausted their supply of cellophane packets, they reported to their caseworker. One bundle of crack contained twenty-eight packets, which sold for $5 each. Ryan turned in $110 and kept $30. For heroin, there were twelve $10 packets in a bundle.

Drugs were all he knew growing up. When Ryan was fourteen, his

cousin gave him some marijuana to sell and taught him the fundamentals: how to conceal your stash from the cops and the fiends, cut and
package the drugs, and calculate the profits. Be prepared to be arrested
at any time, he was told. If the cops come running, don't surrender. It's
their job to chase you. Ryan knew that heroin and crack busts carried
much harsher penalties than marijuana. The terror of a police raid and
being put behind bars never left his mind during that shift. What Ryan
didn't know was that the Narcotics Field Unit was watching their operation. The trio were sitting ducks.

* * *

THE OFFICERS HAD set up a surveillance post within eyeshot of the dealers. Just after 4, Nilsa handed a green bundle to a twenty-six-year-old
white man. A few minutes later, two officers stopped him as he opened
the door of his Honda SUV. He had eleven green glassine packets of
heroin in his possession. His passenger, a twenty-nine-year-old white
woman, was carrying three bundles of heroin containing thirty-three
glassine packets stamped with the name BLACK LABEL. Dealers
named their heroin, so buyers knew which corner to frequent for their
next hit. There were monikers such as Superman, Applebottom Jeans,
Rock, Adidas, and Red Hot. Both of the buyers were arrested.

Ten minutes later, a white man wearing a white tank top and dirty
tan pants offered Ryan cash in exchange for drugs. Another officer trans-
mitted his details to backup cops, but they didn't track him down.
The next buyer paid Nilsa, who retrieved the drugs from under the
car. The officer watched as the buyer walked away, opened the green
packet, snorted the heroin, and sat in a nearby playground to enjoy
his high. Ryan sold to one more customer, but the backup police were
unable to locate the buyer.

When Nilsa depleted her last bundle, she hopped on her bike. One
officer alerted his colleagues, who placed her under arrest and stuck her
in the back of their vehicle. Avry had snuck away to the corner store while
Ryan was sitting on a stoop mentally counting the remaining drugs. He
still had eleven bags of crack left. Once he sold them, his shift would be
over, and he could go home and chill. But the universe had other plans.

Abruptly, a black Ford Edge rolled up smoothly on the curb. It was unmarked, but Ryan knew right away that it was undercover police. Before he could take flight, two officers leaped out. Officer Carl Stubbs, a rugged, six-foot-three Black man in his forties with a graying goatee and dreadlocks, aimed his gun at Ryan's chest and ordered him to get on the sidewalk. As his face kissed the concrete, the officers patted him down and found $90. Ryan said he had just cashed a check and was going to buy a birthday gift for his mother.

"We got a call about a person with a gun," said Stubbs as he cuffed him. It was a common police line so the target would think that's all the cops had and wouldn't consider running.

"I don't got a gun," Ryan said, smirking. He thought the misunderstanding would be resolved quickly. Two minutes later, a phalanx of police cars screeched to a halt. The doors were flung open, and officers began scouring the area for drugs.

Officer Bill Hardy pointed at Ryan. "What are you smirking about?"

"I ain't smirkin'," he replied.

"Just sit tight. You know you're going to jail." Hardy walked up the block and dropped to the ground, poking under the white Mustang. He saw a blue packet of heroin stamped "Apples" and a white Advil bottle. "I'm getting close, ain't I?" he yelled. "Don't even worry about it. I got it." He cranked the bottle open and pulled out eleven packets of crack. Ryan, sitting on the curb in cuffs, dropped his head. *Busted.* In that moment, he realized he was screwed—and he could be locked up for years.

Less than six months after turning eighteen, Ryan was achieving in record speed his family's rite of passage. He was the newest Rivera to come of age under the custodial arm of The Man. This was not the outcome of what has been called the culture of poverty, a debunked concept, but rather the machinery of social reproduction, where "the son goes and independently experiences the same failures, in the same areas, and for much the same reasons as his father," as urban ethnographer Elliot Liebow put it.[3]

As Avry was walking back to the block, he saw Ryan and Nilsa surrounded by police. He pulled on his hoodie and made a beeline for home, telling Rayni that Ryan got arrested, fulfilling her morning prophecy.

Remembering the last time he was in a police van, Ryan told Officer Stubbs about his claustrophobia and begged him to drive to the district in his SUV instead. Stubbs obliged.

Ryan began chatting with him as they sped past El Campamento, the rubbish-strewn swath of Kensington bounded by train tracks where people without homes and on drugs found shelter and community. "You ain't built for this," Stubbs told him.

"I know it sounds crazy," Ryan said. "I want to be a police officer. You think this is going to mess this up?"

"It might," said Stubbs, restraining his laughter. "You gotta change your way. You're better than this. I can see it all over your face."

"Do they rape people in jail?"

"You're not going to get raped up in holding. When they send you to the big jail, you're a pretty boy. They're definitely getting you." Stubbs was poking fun, but Ryan was visibly upset, so he changed his tune.

"You don't gotta worry about that. You're not going to be doing this anymore, right?" Stubbs said, trying to calm him down.

"You're right. This is it." Ryan had made up his mind. "I'm changing my life." He thought he might still be able to talk his way out of it, so he told Stubbs why he had ended up selling. There was no money coming into the house since nobody was working. His stepfather was locked up. His mother had been treated for breast cancer. He was buying the groceries and cooking for everyone. He didn't mention that he had recently become a father to a baby boy, but it wouldn't have helped him get off scot-free.

*　*　*

PHILADELPHIA WAS NOTORIOUS for having the highest per capita incarceration rate of the ten largest cities in the United States. Hyperincarceration accounted for the fact that more than 40 percent of the city's Black male population aged twenty-five to fifty-four, or 36,000 people, were "missing from everyday life."[4] Poor and working-class Latinos were also imprisoned at disproportionate rates. Urban sociologist

Loïc Wacquant examined the symbiotic relationship between the ghetto and criminal justice system, which he observed "entraps a redundant population of younger black men (and increasingly women) who circulate in closed circuit between its two poles in a self-perpetuating cycle of social and legal marginality with devastating personal and social consequences."[5] The same could be applied to Latino men and women.

Ryan was hoping that he would avoid being transferred to the county jail. After being processed in the 24th/25th District, he was plopped into a tiny well-lit cell with a metal sink and toilet. A Latino man sleeping on the concrete bench with a white shirt covering his head reminded Ryan of a turtle, so that's how he nicknamed him. Turtle peeped his head out of his shell to greet Ryan. He said he'd been jailed for a domestic dispute and returned to his slumber.

Over the next few hours, the cell grew more congested as drug dealers and customers were brought in. *There must have been coordinated raids*, Ryan thought. Everyone had a yellow wristband printed with their name, date of birth, and the charge. Ryan sat on the bench with Turtle and hugged his knees, trying to pass the time by napping.

A little before midnight, Ryan was brought to an empty room with a phone. He was instructed to pick up the phone and then answer a list of questions: Have you been arrested in the past? Where do you live? How old are you? Have you graduated high school? Then he was moved to another room to have his mug shot and fingerprints taken.

Back in the cell, Ryan hunched in a corner. An officer stopped by with a box of cheese sandwiches and mini bottles of water. "Don't be using them fuckin' sandwiches for no pillows," the officer called out. Some liked to stack them up and rest their heads, getting a temporary respite from jail. Ryan refused to eat anything. He was used to fighting hunger.

More time passed. Through the cell window, Ryan's gaze fell upon a stocky officer escorting a staggering drunk man. The man was mouthing off to the officer as he shoved him into a cell. "Shut the fuck up," the officer said. The man slurred the same back. Then Ryan heard the sound of shoes scraping across the floor. The officer and the man spilled out of the cell into the hallway, and Ryan watched as the man took a battering and eventually fell to the floor. Rocky Balboa pounding away at the slabs of beef in a meat freezer flashed in Ryan's mind.

A puddle of blood pooled on the floor. The inmate was wheeled out on a stretcher. An inmate in the opposite cell noticed Ryan's distress. "Young boul, this is some grown man shit right here. Don't be scared now," he said. *If this is what goes down in the district, imagine what the county jail must be like*, Ryan thought. He began preparing himself. *Ain't nobody going to think of me as weak.* He wondered how he could make a weapon for protection.

The officer realized that his gold cross chain was missing. It must have broken off during the beating and slid into one of the cells. He opened each door and ordered everyone to stand with their backs against the wall. "Don't nobody fucking move," he growled. "If you got it and you're hiding it, I'm going to fuck you up." Then he located his jewelry.

The night was not over yet. Ryan, now sitting on the floor and resting his eyes, suddenly felt one of the other inmates touching his leg. He was scared of getting assaulted in confinement, and he jumped up with his fists in the air ready to pounce.

"No, no. I'm sorry. I fell," the man yelped. His eyes were partially closed. He was strung out and had lost control of his arms. Ryan calmed down.

Another man was slouched by the cell door. He hadn't had his fix and was sweating profusely. The sweats were joined by rancid farts until he finally defecated, the signal for officers to pull him from the cell. The poorly ventilated cell smelled of death.

In the morning, Ryan and a few others were brought to a room with a bank of phones. He was directed to a chair, picked up the phone, and squinted at a screen. A magistrate appeared and told him that he was being charged with multiple offenses: selling and possessing illegal drugs plus conspiracy to distribute them.

Before long, an officer clipped his yellow wristband and handed him his belongings. He didn't have to pay bail since he had no priors, and the charges were relatively low-level. Free at last. No need to make a shiv. The sun was out as he walked home. He was whipped and famished but relieved to have dodged the county jail. Rayni opened the door, and

Ryan nodded that he was okay—he didn't want a conversation. He took a shower, picked up a bacon, egg, and cheese sandwich at the corner store, and passed out.

He woke up to Avry telling him that he'd posted a picture on Instagram of Nilsa and Ryan sitting on a stoop with his middle finger up. "Free my brother Ryan," he'd written. Had any women commented, Ryan wanted to know. A few. It was the sole redeeming part of his day.

Sunbeam, Flu-Flu, Ju-Ju

Mehmet Oz and his guide, special agent Gary Tuggle of the Drug Enforcement Administration, ducked inside a rickety dwelling where quacks helped people who required assistance injecting drugs. A bilingual sign read, "Attention! Service must be payed before any is given! No exceptions!" The pair were touring El Campamento. Going through the camp, they passed needles caked in dirt, excrement, bags of heroin, mirrors, tires, mattresses, chairs, tables, debris of all kinds, and a tree stabbed with syringes.[1]

"If you think of what hell might look like, this is it," said Oz. "I just walked into hell." He had learned of the camp from a *Philadelphia Inquirer* article headlined "A Hidden Hellscape." The "squalor and chaos along the rail line resembles a scene from Hieronymus Bosch," journalists Stephanie Farr and Sam Wood wrote. "Addicts—many with needle marks so fresh that still-drying blood glistens in the sun—twist their bodies into unnatural forms to crouch and teeter on the trash-covered banks as they shoot up. Others sleep under nearby bridges or in makeshift shelters surrounded by garbage, drugs, and death."[2]

Buried underneath an estimated half million used syringes, the camp fluctuated between 75 and 125 denizens.[3] In 2016, it was the site of 17 of the city's 907 fatal drug overdoses and at least 29 emergency medical service responses to nonfatal overdoses.[4] Philadelphia had the second-highest drug-overdose death rate of U.S. counties with at least one million residents.[5] The rate skyrocketed with the emergence of fentanyl, a powerful synthetic opioid fifty times more potent than heroin and one hundred times more potent than morphine.[6] There was a 113 percent average spike nationwide in fentanyl-involved overdose deaths from 2013 to 2016.[7] Fentanyl was manufactured in China and shipped to the United States by the Postal Service.[8] Alternatively, Mexican cartels, using Chinese chemicals, cooked and transported the product across the southern border.[9]

During the glory days of Kensington's industrial might, more than forty freight trains passed through the viaduct on its eleven tracks daily. That activity slumped accordingly with deindustrialization. Conrail took over ownership of the tracks and the gulch in 1976. For at least the past two decades, the encampment housed drug consumption, which stretched below East Gurney and Tusculum Streets and was mostly shielded from the public eye.[10]

A few days before the segment ran on Oz's show, Philadelphia mayor Jim Kenney ordered code violation notices to Conrail for letting the area deteriorate into a public health nuisance and demanded that the company clean it up. The city and Conrail later came to an agreement for a historic cleanup, and workers removed trees, wild vegetation, and 2,700 pounds of trash and installed ironclad fencing. Social services provided food and medical tests and gave referrals for housing and treatment services.[11] However, some of the camp's residents simply migrated above ground and occupied tents in four bridge underpasses in the neighborhood. "Drug tourists" continued to arrive in the neighborhood on the daily.[12]

* * *

"You just gotta keep hitting, keep hitting them to take them down," insisted Sergeant Paul Perez of the 25th Police District, speaking of the corners. The antidrug strategy executed by Philadelphia police involved surveillance cameras, foot patrols, and raids. But Perez readily admitted that his officers would confiscate a corner's stash, and the supply would just be replenished. The quick fix of rounding up dealers and putting them behind bars appeared futile, because there are "ten more to take his place," noted Captain Michael Cram, ex-commander of the 25th and 26th Districts.

DEA special agent Patrick Trainor recognized the dilemma. Do you expend resources going after the users and dealers or the major traffickers? "Are you going to lock up everybody in Kensington? You can't. From a drug trafficker's perspective, anybody you see on a corner is completely and utterly expendable. They are crash test dummies. Those people who are slinging have probably no more than one or two bundles. There are a bunch of reasons for that. One, in case they are arrested, they will have as little drugs on them as possible. If they get robbed by a rival drug dealer, they have minimal product."

In 2018, Philadelphia had 353 homicides, the highest level recorded in more than a decade.[13] The homicides were increasingly associated with the drug trade.[14] The 24th and 25th Districts, which include much of Kensington, were the nucleus of the violence. In 2016, there were 31 homicides and 111 shooting victims in the 24th and 40 homicides and 189 shooting victims in the 25th.[15] Research found that police enforcement of the drug market can fuel greater violence and more homicides.[16] Leo Beletsky and Jeremiah Goulka argued that the DEA's "heroin seizures and high-profile prosecutions . . . encouraged traffickers to create more compact, potent drugs" such as fentanyl. Disrupting a drug faction on a corner can also cause rivals to scramble for control of the territory, which generates violence.[17] Unlike in other cities where gangs ran the show, Philadelphia had a decentralized network of small groups of dealers.[18]

Boasting of a "PhD in streetology," Cram explained that the police had become "the Band-Aid" for all the economic and social ills in the community. To understand crime, he said, you need to understand the underlying conditions, which generate "a perfect storm": poverty, hunger, unemployment, cheap heroin, low graduation rates, high incarceration rates, and the breakdown of the family structure. On the drug corners, the dealers hustling "are good, decent people trapped in a bad environment" who are trying to "keep food on the table and the lights on."

Instead of locking people up, he argued, resources should be channeled into slowing the demand for drugs. "Mass incarceration does not work. There needs to be a comprehensive, nonnarcotics-related treatment program." As journalist Jill Leovy pointed out, communities of color have been overpoliced for trivial offenses and underpoliced for deadly, violent crimes.[19] If targeting low-level drug users and dealers wasn't a priority, this would free up resources for the police to tackle the more serious problem of violent crime, Cram noted. Philadelphia police solved fewer than half of the homicides committed each year, which fueled a crisis of trust and legitimacy among the public.[20] "These people want to live in safety," he said. "Can you imagine living in a neighborhood where kids can't sleep in a living room" for fear of bullets? "Kids can't play in the playground because the junkies are dropping their needles."

* * *

ON THE MONDAY after his arrest, Ryan arrived on time for his first day at EOP. Early on, he recognized that the computer-based instructional approach was not a good fit for him. It was similar to his brief trial with Penn Foster in ninth grade. He would read a chapter, take the corresponding test, and assuming he passed, move on to the next chapter. Cut and dried and mind-numbing. There was some live instruction for math, science, and English, an easier format for learning. The classes had about fifteen students, and he was one of the youngest. Some were in their late twenties, plus a few in their thirties, and even a grandmother in her eighties who hoped to inspire her grandchildren to get their high school diploma.

The building seemed to secrete mediocre education, but Ryan thought he had to stick with EOP if he wanted to graduate high school. And he did. It seemed to be the only way out of the low-wage service industry, which, along with the drug economy, filled the void left by vanishing manufacturing. The budding opioid crisis also created a steady demand for workers on the corner, especially when formal employment that paid a living wage was not universally available. As Marquan, an El Centro de Estudiantes student, put it, "You expect us to just be dead broke for our families sitting there hungry or while our electric about to cut off or our water about to cut off. No. We going to do what we got to do. And it's like y'all trying to say you're trying to better the community but what're you doing for it? It ain't nothin' in my community, nothin' but abandoned cribs and corner stores."

Ryan wanted to see his son on Halloween. Bianca brought Marc, adorably dressed as a white dog with gray ears, in a stroller to McPherson Park. She knew that his first Halloween would only happen once, so she had pulled together $20 to buy him a costume from the rack at Family Dollar. Trick-or-treaters in colorful costumes milled around the area. Ryan showed up in ragged, wrinkled clothes. His wardrobe rotated among four shirts and three pairs of pants, shared with Avry. Bianca and Ryan chatted cordially for a bit. Then she asked him for some money; he wasn't giving her child support at this point. He didn't mention his arrest but said he was struggling and if he had any money, he'd give it to her.

Instead, Ryan offered to watch Marc more often. Bianca replied, "When you're able to provide Pampers in your house for him, then you can take him. I don't think it's fair that I scrape up the little money I have to pay for diapers and clothes."

Ryan grew mad. "Do you know how many bitches are dying to buy my son diapers?"

"Do you know how many niggas are dying so I can let them step up and be a father to your son?" Bianca bristled.

Insults and a smack or two were exchanged. Ryan claimed that Bianca slapped him, leaving visible marks, and Bianca claimed that Ryan had slapped her and broke her phone.

Ryan left the park and walked home.

Soon after, Bianca drove over to Ryan's house with Marc, her sister and her children, her sister's boyfriend, and his friend. The aged white Toyota Camry was parked sideways to block entry onto Ryan's street. The sister's boyfriend came to the door. "Tell your son to come outside," he said to Rayni.

"My son isn't coming outside," she said. "So you can jump him?"

"He like to hit girls."

"He ain't never hit Bianca," said Rayni. "Bianca is the one who hit him."

They continued exchanging words. Ryan was angling to go outside, but Rayni pushed him back. Then Bianca's sister stepped out of the car and began quarreling with Rayni.

Meanwhile, Avry's girlfriend called 911, and two police officers responded.

"Who did that to your face?" one of the cops asked Ryan, who pointed at Bianca. She denied touching him.

"I need you to turn around and put your hands behind your back," the officer told her. Bianca began grousing. He raised his voice. "I'm not going to ask you again."

As Bianca cried, the officer cuffed her and put her in the back of the police van. Ryan felt vindicated. Her time was up.

Ryan went along in the police van to the 24th/25th District. Bianca said nothing, but he could tell that she was enraged. At the district, a detective snapped photos of his face. He gave a statement, narrating the chain of events and signing his name. His elation faded as he began to worry about how she would retaliate—not physically, but in the courtroom. What would she do to prevent him from gaining custody?

Bianca, who was seventeen, was charged with simple assault, but she avoided jail. She completed community service and attended an anger management class. The incident served as the basis for Ryan's application for a temporary Protection From Abuse order against her, which was granted.

* * *

JUST AS RYAN and Bianca got into their fight, George was on his way to his probation officer, Monica. For the previous year's drug offenses, he had been sentenced to one year of probation, six months of house arrest with electronic monitoring, and an intensive outpatient program. He had to live at the Richard Jones Recovery House, where he roomed with an older Black man. During the day, he attended Northeast Treatment Center for group therapy sessions, which were spent shooting the shit. Some of the participants were dealers who didn't actually have substance abuse issues.

To George, it was just one more box he had to tick off on the path to gaining his freedom. He was under no illusions that the program addressed addiction. It had no rehabilitative treatment services. It did not provide economic support or stable, permanent housing in better-resourced neighborhoods where dope wasn't peddled on the corners. The diversion program, as it was called, held largely poor people to arbitrary measures that few could meet, with severe penalties for any deviation. While it kept some people out of jail, the program didn't mean they could escape the criminal justice apparatus. They were still subjected to electronic monitoring, court appearances, probation officers, and urine tests. Philadelphia was one of the "most supervised" cities in the United States, with one in every twenty-two adults on probation or parole.[21]

At George's appointment, Monica told him that his most recent urine had come back positive for marijuana. It was a violation of the terms of his probation, so back to jail he went.

Ryan didn't want to believe that George was addicted, despite all the mounting evidence over the years. He saw addiction as a character defect and respected George too much to think of him in an unfavorable light. When Ryan was in middle school, George had been arrested for buying heroin that he said was intended for a friend. Another time, George was riding home on his bike, and the cops pulled him over, alleging that they saw him buy something on a known drug corner. The police found nothing on him, but there was a crack pipe nearby. Then Ryan noticed that cash and PlayStation games were going missing at home.

Rayni finally told him the truth after George's latest jail sentence. Ryan wanted to talk to him, frankly, so he arranged a visit at the Detention Center on State Road. There was no better time or place. George's back would be up against a wall. He wouldn't be able to escape or make excuses.

They hugged in the visiting room. Ryan asked how he was faring. George was mostly in good spirits. His commissary account was running low, so he asked for some funds. With the niceties out of the way, Ryan got down to brass tacks, saying, "You can't lie. We know you've been using crack." George began choking up and confessed.

He pledged to Ryan he would stop using and do better. "I hope so,"

Ryan replied. "We love you. Our family needs you. You got to send an example to the kids." As they were sitting there, they saw a woman transfer a small balloon to an inmate via a French kiss. He swallowed it. He'd probably go back to his cell, take a swig of shampoo, and vomit the balloon and its drugs inside. George knew that the guy must have gulped a ton of water before the visit—he had to, for the scheme to work. He'd once seen a group of men stalking another inmate each time he went to the bathroom. They carefully combed through his feces to unearth the drugs. If he had only drunk enough water, the wait might have been avoided.

* * *

RYAN HAD INITIALLY planned to plead not guilty to his drug offense. He wasn't necessarily confident that he would win, but he thought it was worth fighting. When he spoke to his public defender, she urged him to consider the drug treatment diversion route. If he was found guilty, he would risk up to a year in the county jail. The only catch with the treatment program was that you had to be a user to qualify. Ryan didn't abuse or consume drugs, he told her. His crime was poverty. Selling drugs was a readily available gig for the interim while he was looking for better work.

"No, no, no. You can be in the program," the public defender said. "You just have to *do* drugs to be in the program." Ryan weighed the pros and cons. On one hand, he would have to say that he did drugs, and it could take more than a year to complete the cumbersome program. On the other, he'd avoid incarceration and could have the case stripped from his record. He reluctantly took the deal and enrolled in the program. Meanwhile, Nilsa pled guilty to the drug dealing offenses and received a maximum three-year probation sentence. She had to pay court fees, participate in an educational program, and work.

During the intake interview, Ryan explained that he was a frequent marijuana user when he had actually only smoked a handful of times. He didn't even like it, comparing getting high to playing Russian roulette. "I never knew what was going to happen," he said. "Either I was going to be out of my fucking mind or on cloud nine." He was twelve the first time he smoked marijuana, sitting in the back seat of an old Honda Civic with Avry, Nilsa, and a few friends. They were passing around blunts. After a dozen puffs, he exited the car and started tripping out. *Is the world even real? Does this exist? If I throw myself in front of a car, will I die?* The delusions wore off after a while. Another time, he started hearing voices. He was walking down the street when a car stopped, and two people got out to switch places—he thought they were going to kidnap him.

* * *

RYAN WAS SPENDING more time in courtrooms than anywhere else. So much was going on: negotiating custody, trying to make money, Rayni recovering from breast cancer, his stepfather grappling with addiction and jail, and now dealing with this drug case and treatment program. And he was working to graduate high school. He was the man of the household, with one headache after another. He would deal with one obstacle only to be hit with a new crisis.

On Christmas Eve, Ryan and Avry made their way downtown to attend George's violation of probation hearing. They were hoping the judge would be sympathetic and let him come home. As the courtroom filtered out, Judge Rayford Means, an older African American man with a salt-and-pepper mustache, came off the bench and asked who they were there for.

The twins waved as George was brought in. His lawyer summarized that George's urine tested positive for marijuana, which violated his probation, so he had been jailed. She proposed that he be given a "thirty-day sanction, immediate parole, and reinstatement of his remaining two months of house arrest."

Means began questioning George, wanting to know how he had gotten the marijuana.

"You know the guy? Can you point him out to me? I'll show you pictures. What's his name, Sunbeam, Flu-flu, Ju-ju?"

"It's all different people."

"Crow, Crow-bird? You don't know they name?"

"No."

"How do you know what they selling you is not poison, going to kill you, give you a heart attack?"

"I don't."

"To be honest, it's marijuana," the lawyer interjected.

"Right, you don't know that, and you just go ahead 'n do it. It could be laced with something," said Means. "You know that stuff will hurt your heart and your lungs and everything." After a brief back-and-forth with the lawyer, Means decided to vacate the house arrest and ordered George to return to the recovery house and stop using drugs. He oversaw the most probation cases in the city and tried to offer alternatives to incarceration to people with nonviolent offenses. He understood that those who stole things like food, diapers, and medicine or sold drugs did so because they were poor or couldn't find stable work.

Ryan was surprised by how well the hearing had gone. Save his youth advocate during his own juvenile case, Judge Means was unlike anyone he had encountered in his tours of the juvenile and adult criminal justice systems. Means listened carefully. He was fair. He took his time. He did not leap to conclusions. He earnestly wanted to hear the perspective of the defendant.

George's detainer was lifted. He went back to jail to pick up his belongings, and in the evening, George's mother drove Ryan and Rayni to the jail to wait for him. An hour later, he came out with his bag of things. They took turns giving him hugs, thrilled that he was home in time for Christmas.

* * *

AFTER A PRELIMINARY evaluation, Ryan was placed in Phase II, a four-step drug outpatient program. The court-mandated, thrice-weekly sessions involved random exercises designed to help the participants change "their mindsets." This was "treatment for the poor man," as Ryan put it. "Not your resort, country club treatment." He and the other participants—mostly men under the age of forty, all races—would sit in a circle and share their war stories from the streets. The counselor,

Latoya, had them jot down their goals and five-year plans. Ryan wrote that he wanted to finish high school, be a police officer, and get an apartment and a car.

One time she asked them to pick a song that described their lives. Ryan chose "Heaven or Hell" by the Philadelphia artist Kur. He rapped about growing up in poverty ("I was the poorest, needed help so bad"), bathing with buckets of water, hustling on the corner, and seeing his friends paralyzed, incarcerated, and unemployed. "I used to always want them sneakers on the Nike shelf," he rapped. "Nigga please you don't know how living trifling felt."[22] When Ryan played the song for the group, which was largely made up of drug dealers, their heads bobbed up and down.

He continued to drop clean urine samples, but he'd learned that Latoya rarely let anybody move on to the program's third phase. Both her parents had been addicted to drugs, and Ryan thought she was immersed in her drug-related traumas and hell-bent on getting her patients to acknowledge their addiction and grapple with it.

In their private sessions, Latoya never inquired about his life or what he was striving to accomplish. "What is your addiction?" is the only thing she asked.

"I don't have an addiction," Ryan would reply.

"I don't believe you," she said. "I think you have an addiction. Everybody has an addiction. You don't just want to admit it."

Ryan thought maybe he could switch to the evening session and get a new counselor who wouldn't keep him stuck in Phase II forever. But the night session turned out to be the Wild West. Nobody paid attention. They threw paper, blasted music, watched television, and loafed around. When it was time to give urine, Ryan looked on astonished as the clean patients would urinate for the ones who were using for $20 a pop. The security guard was on the gravy train, paid off to stay mum.

After two weeks of this, Ryan realized he could use the chaos to his benefit. He went to the director's office. "Listen, I got some information for you," he said. "But I'm not going to give you the information until you tell me I'm going into Step Three." The director looked at his file and agreed. But she paused over the paperwork. "I ain't going to sign it until you tell me."

Ryan spilled the beans about the urine tests, and the director, who was upset, thanked him for the information. She transferred him to Phase III, several months after he'd first started the program.

* * *

RYAN WAS TRYING to do better. He had kept up attendance at EOP, mostly, and got work at McDonald's at another location. He also had a new girlfriend, Yamilet. They had connected through Instagram and Kik, an instant messaging app, and soon met up. Sometimes it felt like they were from different worlds: Yamilet's family was working-class with stability; her father had a job in a packing company and her mother was a school cafeteria aide. Their row home in Kensington was a cocoon, sheltering their children from the streets and keeping their focus on education. Yamilet had been born in Philadelphia but spent her first few years in Quebradillas, Puerto Rico. She graduated from Edison High School and was now a student at Esperanza College of Eastern University, studying for an associate's degree and hoping to be the first one in her family to graduate college.

She encouraged Ryan to finish high school, but she could tell from his streaks of anger and frustration that he was consumed by other pressing matters. He shielded parts of his world from her to avoid stoking drama. Initially, her parents hadn't approved of their relationship, thinking Ryan was "from the streets." He would wear cardigans to hide his tattoos.

Undermining Ryan's progress and taking a toll on his relationship with Yamilet was the situation concerning Marc. Custody negotiations had dragged on and on, and Ryan hadn't seen him in nearly six months. He'd missed the baby's first steps, first words, and first birthday—one milestone after another. It was heartbreaking for him to feel that he was failing his son, repeating the pattern set by his own father. Bianca asserted that she never stopped him from seeing their son and fulfilling his fatherly responsibilities, countering that he pulled out every excuse in the book: "I don't have a ride." "I don't have enough diapers." "I have to work."

Walking into Family Court a year after the custody case had begun, Ryan decided it was time to wave a white flag. He was tired of fighting with Bianca and Hermosa.

"I'd like to withdraw my petition and sign my rights over," he announced at the start of the hearing. He had never imagined saying that. Judge Peter Rogers asked him why.

"I just don't want to deal with it no more," said Ryan.

"You don't want to deal with the child?" asked Rogers.

"It's not the child. I would love to deal with my child. It's just I don't want to deal with them no more," Ryan replied, exasperated, gesturing toward Bianca and Hermosa.

Hermosa claimed that Ryan wasn't cooperating: he didn't want to do the exchanges at the police district, asking that she drop Marc off and pick him up at his house. "I have a life, too," she declared. "You have a life. I have a life, too . . . But he said that he will deal with the baby when he grown enough." Ryan countered that sometimes Bianca would text him without warning, asking him to watch Marc that night. He couldn't do it on such short notice.

"You had business out in the street?" the judge interjected.

"Huh?" Ryan said, offended by the question. "I ain't had no business on the street. It was the daughter texting me . . ."

He and the judge went back and forth. Ryan had been driving with an expired learner's permit, and the judge wanted details of his ongoing drug case. Ryan explained that he didn't have a drug issue, but he was in a treatment program to avoid jail, on the advice of his lawyer. He did urine tests twice a week.

"So, Mr. Rivera," the judge said. "If I send you over there to give up some urine today, you really need to tell me what I'm going to find."

"Nothing," said Ryan, before acknowledging that his urine had come back positive for morphine the previous month. He agreed to the judge's request for a urine test and noted that it might be positive for marijuana or pills. But he insisted that he never took morphine, so he didn't know why it had shown up in his system. He had a phobia about swallowing pills, afraid they would get stuck in the back of his throat.

Ryan tried to return to the matter of his child. "You could also see . . .

there's been multiple restraining orders took out, and they've all been dropped. That's all the drama I don't want to deal with. It's not about my son. I'll take—if you give me Saturdays at—"

The judge offered him supervised visitation on Sundays at Family Court. Ryan knew what that was like—he had been through it with his own father, and he didn't want his son to endure it as well.

"I wish to see my child, but I don't—"

"Do you wish to see your child at 1801 Vine?"

"No, sir."

"Let the record reflect that he does not wish for the Court to give him contact," Rogers said, winding up. "Therefore, he has no contact with the child. This is not being done with prejudice to the biological father, who may file his own petition to get some level of contact with his child. The reason why the Court is cutting him off is because he refuses—well, he's telling the Court he doesn't want to have contact over at 1801 Vine."

"Sir, I just want the drama to stop . . . I'm not trying to get in trouble," Ryan firmly stated. With that, he surrendered his rights to custody of Marc for the time being. From here on, he would only see him on rare occasions. Ryan hurried out of the courtroom with a nasty taste in his mouth. Not only had he given up his son, he also felt Rogers had added insult to injury by trying to trap him with aggressive questions and get him locked up as if he was on trial. This wasn't the outcome he envisioned when he first started going to Family Court, repeating the cycle of a Rivera growing up without a father.

I Am Not a Number

In tenth grade, Giancarlos made a decision that would change his high school career and maybe even his life. He was leaving school for the day when he spotted Steven, his girlfriend Natalia's stepbrother. A short, thick Puerto Rican boy who attended Kensington Business, Steven said he was heading to Towey Playground to fight Jesus, another Puerto Rican student, who had been harassing Natalia. Giancarlos wanted to tag along.

As they were walking over, Jesus crept up behind them and clubbed Steven, who fell on a parked car. Giancarlos and his friend Kenneth, a Black kid with an athletic build, ran up and pushed Jesus against another car. "We don't do that around here," Giancarlos shouted. "You're not going to sneak up and beat him while he wasn't looking. Y'all want to fight. Fight at the park."

A crowd of students made their way to the park to watch the one-on-one fight.

Jesus started spitting at them. "Since y'all like breaking up fights, I've got two big niggas for y'all."

"Why get somebody if you right here?" Giancarlos jeered.

That sent him and Jesus going at each other in the middle of Berks Street. Giancarlos ducked Jesus's swing and got in a good punch, and

Jesus dropped to the ground. Before Giancarlos could land another blow, the KCAPA school resource officer, Angel Rodriguez, appeared. Rodriguez grabbed him and dragged him to his office. He shouldn't have butted in other people's business, Rodriguez said, and when Marta came to pick him up, she scolded him for acting out in violence. Giancarlos thought the rationale was clear-cut: Jesus snuck up on his friend, so he had to even the score. He couldn't be seen as soft. That was the basic code of the streets.

To Giancarlos, this was business as usual, but he was suspended. He had violated rule 21 in the district's code of conduct: "instigation and/or participation in a group assault."[1] A disciplinary hearing was scheduled for a few weeks later. He figured he would make his case in the hearing and get this bullshit resolved.

The thing Giancarlos didn't realize was that the KCAPA dean, Brandon Walker, had been pushing disruptive students out of the school and into El Centro de Estudiantes, which was a few blocks away, through cajoling (*You get to school late every day; you can arrive at El Centro any time of day*) and disciplinary infractions. Once a student committed a serious violation, the formal transfer process started rolling. Walker seemed less interested in massaging test scores and graduation rates, one of his colleagues felt, than in alleviating the overcrowding and disciplinary crisis at KCAPA. Pick the ones creating the most problems and issues in the hallways and turf them out. That was the strategy.

* * *

GIANCARLOS WAS WELL acquainted with the school district headquarters, where the hearing was held, since it was the site of many protests. He listened as Dean Walker told the hearing officer, Hakeem Carter, that Giancarlos had been involved in a group assault. He had also been organizing students at the school, such as engaging in walkouts.

"You're telling me a fifteen-year-old had the students walk out?" Carter said incredulously. He turned to Giancarlos. "I want to see you in the news doing something positive. You should be in class. When you run for president, I'm going to vote for you."

Walker argued that Giancarlos was interfering with other students' education. El Centro de Estudiantes would be a better fit. Giancarlos was offended. He'd just been accepted at the All-City Choir for the second year in a row. Why would he give that up? He didn't think El Centro would have the same diversity of dance and music offerings that KCAPA had. What would be the point of going to school?

Giancarlos explained that he hadn't initiated the brawl—he was defending his girlfriend's brother. But Carter wasn't convinced. He ruled that Giancarlos would be expelled from KCAPA. The district had taken the most severe action possible. Giancarlos felt he was being punished for his activism. Under the behavior matrix, he could have been given an out-of-school suspension and allowed back after a period of time. But there was no way to appeal the ruling, so he and Marta went to school to empty out his locker and say his goodbyes.

* * *

GIANCARLOS WENT TO Penn Treaty, where his sister, Isabelesse, was in middle school, until a spot opened up at El Centro de Estudiantes. The day after the disciplinary hearing, Giancarlos met with Penn Treaty's principal, Dennis Cooper, and asked that his class schedule wouldn't overlap with a few particular kids from the neighborhood who would try to get him into fights or pranks—there was an ongoing beef between KCAPA and Penn Treaty.

No fights went down, but it was a real slog getting through the days. The classes were the same as at KCAPA: filling out worksheets, reading chapters, and answering questions from a textbook. He didn't have choir or dance class to keep him motivated. But he did play the snare drum and saxophone in instrumental music class and was able to convince Principal Cooper to let him join the drum line. Charlie, a KCAPA teacher, dropped by Penn Treaty during the week to practice with him and four other students. Sometimes they played in the KCAPA parking lot with the rest of his students since Giancarlos was banned from entering the school. His old choir teacher arranged for the bus to pick him up from Penn Treaty for All-City Choir practice.

Keystone state testing season was around the corner. Through his involvement with YUC, Giancarlos knew that standardized testing was a flawed measure of achievement, ignoring the subjects not tested and used to justify punishing and closing schools, firing teachers, and pushing out students. Starting with his year—the class of 2017—passing Algebra I, Biology, and Literature Keystone exams was made a graduation requirement.[2] Parents had the right to opt their children out on religious grounds, but the student would have to sit for a project-based assessment in each subject to graduate. Giancarlos had learned about students organizing to opt out in other parts of the country, and he floated the idea of encouraging Penn Treaty students to boycott the Keystones and walk out of school on the first day of testing. He discovered that none of his classmates were aware the tests were noncompulsory.

Cooper caught wind of talk about the proposed walkout. He called an assembly to announce that any student who walked out of school during testing would be suspended. Cooper had frightened them into submission. Scores of students came up to Giancarlos afterward to say they couldn't have anything to do with his action. He tried to explain that they had the right to take a stand for their education no matter what the principal or any adult claimed.

In mid-May, the day before the first test, Giancarlos printed out hundreds of flyers for the walkout at the YUC office with a plan to distribute them the next morning. In spite of having been kicked out of KCAPA in large part due to his rabble-rousing, and that he'd be identified as the ringleader, he thought it was worth taking a risk to protest the injustice.

In the morning, he sketched out the logistics, skipping his usual pickup basketball game. Coming to the entrance of Penn Treaty, he ran into a teacher, Parker.

"Hey, you're Giancarlos, right?" Parker said, as she emerged from her car. "I hear you're doing the walkout." She popped her trunk and offered to let him borrow her two megaphones. She sneaked him into the building early, and Giancarlos proceeded to tear down the hallways and fling the flyers in the air. He met up with his classmate Juan and handed him one of the megaphones. Students slowly filtered into school. Once the day began, Giancarlos stood outside the building and started chanting. "No justice, no peace!" "Walk out! Everybody walk out!" An incensed Principal Cooper got on the loudspeakers to repeat his threat: any student who walked out would get suspended. That stunted most of the turnout, so only three students joined Giancarlos and Juan.

The small but spirited group chanted and marched over to KCAPA, where a dozen or so students who were also boycotting the tests had congregated in front of the building.[3] KCAPA students were outraged— the school administrators had told them they had forfeited the right to attend prom and the graduation ceremony by opting and walking out.

Opt-out activist and district parent Alison McDowell filmed interviews with the students. "We deserve to learn whatever we want to do as we grow up in life," insisted Giancarlos, who sported a red Philadelphia Phillies T-shirt. "I want to be a dancer when I grow up. I'm in Penn Treaty but don't have dance class. Y'all training me to be something else that I am not. I just want to be who I want to be but I can't—just because of budget cuts and because the Keystones."[4]

"Y'all got to start listening to the youth," he continued. "We think in our opinion we shouldn't be like learning throughout the whole school year just for one test . . . All the work we did is about the Keystones. It sickens me. We tryin' to take away these kids' dreams. Just so you can get more money to build more prisons."

Critics like Secretary of Education Arne Duncan accused the opt-out movement of lacking diversity—that it was dominated by loud white suburban parents. But here were poor and working-class Black, Latino, and white youth together resisting the high-stakes testing regime and sending a message to the testing executives and the city and state's political class: we refuse to be ranked, sorted, labeled, and commodified.[5] Unlike for many of their suburban peers, for Giancarlos and students like him, the tests were truly high-stakes. The requirement would make the path to graduating high school even tougher. "A high school diploma is everything," Juan said. "If you don't have a high school diploma, you might as well call yourself a bum on the streets."[6] And if test scores were flat or declined, their schools might be put on the chopping block or taken over by a charter. Their families didn't have the economic clout to sway politicians. Their power derived from collective and sustained action.

*　*　*

THAT EVENING, GIANCARLOS phoned into the *Rick Smith Show*, a progressive radio program based in Central Pennsylvania, for an interview about the protest.[7] "Telling us we have to pass the Keystones in order to get a diploma is ridiculous," he argued. "The Keystones is basically meant to make you fail, and it's a part of the school to prison pipeline, which is basically the system that wants kids to drop out. When they drop out, they can't get a job 'cause we don't have a diploma. So they end up selling drugs or getting into something bad. And they go to jail. And that's more money in the government's pocket. We don't agree with that." The tests reduced students to statistics, he continued. *I am not a number*, he thought to himself, and then read out his student ID number to drive his point.

Rather than preparing students year-round to pass the Keystones and become worker bees, he asked why the schools weren't helping students follow their dreams. "I want to be a dancer when I grow up. I don't even have a dance class anymore," he said. "It kills me . . . We have music class, but we have it only one period every Tuesday and Thursday. Probably not even that because our music teacher also works at KCAPA. He's busy. What am I learning in school? Why would I come to school? No. I'm not learning what I want to learn. I'm not learning baseball, music production, dancing. I'm learning how I'm gonna get a job."

Giancarlos called for the abolition of the School Reform Commission as an unelected, undemocratic body. He proposed having one student from each school in the district serve on a board and make decisions. To him, it was critical that students understood they had rights and that adults respected them.[8]

When Giancarlos showed up at school the next morning, he knew that Cooper was bluffing on his threat of suspension. But he was done with Penn Treaty. He was still on the waiting list for El Centro de Estudiantes. He had been skeptical of the school's approach, but he had begun to see how it had transformed his cousin Edgar. Once a clown kid, he was now respectful and mature. Edgar told him that students graduated quicker, dressed as they wished, and moved about freely.

In the final weeks of the school year, Giancarlos would check into Penn Treaty in the morning and leave an hour later. By the end, he had accrued dozens of tardies and absences. Nearly all his grades were failing, except for instrumental music class, in which he earned an 88. He often passed the day chilling with his friend Joshua Caraballo at Graffiti Pier, a colorful and deserted hangout spot along the Delaware River. Joshua, a skinny Puerto Rican boy with curly black hair and glasses who went by the nickname Kito, was also playing hooky. He had grown up and spent the first decade of his life in Ponce, a town in southern Puerto Rico, before he, his mother, Ana, and his siblings moved to Philadelphia. For hours on end, Joshua and Giancarlos nursed blunts and filled sheets of rap lyrics together.

Ana was at her wit's end with her son's mischief. Joshua didn't want to go to school or come home. He wanted to run the streets. She called the police more than a dozen times and reached out to her local council member, who had no answers. What else could she do? When Joshua was ordered to appear in truancy court, he didn't show up. Out of options, Ana had him placed in The Bridge, a city-based residential treatment program for youth with substance use disorders and mental health and truancy issues.

One Sunday morning, draped in a baby blue robe and with a bruised leg, Joshua had knocked on the door of Giancarlos's great-aunt's house. As he'd caught his breath, he explained that he had escaped the facility, scaling a wall on the grounds and running four miles in socks to Kensington. Giancarlos hadn't heard from Joshua in a while and didn't know where he had been. He anticipated what Joshua was about to ask him. "Yo, bro, it's not like you can stay here," he said. "I can give you clothes, but that's the best I can do for you." Giancarlos advised Joshua to go home and come clean to his mother.

Ana and Joshua talked and she decided to allow him to stay home as long as he obeyed a curfew. He was still a minor, so he had to enroll in Camelot Academy, a disciplinary school. There was a cudgel hanging over him: truancy would land him in a less than desirable placement far from home, Saint Gabriel's Hall or Glen Mills Schools. But Joshua was willing to take that risk.

Meanwhile, Giancarlos spent a few more days at Penn Treaty and then stopped going. He wouldn't spend another moment at the school.

It was El Centro de Estudiantes or nothing. Marta warned him they could find themselves in truancy court. "You have a better chance of letting me stay home than sending me to Penn Treaty, where I could get into trouble," he argued. After missing so much school, Marta was proved right: Giancarlos received a subpoena requesting his appearance in truancy court.

* * *

TRUANCY COURT WAS in session, cycling through a docket of cases involving mostly Black and Latino single mothers and children who had been referred after accumulating at least ten unexcused absences. Cases were discharged, continued, or transferred to Family Court, where children might be sent to juvenile placement.

One mother, Kennedy, raised her right hand as a white court official swore her in. She stood behind a table facing a white court master who was perched at a tall wooden desk flanked by flags. Her daughter's case had been in and out of court for several years, periodically discharged and revived. The previous year, the girl, Deja, had been a student at Potter-Thomas Elementary and now was supposed to be attending Edison.

"This is the one the district is recommending Family Court," said Ayla, representative for the school district, before noting that Deja had missed twenty-three days last year and fifty-nine this year. It was the third hearing. The court master asked why Deja wasn't enrolled in Edison. Families were not afforded free counsel in truancy court. The case manager assigned to the family explained that they were waiting for a referral from the district to a different school since Deja was a special education student with an IEP. They had an appointment for a specialized school last month, but the child had been ill, so it was postponed. Requests for placement at four schools with appropriate resources had all been denied due to lack of space.

The court master agreed with the district's recommendation to transfer the case to Family Court. "In the next five days, she needs to be enrolled in the cyber-school," he concluded, so that Deja would receive an education until a permanent place could be finalized.

In the cases before the court, there was a profusion of health issues, such as chronic asthma. Children with asthma miss millions of days of school nationwide.[9] One case before the court involved a young child with alpha-thalassemia, a blood disorder that causes lethargy. He was being bullied and had trouble walking up flights of stairs, so he stopped going to school. In another case, a third grader had missed seventy days the previous year and forty-seven in the current year due to housing instability and lack of transportation. Evictions and homelessness posed serious challenges to regular school attendance.

Studies of Philadelphia's child welfare policies showed that the district referred Black and Latino families to truancy and family courts at much higher numbers than their overall racial representation in the system. Even with that, the overall truancy rate continued to rise.[10] Alex Dutton, a Family Court lawyer, described the system as a "school-to-child-removal pipeline." The vast majority of the cases, he argued, didn't involve abuse but rather neglect, which is "often a proxy for poverty."

Later in the court session, a Latino mother arrived for the eighth hearing regarding her two children, one in fifth grade and the other in ninth grade. Adrian had nineteen unexcused absences from Kensington High School. The previous month, he had run away from home. Through a translator, his mother said she was in touch with him every day, but she didn't know where he was. He was afraid of coming home because he didn't want to go to juvenile placement, she reported. Students knew that placement was the most severe repercussion of skipping school.

"We're sending this case to Family Court," said the court master. "If he doesn't show up for this court date, there could be a warrant for him. The judge could put a warrant out for him. The sheriff could bring him in. We also need to get him back in school." Adrian's high school had dropped him from the rolls for nonattendance. The woman's second son, Ricky, had ten unexcused absences. Both Ricky and Adrian had been sent to Florida to stay with their mother's brother while she was getting cancer treatment. Their father said he couldn't handle taking care of the children.

In many of the cases, parents reported abusing drugs and alcohol, incarceration, illness, and working extended hours as reasons for their children's absences. One of the mothers had recently given birth to her eighth child. She wasn't making enough money as a sex worker, so she planned to give one of her children up for adoption.

A few years earlier, the state's truancy laws had been revised following the death of Eileen DiNino, a Berks County mother who died in jail while serving a two-day sentence for failing to pay $2,000 in fines and court fees. The new laws were intended to "preserve the unity of the family whenever possible as the underlying issues of truancy are addressed. Avoid the loss of housing, the possible entry of a child to foster care and other unintended consequences of disruption of an intact family unit. Confine a person in parental relation to a child who is habitually truant only as a last resort and for a minimum amount of time." It added new interventions, such as a school attendance improvement conference to nip truancy in the bud before it escalated. Fines were maxed at $300 for the first offense, $500 for the second offense, and $750 for the third and additional offenses, with court costs. Parents could only be incarcerated—for no more than three days—if it was determined that the individual had the financial means to pay the fines and the violation was deliberate. Furthermore, the law prohibited schools from suspending, expelling, and transferring students for truancy.[11]

The new reforms tightened the flow of youth referred to Family Court, but they preserved carceral actors and tools—courts, incarceration, fines—for truancy and did little to address the root causes. It's often said that truancy is the tip of the iceberg. The truancy court proceedings reveal educational disengagement, a gamut of health ailments, and the problems associated with grinding poverty that fall through holes in the social safety net. "You have Black and brown people standing in front of white males," noted Heather, a staffer who worked for the district's Office of Attendance and Truancy. "This is so Jim Crow, Northeast racism. It's an undercurrent. You have these people explain themselves to someone who doesn't understand you, your culture, and what you're up against. Until we have fair schools and fair housing and fair wages and fair health care, you can't incriminate families for doing the best they can. They don't have a lot of resources . . . ninety-eight percent of the time I don't fault the families."

* * *

Soon after receiving the truancy court subpoena, Giancarlos's mother got a call from JuDonn, who was now co-principal, to say that he'd been accepted to El Centro de Estudiantes. When he arrived at the school for orientation, he immediately saw there were no metal detectors or school resource officers. *I'm going to be treated as an adult, not a prisoner*, he thought. He appreciated their down-to-brass-tacks approach. He saw a few kids from his neighborhood, including a boy he once fought. Preemptively, he told them he was there to learn and graduate. He would not be involved in their dumb shit.

The truancy court hearing still loomed. Giancarlos was worried that he'd be forced to finish high school in juvenile placement or get transferred to a violent disciplinary school. As he was called up, he pulled out a chair for Marta. The court master remarked that she had never seen a student do that before. He handed her a letter from El Centro de Estudiantes attesting to his excellent attendance thus far. She told him to keep it up and discharged the case. Resolved within minutes, it was one of the court's quickest hearings to date.

* * *

Like Giancarlos, many of his classmates had stories of being pushed out of their old schools by zero-tolerance, exclusionary discipline. Before transferring to El Centro de Estudiantes, Zion had been at Mastery Charter School. "Everything was very structured," he said. "Walk in, do now, direct instruction, independent work, review. You had to have socks. If you didn't have socks, you'd be sent home. You needed to have your shirt tucked in, lanyard showing, or you'd get detention. Needed to have a belt on. Getting to class on time was strict." He was an artist and an avid reader, and the rigid, authoritarian culture crushed his spirit. "There was no room for you to be an abstract person or be your own individual," he said. "I couldn't deal with that." Students who had gone to charter schools reported getting suspended over minor infractions.

It was worse in the disciplinary schools. When students switched classes, they were required to walk in a line with their hands behind their backs. "If you don't follow their directions, they slam you down," said Hakeem. "It's like jail. I don't think that's right. We're still children." Kayla once brought her phone to Camelot Academy. As she passed the metal detector, one of the security guards spotted it in her pocket. She refused to give it up because she knew her mother would have to come to school to retrieve it. "So he like, 'Give me your phone already,' and I was like saying no 'cause I didn't want to get in trouble," she recounted. "So then he just stood me against the wall and that dude was like, I'm raw, mean, and stuff like that but I do got soft feelings so that dude was hard as shit, was treating me like I was a boy so I started crying and shit. They got my hands all locked up and stuff like that, all over a phone."

"On any given afternoon, the cafeteria is filled with students in detention who have violated one of the school's meticulous rules," sociologist Joanne Golann wrote, drawing on fieldwork at a charter school. Those rules included "refusing to lift a head off a desk, talking in the hallway, leaving a homework problem blank, chewing gum, getting out of their seat without permission, and the catch-all, disrespecting a teacher." Golann concluded that these practices created "worker-learners—children who monitor themselves, hold back their opinions, and defer to authority—rather than lifelong learners."[12] In this quasi-carceral apparatus, the disciplinary measures, which regulate and govern through classification, objectification, surveillance, and punishment, ultimately condition the bodies of poor and working-class children, especially African American and Latino, for state containment. It is a system that produces "a whole population of criminalized, excluded youth," argued Princeton scholar Kathleen Nolan in her book *Police in the Hallways: Discipline in an Urban High School.*[13]

Such schools were an extension of the violence in the streets, so students came shell-shocked and prepared for "violent shit to happen. Just another day some more bullshit, somebody got to die," said El Centro de Estudiantes advisor Douglas Cox. "If you're always in a state of alertness or fight-or-flight, then you're not able to think," added Katie, director of special education. "Your brain can't do both of those things at the same time . . . It's not physically possible. You can't use your intellect when you're scared and hyperalert and worried and looking over your shoulder." For at least a few hours, the hope at El Centro was for the students to be able to "unzip and put their outer selves away" and shed the tensions of their worlds.

There was one zero-tolerance offense at the school, and that was for fighting. "We need some sort of boundary line that students can respect," JuDonn explained. The rule was a kind of holding measure until students became acclimated to the school. "By their second trimester, veteran students had bought into the culture," JuDonn continued. "It was no longer about this no-tolerance policy. It was, 'We don't do this here.'"

There were usually no more than five fights a year. Students who fought had to sit out a trimester followed by the option to return. Other than that offense, detentions and suspensions were not used. The school had been able to add, through private donor funding, a resiliency specialist on each of its three floors, giving it a student to counselor ratio that matched wealthier private schools. El Centro's approach to conflict was rooted in trauma-informed and restorative justice practices, such as peer mediation to address drama.

If students were caught with drugs, the staff handled the situation in-house and worked it out with their parents. And if they came to school high, they were told to go home. The idea of involving the police was rejected, a recognition that the criminal justice system could inflict a cruel form of punishment.

* * *

For Emmanuel, things at home were getting worse. Freddie's white pit bull, Blanca, gave birth to a litter of puppies, and then she tore up Emmanuel's mattress to use as their bed. They urinated and defecated all over the house—on the floors, the bed, and the couch, so it reeked of *abombao*. "I'm tired of cleaning up after them," Ivette told Freddie. "I'm not a dog sitter." But Freddie cherished his dogs. When she put them out in the backyard, he would get aggressive and bring them back inside. She didn't push further, afraid of stoking his wrath. Emmanuel slept on a moldering, smelly green and beige couch that he and Freddie lugged home off the street.

One night, Emmanuel woke up to a sharp pain on his upper lip. He tasted something metallic. He could tell that a rat had just scurried off his chest. He touched his lip, which was hot and stinging, and in the glow of his phone screen could see that his finger was stained with blood. He stumbled upstairs to Ivette's bedroom. "Mom! I'm bleeding," he screamed, as blood gushed from his lip. "A rat fucking bit me. What the fuck? I can't do this."

In the bathroom, which was lit by a flashlight, Ivette applied some hydrogen peroxide on his lip to suppress an infection and sent Emmanuel back to bed. He was too afraid to fall asleep. When sunlight peeked through the windows, he saw he had a scab wound. Emmanuel demanded that they go to the hospital—what if he contracted rabies? A doctor gave him a tetanus shot, but the whole experience was too much.

Emmanuel wasn't alone in his family's substandard living conditions. In 2019, 121,000 occupied housing units, or 5 percent of the Philadelphia metropolitan area, were deemed inadequate, and nearly 19 percent of units reported rodent sightings, the highest percentage of the country's most populated areas.[14]

As Emmanuel and Ivette left the hospital, he began spitting fire about their living situation and gave his mother an ultimatum: if you don't ditch Freddie and this house, I will leave. Ivette didn't believe him, but Emmanuel's Facebook posts revealed his mental state. "I'm over it," he wrote. "I just need to run and escape." Another status read, "I can never have a happy day. It always ends up ruined I swear. Where did the good times go?" To this one, Ivette responded, "What happened now my son, Emmanuel you were happy. You know I know you. What's going on."

The night after the rat incident, Emmanuel struggled to sleep. Winter was coming, the room was freezing, and Freddie wouldn't share the space heater. He made little effort to support Emmanuel—he even criticized him for "wasting time" in school when he could be earning money—and Ivette showed no sign of being willing to leave him. Freezing, Emmanuel decided he couldn't live like this anymore. If he didn't break free of the Lippincott Street shithole, nothing would change for him.

Stuffing three outfits and four pairs of underwear in a bag, he flipped through his mental Rolodex, trying to think of someone who might take him in for a while. He texted his friend Hannah, who had recently moved into an apartment, and asked if he could crash with her. She lived in a two-bedroom, one-bath apartment with her girlfriend Naomi, Naomi's sister Maeve and her boyfriend, Charles, and another friend, Elisha. Despite the crowding, Hannah welcomed him. Without saying goodbye, Emmanuel left, withdrew his monthly $205 in TANF money from the EBT card, and took the El and a bus up to Northeast Philadelphia. Hannah was just getting off her shift at Walmart and met him at the bus stop.

In the apartment, swigging one shot of E&J after another, Emmanuel got smashed with his new roommates, trying to put the past week behind him. He was relegated to sheets on the floor, but at least there were no dogs defecating and no rats or other vermin. And though she was heartbroken that he had left, Ivette understood why he had done it. She herself was depressed and anxious, and at one point she was admitted to the hospital. When she lay in bed, she imagined that the ceiling was collapsing and the walls were closing in on her. She wanted to leave Freddie, but she had no income and nowhere to go.

When Emmanuel's phone alarm buzzed him awake at 5 a.m., everyone else in the apartment was passed out. He had a killer hangover, but he was determined to get to school on time. He couldn't miss a day. He had to graduate and prove his struggle was worth something. After the evening's drunken festivities, he threw up in the toilet and then jumped in the steaming shower. Used to bathing with buckets of lukewarm water, the piping hot spray whipping at his flesh felt almost purifying. He took his time shampooing and conditioning his curls and scrubbing his tired face and body before catching the 66 bus and southbound El to get to El Centro for breakfast.

Using Ivette's TANF money, Emmanuel bought frozen pizza, ramen noodles, and other groceries, as well as an air mattress at Walmart. But he tried to limit his time in the apartment, staying late at his two internships, one at Galaei and the other at the Institute of Contemporary Art on the University of Pennsylvania campus. His commutes were long and tiring—school was an hour's trip each way. But he was ready to weather the punches, so long as none of them forced him to crawl back to Lippincott. With less than a year of high school left, he could see the finish line off in the distance. Emmanuel told himself that if he stayed the course, he'd make it. He imagined tossing that graduation cap in the air and holding up his diploma. One day, he would look back at Lippincott as a tragic chapter that he had closed. This was how God had decided to test him.

OG Bobby Johnson

Rayni, George, Tino, and Armando moved into a cramped, one-bedroom apartment in the Juniata area. Avry had left the nest, and Ryan was living on his own in an apartment not too far away. The neighborhood was peaceful, quiet, and working-class. Their first morning in the house, when he woke up, George turned to Rayni. "You hear that?" She didn't know what he was talking about. "You hear the birds chirping." He sighed. It felt like they were in the suburbs: no horns, no yelling, no gunshots. Rayni no longer needed to worry about her boys falling to a stray bullet. For George, who just a year ago had been getting high despite entry into a court-ordered recovery house, there was, for the first time he could remember, no thought of drugs. He hoped living in Juniata would keep him on the path to sobriety.

Although it would take another year for Ryan's offense to be expunged from his record, he had finally been discharged from the drug treatment program, many months after he had entered. The regular therapy sessions with drug users had radically changed his view of the drug trade. He heard the men and women talk about turning to drugs to dull the pain of trauma or abuse. One longtime user argued that dealers had been complicit in his addiction. A woman echoed his point. "We're adults and we buy it ourselves, but you guys know that you have family members who are on drugs or a close friend of yours who is starting drugs. You're there for them, and you don't want them to do it because you love them. But you say you don't know us."

For Ryan, dealing had been the basis of the livelihood for his father, stepfather, and uncle. But hearing the others talk, he thought of George. Would I sell drugs to George? he asked himself. Of course he wouldn't. *So how could I sell to other people?* He knew he could no longer feed poison to his community, to the aunts, brothers, mothers in the same predicament as George.

So Ryan had to find some way to pay the bills. The first job he landed was in a dingy electronics recycling factory on the outskirts of the city, where he was one of the youngest workers in a mostly Latino and African American workforce. When he started his 5 a.m. shift, Ryan's task was to sort what came down the conveyor belt into three bins: metal, copper, miscellaneous. In this job, he also picked up recycling in counties across New Jersey.

The work was hard and dirty. He had to wear goggles and a vest, but even so he could feel his lungs filling up with dust. His mucus was as black as tar. To protect himself from the toxic elements, he brought a mask, but his supervisor wouldn't allow him to use it. The Occupational Safety and Health Administration violations stacked up. Being on his feet for the eight-hour shift was also exhausting, so he quit after a few months and started delivering pizzas.

Throughout, the flexibility of EOP allowed Ryan to continue attending. But just when he thought Bianca was a thing of the past, he heard that she was planning to enroll there. He told the administrators that he didn't want to bring the drama of their relationship into the school. They gave him an offer: he needed to graduate by the end of the trimester, or she would be permitted to enroll. He failed English and fell a credit and a half short, so that marked the end of his time at EOP.

His last shot at graduating was to go back to the hallowed grounds of El Centro de Estudiantes. So one afternoon, he set aside his pride and stopped by the school. David Bromley was no longer principal, and Ryan found himself facing the new co-principals, JuDonn and Matthew Prochnow.

"I'm trying to get this done so I can get my diploma," Ryan said. "No bullshit. No games."

"It has to be no bullshit," Matthew said sternly. He was dubious. Ryan was a sweet-talker and rarely seemed committed to following through on his promises. JuDonn, who was endlessly forgiving, took a softer angle. "We want you to come back," he said. "We want to support you in your dreams and help you finish strong." The school didn't normally accept students so close to graduating—it wasn't intended to be a stopover—but because of Ryan's long and tortured history, they decided to give him one last chance.

At twenty years old, Ryan returned to El Centro de Estudiantes. The space was as calm and welcoming as ever, but Ryan had been through a lot in his time away—the birth of his son, the fighting with Bianca's family, the ugly custody battle, the drug arrest, a new girlfriend, drug court, and an array of low-wage jobs. He felt not just older but more mature and focused on getting his diploma and graduating.

He was assigned to a new advisor, Tim Spady, a sinewy Black man with a long, angular face and a fuzzy goatee. A graduate of Franklin & Marshall College, Tim had joined the school after teaching for a year at KIPP DuBois Collegiate Academy, a charter school with a vastly different pedagogy, culture, and disciplinary methods. On Ryan's first day, Tim wasn't sure about him—he walked in as though he ran the place. But he realized that Ryan was singularly focused on graduating. He wasn't loud or disruptive, and while he got along with the other students, he didn't seem to seek out new friendships.

As with the other students, he had to find an internship. Ryan did a day shadowing salespeople at Live In Color, a shoe store on Front Street, but he didn't enjoy it. He had a sudden idea. *What about a courtroom?* Judge Rayford Means popped into his head. He remembered how Means had run his courtroom—it was unconventional, and he had been kind enough to release George before the Christmas holiday. Matthew wasn't optimistic—students rarely managed to land internships related to criminal justice. Undeterred, Ryan caught the train to the Court of Common Pleas. Means's courtroom was teeming with attorneys, defendants, and their friends and family, so crammed that people were pressed against the walls. Ryan managed to squeeze through to the middle of a bench in the third row. He wasn't sure how or when he'd be able to speak with the judge or someone on his staff.

Before court got underway, Means scanned the crowd. "There's a lot of people," he said. "Let's start clearing them out." He asked the people in each row to stand up and state their name and purpose. Ryan mentally rehearsed his pitch. When his turn came, he was confident and direct. "Good morning, my name is Ryan Rivera," he began. "I'm a high school senior at El Centro de Estudiantes. I have to maintain an internship in order to graduate. I've been in your courtroom before, and I was wondering if I can be your intern." Means peered at him for a few seconds. "I'm going to send someone to speak to you."

Eventually, a clerk named Katie called to Ryan and told him he could start on Tuesday. Ryan was struck dumb. He ran to school to deliver the news to Matthew.

On his first Tuesday, Ryan chose a button-down shirt and khakis and took the El train to court. He was directed to sit in a section to the left of the judge and observe the hearings. He began to track the different responsibilities of the prosecutors, lawyers, and judicial staff: crier, coder, stenographer, and court officer. Before long, he was assisting with getting subpoenas signed and distributing plea colloquy to Means.

Means's courtroom was the first stop for cases in Southwest and West Philadelphia. It was designed to reduce the congestion of cases that flowed throughout the city. Only pleas and waiver trials were negotiated and litigated in his room. Cases with jury trials were transferred to another judge. Ryan was learning legal terminology and the punishment for certain crimes. He saw Means act as a fair judge, giving defendants breaks when he felt they were merited. As he watched the lawyers, listening to them defend their clients and argue their cases, Ryan began to think he might want to do that himself someday. Who could have imagined that he'd be working in the belly of the beast after all that he'd gone through?

* * *

GIANCARLOS CONSIDERED DOUG, his advisor, to be the closest thing to a father. In his late thirties, Doug was a veteran Black educator with cornrows and a graying beard. He taught mathematics and organized the school's robotics and Dark Knights chess teams. Doug was a de facto father figure to many of the students, especially the boys in single-parent homes.

Doug and Tim, Ryan's advisor, were outliers in the nationwide teaching force, where Black men comprised only 2 percent.[1] Their influence, even this far along in a student's education, could mean the difference between graduating and dropping out. Research found that for "persistently low-income" Black students, having at least one Black teacher in grades three to five slashed the chances of dropping out of high school by 39 percent and increased their interest in pursuing a four-year college degree by 19 percent (and 29 percent for boys).[2]

On the top floor of El Centro, Doug's classroom had long wooden tables, a row of desktop computers at the back, and banged-up wood floors. A radiant graffiti mural with the words "El Centro" painted in lime green, true blue, hot pink, and black hung above the whiteboard. Chess sets were stored in the closet, which also served as a makeshift recording studio. His roster had some of the most behaviorally challenged students in the school. He became a de facto father figure to many, especially the boys in single-parent homes. "You should be able to relate a little bit to the struggle that they see, because they're going to basically put you into the box of 'you don't really understand where I come from,'" he believed. The hardest part was teaching his students that while you can't "eat that book," you can "eat off of a degree for the rest of your life." Once you got buy-in, "then you have a soldier that will ride for education."

Giancarlos felt that Doug knew what it was like to walk in his shoes. In the mornings, he had to help his great-aunt with her morning routine: fetching her coffee and breakfast, making sure she took her insulin, and pulling down one side of her diaper so she could use the toilet. If he was running late, he would text Doug, who would mark his lateness as excused. When he was absent, Doug would check in—first by text and then by repeated phone calls until he made contact. This wasn't unusual.

Doug did the same with his other students, committed to pushing them on in their education. When they were trying to keep earning credits during pregnancy or bereavement leave, he would collect and drop off their schoolwork. When his student Marquan didn't have money for the laundromat, Doug did his laundry. When Marquan was hungry, Doug bought him food through Uber Eats and Grubhub. And he sometimes drove him to school.

Doug was an all-in-one teacher, social worker, and counselor. "That's OG Bobby Johnson right there," exclaimed Marquan of Doug. "He really understand me. He understand what we be having, what we be going on, so he just talk to me, try to keep me on the right track. He be telling me real life stuff, and the other teachers they ain't care. They just let me do what I want, but Doug and I with it. He the type that will pop up at your crib like 'yeah, come on school's on.'"

Neither Giancarlos, Ryan, Emmanuel, nor Marquan had fathers present in their lives. Doug had a sense of what that was like. His Irish-Scot mother, Kathleen, raised him and his two sisters, Kerry and Shana, in the Germantown neighborhood of Philadelphia on her public school teacher salary. When he was in fourth grade, Doug was playing a soccer match in Port Richmond. He slide-tackled an opposing player, who fell and got a few scrapes. He retaliated by calling Doug a "nigga." Doug knew it was a racial slur against Black people and ran to tell his mother: "He called us 'nigga.'" He thought she was Black like him, even though she had white skin. Kathleen told the coach, who made the boy apologize. She explained to Doug that she was different from him. Until then, she had tried to protect him from the cruel realities of racism.

His exceptional scores on the California Achievement Test got him admitted into Central High School. But lacking intrinsic motivation, he wandered listlessly from class to class, pouring his energy into playing the drums in hip-hop and classic rock bands with friends. During his junior year, Kathleen died from cervical cancer. Reeling from the loss of the most important person in his life, Doug somehow still managed to pass his classes.

Eventually, Doug's father reappeared in his life and helped him land a full scholarship to Claflin University, a historically Black university in South Carolina. "I took the street knowledge, and I married it with the academic," said Doug. And then he entered teaching to carry on the family tradition. His first gig was at Impact Services Corporation, a Kensington-based nonprofit founded in 1974 with the mission to "rekindle hope in the hearts of Philadelphians who have seen factories close, jobs disappear, and life chances dim." He taught GED classes in the Help Offenders to Work program for people who had been released from prison. Doug tried to enliven the hackneyed GED curriculum by introducing plays and books such as *Othello* by Shakespeare and *Native Son* by Richard Wright and showing films like *Once Upon a Time in America* and *City of God*. He stayed in adult education, but he'd notice his former students loitering on drug blocks or taking on menial, low-paying, backbreaking jobs—a similar fate as his future El Centro de Estudiantes students.

In his late twenties, Doug was burned out and wanted to try something new. He taught young children in South Korea, then math at an Afrocentric charter school back in Philadelphia, where the students called the teachers mama or baba, and he was affectionately known as Baba Ndirangu. He had been unemployed for several months before securing an advisor position at El Centro de Estudiantes. It was an ideal fit for his progressive teaching philosophy, an antithetical approach to traditional education, which he described as "Don't talk. Don't move. Don't speak. Fold your hands. Attend and obey."

With freedom over the curriculum and pedagogy, Doug used the city as the classroom. He brought his students to many of the same places his mother had taken him as a child: the Schuylkill Center for Environmental Education, the Kimmel Center, the Franklin Institute, and the Pennsylvania Horticultural Society. He worked to foster a reciprocal relationship with his students. "They're not something to be controlled and dominated. It's a two-way street . . . We believe in the maturity of the young people and I think that's why they're willing to learn. If you're coming in and you already think I'm a thug or I'm a killer or I'm a criminal, it's probably hard to teach me. If I'm coming in as a young man, a young lady, a young scholar, it's a little easier."

* * *

GIANCARLOS PULLED ON a crisp black suit and black-and-white striped tie. It was his second month at El Centro de Estudiantes, and for weeks, he had been trying to land an internship, working on his interpersonal skills and learning how to write résumés and ace interviews. He was preparing for Demonstration Day, where he would participate in a mock interview.

He strolled into the classroom that afternoon, confidently shaking hands with Francisco Cortes, the youth program manager at Galaei, telling himself to stay focused and keep smiling. But Giancarlos was distracted by a beige muscle car with tinted windows that he could see outside on Dauphin Street. Out of the corner of his eye, he spotted a hand emerging from the vehicle, holding a gun. Before he could move or even warn Francisco to duck, the sound of gunshots rang out. "Get down!" Giancarlos screamed. They instantly fell to the floor. When it was quiet, Giancarlos craned his neck to peek out of the window. Two bodies were splayed on the sidewalk. One of them was his friend Shawn, who had graduated from the school. The other was a man he didn't know; the police later identified him as Norman Fletcher.

JuDonn had also heard the shots and met up with Matthew at the school entrance. They dashed across the street, where friends of Shawn and Fletcher were hovering around the bodies. A friend of Fletcher's was sobbing as he held Fletcher's bloody head. Shawn, who was lying on his back, was drifting in and out of consciousness. JuDonn saw no blood, only that Shawn's sweatshirt was pocked with bullet holes. Shawn's friend Nasir, who had also attended the school, was crying and pleading, "You can't go. You got to stay awake."

As JuDonn was on the phone with 911, first responders tore down Dauphin. An ambulance took Fletcher to Temple University Hospital, whose trauma center treated the most gravely injured patients. Having suffered two gunshot wounds to the head and one to his left arm, Fletcher was pronounced dead at 2:13 p.m., less than an hour after the shooting.[3] Shawn had been thrown into the back of a police car and taken to Temple as well.

Giancarlos had kept his distance from the crime scene. Shaken, he started blowing up his friends' phones with the news about Shawn. To calm himself, he drank some water and ate a slice of pound cake from the corner store. About an hour later, he mustered the resolve to resume and pass the mock interview.

Resiliency specialists led discussion circles the next day to help the students process the shooting. Some of them said that their parents were rethinking the decision to send their kids to El Centro, while those who knew Shawn were visibly distressed—they hadn't received any updates about his condition. But for most of the school, it was a fairly normal day in North Philadelphia. Killings of friends and family who happened to be in the wrong place at the wrong time were something they were used to.

Eventually they heard that Shawn was in stable condition. Before heading home in the evening, JuDonn went to the hospital, bringing a light-gray Eagles sweatshirt and a copy of *Between the World and Me*, Ta-Nehisi Coates's raw, poetic letter to his teenage son. In the book, Coates argues that the education system and the streets are "arms of the same beast" where "those who failed in the schools justified their destruction in the streets." He continues, "The society could say, 'He should have stayed in school,' and then wash its hand of him.'"

To JuDonn, Shawn had been a success—he had graduated high school—yet he still got caught up in street violence. Shawn's mother waved him into the room ahead of visiting family and friends (*Who am I?* he thought. *I should have been last in line to see him*), where he found someone showing Shawn texts from people urging him to strike back at whoever had shot at him. JuDonn thought that Shawn, who seemed to be in excruciating pain, wasn't caught up in the prospect of vengeance. He hoped this would be a moment of reckoning for him.

18

...

He Is a Miracle

Emmanuel and Elisha were nursing cups of tea with honey and lemon from 7-Eleven as they stood in a long line that snaked around the Philadelphia Convention Center waiting to audition for *The Voice*. They were terribly nervous but determined to try out anyway, even though Elisha's nerves had led her to walk out of an audition a few years ago, and Emmanuel was insecure about singing in public. He had grown up watching *American Idol* and aspired to become a professional singer. In the apartment, they would sing Ariana Grande, Adele, Beyoncé, and Sam Smith together while he fixed chicken and rice for dinner. Maybe *The Voice* would be his ticket to fame.

After a few boring hours, Emmanuel and Elisha checked in and found their assigned prescreening room. There were two rows of chairs and a table at the front, where a white man with short blond hair and thin lips sat with a MacBook and a stack of paper. The other hopefuls represented a cross section of young Philadelphia: Black, white, Latino, and all along the gender spectrum. One by one, they were called up to stand on a taped white X on the carpeted floor, and sing for about a minute until the producer raised his hand to cut them off. Emmanuel was quite impressed with a woman who hit all the high notes in Whitney Houston's "I Have Nothing."

Elisha was torn between singing Beyoncé's "I Was Here" or Adele's "Hello." Adele's song had some difficult high notes, and she was ill-prepared and tired, having worked until midnight the night before. So she chose "I Was Here," and even though she was a little shaky at first, she felt by the end that she had hit her stride. Then it was Emmanuel's turn. He had been practicing "Who You Are" by Jessie J, a song that had got him through tough, weepy days. "I stare at my reflection in the mirror," went the lyrics. "Why am I doing this to myself? Losing my mind on a tiny error. I nearly left the real me on the shelf." The lyrics reminded him of feeling that he had to pretend his life and family were stable and not in utter turmoil.

But in the moment, anxiety took over, and Emmanuel switched to Bon Iver's indie rock song "Skinny Love." "Come on, skinny love, just last the year," he began. The producer raised his hand after a minute and a half. Emmanuel walked back to his seat, thinking he had done all right but probably not well enough to get a callback. Maybe he should have stuck with "Who You Are" or worn something more stylish than his shabby green sweater and beige pants.

When all the singers had finished auditioning, the producer made his announcement. "You're all awesome," he said, "but there are no call-backs." A few people started crying. Emmanuel felt disappointed as well; despite his doubts, he had hoped for a callback—it would be a validation of his singing and encourage him to devote more time and effort to it.

The winter sun was gleaming when they left the convention center, walking to a nearby McDonald's to get lunch. Emmanuel got four McChicken sandwiches off the dollar menu while Elisha got a meal with a double cheeseburger and fries. They sat in the restaurant and tried to cheer each other up by trash-talking the arbitrariness of reality TV singing shows. Elisha was shocked that the woman who'd sung Whitney Houston hadn't been called back. If she wasn't up to the show's standards, what on earth were they looking for?

* * *

TENSION HAD BEGUN to flare in the apartment. Emmanuel found himself getting into constant shouting matches with Hannah, arguing about

politics and racism. Hannah, who was white, didn't think white privilege was real. She hit back by demanding that Emmanuel either pay
her $300 a month in rent or get out. Worse, his mattress had deflated
after her cat clawed a hole in it, so he was left sleeping on the floor with
sheets.

Those conditions weren't worth plunking down hundreds of dollars, so Emmanuel talked to Deja Lynn Alvarez, who worked with the
Trans-Health Information Project at Galaei. She was also founder and
executive director of the LGBTQ Home for Hope, a homeless shelter
for LGBTQ people struggling with trauma, drug and substance abuse,
and mental health challenges. Emmanuel explained his situation to
her. If he wanted to move into the shelter, he had to stop using drugs,
she told him—she knew he smoked marijuana. Emmanuel agreed to
comply; he had nowhere else to go.

The shelter was housed in a four-story gray stone building on an
eerily desolate block in Kensington. Once the rectory for St. Bonaven-
ture Catholic Church, which closed in 1993 and was demolished in
2014, it later became a halfway house for formerly incarcerated women.
It sat across from the old church's school building and in eyeshot of the
Fair Hill Burial Ground, a historic Quaker cemetery established in 1703
that housed the remains of notable abolitionists and women's rights
activists such as Robert Purvis and Lucretia Mott.[1]

Emmanuel moved in one afternoon after school. His room was
on the third floor. When he walked in, he couldn't help but cry out,
"A bed!" It was his first real bed in years. And at that moment, he
had the huge room to himself. That first night, he slept better than he
had in years.

The shelter, which housed two to three dozen residents, provided
routine and structure. Every morning, they had to be up at 5:30 a.m.
for meditation, which began and ended with the Serenity Prayer. Since
he was a student, Emmanuel was usually excused from participating.
Then there were chores. Emmanuel, the youngest and one of the few
who weren't dealing with addiction, had to sweep, mop, and do laundry.
After a breakfast of eggs, sausage, oatmeal, and grits, he would shower,
get dressed, and catch the 39 bus to school.

He had been at the shelter for a month when a few single beds were moved into his room and four new roommates arrived. They groused that he got to skip morning meditation and pestered him for money. One day, someone stole his silver watch and $120 in cash from his dresser. After that, Emmanuel stored his valuables more carefully. Despite the theft, Emmanuel warmed up to the fellow residents. He became close friends with Lucas, a gay white man, who was addicted to methamphetamine. They would put on makeup together as Emmanuel got ready for school. He wore foundation, black eyeliner, layered eyeshadow—brown on the outside and pink on the lids with a tap of gold—and brown bronzer on his cheekbones, finishing the look with matte brown lipstick. He would have never felt comfortable wearing makeup at Esperanza, but at El Centro de Estudiantes, he got compliments from some of the girls— "Oooo your makeup is really cute"—and the shelter was a safe space for Emmanuel to explore the fringes of his gender identity.

He was surrounded by people who spanned the gender spectrum and rejected normative gender roles, people from broken homes or families who didn't accept them—people like him. On weekends, he watched some of the trans women vogueing in the dining room and occasionally joined in. They taught him Vogue Fem moves, such as the catwalk, duckwalk, and spins and dips. A few months into his stay, he was informally adopted by Jamila, a trans staff member who worked the night shift, and Tre, one of his roommates. "She's not just yo daughta, she's my daughta too," Jamila would say to Tre. Jamila, his gay motha, would save Emmanuel some dinner when he came home late and once took him to Dorney Park. Tre, his gay fatha, braided his hair and made sure it was neat for school. He also bought him ramen noodles, honey buns, and Day's Blue Pop soda.

Being in such a supportive queer community helped Emmanuel feel less alone. Nobody judged him. He barely thought about his mother or Freddie or his old home. After school, he participated in the Raíces de Cambio apprenticeship through the Norris Square Neighborhood Project, learning about urban agriculture from planting to harvesting tomatoes, lettuce, kale, and other vegetables. Toiling under the sun was physically demanding, but Emmanuel was glad to be shedding some of the weight he had accrued being confined to the house in Lippincott.

He also taught nutrition and cooking to other high school students. For this work, he earned $120 every other week.

When these activities were done, he'd hang out with his friend Esther, who lived near the shelter, until the 9 p.m. curfew. They occasionally popped Xanax and regularly smoked marijuana. The shelter residents were often urine tested, and his continued to come back positive. "We couldn't smoke weed, but we could smoke cancer," he complained. The staff gave him multiple warnings and advised him to enter rehab, but Alvarez knew that his circumstances warranted some leeway. Things were obviously better than they had been before, but he still suffered from chronic depression and the fear of what lay ahead, and the marijuana provided some solace.

* * *

RYAN's ADVISOR, TIM, gave him the surreal news: he was passing his classes and on track to graduate next month with a 2.20 grade point average. Ryan, holding back tears, paused to take it in. He had done it. He was going to be a high school graduate. It felt like the final stretch of the longest marathon of his life, a race in which he'd been repeatedly knocked down, doubting he'd ever cross the finish line. He hadn't thought much about what would happen after graduation, but he figured he could find a decent job with a diploma under his belt.

El Centro de Estudiantes's graduation was held in a large carpeted room with tall windows on the Temple University campus. Ryan, who had a new bushy goatee, was amped up. He was wearing a black gown over a red, yellow, and blue plaid shirt and navy pants with immaculate white sneakers—"ghetto fabulous," as he described himself. He brought along an entourage: Rayni, Yamilet, Tino, Armando, Amir's uncle Albert, his friend Drew, and law clerk Katie.

"It's been a bumpy trimester," Matthew told the more than two dozen graduating students, who were huddled together. "This group could have been quite a lot bigger, so I'm very proud of you for having made it. This group could have also been quite a lot smaller. Congratulations for having made it this far. I'm super proud of all of you. I'm very much looking forward to this. We have one of the best graduation traditions that I've ever seen. I'm happy to invite you into it and become part of our alumni family."

"What do you think of the sound of that?" a student poked fun. "Alumni."

"I was trying to figure out how to describe all of you as a group the other day, and I must admit a few cuss words came to mind," Nia, a staff member, said. "Frustration. I love these kids so much, but sometimes. And someone said spirited. I think it was JuDonn . . . All of you together and individually are so powerful. You're such an amazingly strong group. Your charisma, your charm, your intelligence, your, just, brazenness sometimes. The way you get out there and get things done."

She went on. "Those of you who were struggling to get to this point or said I wasn't going to come today and you showed up. Or people aren't here that you wanted to be here today. It's their loss if they didn't come by choice. If they aren't here and they couldn't prevent that, I'm sorry that they're not here for you, but know that your El Centro family is. And we will always love you as much as we do today. Come back and visit us. Don't be strangers. We want to make sure you're okay out there in the world."

JuDonn gave the formal address, pointing out that the students' efforts to graduate had upset all the dominant societal expectations for poor kids in their section of Philadelphia:

The dictionary defines magic as "the power of apparently influencing the course of events by using mysterious or supernatural forces." If we look at the course of events facing our young people in schools, in North Philadelphia, in the real world, if we're honest about that for a second, we see communities rooted in love, fragmented by a lack of safety, opportunities sapped by senseless violence and selfishness, 50 percent graduation rate, the list goes on.

The magic here in this room is in the conscious choice and action of young people in front of us. The choice to change the expected course of events that lay before them. The magic is in courageously re-enrolling in school after suffering the shame of being pushed or dropped out. The magic is in sitting in circles and sharing feelings, being vulnerable to strangers. The magic is in venturing out to organizations, businesses, and places in the city that are not often represented by young people in North Philly and demanding to have an opportunity to be engaged in the real world.

The magic is in resorting to resolution and putting fists aside. The magic is in seeking to change old and stifling behaviors to help someone new. The magic is in parents and other supporters putting their faith back in schools that they previously cast to the side. In teachers and other staff going above and beyond the call of duty to advise, coach, and support students to the finish line. This is the magic we have come to celebrate.

A few students spoke next. Ivanna read a poem and talked about dropping out of high school after her son was born before coming to El Centro, which gave her "a second chance."

Simona had once been told that she would never achieve her goals or be anyone in life. "I thought all teachers were cruel and selfish just like him," she said. Her teachers at El Centro were different. She thanked them for believing in her mission to get an education. "I think what that teacher told me," she triumphantly declared. "I kept that negativity with me, and I used it as my motivation. I thank him because look at where it got me now."

Then it was Ryan's turn.

Good afternoon. My name is Ryan Rivera. I started at El Centro in 2011. Man, I tell you that feels like a lifetime ago. I had a lot of family issues my first two years of school. I made some wrong decisions, and I left school. My mother had breast cancer in 2012, and I had my son in 2013. But El Centro has always been like a second home to me.

My first advisor-teacher ever was Mr. Andrew. Mr. Andrew has done a lot for me from teaching me how to drive to even renting me a tux so I could go to my first prom. He really had become like a father figure to me.

Coming back to school was hard for me. But I had to thank my principal: Mad Money sitting in the front. He really sat with me and made out a plan for me so I could come back and finish school. Without him, I wouldn't be here today.

Coming back to school in 2016 is when I met my second advisor-teacher Tim. Tim is a funny dude . . . Deep down inside, he wants to see us succeed in life. He will help you with anything you need as long as you put in the effort to better yourself. He's a great teacher, also a great mentor.

When I came to El Centro, I was just a young, immature kid. I never thought or had any idea that this school would mold me into the man I am today. I'm going to miss El Centro. I feel like I'm leaving my childhood home. I'm sad but, at the same time I'm happy. I never thought I'd get my high school diploma.

But here I stand before you today a high school graduate. I'm still going to visit El Centro on birthdays and holidays. It will always be my home. I also got to thank my mom, my girlfriend, my little brothers, my grandmom, my brothers that came today, everybody who supported me throughout my whole trials and tribulations of stopping school and starting school. We made it, baby!

Matthew closed out the ceremony with some words about tassels.

We have one last thing to do . . . What's the deal with the tassels? What's that for? . . . The tassels signify something, guys. The tassels signify wealth. The tassels signify richness . . . You have something that has given you wealth. That's your education. Nobody's going to take it from you. Now it's yours. To signify turning the page of this chapter of your life, take that tassel from right to left, and I'd like to introduce to you, the March Class of 2016!

* * *

FOR HIS FINAL project, Emmanuel interviewed students about their internships and goals and made a promotional video for the school that featured classroom scenes, student projects, prom, and a somber monologue. "I honestly don't know where I would be if I had never chosen to go to this school," he said. "I remember sitting on my couch and just being nobody and then I became a leader . . . I never once believed in myself until I attended El Centro, from getting good grades and making new friends. It's just a great experience. I came from a broken family, and I think I found mine at El Centro."

It had been an arduous seven months of homelessness, insecurity, cynicism, loneliness, and teetering on the edge of giving up, but he had made it. On the morning of his graduation—the school's third and final ceremony of the year—Emmanuel skipped breakfast and went over to his friend Ada's house to put on the black cap and gown. He thought of being curled up in the Lippincott house, a bisexual high school dropout at the apex of his depression.

The twenty-nine graduating students gathered around. Nia reassured them: "Know that you can always come home." Then Pamela, another staff member, asked them to repeat the words "I have a voice."

"I have a voice," they said, their voices booming louder with each repetition.

"I am powerful," she said. "I am powerful," they chanted back at her.

"I am a graduate."

"I am a graduate!"

As the graduating class filed in on the cue of "Pomp and Circumstance," Emmanuel spotted his mother in the audience and waved. He had invited her, and she'd assured him she'd be there for him, but he had no expectations because Freddie would rarely drive her anywhere. Ivette had made sure a friend would bring her. Emmanuel was glad she had come. They were still scarcely on speaking terms or ready to mend ties, so their reconciliation would have to wait.

JuDonn had a different message for this graduating class:

By crossing this stage today, you, the graduates, become something that in the words of my poet activist friend in Oakland named Bailey calls "dealers of hope." For someone sitting in the audience wondering if they had done a good enough job of parenting or mentoring or serving as a role model for you, today right here, right now, says yes.

For an advisor, a counselor, a principal even, wondering if the stress, long hours of seemingly endless setbacks, are worth it, today says yes.

For your kids, who are sitting in the audience and will one day wonder if their future is bright, today says yes.

For a random person walking down the sidewalk who sees you walking proudly with your diploma after you leave here and wondering if kids from North and West and South Philly are worthy of a second chance, today says yes.

For your friends who see your Facebook, Instagram, Snapchat, those friends who serve as the other 99 percent of out-of-school youth, the friends who wonder if getting back to school to make a difference in their own lives, to change and pursue a high school diploma for a second, third, fourth time, today says absolutely yes.

Emmanuel began his speech and then halted. "I'm sorry. I'm a little emotional today."

"Get it!" some students cheered him on. "Get it, Manny!"

Here I am, June 17th, 2016. I am excited and scared as I am about to receive my diploma. This journey has not been easy whatsoever. I remember laying in bed giving up. I was a dropout. I had no friends. I was heading towards a life of a statistic. I was ready to live off of public benefits. Something in me, something deep within me told me that I was capable of so much more. I was referred to El Centro by a friend who happened to be godsend. She told me that the school was perfect for teens who needed second chances. At first I was hesitant about attending. Fear trickled up and down my spine. I had terrible experiences at my old high schools. I always seemed to withdraw from my academics, continuously hitting the snooze button until I decided not to go to school that day.

El Centro was different. I woke up before my alarm. I was actively interested in the academic curriculum. And I was finally starting to blossom. I became a source of positivity, and I finally became a leader. My GPA went from a 1.0 to a 3.6. I became resilient. I really need to give my resilience a shoutout, because everyday was not easy for me. Depression, homelessness, doubt, and fear tried to get in the way of my education, but I did not allow it. My resilience brought me to school every morning. When I walked to school with tears running down my eyes because I hadn't eaten the day before. When I rushed to school in my bike on a snowy January day, and my fingers were numb to the touch, and I really wanted to give up, but I didn't allow myself.

El Centro made my problems evaporate into a thinness and truly became my home. Literally I never wanted to leave the building. If it wasn't for the kind and loving staff, I don't think I would have stayed. Teachers like Adriana, who become my second mother, really pushed me to reach higher goals and was always a shoulder to cry on. She even cried on my shoulder once. Or maybe it was the coolest principal in the world. Or the counselor that directs you to important opportunities. Maybe I stayed because all of the mentors I acquired through my LTIs: the Frans, the Jinays, the Sergios, and the entire Galaei staff. Without you guys, I would not be here. Maybe it was the friends I made along the way from the Adas to the Mollys to the Esthers. You really build a family and maybe rebuild a broken one, too.

I love my Honey Badgers! Congratulations to each and every one of my peers who are about to move forward to adulthood, and to the ones who are almost there, don't give up. You may be a small atom in the universe, shout out to Doug, but in our world your potential is bigger than a thousand stars.

Remember me as a resilient leader who defied gravity and stepped above all issues. Remember me as Handy Manny.[2]

It was time for the El Centro Award, given to one standout senior at each graduation. While the school commended students who achieved high grade point averages, Matthew said, "we also find a number of things to be more important: the ability to speak up for yourself, the ability to keep going when it gets hard, the ability to work with others, to grow . . . While all of you have showed these traits over the years, a number of you have stood out and one person in particular. So I'd like to call that person to the stage. Please give a round of applause to Emmanuel Coreano!"

"He has struggled so much," Ivette said after the ceremony. "He is a miracle."

Another Boy in a Box

Ana Caraballo woke up with a blinding migraine on the morning of November 7, which she interpreted as a bad omen. Joshua had fled the house again and was rooming with friends and girlfriends, at one point staying in an abandoned trailer. He called her in the early afternoon. "Mommy, can you pick me up? I'm going to take a bath." She met him on East Firth Street, a gritty block in the shadow of the soaring St. Michael's Lutheran Church in East Kensington.[1] At home, she tried to entice him to stay by offering to cook something, but he said he'd come back to eat later.

Shortly after 2 p.m., Ana reluctantly dropped Joshua off on Firth then went back home. As she walked through her front door, she got a call from his girlfriend, Crystal. Joshua had been shot in the head.

Minutes earlier, a man, Alexandro Doroshenko, had been smoking a cigarette while waiting for his ride when he saw Joshua arguing with Crystal and another girl down the block. Doroshenko walked over to intervene. Before long, a few kids joined in the melee, jumping Doroshenko and Joshua. Doroshenko returned to the Hilmarr Rubber Company, where he worked, and retrieved a 9mm handgun. Somebody yelled out that he had a gun. As children started to run, Doroshenko fired off three shots from a distance, hitting Joshua in the head. A contractor nearby found his body on the ground and called the police. They whisked him off to Temple University Hospital in the back of their squad car in a "scoop and run," saving precious minutes rather than waiting for emergency medical services.[2] Doroshenko was arrested.

Ana raced to the hospital where Joshua was being treated. Giancarlos and his friend Marcus stopped by his room in the trauma unit in the evening hours. Giancarlos began bawling when he saw his best friend hooked up to life support, with his head bandaged and his face severely bruised.

On the way over, Giancarlos had scrawled a short rap for him and recited it as Marcus and Joshua's family listened.

> K. I. T. O. That's my bro, my compadre, my amigo
> You used to eat the game up like some Cheetos
> How you gonna die but you didn't write a will
> We supposed to have each other. I got more love for you than I have
>   for my mother
> This ain't cool, bro. Get back up, so you can get back to your school
>   stuff
> So we can leave Philly and fall back on some cool stuff
> You can't leave me now because I ain't tryin' lose stuff

Joshua didn't pull through. As Ana struggled to grasp what had happened, she agreed to donate her son's organs. Sixteen-year-old Joshua Caraballo was "another boy in a box," as Senator Cory Booker put it, another victim of the killing fields of Philadelphia.[3] He was one of the city's 277 homicide victims in 2016.[4]

Joshua had been looking forward to starting El Centro de Estudiantes and turning his life around. He had recently visited the school, and JuDonn had noticed how animated he had become when they talked about potential music internships. He had a whole life ahead of him, with dreams of moving out of Philadelphia, going to college, helping children, and playing music, all stolen by the hotheaded actions of a man with a gun. In 2021, Doroshenko, after several years of refusing to cooperate with the prosecution, entered a guilty plea for voluntary manslaughter and was sentenced to nine to twenty years in prison.

"See where the deaths come quickest," political economist Henry George wrote in 1885. "See where it is that little children die like flies—it is in the poorer quarters."[5] The homicide epidemic was concentrated in the economically distressed Black and Latino neighborhoods of North and West Philadelphia, a consequence of poverty, unemployment, hypersegregation, and toxic masculinity—amplified by a surplus of readily available firearms.[6] "Because crime and violence are strongly correlated with income deprivation," sociologist Douglas Massey observed, "any social process that concentrates poverty also concentrates crime and violence to create an ecological niche characterized by a high risk of physical injury, violent death, and criminal victimization."[7]

> *You really gone man. . . . My Hype Man, My LeftHand, and my Lil Brother. They took you from me. . . . But I know your happy. I love you nigga Rs Ima see you another day just don't forget me.*
> —Giancarlos on Instagram

Like many of the neighborhood's dead children, Joshua was laid to rest at Guckin Funeral Mansion, a majestic, family-run funeral home in Kensington. Giancarlos began weeping when he saw Joshua's open casket topped with flowers and balloons; his head was covered with a blue beanie. Giancarlos felt that a part of his soul had been ripped out. Joshua's sister asked him if he would perform his rap again. As Giancarlos wiped his eyes, he faced his friend's lifeless body and croaked out a few lines. Another friend, Jonathan, comforted him, rubbing his back. (Two years later, Jonathan killed a man named Tevin Hill in a robbery that went wrong and was sentenced to forty-five to ninety years in state prison.[8]) After the funeral, Giancarlos and his friends hosted a small vigil, celebrating Joshua's life by smoking marijuana and getting drunk on one of his favorite libations, Christian Brothers Brandy.

In the weeks and months after Joshua's death, Giancarlos found the pain of losing his best friend unbearable, and he started popping Xanax.

He thought the pills would take away the misery, but he just felt a gaping void. He started skipping school, but each day he thought Doug would want him to be there. *You can't fuck this up.* Doug texted to see how he was doing and came over with a turkey hoagie from the corner store. He counseled Giancarlos that he was going to lose friends and family, but he couldn't let their deaths stop his pursuit of education.

In the end, it was the thought of Joshua that motivated Giancarlos to stay in school for the final months and graduate. He didn't want his failure to finish tied to losing his best friend. "He wasn't my blood brother, but blood wouldn't have made us any closer," Giancarlos said in his end-of-trimester exhibition. "Even though he's not physically with me, he helps me with his spirit." He did his final internship at Marsten House Recording, a studio where he learned how to make beats and mix. "Whenever I felt stressed or got too deep in my thoughts," he said, "I would go to the studio and release my stress with music." He would try to imagine Joshua beside him, rapping along.

For one of his projects, he applied what he had learned to "Slick Moves," a music video he created with a friend, which they filmed in Fairhill Square Park.

Slick moves made a trick loose
But don't do my moves if you can't fit these shoes
A bitch move get your shit blew
That's rule number one and rule number two
Grow in the hood and you do what you do, you do what you know, you
    say fuck the hoes, then go chase the gold.
Never stop it until you see a profit or your momma out of the projects
Damn, I said I'm earning to bag. Counting all the cash, I'm learning the
    math.
A couple of years later started teaching the class
The system got them thinking that the streets where it's at
Now we killing our own, that's why nowadays I'm just chasing the throne
I was always taught just to stick with what you know
I know myself and now I own my wealth

* * *

GIANCARLOS WOKE UP on graduation day with a mean hangover. He and Marcus had spent the night at a lounge, getting hammered with Hennessy and smoking blueberry mint- and watermelon-flavored hookah. He posted a photo of himself in his black gown and cap and Timberland boots, captioned: "Oh Yaw Ain't Know. They Ain't Wanna See Me Win #Graduated #Yak." It had taken three different schools, KCAPA, Penn Treaty, and El Centro de Estudiantes. Expelled from KCAPA, pushed out of Penn Treaty for his activism, he found a home, respect, and dignity at El Centro.

His mother, sister, Isabelesse, great-aunt, grandmother, and uncle were in the audience to hear Giancarlos's speech. He felt that Kito was with him, too, looking down with pride. "Always remember even if high school is over right now," he told the assembly, "your education is not yet finished. I want you to take your education to a new level and go educate yourselves on what you want to do in life and the goals you have set for yourselves . . . You did it. We made it. We are now high school graduates!" These weren't just words—Giancarlos was one of three El Centro students who had won a scholarship to Experiment in International Living, a program for high school students. He was off to Nicaragua and Cuba in a few days.

On the way home from graduation, Giancarlos asked Marta to pull up to KCAPA. He had Isabelesse take a photo of him standing on the sidewalk, giving the school the middle finger. "Fuck KCAPA fr they ain't do shit for my education," he posted. "#ElCentroAllDayBaby #TheyAintWannaSeeMeWin."

* * *

WITHIN A WEEK, Giancarlos was listening to an ex-Sandinista guerrilla fighter rhapsodize about the glory days of toppling the U.S.-backed Somoza dictatorship in Managua. Each day was filled with scavenger hunts and visits to cathedrals, art galleries, parks, and museums around Nicaragua. There were about two dozen youth on the trip, all girls except for Giancarlos and another boy.

He was chewing on boneless wings dipped in ranch at Buffalo Wings Nicaragua, a copycat of an American restaurant chain, in the Galerías

Santo Domingo mall in Managua, when he connected to Wi-Fi for the first time in days. His phone blew up with messages telling him about the death of TJ. This was an El Centro classmate, Timothy A. Michael Jr., a biracial twenty-year-old, who had been found lying between two parked cars on a street in Germantown in the early hours of a July morning. He succumbed to multiple gunshot wounds and was pronounced dead at Temple University Hospital.[9] Trying to escape the dangers of the city, TJ had been scheduled to fly the next day to Dubai to live with his mother and her fiancé.[10]

Giancarlos excused himself from the table. He walked blindly around the mall, crying. He'd known TJ since they played tee ball together in the neighborhood as kids. Another friend gone, just like that. He was still raw from mourning Joshua's death. This trip was supposed to be an escape from the chaos and bullshit of Philadelphia. He'd been unwinding, eating great food, and generally enjoying himself. News of TJ's murder jolted him back to his real world.

Giancarlos returned to the table. He told the staff what he'd heard and asked if he could go back to the hotel. Over the next two days, he processed the tragedy alone, smoking and guzzling bottles of beer. He couldn't have articulated it, but the constant blows of losing friends to gun violence had desensitized him. Otherwise, the pain would have been intolerable.

He tried to remind himself that this was his trip; it wasn't every day that he would get the chance to explore a foreign country. TJ would have wanted him to enjoy himself. In one of the group's evening chats, he explained that he was grieving the death of a childhood friend. Two Black girls who lived in urban neighborhoods understood, but the others didn't really register what he was going through; they had grown up in a very different world.

Talking to one of the girls, Stephanie, a wealthy Latina, Giancarlos was explaining how to make Chi chi noodles—a penitentiary delicacy of crushed ramen noodles, cheese curls, beef sticks, and green peppers mixed in a plastic bag with steaming water. The final product looked something like Hamburger Helper. Stephanie, who thought it sounded disgusting, called it a "struggle meal."

"You wouldn't survive a day in my shoes," Giancarlos told her, frustrated. He tried to explain the basics of class stratification using a pyramid. There's "a little piece cut at the top for the high class, some space in the middle, and then a big space for the low income." His time at YUC had helped him see that income and wealth inequality were largely by design. "They don't want us to climb that ladder," he said. "The more people who don't got no money, it's better for the people at the top. More money in their pockets." He'd once dreamed of being a millionaire, but his view had changed. "I don't know if I want to be a millionaire if I can't make others millionaires. It would kill me to see people struggling if I got there."

* * *

TJ WAS THE third El Centro de Estudiantes student to die that year. His death was preceded by the murder of two brothers, Symir and Raheem, both in their early twenties.[11] They had been friends with Ryan during his first tour of the school, but they hadn't kept in touch. He'd lost count of the number of funerals he'd attended. "Niggas die every day," he said. "Niggas get shot every day." He had resigned himself to the situation that violence and premature death were a fact of his life.

Following the string of losses, TJ's death was devastating for JuDonn. He remembered TJ at his graduation, declaiming his grand plans for the future, counting on his fingers all the cars and houses he would own. It made him wonder whether his work had any tangible value. "If a high school diploma can't protect you from the streets, how important is our work really?" he asked. "We got to the proverbial finish line, at least for us, and it still wasn't enough. It forces you to think critically about the reality of what education is for young people who are living in deep poverty in underserved communities. It's not just this piece of paper. We've got to be real with ourselves. Your diploma does not immediately change your day-to-day surroundings. It has the potential to, but in the immediate, it's not going to do that for our young people."

Since founding El Centro de Estudiantes, David Bromley had come to see that he had sorely underestimated the effect of North Philadelphia's abysmal social and economic conditions on the school's students.

Unlike the students at his first Big Picture Learning school, MetWest in Oakland, virtually all of the El Centro population lived in poverty—more often, deep poverty—and faced homelessness, evictions, teenage pregnancy, sexual, physical, and anti-LGBTQ violence, involvement in the drug trade, incarceration, hunger, and extraordinary loss. They also often entered with elementary or middle school levels of reading and mathematics—huge formal learning challenges that were hard to address. How much growth was really feasible within two or three years, even assuming that the student was fully invested and didn't get derailed by circumstances? Educators were essentially performing triage, and few of their charges—a quarter to a third, depending on the year—pulled through to graduation.

* * *

AFTER A VISIT to the colonial city of León, Giancarlos and the group were taken by bus to El Lagartillo, a rural village set in luscious, rolling mountains where they stayed with host families. Giancarlos was placed with a couple who lived in a gray clay and brick home with two bedrooms, a wood-burning brick stove, and an outdoor latrine. He slept in their son's bedroom, which had mosquito netting over the bed. In the mornings, he'd hit the walls with sticks to scatter the big black spiders that came in through a gap between the roof and wall. His host mother fed him eggs, rice, beans, chicken, juice, and freshly made bread.

During their weeklong stay, Giancarlos and the group had daily Spanish-language classes in the community garden and learned about the area's history. They saw a memorial to the people killed defending the community from the Contras, the right-wing group armed and financed by the U.S. government.[12]

From Nicaragua, they flew to Havana. Giancarlos had talked about the trip to his Cuban grandfather, Vincente, who had immigrated to Florida as a child. But he hadn't spoken to his family in years and didn't know who was alive. Yet Giancarlos had dreamed of visiting the motherland. He spent the days there wandering the streets, hanging at the beach, visiting museums and landmarks, watching capoeira performances, and relishing the local food—his favorite dish was steak with peppers and grilled shrimp. He was browsing the shirts in a store when a young woman approached him. She knew he was from America, she said, and asked for money. Giancarlos said he didn't have any. "Not everybody's rich in America," he told her, and then took out his phone and found a video of people injecting needles in their arms and nodding off in Kensington.

"Why do they look like that?" the girl asked in horror. "Drugs," he replied.

* * *

BACK IN PHILADELPHIA, Giancarlos felt a rush of stress. First, his girlfriend, Veronica, confessed that she had cheated on him, a devastating blow since they had talked about having a baby. And Giancarlos had nipped his itch to hook up with women in Nicaragua and Cuba. Then his mother said he had to contribute to the family finances now that high school was over.

He got a job with the city's Parks and Recreation department, picking up trash, emptying bins, and clearing pathways for $12.75 an hour. He had been selling marijuana before the trip and restarted. His corner had been raided a few times when he was away. The new junta of dealers who had been brought in had failed to follow protocol: hide the drugs in the nearby stash and carry only a small quantity to avoid charges in the event of a bust. Instead, they got cocky and stowed the bundles in their fanny packs, making them easy targets.

Giancarlos was on the corner when he saw a short, light-skinned girl with long black hair pushing a stroller. As she hugged one of his friends, Giancarlos called out, "Hey, how you doing?" She smiled and continued walking. Her name was Jennifer. He looked up her Instagram profile and decided to shoot his shot—send her a message. She didn't answer until Isabelesse texted her that he was her brother. Jennifer's younger brother had gone to school with Isabelesse. Jennifer was fresh out of a long-term relationship with her son's father, and she and Giancarlos started dating.

Born to an Irish mother and a Puerto Rican father, she'd had a rough childhood: stints in a group home and with several foster families before getting expelled from KCAPA and evicted from her home. She floated from house to house of friends and family, growing used to living out of a backpack. Eventually, she got into a relationship with Camilo, and they had a son, Felix.

Jennifer's father's dying wish had been for her to graduate high school. After KCAPA, she tried Agora Cyber Charter School, but the "chalk and talk" mode of learning didn't suit her, and she couldn't afford the Internet bill. In a Google search, she came across YouthBuild Charter, a yearlong school for dropouts. In her mind, she ran a cost-benefit analysis: Can I manage caring for my baby while attending school? Am I forfeiting time and income by giving school another go?

At YouthBuild, she found she was just one of many young parents. The teachers recognized that she was a mother first and a student second, juggling an array of responsibilities on top of school. She enrolled in the health care track and obtained home health aide and CPR certifications. The hands-on approach to learning didn't feel like school. *It was just everyday life*, she thought. Six years after entering ninth grade at KCAPA, she fulfilled her father's dream.

By the time Jennifer and Giancarlos got together, she was staying with her aunt in Kensington. She'd recently left a $10.50 hourly job unboxing shipments at an Old Navy store in North Philadelphia. Her male co-worker was grabbing her butt and hitting her with a broomstick, and her manager refused to shuffle her work schedule, so she quit.

One Sunday, Jennifer's friend Astrid was driving her to her aunt's house. She and Giancarlos were taking a break after she found out he was still talking to his ex-girlfriend Veronica. As they approached the intersection of Second and Norris Streets, Astrid slammed on the brakes to avoid hitting the police car idling in front of them. Jennifer wasn't wearing a seat belt, and her head smashed against the windshield.

As they drove off, Jennifer asked, "Hey, you always had a crack in your windshield? I never noticed that before."

"No, you OK?" Astrid replied.

"I don't feel nothing," said Jennifer. Her head felt fine. No bruises or swelling.

Later, Jennifer noticed blood in her urine and had her friend ferry her to the hospital. She learned that she was seven weeks pregnant—she and Giancarlos had not wasted time—and had suffered a miscarriage. She wasn't too upset. She accepted the loss, figuring it was in God's hands. When Giancarlos found out, it brought them back together. He saw the miscarriage as a message from God: Sometimes you're ready to have a kid. Sometimes you're not.

March for Our Lives

On the Friday ahead of the Super Bowl, Giancarlos was hanging out with his uncle Leo, his uncle's girlfriend, Madeline, and a cousin, Marissa. They were watching *The Avengers* and hotboxing in Leo's white Lincoln, parked on a quiet Kensington street. Giancarlos was taking a drag when several vehicles drew up and boxed them in. Police officers leaped out of their cars and drew their guns. *Get the fuck out of the car! Put your hands on the ground!*

All Giancarlos could think was, *Don't shoot. Don't shoot.* The officers cuffed them. Giancarlos ended up getting stuffed in one of their cars. "You have to let me go," he insisted. "I have half a dub." The police found a few tubes of marijuana, but he said he was smoking, not selling.

"You're not going anywhere," the officer said. "We found pills in the back seat." They'd found $300 on Leo, along with a pink tube of marijuana and nearly five hundred blue Xanax pills in his seat pocket and more weed and money on Marissa. Giancarlos knew the pills were his uncle's and thought the trap was so precise and perfectly timed that it must have been orchestrated. A white police officer, Jason Seigafuse, had been sitting in his car behind the Lincoln, watching for a while before calling for backup.

Giancarlos didn't want to go to real jail. More important, he had to watch the Super Bowl. The Philadelphia Eagles were playing the New England Patriots. He had a hunch that the juvenile detention center would be showing the game. So when he arrived at the 24th/25th District, he lied about his birthday, claiming he was seventeen, not an adult.

Sitting in the cell, he recognized an officer walking by and tapped on the window to get her attention.

"Aren't you Giancarlos?" She knew his mother. "Boy, what you got into now?"

"They grabbed me over something with my uncle," he said. "I need you to help me to get out. I was just chilling smoking with him. Can they keep me here if I'm a youth?"

She said that as a juvenile, he'd be taken to the Juvenile Justice Services Center, the city's gleaming new $110 million detention center that had replaced the Youth Study Center.

At home, Jennifer heard Giancarlos's grandmother rush into the house screaming, "They took them!" She rushed outside and saw that the doors of the Lincoln were open. The key was in the ignition, and their phones were on the seats. And there was a stub of a blunt on the floor. At first she thought her ex, Camilo, had called the cops on them. Earlier that day, he and Giancarlos were arguing, and Jennifer was supposed to fight Camilo's girlfriend because she'd been running her mouth, saying Jennifer was a bad mother.

"You wanna smoke it?" Jennifer asked Luna. They polished off the remaining stub of the blunt.

* * *

Two officers drove Giancarlos over to the JJSC in West Philadelphia, where a guard put him in hand and leg cuffs. He was irritated. Where did they think he was going to run? The first order of business was taking a shower. Giancarlos insisted that he be given clothes fresh out of the pack. He inspected the underwear, blue short-sleeve shirt, and stretchy blue pants. The garments appeared clean, so he slipped them on.

He managed to call his mother, coaching her what to say and not to reveal his real age. He asked her to let Jennifer know that he was doing okay. When he was brought to his cell, he saw the TVs in the common room and heaved a sigh of relief. His cellmate was already asleep. In the morning, Giancarlos scarfed down scrambled eggs and toast and was transported by van to Glen Mills Schools, a juvenile placement in Delaware County, Pennsylvania. He was awed by the amenities: basketball courts, an indoor running track, and weight machines. He joined a group of boys playing *Madden NFL* and *NBA 2K* on a PlayStation to kill the time until dinner.

His stomach was flaring up, probably from anxiety, so he refused dinner. His first real meal in more than twenty-four hours was breakfast the next morning—the day of the Super Bowl. His master plan had worked. He talked to Jennifer and his mother on the phone. "You just need to worry about you and not doing the dumb shit when you come home," Marta said. She'd been notified about his hearing the next day. Giancarlos said a boy at Glen Mills had advised him to tell his counsel his real age. Otherwise, he might end up having to do extended time in a juvenile facility.

The boys in Glen Mills gathered around the screen to watch the Super Bowl, eating cheese pizza with Tastykake Chocolate Cupcakes and Koffee Kake Juniors. When the first quarter started, Giancarlos snuck out to take a quick shower. He wanted to avoid the two boys who were known for pouring body wash above the curtains to muck up people's eyes.

After a last-second Hail Mary by Patriots quarterback Tom Brady flopped, the Eagles were crowned Super Bowl champions, the first time in the team's history. The boys went berserk, punching at the walls and chasing each other. Giancarlos ran back to his dorm so he wouldn't be there when the guards broke up the ruckus.

* * *

FOR THE HEARING, two guards transported Giancarlos back to JJSC. He asked them what would happen now. Either you're coming back here or you're going home, they said. In the courtroom, Marta greeted him with a hug and a peck on the cheek. He confessed his real age to the public defender, but despite his lie, the hearing went quickly. The judge said he could be thrown in jail for falsifying his age and not to do it again before he was remanded to the adult system for reprocessing.

For the rest of the day, Giancarlos sat on a cold metal bench. He was given cheese sandwiches and bottles of water, but the sandwich tasted rotten when he bit into it. So he wrapped the sandwiches with toilet paper to fashion a pillow. Another inmate was yelling, banging on the walls, and pacing back and forth; Giancarlos assumed he was high—possibly on K2. Other guys yelled back for making too much noise. "Chill out; you're loud as shit!" Giancarlos began to wonder whether watching the Super Bowl had really been worth it.

Early on Tuesday, Giancarlos was woken up and taken to another room. His mother, who was streaming in, and a magistrate judge appeared on the split-screen television. The judge outlined the charges against him: selling and possessing illegal drugs and conspiracy. He decided to release Giancarlos on unsecured bail—he was a first-time offender. "Mom, you can go pick him up," the judge said, wrapping up the proceedings.

"Next time you get locked up, don't call me," Marta snarled as they drove home in the dead of night. "If this is the lifestyle you're choosing, don't be bringing me into it."

At the sight of him, Jennifer started crying. He told her how much he had missed her, then he took a beeline for the kitchen. When pizza rolls and an egg and cheese sandwich failed to sate his hunger, he had his brother Frank drive him to Max's Steaks, an iconic Philadelphia eatery.

Tearing into a cheesesteak, Giancarlos said he was planning to propose to Jennifer. "Be careful," Frank advised. "Don't rush into things. You have your whole life ahead of you."

"I've lived a lot," Giancarlos replied. His mind was made up.

Jennifer had been a nervous wreck while he was in custody. Home from his cheesesteak, he talked to her. "When stuff like this happens, I really need you to help my family more," he said. "I need you to be their backbone. You gotta hold it down if I'm ever gone. God forbid if I had been in there longer."

"I didn't know how to handle it because you hadn't been doing nothing," Jennifer replied.

"Well, put this on," Giancarlos said. He got down on one knee and pulled out a gold ring with two fake diamonds. "The reason I'm giving you this is because I want to be with you." Tearing up, Jennifer said yes.

* * *

GIANCARLOS CAUGHT HIS case in the second month of Larry Krasner's tenure as Philadelphia district attorney. Krasner, a civil rights attorney of more than three decades, had been elected in 2017 with a mandate to end mass incarceration in one of the most incarcerated cities in the country. He promised to eliminate cash bail for nonviolent offenses, curb the practice of prosecuting juveniles as adults, refuse to seek the death penalty, expand diversion programs for drug offenses, and crack down on police misconduct and abuse.[1]

In a memo, he instructed prosecutors to decline prosecuting possession of marijuana cases of any amount and some prostitution cases against sex workers. He also instructed them to divert some illegal gun possession cases, and seek shorter probation sentences. "Pennsylvania's and Philadelphia's over-incarceration have bankrupted investment in policing, public education, medical treatment of addiction, job training and economic development—which prevent crime more effectively than money invested in corrections," Krasner wrote. "Over-incarceration also tears the fabric of defendants' familial and work relationships that tend to rehabilitate defendants who are open to rehabilitation and thereby prevent crime. As a result, a return to lower rates of incarceration for those defendants who do not require lengthy sentences is necessary in order to shift resources to crime prevention." At sentencing hearings, he told prosecutors to state their rationale for recommending a particular sentence and the specific benefits and costs, including the economic burden on the public. He emphasized that it cost $60,000 a year to imprison someone in the city's correctional system, on par with the annual salary of a teacher, police officer, firefighter, or social worker.[2]

Krasner later announced that he would eliminate cash bail for twenty-five nonviolent offenses. "We don't imprison the poor in the United States for the so-called crime of poverty."[3] Following an ongoing trend, the jail population fell by 9 percent in Krasner's first hundred days and continued to fall in his first term.[4] In a city once ruled by Frank Rizzo, dubbed "The General" by the police, and Lynne Abraham, known as the "Deadliest D.A." or the "Queen of Death" for pursuing the death penalty more than any prosecutor in the nation, Krasner was preparing to take a machete to the heart of the carceral beast. He intended to reverse decades of criminal justice policies that targeted low-income people and people of color and reimagine public safety based on justice, fairness, and dignity.[5]

* * *

ON A FRIGID March morning, some two dozen El Centro de Estudiantes students, educators, and counselors convened in a garden across the street from the school, steps from where Shawn and Fletcher had been killed two years earlier. They walked out to commemorate the one-month anniversary of the shooting at Marjory Stoneman Douglas High School in Parkland, Florida, which left fourteen students and three staff dead. The surviving students had channeled their mourning into taking on the gun lobby—the National Rifle Association and their bought-and-paid-for politicians—by demanding the passage of gun control measures to stop school shootings and gun violence. The moral clarity of the mostly white teenagers in the face of government inaction catapulted them into the national limelight, attracting the backing of celebrities and hauling in millions of dollars for their cause.

Some scholars and organizers pointed out a double standard. African American and Latino youth who had raised the issue in their urban communities for decades had been ignored by the glossy magazines and passed over for the financial contributions given to the Parkland students. As one columnist put it, "Black youth, who've been passionately advocating for gun control measures, have been demonized, obfuscated, and overlooked."[6]

The Trump administration endorsed arming teachers and installing more police officers in schools, which was already the norm in many urban schools for Black and Latino youth.[7] The underlying assumption, noted Mari Morales-Williams, an advisor at El Centro de Estudiantes, was that children need to be policed and controlled to be kept safe. "We know historically that's how Trayvon Martin passed," she said, "how Mike Brown passed, how Aiyana Stanley-Jones passed, how Rekia Boyd passed." She called for listening to students in the city agitating for more social workers, mental health services, and restorative justice and for educational spaces to feel safe and nurturing. The most vulnerable youth, in particular, often attend "schools that don't see them."

Two students read the names of the seventeen dead in Parkland, and Morales-Williams invited those gathered to name people in their lives who had been lost to gun violence. Five names were offered. Afterward, the group took the El to the school district headquarters, where they joined other students from the city.

The hundreds of students had come prepared with signs: "Shoot Your Shot Not Your Classmates," "There Should Be a Background Check B4 the NRA Can Buy Senators," and "Less Guns. Less Deaths. More Chance." Superintendent William Hite had approved the seventeen-minute walkout so that students wouldn't be disciplined.[8]

Surrounding the sound system, a lineup of students broadened the protest beyond school shootings to criminalization in their schools and neighborhoods. Nyla Brooks said, "I'm sick and tired of not being able to go to the store and I want a water and they're shooting down the block. I'm tired of being scared to have to go to practice after school and it's dark and I might get mistaken for somebody else."

Jahyad Thomas-Thorton said that police violence is gun violence, too. "I shouldn't have to fear for my sister's life, my brother's life, any of my friends' lives. Little innocent kids being victimized by cops." Before setting out to march, they recited Assata Shakur's chant: "It is our duty to fight for our freedom. It is our duty to win. We must love each other and support each other. We have nothing to lose but our chains."

Outside city hall, the rally featured, among others, Helen Gym, activist turned city councilwoman. Before the boisterous crowd, Gym gave a fiery speech imploring young people to use their power to demand transformative change: "It means that we get rid of the surveillance cameras, the police officers, and the metal detectors, and you put back in the social workers, the nurses, and counselors that every child deserves. It means when there's tragedy that hits one of our schools, you don't go out and tell young people to ignore it, or to buck up, or get back to work, you help heal them. We give space to talk about our pain, to figure our solutions, and we learn to love each other. That's what this movement is all about."

*   *   *

EMMANUEL WAS BRONZED after hours of gardening in Las Parcelas, a community garden in West Kensington, and was resting on a bench near the Wall of Community Heroes mural. Designed by artist Jane Golden, it featured portraits of the members of Grupo Motivos, a group of local Latina women who were the architects of the community gardens.[9]

In the 1980s and '90s, with the support of the Norris Square Neighborhood Project, Iris Brown, Tomasita Romero, and more than two dozen women did the painstaking work of clearing out vacant lots and planting several gardens. Many of the women had lost family to the drug trade. "It was an incredible group of women," said Brown. "It was a friendship that became a family of women. We were doing the impossible." Each garden was a classroom, Brown explained, designed to prompt conversations and pay tribute to the history of Puerto Rico. There was a children's garden, one honoring the indigenous Taino people, and another that showed the West African influence on Puerto Rican culture, music, and art. They grew beans, sweet potatoes, cucumbers, yuca, okra, pigeon peas, tomatoes, and chili peppers. Some of the food was sold in a nearby farmer's market or donated to the St. Francis Inn soup kitchen in Kensington.[10] As Brown once put it, "Gardening is what I can do for children. I can't patch their broken families. I can't give them schools that work. I can't even promise them that if they do finish school they'll get a job. But I can help them grow a garden. They can feel safe in it. They can enjoy its flowers and eat its fruits. That I can promise and deliver."

Emmanuel had done a few different jobs before getting this current position as garden coordinator at NSNP. They had also changed their name to Corem and adopted they/them pronouns, embracing their gender fluidity. It had been a torturous journey until Corem had found peace and solidarity in queer spaces as their devotion to Christianity faded away. They still believed in a higher power, but not "a higher power that believes my existence is an abomination," they said.

After leaving the shelter, their housing situation became erratic, temporarily staying at NSNP or with friends. Housing had always been the toughest nut to crack and Corem's greatest source of anxiety. Now, they were living with a roommate in an apartment in West Philadelphia, the rent covered by Valley Youth House's Pride program. Knowing they had a home where they could eat, sing, shower, and sleep was both liberating and conflicting. "So even though I'm in this stable place," said Corem, "it still feels like I could lose it at any second. Anything could go wrong and I could lose my housing. That's kind of just the residual trauma that's lingered from before in my past experiences. But I'm also not afraid of losing housing and being like, okay, I lost housing once, and I can live through this again."

Corem was hoping to enroll in the Community College of Philadelphia, a goal since graduating high school. The supervisor at NSNP had advised that the tuition would be waived, but Corem was skeptical. The government had done so little when they and Ivette were on their knees. It had failed them in too many ways to count. Why would this time be any different?

Still, Corem filled out a Free Application for Federal Student Aid and submitted a letter to CCP explaining why they should qualify for a dependency override. Corem noted that they had been self-supporting and separated from their parents for a few years. Corem wrote about Ivette and Ivan's split, about Ivette living in poverty, about learning of Ivan's death only when they had an eye exam and the examiner happened to be a distant cousin. The news had made Corem feel sad; there had always been a small hope that perhaps they would reunite one day.

"Growing up I faced extreme poverty and harsh living conditions," Corem continued. The family's home on Lippincott Street, where Ivette still lived, "is in a deteriorated condition and my mother lacks the necessary money to pay the bills like gas, electric and water. There were many winters where I was forced to take cold showers in a home that was 39 degrees. The house is infected by trash, insects, covered in mold and completely unsafe to reside in." Corem closed by describing running away from home, being serially homeless, and then succeeding in finding employment and housing.

On the day Corem heard they had been awarded a full ride to CCP, they hardly knew where to put their joy. Corem was going to college. It was actually happening. As a homeless student, Corem was given a Pell Grant of $6,095, which would cover tuition and fees, books, supplies, and some housing costs. They took out a student loan of $3,500 to cover the rest of the rent, groceries, and other expenses. Corem would soon move into a house in North Philadelphia with three roommates. The nation was investing in their future.

* * *

OFFICER JASON SEIGAFUSE of the 26th District began his testimony in the preliminary hearing of Giancarlos and his uncle Leo's drug cases in Judge Marissa Brumbach's courtroom. Giancarlos wore a red Nike T-shirt and black Adidas sweats—if he'd felt guilty, he would have dressed in a suit. Just before court, he had vomited the previous night's dinner of a Crispy Chicken sandwich and Whopper burger. Jennifer was pregnant, presumably the result of his birthday festivities, and he seemed to be suffering from sympathetic morning sickness. Neither of them believed in abortion, and familiar with the challenges of single-parent households, they wanted the child to grow up with both parents. The pregnancy had raised the stakes in his case.

Officer Seigafuse recalled that at 7:45 p.m. on the day of the arrest, a white man approached the corner, and Giancarlos, who was sitting in the front passenger seat, got out and handed him a purple tube. According to Giancarlos, the man had rolled up marijuana for him in the past, and this was his way of returning the favor; there was no exchange of money. Fifteen minutes later, Seigafuse said, a yellow Ford Focus drove up and parked across the street. Another man walked to the driver's side, where Marissa was sitting, and she exchanged pink tubes for cash, he said.

Finally, in exchange for cash, Seigafuse said, Giancarlos gave a third man a purple tube that was later determined to hold marijuana (Giancarlos denied this).

"Where were you parked?" asked Zak Goldstein, Giancarlos's lanky, bespectacled lawyer.

"Immediately behind the Lincoln," Seigafuse answered.

"When you say immediately, how far is that?"

"There was no vehicle between myself and the vehicle," replied Seigafuse.

Goldstein directed a volley of questions at Seigafuse, who acknowledged that Giancarlos had no money on him at the time of the arrest. Seigafuse also confirmed that he couldn't hear or see activities inside the car. He had lost sight of the alleged buyers before they were arrested. And he hadn't taken any photos or videos.

Leo's lawyer, Richard Giuliani, was up next. He argued that the evidence indicated that none of the transactions involved his client. His culpability was limited to him holding money and that the car was registered under his name. He continued, "He's sitting in the back seat of the car where there are drugs found in a common area close by him, as well as two other people. That is not enough. Had he been doing something else, if there was other activity, accepting money, handing something out of the window, getting out of the car, speaking to alleged buyers, then they've made their case. They haven't made their case out based on this evidence and I would ask for a discharge."

Goldstein stated there was no evidence that Giancarlos was selling pills and requested that he be remanded on the count of possession with intent to deliver marijuana to municipal court.

Alexandra McNulty, legal intern for the District Attorney's Office, rebutted that the officer testified to observing individuals in the car sell marijuana to various customers and the large volume of pills was beyond reasonable personal use and signified that Leo had intent to deliver. "The two defendants were both recovered with money on them and you can make a reasonable inference that they were all working together to make these drug transactions," she said.

"My client did not have any money on him," interjected Goldstein.

Brumbach announced that she was dismissing the charge of conspiracy and possession with intent to deliver for both defendants. In August, Giancarlos and Leo had another court date for their possession charges. Through Pennsylvania's Section 17 drug diversion program, Giancarlos pled no-contest for the Intentional Possession of a Controlled Substance by Person Not Registered offense. He was sentenced to probation for one year and ordered to pay $782.94 in court fees. Leo, who had a vast criminal record, was found guilty on the same offense plus possession of marijuana. Both he and Giancarlos's cousin Marissa entered diversion programs—in line with District Attorney Krasner's agenda.

Giancarlos was delighted that he had avoided jail time, and probation would be a cinch. Every two months, he had to call a MonitorConnect line and answer an assortment of questions: "What's your Social Security number? Have you been going to work? Have you been paying your restitution? Do you want to kill yourself?" This was followed by a confirmation code and the date of his next call. And no urine tests meant he could still blaze.

*　*　*

Too often El Centro de Estudiantes students graduated without a plan or any notion of filling out a FAFSA form. Some went off to community colleges or trade schools. With sizable learning gaps, they frequently had to take remedial courses. They usually had to work long hours to cover rent, food, child care, and other essentials. With these academic and economic barriers, they rarely completed their degrees. The majority of graduates entered the labor market, working in low-wage service jobs at fast-food restaurants and retail stores, home health care, and automotive, construction, and other forms of manual labor. Others fell into the local drug economy, which often led to incarceration.

After graduating, Ryan worked as a security guard at Temple University, which was followed by a stint as a peer recovery specialist in the same drug treatment program where he had once been a participant. It gave him a stable flow of income for the first time. But he was still committed to joining the police force. Once he turned twenty-one, he applied to the Philadelphia Police Academy, but learned, before taking the police academy exams, that his criminal record made him ineligible. Ryan was shattered. It was all he ever wanted to be. What was he supposed to do now?

He tried to move on, but he couldn't shake the disappointment. And then his fortunes flipped. He had kept in touch with Judge Rayford Means since his El Centro internship. Means called to say that there was an opening on his staff, a personal assistant position, and he wanted to hire Ryan.

"For real, Judge? Don't play with me," Ryan said. There was a time when he couldn't have imagined living beyond twenty-one, let alone having a well-paying professional job. He should have either been incarcerated or dead. Okay, he wouldn't be a police officer, but he felt he had made it out of Kensington.

*   *   *

RYAN WAS BACK at El Centro de Estudiantes, running a student-police forum. He organized events like this through the Philadelphia Disproportionate Minority Contact Working Group, with the goal of breaking the ice between youth and police officers so that the two groups had a better understanding of each other.

The students were deep into a discussion about talking to the police. A few of them said they would never voluntarily speak with a cop. "What I've seen on the news, what I hear, I'm not going to talk to a police," one boy said. "I'm not trying to be in that predicament."

"You say you don't talk to police officers based on what you see or what you hear from other people," a woman cop replied. "The news only tell you the bad stuff. They don't tell you the full story."

"I didn't say all cops are bad."

"They only tell you part of the story. They don't tell you the whole thing from beginning to the end. They don't tell you what happened. They don't tell you the good stuff that us as police officers out here do. So if that's the case, then police officers stereotype all children. Because we feel as though half of y'all are ignorant, y'all rude, y'all disrespectful to adults, teachers, staff, whatever, so is that fine for us to put y'all in a group based on what we see on TV, what we see on the news?"

A girl who had her hand up joined in. "Some cops got no respect, and they talk about us having no respect for cops. Some cops come curse at you. They'll come at you regularly. But if you come at them regularly, you're the bad one. Some cops be nice, some cops be assholes.

How we supposed to act toward y'all—we can't fight y'all. No matter what we do, we can get locked up like this." A few students snapped their fingers.

"Some people are good; some people are bad," an officer said. "Now we're getting to a human level. Because you said it depends on the cop. Just like people, it depends on the person."

"And cops are people," another one added.

Ryan said he often got pulled over because his car had tinted windows. "I roll my windows down. I say, 'Yes sir, no sir.' I give my license and registration. I get sent on my way nine times out of ten." A girl mumbled, "He's light-skinned." Ryan didn't mention that he had been subjected to random stop and frisks since childhood. He felt he'd been viewed suspiciously for being Puerto Rican in a "dangerous neighborhood." The predominantly white Philadelphia police force did not reflect the city's diversity, and a lot of the officers lived far from the neighborhoods they patrolled.

Putting the police and marginalized youth together made the asymmetrical power dynamic starkly clear. One has state power to inflict pain and kill; the other does not. To many Black and Latino youth, the police are not a neutral entity that serves and protects but a rogue force that occupies, maims, brutalizes, and executes with impunity.

Ryan also ran meetings at the police academy between Black and Latino teens and the mostly white cadet recruits. He'd begin by asking the recruits if they thought the job was going to be a culture shock. Most said no. Then he'd ask if they knew who Chinos were or what the papi store is. The kids would giggle while the recruits looked clueless.

"I just asked you if this was going to be a culture shock and you guys said no," Ryan said. "I'm here to tell you that you can't be like that. Everything you see in the movies, you have to wipe the slate clean."

Conclusion

Corem was taking notes in psychology class as their professor lectured about the various effects on child development of enriched and impoverished environments. Identifying with the concepts was easy, since Corem knew what it was like to be deprived of good nutrition, stable shelter, economic security, and material comforts. Their first semester in community college was going well. Unlike at El Centro de Estudiantes, Corem wasn't plagued by self-doubt, instead feeling confident in their intelligence and abilities. This was where they were supposed to be. They were taking four classes: psychology, arithmetic, English, and First Year Experience, and they were able to apply their rich array of lived experiences.

In English class, Corem wrote an essay responding to a video, "15 Things Poor People Do That the Rich Don't" on the Alux YouTube channel, which called itself "the largest community of Luxury & Fine Living enthusiasts in the World." It was a hackneyed, blame-the-poor tirade that checked off what "poor people do to guarantee their mediocrity": eating fast food, buying clothes on sale, not saving money, and not showering "as often as rich people."[1]

Corem lambasted the video for ignoring "the socio-economic and systemic structures that exist in our society that play a role in poverty. It failed to acknowledge the experiences behind the scenes." Corem hadn't been able to shower sometimes not out of laziness but because there was "no access to water." The essay cited an MTV News segment about the history of the racial wealth gap and how redlining, educational inequality, and other forms of exploitation and racism had contributed to it. "As a person of color, the system was placed against me from the very beginning," Corem wrote. The Alux video had no such analysis and was riddled with distortions. In conclusion: "Videos like this promote the idea that poor people are just 'weak,' 'lazy,' 'aggressive,' and that their status is 'easily changeable.' When in all actuality, my 'poor' mother is the strongest person I know."

After years of keeping their distance, Ivette and Corem reconciled when she finally found the courage to break up with Freddie. With the help of her pastor and her brother, she left the Lippincott dump and moved into a small, habitable apartment in another section of Kensington. It was a major upgrade, but it brought her back to the perpetual violence of Kensington Avenue. Corem had been clear that leaving Freddie was a prerequisite for them to move forward. Ivette had apologized for her mistakes. She had grown, she said, and accepted her child unconditionally. "God loves you for who you are. I hope one day we can rebuild what we had," she said. Corem wanted nothing more.

* * *

GIANCARLOS PICKED UP extra shifts at Burger King to get ready for the birth of his son and cover the flood of new expenses. He and Jennifer had thrown a gender reveal party with balloons and confetti poppers on the sidewalk in front of their house. At a prenatal appointment at Temple University Hospital, she was told that she had preeclampsia, and labor was induced the same day, weeks ahead of the due date. Labor went on for an agonizing thirty-plus hours, with Jennifer restricted to eating Jell-O, chicken broth, and ice chips. In the end she needed a C-section. Elias was born at 5 pounds and 2.7 ounces. Giancarlos was waiting nearby, and when he heard his son cry, he looked over the curtain and flashed the biggest smile.

A few days after the birth, Giancarlos posted a black-and-white picture of him gently cradling Elias, who was swaddled in a blanket and locking eyes with him. The caption said "My Soul" followed by a string of exclamation points and hearts and footprints emojis. He had done the easy part. He was a father. Now he had to be what his own father never was: a dad.

* * *

RYAN HAD STUCK with Judge Means and was living in an apartment in Juniata with Yamilet, who was pregnant. He had turned his life around, and it almost seemed mundane after his turbulent teenage years. Secure housing, decent employment, and health care—the bedrocks of a livelihood—had erased the social dislocations that had defined his life. At twenty-four, he had a second boy, Noah Rayford Rivera, the middle name chosen to honor the judge. This time, the birth was on his terms, and he had no doubt that he was the father.

From his perch of stability, Ryan looked back on the arson episode in middle school and what followed as a seminal moment. Recalling the play-by-play, with every blow to his dignity, could still prompt rage. Had he been a white kid at a good school in the suburbs, the principal would have called his mother. He might have been given a stern talk and a slap on the wrist—maybe a week of detention or a short suspension. Life would have gone on. No arrest, no juvenile detention, no disciplinary school, no court dates, no probation, and no sweat-drenched nightmares. But that wasn't how it worked for a poor Puerto Rican kid in the barrio. His lot was the shame of the perp walk, of wearing someone else's shit-stained underpants, the dehumanizing rituals of frisks, restraints, metal detectors, and surveillance at school. The potential superpredator had to be contained for the public good. No mercy. No justice. A politics of revanchism.

* * *

"POVERTY IS A crime," declared Henry George. "I hold, and I think no one who looks at the facts can fail to see, that poverty is utterly unnecessary. It is not by the decree of the Almighty, but it is because of our own injustice, our own selfishness, our own ignorance, that this scourge, worse than any pestilence, ravages our civilisation, bringing want and suffering and degradation, destroying souls as well as bodies."[2] In the richest country in the history of the world, it is a profound moral stain.[3]

And poverty is violence. Children's lives in Kensington are dominated by the exhausting need to negotiate, avoid, and neutralize violence: the violence of stomachs twisting from hunger, sharp drafts striking flesh while bathing in buckets of water, sadistic security forces, confinement to cages, unlivable shelter, and navigating the hypermasculine logic of the streets. These are the shameful failings of the state, not character defects of the people.

In Philadelphia, the chances of a child born into a family in the bottom quintile of income distribution making it to the top quintile was about one out of thirteen.[4] Children like Ryan, Giancarlos, and Corem have predestined slots at the bottom of the social and economic hierarchy. A lucky few make it to the top, which gives the impression of a functioning meritocracy.[5] The violence of this plutocracy steals childhoods, crushes dignity, and curses dreams. It pathologizes, stigmatizes, and ultimately reduces communities to a condition of social death.[6]

How does multiracial liberal democracy reconcile with the violence meted out against people who live in the Kensingtons all over the United States? They are found in the Northeast Kingdom of Vermont and McDowell County in West Virginia, in the South Side of Chicago and the Black Belt of the South, the Native American reservations at Pine Ridge and San Carlos, and the San Joaquin Valley in California.[7]

Political economist Karl Polanyi warned of the catastrophic repercussions of maximal market fundamentalism as "the demolition of society." "Robbed of the protective covering of cultural institutions, human beings would perish from the effects of social exposure," he argued. "They would die as the victims of acute social dislocation through vice, perversion, crime, and starvation. Nature would be reduced to its elements, neighborhoods and landscapes defiled, rivers polluted, military safety jeopardized, the power to produce food and raw materials destroyed."[8]

In 2020, the COVID-19 pandemic showed the result of letting markets rip for a half century. Decades of neoliberal policy—defunding

education, housing, health care, transit, infrastructure, and other public services while expending trillions on locking people up and foreign
military adventures—left the country with weak institutions and a
shredded social safety net offering minimal protections for working-
class people, children, the sick, elderly, and disabled.[9]

The pandemic sparked new support for a New Deal–style economic
agenda that could shift wealth and power to working people and their
communities. The ground had been laid by the presidential campaigns
of Senators Bernie Sanders and Elizabeth Warren and social movements
such as Occupy Wall Street, Black Lives Matter, and Fight for 15. Taken
together, the stage was set for Joe Biden's presidency to break with the
bipartisan neoliberal consensus.

Millions of American families began receiving monthly expanded
Child Tax Credit payments of $300 per child ages 0–5 and $250 per
child ages 6–17. The credit, which had no work requirements or time
limits, would be phased out at income levels of $75,000 for single fil-
ers and $150,000 for joint households. Previously, the CTC gave fami-
lies up to $2,000 a year and had a minimum income requirement. It was
also only refundable up to $1,400. Some 23 million children, or 35 per-
cent, including more than half of Black and Latino children and those
in single-parent women-householder families, did not receive the full
$2,000 credit because their parents did not earn enough income.[10]

The expanded CTC, a temporary, six-month measure and passed as
part of the 2021 American Rescue Plan, represented the most sweeping investment in the social safety net for children in modern American history. President Joe Biden was on pace to achieve what Franklin
Delano Roosevelt and Lyndon B. Johnson did for seniors by creating
Social Security and Medicare. Within a month of the first payments,
millions of children and families ceased experiencing food insecurity
and economic hardship. By December 2021, the CTC had reached 61.2
million children, slashed child poverty by 30 percent, and alleviated the
economic insecurity of low- and middle-income families. Contrary
to unfounded claims that CTC would be wasted on drugs, Americans
overwhelmingly used their payments for food, utilities, clothing, rent,
school supplies, and child care.[11] The program showed what happens

when government is committed to making life more affordable for ordinary people.

But the good times would not last forever. When the expanded CTC expired on December 31, 2021, nearly 4 million children were immediately plunged back into poverty and the child poverty rate hit 17 percent.[12]

According to the National Academies of Sciences, Engineering, and Medicine, the economic cost of child poverty ranged from $800 billion to $1.1 trillion each year, based on 2018 figures.[13] For years, scholars and activists have championed a child allowance to address this colossal loss and bring the United States in line with the rest of the industrialized world.[14] Studies show that cash transfers lead to huge reductions in poverty, higher educational attainment, improved health, reduced criminal activity, increased longevity, and other positive outcomes.[15]

What if Emmanuel, Ryan, and Giancarlos and their families had received a monthly child allowance starting from birth? They may have been able to consistently live in safe housing and afford groceries, utilities, and other necessities. They may have been spared the evictions and loss of homes. They may have been spared skipping meals and wearing dirty clothes. They may have been spared joining the underground economy as a means of survival. Most certainly, the economic cushion would have reduced stress, anxiety, depression, dependency, and domestic abuse. It would have helped their physical, social, and emotional development, especially in the earliest years. They would have been healthier, adding years to their lives.

Economist Amartya Sen made the case that poverty is not only the condition of low income but also "the deprivation of basic capabilities," which he defined as "the substantive freedoms he or she enjoys to lead the kind of life he or she has reason to value." In other words, capabilities constitute the core necessities that enable people to enjoy dignified lives.[16]

What is required to achieve this vision? We must first recognize that we cannot educate our way out of immiseration. We should ensure every young person graduates high school with the necessary skills and knowledge for work, higher education, and life. We should fully fund public education, provide universal early childhood education, rebuild and modernize school infrastructure, respect and pay teachers and staff decent salaries and benefits, reduce class sizes, turn every school into a community school with primary, dental, vision, and mental health care and afterschool and summer programs, offer universal, free school meals, and implement experiential, project-based pedagogy and restorative justice measures. But that isn't enough.

While it's helpful for pursuing higher education, obtaining some types of employment, and for validating achievement, resilience, and hard work, a high school diploma can be a hollow prize, hardly changing material conditions for many graduates. What's more, as scholars have explained, schools are not the great equalizer; they reproduce existing inequalities that originate in the political economy—the central site of this struggle.[17] A decent, fair society will only come about with a New Deal for the Twenty-First Century that produces a cradle-to-grave social democracy with economic and social freedoms and a sufficient standard of living for all. A New Deal means well-paying unionized jobs, living wages, social housing, universal health care, affordable child care, community-based, well-funded public education, tuition-free public college, paid family and medical leave, expanded Social Security and stable pensions, high-speed broadband, and reliable public transit.[18]

Under Senators Bernie Sanders and Chuck Schumer, the Build Back Better bill was designed to provide those crucial capabilities—paid for by progressively taxing the wealthiest Americans and corporations. The bill's passage would have generated millions of good jobs, lifted many out of economic insecurity, and narrowed widening class, racial, gender, and educational inequalities and polarization. It would have gone a long way to making the United States a true social democracy and achieving a decent life for all.[19]

Ultimately, Build Back Better was hacked and whittled down to a scaled-back version, still enacting significant legislation to invest in clean and renewable energy and health care, allow Medicare to negotiate prices on some prescription drugs, and impose a 15 percent minimum tax rate on profitable American corporations.[20] As the bill passed, economist Paul Krugman observed, "We will be a poorer, less just society than we could have been" had the original social and economic programs been preserved.[21]

Eradicating the miserable conditions in the Kensingtons of America is both feasible and essential to protect American democracy from the rising reactionary forces that threaten our rights, our way of life, and our planet.[22] Nearly a century ago, President Roosevelt understood that he had to crush the Great Depression to save democracy. "Democracy has disappeared in several other great nations—not because the people of those nations disliked democracy, but because they had grown tired of unemployment and insecurity, of seeing their children hungry while they sat helpless in the face of government confusion and government weakness through lack of leadership in government," he said in a fireside chat in 1938, on the brink of the Nazi conquest of Europe. "Finally, in desperation, they chose to sacrifice liberty in the hope of getting something to eat."[23]

This mighty nation has the wealth, power, and imagination to end the suffering. As Langston Hughes said, let us birth a new America, one that becomes "the dream the dreamers dreamed . . . that great strong land of love."[24]

ACKNOWLEDGMENTS

Most of all, I am indebted to Ryan, Corem, Giancarlos, Rayni, Ivette, Marta, and others who took me under their wing and showed me their remarkable neighborhoods and city. They endured my incessant questions, connected me with their friends, mentors, and resources, and shaped the scope and direction of the book. I am awed by their kindness, brilliance, courage, vigor, and friendship. No words can fully capture my gratitude and appreciation.

This book would likely not exist without Andrew Frishman's introduction to David Bromley and El Centro de Estudiantes in 2015. David, JuDonn, Matthew, Doug, Andrew, Marie, Madeline, and many other members of staff graciously welcomed me into their school, put up with my interviews, and allowed me to freely wander, chat with students, and sit in on classes. Their trust and support made the project possible. Despite appallingly few resources, they went to bat for the children and families of Philadelphia, day in and day out. They are our nation's heroes.

The greatest honor of my life was serving as a senior policy advisor to Senator Bernie Sanders and working on behalf of the beautiful people of Vermont and the United States over the past few years. He reminds us that we must never stop struggling for a world rooted in justice, democracy, and freedom. Not Me, Us. Solidarity forever.

I am grateful for my dear friends who provided joy, laughter, sanity, and insights during the research and writing: Sumaiya Ahmed, Arvin Alaigh, Essam Attia, Viraj Ayar, Isabel Balazs, Mitchell Bradford, George Camerlo, Ariel Charney, Deana Davoudiasl, Aashna Desai, Astrid DuBois, Zach Hammer, Jonathan Hiles, Max Kenner, Maria Khwaja, Parijat Lal, Maya Major, Zak Malamed, Erik Martin, Mike Meaney, Katrina Menard, Chloe Miller, Mandeep Minhas, Israel Muñoz, Sydney Myong, Daniel Novack, Gabe Nussbaum, Lili Pike, Seth Pollack, Ari Rabin-Havt, Natalie Scavuzzo, Adora Svitak, Jenny Zhang, Robert Zimmerman, and especially Sion Bell, Ravi Gupta, Richard Phillips, and Aastha Uprety for reading the entire manuscript and offering helpful feedback.

I had the great pleasure of working with Katherine Flynn, who championed this book from proposal to final product and has been one of my best advocates during this process. She and Astra Taylor introduced me to the brilliant Riva Hocherman. I am very appreciative of Riva's kindness, wit, sharp editorial hand, consistent support, and unflagging commitment to building a more decent society. I also thank Aileen Boyle and the Metropolitan and Henry Holt staff: Elisa Rivlin, Hannah Campbell, Chris O'Connell, Christopher Sergio, Julia Ortiz, Lisa Kleinholz, Arriel Vinson, Laura Flavin, and Catryn Silbersack, and the printers, warehouse and delivery workers, booksellers, and librarians.

Betsy Lerner was involved in this project early on. She read and reread umpteen drafts and offered numerous constructive revisions and thoughts. Without her input, the book would not read as smoothly as it currently does. Alexis Gargagliano, Katie Adams, and Hasan Altaf also provided excellent editorial support. I thank my outstanding fact-checker, Claire Wang, for diligently examining the full manuscript and catching several errors. Jo-Anne Dillabough, an exceptional sociologist and ethnographer, was my primary supervisor at Cambridge. I am enormously grateful for her mentorship and friendship during my PhD. Another wonderful sociologist, Susan Robertson, was insightful in her comments and guidance early on. I am very fortunate to have had the opportunity to study with Jo and Susan.

My thanks go out: To the librarians and staff at the University of

Cambridge and New York University for their research assistance and indulging my book requests. To the staff at the Library Company of Philadelphia, Historical Society of Pennsylvania, Temple University Urban Archives, and City Archives for their insight and assistance during my research. To my teachers at the Middlebury Language School who helped me achieve an adequate level of Spanish proficiency so I could conduct interviews and fieldwork (and thanks to the Kathryn Davis Fellowship for Peace). To the Philadelphia court staff who handle records and transcriptions. To the historians and sociologists of Philadelphia, especially Elijah Anderson, John F. Bauman, Peter Binzen, Philippe Bourgois, W. E. B. Du Bois, Kathryn Edin, Alice Goffman, David Grazian, Saidiya Hartman, Marcus Anthony Hunter, Maria Kefalas, Walter Licht, Timothy Lombardo, Joan D. Koss, Joan Maya Mazelis, Kenneth W. Milano, Charles Nier, Philip Scranton, Patricia Stern Smallacombe, Carmen T. Whalen, Frederick Wherry, and James Wolfinger. To the reporters at the *Philadelphia Inquirer, Philadelphia Public School Notebook, Philadelphia City Paper, Hidden City Philadelphia, Philadelphia Citizen,* and WHYY for their terrific coverage of education, poverty, incarceration, gun violence, the opioid epidemic, and Kensington.

Sociological and ethnographic research requires extensive resources and patience. The NoVo Foundation provided generous funding and the freedom to pursue this project. I am deeply appreciative of Peter and Jennifer Buffett and Stephanie Hartka.

I thank my family for being there for me over the past eight years. Harshita Bhabhi and Mayank Bhaiya took care of me during my initial trips to Philadelphia. Maasi, Mesho, Anisha Didi, and Sanjeev cheered me on and were the most enjoyable company. Finally, I thank Mom, Dad, and Nikita, and our late dog, Bobby, for their endless love and support during this journey.

BIBLIOGRAPHY

Abrams, Samuel. *Education and the Commercial Mindset*. Cambridge, MA: Harvard University Press, 2016.

Abramsky, Sasha. *The American Way of Poverty: How the Other Half Still Lives*. New York: Nation Books, 2013.

Adams, Carolyn, David Bartelt, David Elesh, Ira Goldstein, Nancy Kleniewski, and William Yancey. *Philadelphia: Neighborhoods, Division, and Conflict in a Postindustrial City*. Philadelphia: Temple University Press, 1991.

Agamben, Giorgio. *Homo Sacer: Sovereign Power and Bare Life*. Stanford, CA: Stanford University Press, 1998.

Alexander, Karl, Doris Entwisle, and Linda Olson. *The Long Shadow: Family Background, Disadvantaged Urban Youth, and the Transition to Adulthood*. New York: Russell Sage Foundation, 2014.

Alexander, Michelle. *The New Jim Crow: Mass Incarceration in the Age of Colorblindness*. New York: The New Press, 2010.

Allen, Theodore W. *The Invention of the White Race: Racial Oppression and Social Control*. Vol. 1. New York: Verso, 1994.

Anderson, Elijah. *Code of the Street: Decency, Violence, and the Moral Life of the Inner City*. New York: W. W. Norton, 2000.

——. "Drugs and Violence in the Inner City." In *W.E.B. Du Bois, Race, and the City: The Philadelphia Negro and Its Legacy*, edited by Michael B. Katz and Thomas J. Sugrue. Philadelphia: University of Pennsylvania Press, 1998.

——. *Streetwise: Race, Class, and Change in an Urban Community*. Chicago: University of Chicago Press, 1990.

Anyon, Jean. *Ghetto Schooling: A Political Economy of Urban Educational Reform*. New York: Teachers College Press, 1997.

Apple, Michael W. *Educating the "Right" Way: Markets, Standards, God, and Inequality*. New York: Routledge, 2001.

———. *Education and Power*. New York: Routledge, 1995.

Aronowitz, Stanley, and Henry A. Giroux. *Education Under Siege: The Conservative, Liberal and Radical Debate over Schooling*. South Hadley, MA: Bergin & Garvey, 1987.

Baldwin, James. *I Am Not Your Negro*. New York: Vintage, 2017.

Balko, Radley. *Rise of the Warrior Cop: The Militarization of America's Police Forces*. New York: PublicAffairs, 2013.

Baptist, Edward. *The Half Has Never Been Told: Slavery and the Making of American Capitalism*. New York: Basic Books, 2014.

Baum, Dan. *Smoke and Mirrors: The War on Drugs and the Politics of Failure*. New York: Little, Brown, 1996.

Bauman, John F. *Public Housing, Race, and Renewal: Urban Planning in Philadelphia, 1920–1974*. Philadelphia: Temple University Press, 1987.

Bauman, John F., et al. "Public Housing, Isolation, and the Urban Underclass: Philadelphia's Richard Allen Homes, 1941–1965." In *African Americans in Pennsylvania: Shifting Historical Perspectives*, edited by Joe W. Trotter and Eric Ledell Smith. University Park: Pennsylvania State University Press, 1997.

Bazelon, Emily. *Charged: The New Movement to Transform American Prosecution and End Mass Incarceration*. New York: Random House, 2019.

Beckert, Sven. *Empire of Cotton: A New History of Global Capitalism*. New York: Knopf, 2014.

Beckett, Katherine. *Making Crime Pay: Law and Order in Contemporary American Politics*. New York: Oxford University Press, 1997.

Beckett, Katherine, and Theodore Sasson. *The Politics of Injustice: Crime and Punishment in America*. Thousand Oaks, CA: SAGE, 2004.

Bell, Derrick. *Faces at the Bottom of the Well: The Permanence of Racism*. New York: Basic Books, 1992.

Benezra, Michael Raymond. *How Policymakers Started the Federal Charter School Movement: A Case Study in Policy Entrepreneurship*. Master of Arts thesis, Harvard University, 2016.

Berlin, Ira. *The Making of African America: The Four Great Migrations*. New York: Viking, 2010.

Bernard, Thomas J., and Megan C. Kurlychek. *The Cycle of Juvenile Justice*. New York: Oxford University Press, 2010.

Beveridge, William H. B. *Social Insurance and Allied Services: Report by Sir William Beveridge*. London: Her Majesty's Stationery Office, 1942.

Biehl, João. *Vita: Life in a Zone of Social Abandonment*. Berkeley: University of California Press, 2005.

Binzen, Peter. *Whitetown, U.S.A.* New York: Random House, 1970.

Bissinger, Buzz. *A Prayer for the City*. New York: Random House, 1997.

Blackmon, Douglas A. *Slavery by Another Name: The Re-Enslavement of Black Americans from the Civil War to World War II*. New York: Doubleday, 2008.

Blauner, Robert. *Racial Oppression in America*. New York: Harper & Row, 1972.

Block, Fred L., and Margaret R. Somers. *The Power of Market Fundamentalism: Karl Polanyi's Critique*. Cambridge, MA: Harvard University Press, 2016.

Bluestone, Barry, and Bennett Harrison. *The Deindustrialization of America: Plant Closings, Community Abandonment, and the Dismantling of Basic Industry*. New York: Basic Books, 1982.

Blyth, Mark. *Austerity: The History of a Dangerous Idea*. New York: Oxford University Press, 2013.

Bonilla-Silva, Eduardo. *Racism Without Racists: Color-Blind Racism and the Persistence of Racial Inequality in the United States*. Lanham, MD: Rowman & Littlefield, 2010.

Boo, Katherine. *Behind the Beautiful Forevers: Life, Death, and Hope in a Mumbai Undercity*. New York: Random House, 2012.

Bourdieu, Pierre. *Acts of Resistance: Against the New Myths of Our Time*. Translated by Richard Nice. Cambridge: Polity, 1998.

——. *Outline of a Theory of Practice*. Cambridge: Cambridge University Press, 1977.

Bourdieu, Pierre, et al. *The Weight of the World: Social Suffering in Contemporary Society*. Stanford, CA: Stanford University Press, 2000.

Bowles, Samuel, and Herbert Gintis. *Schooling in Capitalist America: Educational Reform and the Contradictions of Economic Life*. London: Routledge & Kegan Paul, 1976.

Brown, Phillip. *Schooling Ordinary Kids: Inequality, Unemployment, and the New Vocationalism*. London: Tavistock, 1987.

Brown, Wendy. *Undoing the Demos: Neoliberalism's Stealth Revolution*. Brooklyn, NY: Zone Books, 2015.

Carney, Caroline. *Diabetes and Food Access in Philadelphia*. Undergraduate senior thesis, University of Pennsylvania, 2012.

Carter, Zachary D. *The Price of Peace: Money, Democracy, and the Life of John Maynard Keynes*. New York: Random House, 2020.

Case, Anne, and Angus Deaton. *Deaths of Despair and the Future of Capitalism*. Princeton, NJ: Princeton University Press, 2020.

Catrambone, Jamie, and Harry C. Silcox, eds. *Kensington History: Stories and Memories*. Philadelphia: Brighton Press, 1996.

Cervantes, Lucius F. *The Dropout: Causes and Cures*. Ann Arbor: University of Michigan Press, 1965.

Chang, Ha-Joon. *23 Things They Don't Tell You About Capitalism*. New York: Bloomsbury Press, 2010.

Chomsky, Noam. *Profit over People: Neoliberalism and Global Order*. New York: Seven Stories Press, 1999.

Clark, Kenneth. *Dark Ghetto: Dilemmas of Social Power*. New York: Harper & Row, 1967.

Conant, James Bryant. *Slums and Suburbs*. New York: McGraw-Hill, 1961.

Coates, Ta-Nehisi. *Between the World and Me*. New York: Spiegel & Grau, 2015.

Corrigan, Paul. *Schooling the Smash Street Kids*. London: Macmillan, 1979.

Countryman, Matthew. *Up South: Civil Rights and Black Power in Philadelphia*. Philadelphia: University of Pennsylvania Press, 2006.

Davis, Angela Y. *Are Prisons Obsolete?* New York: Seven Stories Press, 2011.

Davis, Mike. *City of Quartz: Excavating the Future in Los Angeles.* New York: Verso, 1990.

——. *Planet of Slums.* New York: Verso, 2006.

Dei, George. *Reconstructing "Dropout": A Critical Ethnography of the Dynamics of Black Students' Disengagement from School.* Toronto: University of Toronto Press, 1997.

Delmont, Matthew F. *The Nicest Kids in Town: American Bandstand, Rock 'n' Roll, and the Struggle for Civil Rights in 1950s Philadelphia.* Berkeley: University of California Press, 2012.

DeParle, Jason. *American Dream: Three Women, Ten Kids, and a Nation's Drive to End Welfare.* New York: Viking, 2004.

Desmond, Matthew. *Evicted: Poverty and Profit in the American City.* New York: Crown, 2016.

Devine, John. *Maximum Security: The Culture of Violence in Inner-City Schools.* Chicago: University of Chicago Press, 1996.

Dewey, John. *The School and Society: Being Three Lectures.* Chicago: University of Chicago Press, 1899.

Dillabough, Jo-Anne, and Jacqueline Kennelly. *Lost Youth in the Global City: Class, Culture, and the Urban Imaginary.* New York: Routledge, 2010.

Dix, Paul, and Pamela Fitzpatrick. *Nicaragua: Surviving the Legacy of U.S. Policy.* Eugene, OR: Just Sharing Press, 2011.

Dolovich, Sharon. "Creating the Permanent Prisoner." In *Life Without Parole: America's New Death Penalty?*, edited by Charles J. Ogletree Jr. and Austin Sarat. New York: New York University Press, 2012.

Drake, St. Clair, and Horace R. Cayton. *Black Metropolis: A Study of Negro Life in a Northern City.* New York: Harper & Row, 1962.

Drinan, Cara H. *The War on Kids: How American Juvenile Justice Lost Its Way.* New York: Oxford University Press, 2018.

Duany, Jorge. *Puerto Rico: What Everyone Needs to Know.* New York: Oxford University Press, 2017.

Du Bois, W. E. B. *Black Reconstruction: An Essay Toward a History of the Part Which Black Folk Played in the Attempt to Reconstruct Democracy in America, 1860–1880.* New York: Free Press, 1998.

——. *The Philadelphia Negro: A Social Study.* Philadelphia: University of Pennsylvania Press, 1996.

——. *The Souls of Black Folk.* Chicago: A. C. McClurg, 1903.

Duff, Anthony, and Ido Weijers, eds. *Punishing Juveniles: Principle and Critique.* Portland, OR: Hart Publishing, 2002.

Duneier, Mitchell. *Ghetto: The Invention of a Place, the History of an Idea.* New York: Farrar, Straus & Giroux, 2016.

Edin, Kathryn, and Maria Kefalas. *Promises I Can Keep: Why Poor Women Put Motherhood Before Marriage.* Berkeley: University of California Press, 2005.

Edin, Kathryn J., and H. Luke Shaefer. *$2.00 a Day: Living on Almost Nothing in America.* New York: Houghton Mifflin Harcourt, 2015.

Ehrenreich, Barbara. *Nickel and Dimed: On (Not) Getting By in America*. New York: Metropolitan Books, 2001.

Elliott, Andrea. *Invisible Child: Poverty, Survival, and Hope in an American City*. New York: Random House, 2021.

Ericksen, Eugene P., and the Institute for Public Policy Studies. *The State of Puerto Rican Philadelphia*. Philadelphia: Institute for Public Policy Research, Temple University, 1985.

Esping-Andersen, Gøsta. *The Three Worlds of Welfare Capitalism*. Princeton, NJ: Princeton University Press, 1990.

Everhart, Robert B. *Reading, Writing, and Resistance: Adolescence and Labor in a Junior High School*. Boston: Routledge, 1983.

Ewing, Eve. *Ghosts in the Schoolyard: Racism and School Closings on Chicago's South Side*. Chicago: University of Chicago Press, 2018.

Fagan, G. Honor. *Culture, Politics, and Irish School Dropouts: Constructing Political Identities*. Westport, CT: Bergin & Garvey, 1995.

Fairbanks, Robert P. *How It Works: Recovering Citizens in Post-Welfare Philadelphia*. Chicago: University of Chicago Press, 2009.

Farmer, Paul. *Pathologies of Power: Health, Human Rights, and the New War on the Poor*. Berkeley: University of California Press, 2003.

Federal Housing Administration. *Underwriting Manual: Underwriting and Valuation Procedure Under Title II of the National Housing Act*. Washington, DC: U.S. Government Printing Office, 1936.

Federal Writers' Project, Works Progress Administration. *Philadelphia: A Guide to the Nation's Birthplace*. Harrisburg, PA: Telegraph Press, 1937.

Ferguson, Ann Arnett. *Bad Boys: Public Schools in the Making of Black Masculinity*. Ann Arbor: University of Michigan Press, 2000.

Fields, Barbara J., and Karen Fields. *Racecraft: The Soul of Inequality in American Life*. New York: Verso, 2012.

Fine, Michelle. Foreword to *Debating Dropouts: Critical Policy and Research Perspectives on School Leaving*, edited by Deirdre Kelly and Jane Gaskell. New York: Teachers College Press, 1996.

———. *Framing Dropouts: Notes on the Politics of an Urban Public High School*. Albany: State University of New York Press, 1991.

Folwell, Nathan T. "The Textile Capital of the World." In *1917 Philadelphia Year Book*. Philadelphia: Philadelphia Chamber of Commerce, 1917.

Foner, Eric. *Reconstruction: America's Unfinished Revolution, 1863–1877*. New York: Harper & Row, 1988.

Forman, James, Jr. *Locking Up Our Own: Crime and Punishment in Black America*. New York: Farrar, Straus & Giroux, 2017.

Foucault, Michel. *Discipline and Punish: The Birth of the Prison*. New York: Vintage, 1995.

———. *Essential Works of Foucault 1954–1984*. Vol. 3, *Power*, edited by James D. Faubion and translated by Robert Hurley. London: Penguin, 2002.

———. *Security, Territory, Population: Lectures at the Collège de France, 1977–1978*, edited by Michel Senellart. Translated by Graham Burchell. New York: Picador, 2004.

———. *The Birth of Biopolitics: Lectures at the Collège de France, 1978–1979*. Edited by Michel Senellart. Translated by Graham Burchell. New York: Picador, 2008.

———. "The Concern for Truth." In *Politics, Philosophy, Culture: Interviews and Other Writings, 1977–1984*, edited by Lawrence D. Kritzman. New York: Routledge, 1988.

Frank, Thomas. *Listen, Liberal: Or, What Ever Happened to the Party of the People?* New York: Metropolitan Books, 2016.

Fraser, Steve. *The Age of Acquiescence: The Life and Death of American Resistance to Organized Wealth and Power*. New York: Little, Brown, 2015.

Friedman, Murray. *Overcoming Middle Class Rage*. Philadelphia: Westminster Press, 1971.

Fuentes, Annette. *Lockdown High: When the Schoolhouse Becomes a Jailhouse*. London: Verso, 2011.

Fullilove, Mindy. *Root Shock: How Tearing Up City Neighborhoods Hurts America, and What We Can Do About It*. New York: One World/Ballantine Books, 2004.

Gans, Herbert. *The War Against the Poor: The Underclass and Antipoverty Policy*. New York: Basic Books, 1996.

Garbarino, James. *Miller's Children: Why Giving Teenage Killers a Second Chance Matters for All of Us*. Oakland: University of California Press, 2018.

Garland, David. *The Culture of Control: Crime and Social Order in Contemporary Society*. Chicago: University of Chicago Press, 2002.

———, ed. *Mass Imprisonment: Social Causes and Consequences*. Thousand Oaks, CA: SAGE, 2001.

Gerstle, Gary. *The Rise and Fall of the Neoliberal Order: America and the World in the Free Market Era*. New York: Oxford University Press, 2022.

Gillen, Jay. *Educating for Insurgency: The Roles of Young People in Schools of Poverty*. Chico, CA: AK Press, 2014.

Gilmore, Ruth Wilson. *Golden Gulag: Prisons, Surplus, Crisis, and Opposition in Globalizing California*. Berkeley: University of California Press, 2007.

Giroux, Henry A. *Theory and Resistance in Education: A Pedagogy for the Opposition*. South Hadley, MA: Bergin & Garvey, 1983.

———. *Youth in a Suspect Society: Democracy or Disposability?* New York: Palgrave Macmillan, 2009.

Goffman, Alice. *On the Run: Fugitive Life in an American City*. Chicago: University of Chicago Press, 2014.

Goffman, Erving. *Stigma: Notes on the Management of Spoiled Identity*. New York: Simon & Schuster, 1963.

Golann, Joanne W. *Scripting the Movies: Culture and Control in a "No Excuses" Charter School*. Princeton, NJ: Princeton University Press, 2021.

Goode, Judith, and Jo Anne Schneider. *Reshaping Ethnic and Racial Relations in Philadelphia: Immigrants in a Divided City*. Philadelphia: Temple University Press, 1994.

Goodman, Paul. *Compulsory Mis-Education and the Community of Scholars*. New York: Vintage, 1964.

Goodwin, David J. *Left Bank of the Hudson: Jersey City and the Artists of 111 1st Street*. New York: Fordham University Press, 2017.

Gottschalk, Marie. *The Prison and the Gallows: The Politics of Mass Incarceration in Amer-ica*. New York: Cambridge University Press, 2006.

Goyal, Nikhil. *Schools on Trial: How Freedom and Creativity Can Fix Our Educational Mal-practice*. New York: Doubleday, 2016.

Grandin, Greg. *The End of the Myth: From the Frontier to the Border Wall in the Mind of America*. New York: Metropolitan Books, 2019.

Graubard, Allen. *Free the Children: Racial Reform and the Free School Movement*. New York: Pantheon, 1972.

Grazian, David. *On the Make: The Hustle of Urban Nightlife*. Chicago: University of Chicago Press, 2008.

Gregory, Steven. *Black Corona: Race and the Politics of Place in an Urban Community*. Princeton, NJ: Princeton University Press, 1998.

Hacker, Jacob. *The Great Risk Shift: The New Economic Insecurity and the Decline of the American Dream*. New York: Oxford University Press, 2006.

Hacker, Jacob, and Paul Pierson. *Winner-Take-All Politics: How Washington Made the Rich Richer—And Turned Its Back on the Middle Class*. New York: Simon & Schuster, 2010.

Hahn, Steven. *A Nation Under Our Feet: Black Political Struggles in the Rural South from Slavery to the Great Migration*. Cambridge, MA: Harvard University Press, 2003.

Hannerz, Ulf. *Soulside: Inquiries into Ghetto Culture and Community*. New York: Columbia University Press, 1969.

Hari, Johann. *Chasing the Scream: The First and Last Days of the War on Drugs*. New York: Bloomsbury, 2015.

Harrington, Michael. *The Other America: Poverty in the United States*. New York: Macmil-lan, 1962.

Hart, Carl. *High Price: A Neuroscientist's Journey of Self-Discovery That Challenges Every-thing You Know About Drugs and Society*. New York: Harper, 2013.

Hartman, Saidiya. *Wayward Lives, Beautiful Experiments: Intimate Histories of Riotous Black Girls, Troublesome Women, and Queer Radicals*. New York: W. W. Norton, 2019.

Harvey, David. *A Brief History of Neoliberalism*. New York: Oxford University Press, 2007.

———. *Social Justice and the City*. Baltimore: Johns Hopkins University Press, 1973.

Hayden, Dolores. *Redesigning the American Dream: The Future of Housing, Work, and Fam-ily Life*. New York: W. W. Norton, 1984.

Hedges, Chris. *The Death of the Liberal Class*. New York: Nation Books, 2010.

Henig, Jeffrey R. *Rethinking School Choice: Limits of the Market Metaphor*. Princeton, NJ: Princeton University Press, 1994.

Hinton, Elizabeth. *From the War on Poverty to the War on Crime: The Making of Mass Incar-ceration in America*. Cambridge, MA: Harvard University Press, 2016.

Hirsch, Arnold R. *Making of the Second Ghetto: Race and Housing in Chicago, 1940–1960*. New York: Cambridge University Press, 1983.

Honig, Bonnie. *Public Things: Democracy in Disrepair*. New York: Fordham University Press, 2017.

Hunter, Marcus Anthony. *Black Citymakers: How The Philadelphia Negro Changed Urban America*. New York: Oxford University Press, 2013.

Ignatiev, Noel. *How the Irish Became White*. New York: Routledge, 1995.

Jackson, Kenneth T. *Crabgrass Frontier: The Suburbanization of the United States*. New York: Oxford University Press, 1985.

Jackson, Philip W. *Life in Classrooms*. New York: Teachers College Press, 1990.

Jencks, Christopher. *Rethinking Social Policy: Race, Poverty, and the Underclass*. Cambridge, MA: Harvard University Press, 1992.

Jencks, Christopher, et al. *Inequality: A Reassessment of the Effect of Family and Schooling in America*. New York: Basic Books, 1972.

Jones, Daniel Stedman. *Masters of the Universe: Hayek, Friedman, and the Birth of Neoliberal Politics*. Princeton, NJ: Princeton University Press, 2014.

Johnson, Walter. *River of Dark Dreams: Slavery and Empire in the Cotton Kingdom*. Cambridge, MA: Belknap Press of Harvard University Press, 2013.

Judt, Tony. *Ill Fares the Land*. New York: Penguin Books, 2010.

Kafka, Judith. *The History of "Zero Tolerance" in American Public Schooling*. New York: Palgrave Macmillan, 2011.

Kasarda, John D. "Jobs, Migration, and Emerging Urban Mismatches." In *Urban Change and Poverty*, edited by Michael McGeary and Laurence Lynn Jr. Washington, DC: National Academies Press, 1988.

——. "Urban Industrial Transition and the Underclass." In *The Ghetto Underclass*, edited by William Julius Wilson. Newbury Park, CA: SAGE, 1993.

Katz, Michael B. *Class, Bureaucracy, and Schools: The Illusion of Educational Change in America*. New York: Praeger, 1971.

——. *In the Shadow of the Poorhouse: A Social History of Welfare in America*. New York: Basic Books, 1996.

——. *The Irony of Early School Reform: Educational Innovation in Mid-Nineteenth Century Massachusetts*. Cambridge, MA: Harvard University Press, 1968.

——, ed. *The "Underclass" Debate: Views from History*. Princeton, NJ: Princeton University Press, 1993.

Katznelson, Ira. "Was the Great Society a Lost Opportunity?" In *The Rise and Fall of the New Deal Order, 1930–1980*, edited by Steve Fraser and Gary Gerstle. Princeton, NJ: Princeton University Press, 1989.

——. *When Affirmative Action Was White: An Untold History of Racial Inequality in Twentieth-Century America*. New York: W. W. Norton, 2006.

Kaye, Kerwin. *Enforcing Freedom: Drug Courts, Therapeutic Communities, and the Intimacies of the State*. New York: Columbia University Press, 2020.

Keels, Thomas H. *Philadelphia Graveyards and Cemeteries*. Mount Pleasant, SC: Arcadia Publishing, 2003.

Kelly, Deirdre M. *Last Chance High: How Girls and Boys Drop In and Out of Alternative School*. New Haven, CT: Yale University Press, 1993.

Kenworthy, Lane. *Social Democratic America*. New York: Oxford University Press, 2014.

King, Robert Pennick. *A Digest of the Laws and Ordinances, Relating to the City of Philadelphia, in Force on the Twelfth Day of December, A.D. 1868*. Philadelphia: King & Baird, 1869.

Klein, Naomi. *The Shock Doctrine: The Rise of Disaster Capitalism*. New York: Metropolitan Books, 2007.

Klinenberg, Eric. *Palaces for the People: How Social Infrastructure Can Help Fight Inequality, Polarization, and the Decline of Civic Life*. New York: Crown, 2018.

Koss, Joan D. *Puerto Ricans in Philadelphia: Migration and Accommodation*. PhD diss., University of Pennsylvania, 1965.

Kotlowitz, Alex. *There Are No Children Here: The Story of Two Boys Growing Up in the Other America*. New York: Doubleday, 1991.

Kotz, David. *The Rise and Fall of Neoliberal Capitalism*. Cambridge, MA: Harvard University Press, 2015.

Kozol, Jonathan. *Free Schools*. Boston: Houghton Mifflin, 1972.

———. *Savage Inequalities: Children in America's Schools*. New York: Crown, 1991.

Kristof, Nicholas, and Sheryl WuDunn. *Tightrope: Americans Reaching for Hope*. New York: Knopf, 2020.

Kupchik, Aaron. *Homeroom Security: School Discipline in an Age of Fear*. New York: New York University Press, 2010.

Kuttner, Robert. *Going Big: FDR's Legacy, Biden's New Deal, and the Struggle to Save Democracy*. New York: The New Press, 2022.

Labaree, David F. *Someone Has to Fail: The Zero-Sum Game of Public Schooling*. Cambridge, MA: Harvard University Press, 2012.

Lamont, Michèle. *The Dignity of Working Men: Morality and the Boundaries of Race, Class, and Immigration*. Cambridge, MA: Harvard University Press, 2000.

Laurent, Sylvie. *King and the Other America: The Poor People's Campaign and the Quest for Economic Equality*. Oakland: University of California Press, 2018.

Lawson, Laura. *City Bountiful: A Century of Community Gardening in America*. Berkeley: University of California Press, 2005.

LeCompte, Margaret D. *Giving Up on School: Student Dropouts and Teacher Burnouts*. Newbury Park, CA: Corwin Press, 1991.

Lefebvre, Henri. *The Production of Space*. Translated by Donald Nicholson-Smith. Oxford: Wiley-Blackwell, 1991.

———. *Writings on Cities*. Translated by Eleonore Kofman and Elizabeth Lebas. Oxford: Wiley-Blackwell, 2000.

Lemann, Nicholas. *The Promised Land: The Great Black Migration and How It Changed America*. New York: Knopf, 1991.

Leovy, Jill. *Ghettoside: A True Story of Murder in America*. New York: Spiegel & Grau, 2015.

Levin, Josh. *The Queen: The Forgotten Life Behind an American Myth*. New York: Little, Brown, 2019.

Licht, Walter. *Getting Work: Philadelphia, 1840–1950*. Cambridge, MA: Harvard University Press, 1992.

Liebow, Elliot. *Tally's Corner: A Study of Negro Streetcorner Men*. Boston: Little, Brown, 1967.

Lipman, Pauline. *High Stakes Education: Inequality, Globalization, and Urban School Reform*. New York: Routledge, 2004.

———. *The New Political Economy of Urban Education: Neoliberalism, Race, and the Right to the City*. New York: Routledge, 2011.

Liston, Daniel P. *Capitalist Schools: Explanations and Ethics in Radical Studies of Schooling*. New York: Routledge, 1990.

Little, Tom, and Katherine Ellison. *Loving Learning: How Progressive Education Can Save America's Schools*. New York: W. W. Norton, 2015.

Lombardo, Timothy J. *Blue-Collar Conservatism: Frank Rizzo's Philadelphia and Populist Politics*. Philadelphia: University of Pennsylvania Press, 2018.

Louis, Édouard. *The End of Eddy: A Novel*. Translated by Michael Lucey. New York: Farrar, Straus & Giroux, 2017.

———. *Who Killed My Father*. Translated by Lorin Stein. New York: New Directions, 2019.

Lynch, Kathleen. *The Hidden Curriculum: Reproduction in Education, a Reappraisal*. London: Falmer Press, 1989.

Macfarlane, John J. *Manufacturing in Philadelphia, 1683–1912*. Philadelphia: Philadelphia Commercial Museum, 1912.

Macleod, Jay. *Ain't No Makin' It: Leveled Aspirations in a Low-Income Neighborhood*. Boulder, CO: Westview Press, 1987.

Madrick, Jeff. *Invisible Americans: The Tragic Cost of Child Poverty*. New York: Knopf, 2020.

Marsh, John. *Class Dismissed: Why We Cannot Teach or Learn Our Way out of Inequality*. New York: New York University Press, 2011.

Marshall, T. H. *Citizenship and Social Class and Other Essays*. Cambridge: Cambridge University Press, 1950.

Massey, Doreen. *For Space*. London: SAGE, 2005.

Massey, Douglas S., and Nancy A. Denton. *American Apartheid: Segregation and the Making of the Underclass*. Cambridge, MA: Harvard University Press, 1993.

Massing, Michael. *The Fix*. Berkeley: University of California Press, 1998.

Mazelis, Joan Maya. *Surviving Poverty: Creating Sustainable Ties Among the Poor*. New York: New York University Press, 2017.

Mazzucato, Mariana. *The Entrepreneurial State: Debunking Public vs. Private Sector Myths*. London: Anthem Press, 2011.

Mbembe, Achille. *Necropolitics*. Durham, NC: Duke University Press, 2019.

McAllister, David. "Realtors and Racism in Working-Class Philadelphia, 1945–1970." In *African American Urban History Since World War II*, edited by Kenneth L. Kusmer and Joe W. Trotter. Chicago: University of Chicago Press, 2009.

McGhee, Heather. *The Sum of Us: What Racism Costs Everyone and How We Can Prosper Together*. New York: One World, 2021.

McGrew, Ken. *Education's Prisoners: Schooling, the Political Economy, and the Prison Industrial Complex*. New York: Peter Lang, 2008.

McKee, Guian A. *The Problem of Jobs: Liberalism, Race, and Deindustrialization in Philadelphia*. Chicago: University of Chicago Press, 2008.

Meléndez, Edgardo. *Sponsored Migration: The State and Puerto Rican Postwar Migration to the United States*. Columbus: Ohio State University Press, 2017.

Milano, Kenneth W. *Hidden History of Kensington and Fishtown*. Charleston, SC: History Press, 2010.

——. *Remembering Kensington and Fishtown: Philadelphia's Riverward Neighborhoods*. Charleston, SC: History Press, 2008.

Milanović, Branko. *Global Inequality: A New Approach for the Age of Globalization*. Cambridge, MA: Harvard University Press, 2016.

Miller, Fredric M., Morris J. Vogel, and Allen F. Davis. *Still Philadelphia: A Photographic History, 1890–1940*. Philadelphia: Temple University Press, 1983.

Miller, Reuben Jonathan. *Halfway Home: Race, Punishment, and the Afterlife of Mass Incarceration*. New York: Little, Brown, 2021.

Miller, Ron. *Free Schools, Free People: Education and Democracy after the 1960s*. Albany: State University of New York Press, 2002.

Mills, C. Wright. *Sociological Imagination*. Oxford: Oxford University Press, 2000.

Mills, Charles W. *The Racial Contract*. Ithaca, NY: Cornell University Press, 1997.

Montagu, Ashley. *Man's Most Dangerous Myth: The Fallacy of Race*. New York: Columbia University Press, 1942.

Moran, Dominique. *Carceral Geography: Spaces and Practices of Incarceration*. New York: Routledge, 2015.

Morgan, Edmund. *American Slavery, American Freedom*. New York: W. W. Norton, 1975.

Morgan, George. *The City of Firsts*. Philadelphia: Historical Publication Society, 1926.

Morris, Monique W. *Pushout: The Criminalization of Black Girls in Schools*. New York: The New Press, 2015.

Morrison, Toni. *Playing in the Dark: Whiteness and the Literary Imagination*. Cambridge, MA: Harvard University Press, 1992.

Moynihan, Daniel Patrick. *Miles to Go: A Personal History of Social Policy*. Cambridge, MA: Harvard University Press, 1996.

——. *The Negro Family: The Case for National Action*. Washington, DC: U.S. Department of Labor, 1965.

Muhammad, Khalil Gibran. *The Condemnation of Blackness: Race, Crime, and the Making of Modern Urban America*. Cambridge, MA: Harvard University Press, 2010.

Murakawa, Naomi. *The First Civil Right: How Liberals Built Prison America*. New York: Oxford University Press, 2014.

Murray, Charles. *Coming Apart: The State of White America, 1960–2010*. New York: Crown Forum, 2012.

Murray, Martin J. *The Urbanism of Exception: The Dynamics of Global City Building in the Twenty-First Century*. Cambridge: Cambridge University Press, 2017.

Neill, A. S. *Summerhill: A Radical Approach to Child Rearing*. New York: Hart, 1960.

Newman, Katherine. *No Shame in My Game: The Working Poor in the Inner City*. New York: Russell Sage Foundation, 1999.

Ngai, Mae M. *Impossible Subjects: Illegal Aliens and the Making of Modern America*. Princeton, NJ: Princeton University Press, 2004.

Nier, Charles. *Race, Financial Institutions, Credit Discrimination and African American Home Ownership in Philadelphia, 1880–1960*. PhD diss., Temple University, 2011.

Noguera, Pedro. *City Schools and the American Dream: Reclaiming the Promise of American Education*. New York: Teachers College Press, 2003.

Nolan, Kathleen. *Police in the Hallways: Discipline in an Urban High School*. Minneapolis: University of Minnesota Press, 2011.

Nussbaum, Martha. *Creating Capabilities: The Human Development Approach*. Cambridge, MA: Harvard University Press, 2011.

Nygreen, Kysa. *These Kids: Identity, Agency, and Social Justice at a Last Chance High School*. Chicago: University of Chicago Press, 2013.

Oakes, Jeannie. *Keeping Track: How Schools Structure Inequality*. New Haven, CT: Yale University Press, 2005.

O'Connor, Alice. *Poverty Knowledge: Social Science, Social Policy, and the Poor in Twentieth-Century U.S. History*. Princeton, NJ: Princeton University Press, 2001.

Oliver, Melvin, and Thomas M. Shapiro. *Black Wealth / White Wealth: A New Perspective on Racial Inequality*. New York: Routledge, 2006.

Omi, Michael, and Howard Winant. *Racial Formation in the United States: From the 1960s to the 1990s*. New York: Routledge, 1994.

Orfield, Gary. *Dropouts in America: Confronting the Graduation Rate Crisis*. Cambridge, MA: Harvard Education Press, 2004.

Orr, Margaret Terry. *Keeping Students in School: A Guide to Effective Dropout Prevention Programs and Services*. San Francisco: Jossey-Bass, 1987.

Oshinsky, David. *Worse Than Slavery: Parchman Farm and the Ordeal of Jim Crow Justice*. New York: Free Press, 1996.

Osnos, Evan. *Wildland: The Making of America's Fury*. New York: Farrar, Straus & Giroux, 2021.

Packer, George. *The Unwinding: An Inner History of the New America*. New York: Farrar, Straus & Giroux, 2013.

Pager, Devah. *Marked: Race, Crime, and Finding Work in an Era of Mass Incarceration*. Chicago: University of Chicago Press, 2007.

Palmer, Gladys Louise. *Philadelphia Workers in a Changing Economy*. Philadelphia: University of Pennsylvania Press, 1956.

Patterson, James. *America's Struggle Against Poverty in the Twentieth Century*. Cambridge, MA: Harvard University Press, 2000.

Pattillo, Mary. *Black Picket Fences: Privilege and Peril Among the Black Middle Class*. Chicago: University of Chicago Press, 2013.

Payne, Charles M. *So Much Reform, So Little Change: The Persistence of Failure in Urban Schools*. Cambridge, MA: Harvard Education Press, 2008.

Perkiss, Abigail. *Making Good Neighbors: Civil Rights, Liberalism, and Integration in Postwar Philadelphia*. Ithaca, NY: Cornell University Press, 2014.

Pettit, Becky. *Invisible Men: Mass Incarceration and the Myth of Black Progress*. New York: Russell Sage Foundation, 2012.

Pfaff, John. *Locked In: The True Causes of Mass Incarceration—and How to Achieve Real Reform*. New York: Basic Books, 2017.

Philadelphia Chamber of Commerce. *The City of Philadelphia as It Appears in the Year 1894*. Philadelphia: G. S. Harris & Sons, 1894.

Piketty, Thomas. *Capital and Ideology*. Translated by Arthur Goldhammer. Cambridge, MA: Belknap Press of Harvard University Press, 2020.

——. *Capital in the Twenty-First Century*. Translated by Arthur Goldhammer. Cambridge, MA: Belknap Press of Harvard University Press, 2014.

Platt, Anthony M. *The Child Savers: The Invention of Delinquency*. New Brunswick, NJ: Rutgers University Press, 2009.

Polanyi, Karl. *The Great Transformation: The Political and Economic Origins of Our Time*. New York: Farrar & Rinehart, 1944.

Press, Eyal. *Dirty Work: Essential Jobs and the Hidden Toll of Inequality in America*. New York: Farrar, Straus & Giroux, 2021.

Provine, Doris Marie. "Creating Racial Disadvantage: The Case of Crack Cocaine." In *The Many Colors of Crime: Inequalities of Race, Ethnicity, and Crime in America*, edited by Ruth Peterson, Lauren Krivo, and John Hagan. New York: New York University Press, 2006.

Purdy, Jedediah. *This Land Is Our Land: The Struggle for a New Commonwealth*. Princeton, NJ: Princeton University Press, 2019.

Quadagno, Jill S. *The Color of Welfare: How Racism Undermined the War on Poverty*. New York: Oxford University Press, 1994.

Quart, Alissa. *Branded: The Buying and Selling of Teenagers*. New York: Basic Books, 2003.

Ralph, Laurence. *Renegade Dreams: Living Through Injury in Gangland Chicago*. Chicago: University of Chicago Press, 2014.

Rauchway, Eric. *Why the New Deal Matters*. New Haven, CT: Yale University Press, 2021.

Ravitch, Diane. *Death and Life of the Great American School System: How Testing and Choice Are Undermining Education*. New York: Basic Books, 2010.

——. *Reign of Error: The Hoax of the Privatization Movement and the Danger to America's Public Schools*. New York: Knopf, 2013.

Reinarman, Craig, and Harry G. Levine. "The Crack Attack: Politics and Media in the Crack Scare." In *Crack in America: Demon Drugs and Social Justice*, edited by Craig Reinarman and Harry G. Levine. Berkeley: University of California Press, 1997.

Ribeiro, Alyssa M. "The Battle for Harmony": Intergroup Relations between Blacks and Latinos in Philadelphia, 1950s to 1980s. PhD diss., University of Pittsburgh, 2013.

Rios, Victor M. *Punished: Policing the Lives of Black and Latino Boys*. New York: New York University Press, 2011.

Roberts, Dorothy. *Shattered Bonds: The Color of Child Welfare*. New York: Basic Books, 2002.

Rooks, Noliwe. *Cutting School: Privatization, Segregation, and the End of Public Education*. New York: The New Press, 2017.

Rosenbaum, James E. *Making Inequality: The Hidden Curriculum of High School Tracking*. New York: John Wiley & Sons, 1976.

Rothman, David J. *Conscience and Convenience: The Asylum and Its Alternative in Progressive America*. Boston: Little, Brown, 1980.

——. *The Discovery of the Asylum: Social Order and Disorder in the New Republic*. Boston: Little, Brown, 1971.

Rothstein, Richard. *The Color of Law: A Forgotten History of How Our Government Segregated America*. New York: Liveright, 2017.

Rumberger, Russell W. *Dropping Out: Why Students Drop Out of High School and What Can Be Done About It*. Cambridge, MA: Harvard University Press, 2011.

Russakoff, Dale. *The Prize: Who's in Charge of America's Schools?* New York: Houghton Mifflin Harcourt, 2015.

Ryan, William. *Blaming the Victim*. New York: Pantheon, 1971.

Sachs, Jeffrey. *Building the New American Economy: Smart, Fair, and Sustainable*. New York: Columbia University Press, 2017.

Saltman, Kenneth J. *The Edison Schools: Corporate Schooling and the Assault on Public Education*. New York: Routledge, 2005.

——. *The Gift of Education: Public Education and Venture Philanthropy*. New York: Palgrave Macmillan, 2010.

Sampson, Robert. *Great American City: Chicago and the Enduring Neighborhood Effect*. Chicago: University of Chicago Press, 2012.

Sánchez, José Ramón. *Boricua Power: A Political History of Puerto Ricans in the United States*. New York: New York University Press, 2007.

Sandel, Michael J. *What Money Can't Buy: The Moral Limits of Markets*. New York: Farrar, Straus & Giroux, 2012.

Sassen, Saskia. *Expulsions: Brutality and Complexity in the Global Economy*. Cambridge, MA: Belknap Press of Harvard University Press, 2014.

——. *The Global City: New York, London, Tokyo*. Princeton, NJ: Princeton University Press, 1991.

Satter, Beryl. *Family Properties: How the Struggle over Race and Real Estate Transformed Chicago and Urban America*. New York: Metropolitan Books, 2009.

Scanlon, Amanda. *School Discipline, Law Enforcement, and Student Outcomes*. PhD diss, University of Pennsylvania, 2016.

Scharf, J. Thomas, and Thompson Westcott. *History of Philadelphia, 1609–1884*, vol. 3. Philadelphia: L. H. Everts, 1884.

Scranton, Philip. "Build a Firm, Start Another: The Bromleys and Family Firm Entrepreneurship in the Philadelphia Region." In *Family Capitalism*, edited by Geoffrey Jones and Mary B. Rose. Portland, OR: Frank Cass, 1993.

——. *Endless Novelty: Specialty Production and American Industrialization, 1865–1925*. Princeton, NJ: Princeton University Press, 1997.

——. *Figured Tapestry: Production, Markets, and Power in Philadelphia Textiles, 1855–1941*. Cambridge: Cambridge University Press, 1989.

——. *Proprietary Capitalism: The Textile Manufacture at Philadelphia, 1800–1885*. Cambridge: Cambridge University Press, 1983.

Scranton, Philip, and Walter Licht. *Work Sights: Industrial Philadelphia, 1890–1950*. Philadelphia: Temple University Press, 1986.

Seder, Jean. *Voices of Kensington: Vanishing Mills, Vanishing Neighborhoods*. Ardmore, PA: Whitmore Publishing, 1982.

Sen, Amartya. *Development as Freedom*. New York: Knopf, 1999.

Shapiro, Thomas. *The Hidden Cost of Being African American: How Wealth Perpetuates Inequality*. New York: Oxford University Press, 2004.

Sharkey, Patrick. *Stuck in Place: Urban Neighborhoods and the End of Progress Toward Racial Equality*. Chicago: University of Chicago Press, 2013.

Shedd, Carla. *Unequal City: Race, Schools, and Perceptions of Injustice*. New York: Russell Sage Foundation, 2015.

Sibley, David. *Geographies of Exclusion: Society and Difference in the West*. New York: Routledge, 1995.

Simmons, Lizbet. *The Prison School: Educational Inequality and School Discipline in the Age of Mass Incarceration*. Oakland: University of California Press, 2017.

Simon, Jonathan. *Governing Through Crime: How the War on Crime Transformed American Democracy and Created a Culture of Fear*. New York: Oxford University Press, 2007.

Simson, Sharon P., and Martha C. Straus. *Horticulture as Therapy: Principles and Practice*. Binghamton, NY: Food Products Press, 1998.

Singh, Nikhil Pal. *Black Is a Country: Race and the Unfinished Struggle for Democracy*. Cambridge, MA: Harvard University Press, 2005.

———. *Race and America's Long War*. Oakland: University of California Press, 2017.

Sitaraman, Ganesh. *The Crisis of the Middle-Class Constitution: Why Economic Inequality Threatens Our Republic*. New York: Knopf, 2017.

Smallacombe, Patricia Stern. *Why Do They Stay: Rootedness and Isolation in an Inner-City White Neighborhood*. PhD diss., University of Pennsylvania, 2002.

Smith, Jonathan A., Paul Flowers, and Michael Larkin. *Interpretative Phenomenological Analysis: Theory, Method, and Research*. London: SAGE, 2009.

Smyth, John, and Robert Hattam. *Dropping Out, Drifting Off, Being Excluded: Becoming Somebody Without School*. New York: Peter Lang, 2004.

Soja, Edward W. *Seeking Spatial Justice*. Minneapolis: University of Minnesota Press, 2010.

Solomon, R. Patrick. *Black Resistance in High School: Forging a Separatist Culture*. Albany: State University of New York Press, 1992.

Spear, Allan H. *Black Chicago: The Making of a Negro Ghetto, 1890–1920*. Chicago: University of Chicago Press, 1967.

Sperling, Gene. *Economic Dignity*. New York: Penguin Press, 2020.

Stack, Carol B. *All Our Kin: Strategies for Survival in a Black Community*. New York: Harper & Row, 1974.

Steinberg, Stephen. *Race Relations: A Critique*. Stanford, CA: Stanford University Press, 2007.

Stevenson, Bryan. *Just Mercy: A Story of Justice and Redemption*. New York: Spiegel & Grau, 2014.

Stiglitz, Joseph. *The Price of Inequality: How Today's Divided Society Endangers Our Future*. New York: W. W. Norton, 2012.

Stinchcombe, Arthur L. *Rebellion in a High School*. Chicago: Quadrangle Books, 1964.

Streatfeild, Dominic. *Cocaine: An Unauthorized Biography*. New York: Thomas Dunne Books, 2002.

Stuart, Forrest. *Down, Out, and Under Arrest: Policing and Everyday Life in Skid Row*. Chicago: University of Chicago Press, 2016.

Sugrue, Thomas J. *The Origins of the Urban Crisis: Race and Inequality in Postwar Detroit*. Princeton, NJ: Princeton University Press, 2014.

Tanaka, Aaron. *The Criminalization of Poor Youth of Color in the Bio-Security State*. Undergraduate thesis, Harvard University, 2005.

Tanenhaus, David Spinoza. *Juvenile Justice in the Making*. New York: Oxford University Press, 2004.

Tardiff, Madeleine. *Social Contexts of the School Closures in West Philadelphia*. Undergraduate senior thesis, University of Pennsylvania, 2014.

Taylor, Keeanga-Yamahtta. *From #BlackLivesMatter to Black Liberation*. Chicago: Haymarket Books, 2016.

———. *Race for Profit: How Banks and the Real Estate Industry Undermined Black Homeownership*. Chapel Hill: University of North Carolina Press, 2019.

Tompkins-Stange, Megan E. *Policy Patrons: Philanthropy, Education Reform, and the Politics of Influence*. Cambridge, MA: Harvard Education Press, 2016.

Tuck, Eve. *Urban Youth and School Pushout: Gateways, Get-aways, and the GED*. New York: Routledge, 2012.

Ture, Kwame, and Charles V. Hamilton. *Black Power: The Politics of Liberation in America*. New York: Vintage, 1992.

Tyack, David. *The One Best System: A History of American Urban Education*. Cambridge, MA: Harvard University Press, 1974.

Vargas, Robert. *Wounded City: Violent Turf Wars in a Chicago Barrio*. New York: Oxford University Press, 2016.

Vázquez-Hernandez, Víctor. "Pan-Latino Enclaves in Philadelphia and the Formation of the Puerto Rican Community." In *Global Philadelphia: Immigrant Communities Old and New*, edited by Ayumi Takenaka and Mary Johnson Osirim. Philadelphia: Temple University Press, 2010.

Violas, Paul C. *The Training of the Urban Working Class: A History of Twentieth Century American Education*. Chicago: Rand McNally, 1978.

Vitale, Alex S. *The End of Policing*. New York: Verso, 2017.

Wacquant, Loïc. "A Janus-Faced Institution of Ethnoracial Closure: A Sociological Specification of the Ghetto." In *The Ghetto: Contemporary Global Issues and Controversies*, edited by Ray Hutchison and Bruce D. Haynes. Boulder, CO: Westview Press, 2011.

———. *Prisons of Poverty*. Minneapolis: University of Minnesota Press, 2009.

———. *Punishing the Poor: The Neoliberal Government of Social Insecurity*. Durham, NC: Duke University Press, 2009.

———. *Urban Outcasts: A Comparative Sociology of Advanced Marginality*. Cambridge, UK: Polity, 2008.

Watkins, Beverly Xaviera, and Mindy Thompson Fullilove. "Crack Cocaine and Harlem's Health." In *Dispatches from the Ebony Tower: Intellectuals Confront the African American Experience*, edited by Manning Marable. New York: Columbia University Press, 2000.

Weaver, Timothy P. R. *Blazing the Neoliberal Trail: Urban Political Development in the United States and the United Kingdom*. Philadelphia: University of Pennsylvania Press, 2015.

Weber, Carmen A., Irving Kosmin, and Muriel Kirkpatrick. *Workshop of the World*. Philadelphia: Oliver Evans Press, 1990.

Weis, Lois, Eleanor Farrar, and Hugh G. Petrie, eds. *Dropouts from School: Issues, Dilemmas, and Solutions*. Albany: State University of New York Press, 1989.

Weiss, Roger D., Steven M. Mirin, and Roxanne L. Bartel. *Cocaine*. Washington, DC: American Psychiatric Press, 1994.

Wells, Henry. *The Modernization of Puerto Rico: A Political Study of Changing Values and Institutions*. Cambridge, MA: Harvard University Press, 1969.

West, Cornel. *Race Matters*. Boston: Beacon Press, 1993.

Western, Bruce. *Punishment and Inequality in America*. New York: Russell Sage Foundation, 2006.

Whalen, Carmen T. "Colonialism, Citizenship, and the Making of the Puerto Rican Diaspora: An Introduction." In *Puerto Rican Diaspora: Historical Perspectives*, edited by Carmen T. Whalen and Víctor Vázquez-Hernandez. Philadelphia: Temple University Press, 2005.

——. *From Puerto Rico to Philadelphia: Puerto Rican Workers and Postwar Economies*. Philadelphia: Temple University Press, 2001.

Wherry, Frederick F. *The Philadelphia Barrio: The Arts, Branding, and Neighborhood Transformation*. Chicago: University of Chicago Press, 2011.

Wilkerson, Isabel. *The Warmth of Other Suns: The Epic Story of America's Great Migration*. New York: Random House, 2010.

Wilkinson, Richard, and Kate Pickett. *The Spirit Level: Why Greater Equality Makes Societies Stronger*. New York: Bloomsbury, 2010.

Willis, Paul. *Learning to Labour: How Working Class Kids Get Working Class Jobs*. Farnborough, UK: Saxon House, 1977.

Wilson, William Julius. *The Truly Disadvantaged: The Inner City, the Underclass, and Public Policy*. Chicago: University of Chicago Press, 1987.

——. *When Work Disappears: The World of the New Urban Poor*. New York: Knopf, 1996.

Wolfinger, James. *Philadelphia Divided: Race and Politics in the City of Brotherly Love*. Chapel Hill: University of North Carolina Press, 2007.

Woodward, C. Vann. *The Strange Career of Jim Crow*. New York: Oxford University Press, 1955.

Yaffe, Gideon. *The Age of Culpability: Children and the Nature of Criminal Responsibility*. New York: Oxford University Press, 2018.

Younge, Gary. *Another Day in the Death of America*. New York: Nation Books, 2016.

Ziegler-McPherson, Christina A. *Selling America: Immigration Promotion and the Settlement of the American Continent, 1607–1914*. Santa Barbara, CA: Praeger, 2017.

Zucchino, David. *Myth of the Welfare Queen: A Pulitzer Prize–Winning Journalist's Portrait of Women on the Line*. New York: Scribner, 1997.

NOTES

INTRODUCTION

1. School District of Philadelphia, *S737001; Washington, Grover Final Site Assessment Report* (January 31, 2017).
2. Center on Society and Health, Virginia Commonwealth University, "Philadelphia Life Expectancy Methodology and Data Table"; World Bank, "Life Expectancy at Birth, Total (Years)," 2020.
3. "Large city" is defined here by having at least one million residents; Pew Charitable Trusts, *Philadelphia 2021: The State of the City* (April 2021); Pew Charitable Trusts, *Philadelphia's Poor: Who They Are, Where They Live, and How That Has Changed* (2017); United States Census Bureau, "American Community Survey 1-Year Data (2005–2021)," 2022; United States Census Bureau, "2016–2020 American Community Survey 5-Year Estimates," 2022; Douglas S. Massey and Jonathan Tannen, "A Research Note on Trends in Black Hypersegregation," *Demography* 52, no. 3 (2015): 1025–34; Martin Luther King Jr., "Letter from Birmingham Jail," April 16, 1963. As many scholars and experts have pointed out, the Official Poverty Measure is a very flawed metric that underestimates the depth of poverty in the country. I am using this measure because OPM provides county and census tract-level data. For critiques of OPM and the Supplemental Poverty Measure, see: Shawn Fremstad, "The Defining Down of Economic Deprivation: Why We Need to Reset the Poverty Line," Century Foundation, September 30, 2020; David Brady, "American Poverty Should Be Measured Relative to the Prevailing Standards of Our Time," Century Foundation, April 27, 2021; Jeff Madrick, *Invisible Americans: The Tragic Cost of Child Poverty* (New York: Knopf, 2020).
4. Mike Newall, "Business and Bloodshed," *Philadelphia Inquirer*, May 23, 2021.
5. Franklin Delano Roosevelt, "Second Inaugural Address" (speech, Washington, D.C., January 20, 1937).

6. John Creamer, Emily A. Shrider, Kalee Burns, and Frances Chen, *Poverty in the United States: 2021*, United States Census Bureau (September 2022); PYMNTS, *New Reality Check: The Paycheck-to-Paycheck Report* (June 2022); Andrew P. Wilper et al., "Health Insurance and Mortality in US Adults," *American Journal of Public Health* 99, no. 12 (2009): 2289–95; Harvard Joint Center for Housing Studies, *The State of the Nation's Housing*, 2021; United States Census Bureau, "Household Pulse Survey," June 29–July 11, 2022.

7. Franklin Delano Roosevelt, "State of the Union Address" (speech, Washington, D.C., January 4, 1935); Eric Rauchway, *Why the New Deal Matters* (New Haven, CT: Yale University Press, 2021); Jamelle Bouie, "F.D.R. Didn't Just Fix the Economy," *New York Times*, April 16, 2021; Ira Katznelson, "Was the Great Society a Lost Opportunity?" in *The Rise and Fall of the New Deal Order, 1930–1980*, ed. Steve Fraser and Gary Gerstle (Princeton, NJ: Princeton University Press, 1989), 185–211; Karl Polanyi, *The Great Transformation: Economic and Political Origins of Our Time* (New York: Farrar and Rinehart, 1944); Loïc Wacquant, "Deadly Symbiosis: When Ghetto and Prison Meet and Mesh," *Punishment & Society* 3, no. 1 (2001): 95–133; David Harvey, *A Brief History of Neoliberalism* (New York: Oxford University Press, 2007); Naomi Klein, *The Shock Doctrine: The Rise of Disaster Capitalism* (New York: Metropolitan Books, 2007); Tony Judt, *Ill Fares the Land* (New York: Penguin Press, 2010); Emmanuel Saez and Gabriel Zucman, "Wealth Inequality in the United States Since 1913: Evidence from Capitalized Income Tax Data," National Bureau of Economic Research (October 2014); Daniel Stedman Jones, *Masters of the Universe: Hayek, Friedman, and the Birth of Neoliberal Politics* (Princeton, NJ: Princeton University Press, 2014); Thomas Piketty, *Capital in the Twenty-First Century*, trans. Arthur Goldhammer (Cambridge, MA: Belknap Press of Harvard University Press, 2014); David Kotz, *The Rise and Fall of Neoliberal Capitalism* (Cambridge, MA: Harvard University Press, 2015); Fred L. Block and Margaret R. Somers, *The Power of Market Fundamentalism: Karl Polanyi's Critique* (Cambridge, MA: Harvard University Press, 2016); George Monbiot, "Neoliberalism—The Ideology at the Root of All Our Problems," *Guardian*, April 15, 2016; Gary Gerstle, *The Rise and Fall of the Neoliberal Order: America and the World in the Free Market Era* (New York: Oxford University Press, 2022).

8. OECD, "Poverty Rate," 2023.

CHAPTER ONE: THE FIREMAN

1. Brent Staples, "Special Education Is Not a Scandal," *New York Times Magazine*, September 21, 1997; Tracy Thompson, "The Special-Education Charade," *Atlantic*, January 3, 2016; Evie Blad, "Why the Feds Still Fall Short on Special Education Funding," *Education Week*, January 10, 2020.

2. Alexander Sutherland Neill, *Summerhill: A Radical Approach to Child Rearing* (New York: Hart, 1960).

3. J. M. Moak, "James Russell Lowell School," Pennsylvania Historic Resource Survey Form, Office of Historic Preservation, May 27, 1987; United States Department of the Interior, "Philadelphia Public Schools Thematic Resources," National Register of Historic Places Inventory—Nomination Form, December 4, 1986; Franklin Davenport Edmunds, *The Public School Buildings of the City of Philadelphia* 8 (Philadelphia: F. D. Edmunds, 1913): 129–32.

4. Barbara Laker, Wendy Ruderman, Dylan Purcell, Jessica Griffin, and Garland Potts, "Toxic City: Sick Schools" series, *Philadelphia Inquirer*, May 3–17, 2018; Dylan Purcell, Barbara Laker, and Wendy Ruderman, "Botched Jobs," *Philadelphia Inquirer*, May 17, 2018.

5. Nina Feldman, "Why Your Neighborhood School Probably Doesn't Have a Playground," WHYY, February 6, 2019.

6. Two names have been changed to account for pseudonyms.

7. Jason P. Nance, "Students, Police, and the School-to-Prison Pipeline," *Washington Law Review* 93, no. 4 (2016): 919–87; Advancement Project, *Test, Punish, and Push Out: How "Zero Tolerance" and High-Stakes Testing Funnel Youth into the School-to-Prison Pipeline* (March 2010); Matthew T. Theriot, "School Resource Officers and the Criminalization of Student Behavior," *Journal of Criminal Justice* 37, no. 3 (May–June 2009): 280–87; Owen Davis, "Punitive Schooling," *Jacobin*, October 17, 2014; Kim Brooks, Vincent Schiraldi, and Jason Ziedenberg, *School House Hype: Two Years Later* (Justice Policy Institute and Children's Law Center, 2000); Carla Shedd, *Unequal City: Race, Schools, and Perceptions of Injustice* (New York: Russell Sage Foundation, 2015).

8. Robert Balfanz, Vaughan Byrnes, and Joanna Hornig Fox, "Sent Home and Put Off-Track: The Antecedents, Disproportionalities, and Consequences of Being Suspended in the Ninth Grade," *Journal of Applied Research on Children: Informing Policy for Children at Risk* 5, no. 2 (2014): 1–19; Russell J. Skiba, Mariella I. Arredondo, and Natasha T. Williams, "More Than a Metaphor: The Contribution of Exclusionary Discipline to a School-to-Prison Pipeline," *Equity & Excellence in Education* 47, no. 4 (2014): 546–64.

9. John J. Dilulio, "Moral Poverty," *Chicago Tribune*, December 15, 2005; John J. Dilulio, "The Coming of the Super-Predators," *Weekly Standard*, November 27, 1995; Robert Mackey and Zaid Jilani, "Hillary Clinton Still Haunted by Discredited Rhetoric on 'Superpredators,'" *Intercept*, February 25, 2016; Alex S. Vitale, "The New 'Superpredator,'" *New York Times*, March 23, 2018; Nancy A. Heitzeg, "Criminalizing Education: Zero Tolerance Policies, Police in the Hallways, and the School to Prison Pipeline," *Counterpoints* 453 (2014): 11–36; Aaron Brand, "Biting the Bullet: Why the Gun Free Schools Act Must Be Repealed to Protect Student Speech," *John Marshall Law Review* 49, no. 2 (2015): 593–624; Kathleen M. Cerrone, "The Gun-Free Schools Act of 1994: Zero Tolerance Takes Aim at Procedural Due Process," *Pace Law Review* 20, no. 1 (1999): 131–88; Brooks, Schiraldi, and Ziedenberg, "School House

Hype"; Sheila Heaviside et al., *Violence and Discipline Problems in U.S. Public Schools: 1996–97* (Washington, DC: National Center for Education Statistics, U.S. Department of Education, 1998); Jeffrey Butts and Jeremy Travis, *The Rise and Fall of American Urban Violence: 1980 to 2000* (Washington, D.C.: Urban Institute, March 2002).

10. Kevin P. Brady, Sharon Balmer, and Deinya Phenix, "School–Police Partnership Effectiveness in Urban Schools: An Analysis of New York City's Impact Schools Initiative," *Education and Urban Society* 39, no. 4 (2007): 455–78; Cathy Girouard, *School Resource Officer Training Program* (Washington, DC: Office of Juvenile Justice and Delinquency Prevention, U.S. Department of Justice, 2001); Nathan James and Gail McCallion, *School Resource Officers: Law Enforcement Officers in Schools* (Washington, DC: Congressional Research Service, 2013); Barbara Raymond, *Assigning Police Officers to Schools* (Washington, DC: Office of Community Oriented Policing Services, U.S. Department of Justice, 2010); Chongmin Na and Denise C. Gottfredson, "Police Officers in Schools: Effects on School Crime and the Processing of Offending Behaviors," *Justice Quarterly* 30, no. 4 (2013): 619–50; Nance, "Students, Police, and the School-to-Prison Pipeline."

11. Michel Foucault, *Discipline and Punish: The Birth of the Prison* (New York: Vintage, 1995), 297.

CHAPTER TWO: LITTLE VIETNAM

1. Abigail Abrams, "Democrats Want to Reform This Program That Helps Poor Elderly and Disabled Americans," *Time*, July 22, 2021; Maggie Astor, "How Disabled Americans Are Pushing to Overhaul a Key Benefits Program," *New York Times*, July 30, 2021; Dylan Matthews, "The Democratic Plan to Smash Poverty for Seniors and People with Disabilities," *Vox*, July 9, 2021; Social Security Report No. 92–1230, *Social Security Amendments of 1972: Report on the Committee on Finance, United States Senate to Accompany H.R. 1 to Amend the Social Security Act, and for Other Purposes* (Washington, DC: U.S. Government Printing Office, 1972), 384; Nancy Altman, "The Pressing Need to Update, Expand, and Simplify SSI," Social Security Advisory Board, 2020; Annie Harper, Michaella Baker, Dawn Edwards, Yolanda Herring, and Martha Staeheli, "Disabled, Poor, and Poorly Served: Access to and Use of Financial Services by People with Serious Mental Illness," *Social Service Review* 92, no. 2 (2018): 202–40; Azza Altiraifi, "A Deadly Poverty Trap: Asset Limits in the Time of the Coronavirus," Center for American Progress, April 7, 2020.

2. MedlinePlus, "Electromyography (EMG) and Nerve Conduction Studies."

3. Code of Federal Regulations, Title 20, *Employee Benefits: Parts 400 to 499* (Washington, DC: U.S. Government Printing Office, 1999), 443.

4. Olivia Golden and Amelia Hawkins, "TANF Child-Only Cases," Urban Institute, November 2011.

5. Dennis Hevesi, "5 Children Die in Fire in Jersey Project," *New York Times*, August 21, 1988.

6. David J. Goodwin, *Left Bank of the Hudson: Jersey City and the Artists of 111 1st Street* (New York: Fordham University Press, 2017); Hamilton S. Wicks, "American Industries—No. 1," *Scientific American*, January 11, 1879; Rick James, "Warehouse Historic District," Jersey City Landmarks Conservancy, 2003; Ted Koppel, "Hassan's Choices: Life in the Woods," ABC News, *Nightline*, May 3 and 4, 1993.

7. Loïc Wacquant, *Punishing the Poor: The Neoliberal Government of Social Insecurity* (Durham, NC: Duke University Press, 2009), 305.

8. Joel Achenbach, "Novelist of the Gutter Instinct," *Washington Post*, June 3, 1992; Isabelle de Pommereau, "Fighting Crime, One Kid at a Time," *Christian Science Monitor*, March 10, 1997; Jeffrey Hoff, "Plan to Raze Housing Irks Homeless," *New York Times*, May 14, 1989.

CHAPTER THREE: DON'T NOBODY LEAVE THIS SCHOOL

1. Bruce Dobie, "Exit Interview," *Nashville Scene*, December 14, 1995; Annette Fuentes, "Failing Students, Rising Profits," *Nation*, September 1, 2005; David Montero, "A Changing of the Guard at Houston's Disciplinary School," *Frontline*, PBS, September 27, 2012; Margaret Downing and Wendy Grossman, "Learning How to Survive (at) CEP," *Houston Press*, May 31, 2001; Wendy Grossman, "Making (Up) the Grade," *Houston Press*, April 6, 2000; Wendy Grossman, "Learning Curve," *Houston Press*, October 5, 2000; Scott Freeman, "Forrest Hill Academy: The Children Left Behind," *Creative Loafing*, May 7, 2008; Paul Socolar, "CEP Clashes with Critics in Texas," *Philadelphia Public School Notebook*, November 28, 2002; Dale Mezzacappa, "CEP's Political Allies," *Philadelphia Public School Notebook*, September 20, 2006.

2. Pennsylvania General Assembly, "Act 30," 1997; Pennsylvania General Assembly, "Act 48," 1999; Education Law Center, *Improving "Alternative Education for Disruptive Youth" in Pennsylvania* (2010); Dale Mezzacappa, "CEP Mystery: Many Pass Through . . . and Then?" *Philadelphia Public School Notebook*, September 20, 2006; Pennsylvania Department of Education, "Alternative Education for Disruptive Youth (AEDY)"; Dale Mezzacappa, "CEP Tells State It Is Leaving Philadelphia," *Philadelphia Public School Notebook*, August 9, 2010; Kristen A. Graham and Susan Snyder, "School District Cancels Contract with Company That Ran Alternative Programs," *Philadelphia Inquirer*, August 10, 2010; Fuentes, "Failing Students, Rising Profits"; Barbara Laker, "Helping Young Felons," *Philadelphia Daily News*, March 19, 2002; Paul Socolar, "New Law Forces Students into Alternative Schools," *Philadelphia Public School Notebook*, September 25, 2002; Rhea R. Borja, "Phila. Students Sue over Ban from Schools," *Education Week*, October 9, 2002; "CEP: City's Largest Disciplinary School Adds More Students," *Philadelphia Public School Notebook,* November

28, 2002; "Outside Providers Play Growing Role in Alternative Schools," *Philadelphia Public School Notebook*, May 28, 2003; Paul Socolar, "CEO Vallas Commits to a Fresh Start," *Philadelphia Public School Notebook*, September 25, 2002; Paul Socolar, "Zero Tolerance Kicks In," *Philadelphia Public School Notebook*, November 27, 2002; Wendy Harris, "A Growing Expulsion Pipeline," *Philadelphia Public School Notebook*, November 28, 2009; Youth United for Change and Advancement Project, *Zero Tolerance in Philadelphia: Denying Educational Opportunities and Creating a Pathway to Prison* (January 2011).

3. Some names in this section have been changed to account for pseudonyms.

4. Paul Socolar, "With Boom in 'Alternative' Schools, Questions Raised About Their Impact," *Philadelphia Public School Notebook*, July 27, 2004; Mezzacappa, "CEP Mystery: Many Pass Through . . . and Then?"; Socolar, "CEP Clashes with Critics in Texas"; Fuentes, "Failing Students, Rising Profits"; Grossman, "Learning Curve"; Downing and Grossman, "Learning How to Survive (at) CEP"; Grossman, "Making (Up) the Grade"; Robert Kimball, "A Study of the Retention and Graduation Rate at an Alternative School in Houston ISD Managed by Community Education Partners," October 2, 2006; Montero, "A Changing of the Guard."

5. ACLU, "ACLU Drops Community Education Partners from Federal Lawsuit After Atlanta Severs Contract," July 30, 2009; Alan Judd, "Shining Image Tarnished," *Atlanta Journal-Constitution*, March 2, 2005.

6. Plaintiffs v. Atlanta Independent School System and Community Education Partners, Inc., United States District Court for the Northern District of Georgia, Atlanta Division (March 31, 2009); Judd, "Shining Image Tarnished"; Montero, "A Changing of the Guard"; Freeman, "Forrest Hill Academy."

7. Mezzacappa, "CEP Tells State It Is Leaving Philadelphia"; Graham and Snyder, "School District Cancels Contract"; Montero, "A Changing of the Guard."

8. Kristen A. Graham, "Perzel Loses Longtime Pa. House Seat to Boyle," *Philadelphia Inquirer*, November 3, 2010; Angela Couloumbis, "Perzel to Plead Guilty to Corruption," *Philadelphia Inquirer*, August 31, 2011; Dave Warner, "Once-Influential Pennsylvania Legislator Sentenced to Prison," Reuters, March 21, 2012; Tony Romeo, "Former Pennsylvania House Speaker John Perzel Paroled from Prison," CBS News Philadelphia, February 27, 2014.

CHAPTER FOUR: HAMBURGER HELPER

1. Sandra Wexler and Rafael J. Engel, "Historical Trends in State-Level ADC/AFDC Benefits: Living on Less and Less," *Journal of Sociology and Social Welfare* 26, no. 2 (June 1999): 37–61.

2. Social Security Administration, "SSI Federal Payment Amounts."

3. Dylan Matthews, "Sweden Pays Parents for Having Kids—and It Reaps Huge Benefits. Why Doesn't the US?" *Vox*, May 23, 2016.

4. Ira Goldstein, "Racial & Economic Correlates of Eviction and Foreclosure Rates

in Philadelphia: Preliminary Observations (presentation, Homeownership & Consumer Rights Unit, Community Legal Services, December 13, 2016).

5. Matthew Desmond, *Evicted: Poverty and Profit in the American City* (New York: Crown, 2016), 5.

CHAPTER FIVE: ALL WEED AND NO SEED

1. Philadelphia Chamber of Commerce, *The City of Philadelphia as It Appears in the Year 1894* (Philadelphia: G. S. Harris & Sons, 1894), 184; Kenneth W. Milano, *Hidden History of Kensington and Fishtown* (Charleston, SC: History Press, 2010); Federal Writers' Project, Works Progress Administration, *Philadelphia: A Guide to the Nation's Birthplace* (Harrisburg, PA: Telegraph Press, 1937); Philip Scranton, "Build a Firm, Start Another: The Bromleys and Family Firm Entrepreneurship in the Philadelphia Region," in *Family Capitalism*, ed. Geoffrey Jones and Mary B. Rose (Portland, OR: Frank Cass, 1993), 115–51.

2. Bob Burns, "Master Streams Contain Philadelphia Mill Fire," *Fire Engineering*, December 1, 1979; Dick Cooper, "Fire Hits Old Mill in Kensington," *Philadelphia Inquirer*, July 30, 1979; Philadelphia Fire Department | Engine 6 / Ladder 16, "Back in Time," Facebook, March 22, 2018.

3. Carmen A. Weber, Irving Kosmin, and Muriel Kirkpatrick, *Workshop of the World* (Philadelphia: Oliver Evans Press, 1990); Buzz Bissinger, *A Prayer for the City* (New York: Random House, 1997); Fredric M. Miller, Morris J. Vogel, and Allen F. Davis, *Still Philadelphia: A Photographic History, 1890–1940* (Philadelphia: Temple University Press, 1983); Alfred Lubrano, "A Struggle to Make an Honest Living," *Philadelphia Inquirer*, December 29, 2010; Patricia Stern Smallacombe, *Why Do They Stay: Rootedness and Isolation in an Inner City White Neighborhood* (PhD diss., University of Pennsylvania, 2002).

4. Nathan T. Folwell, "The Textile Capital of the World," in *1917 Philadelphia Year Book* (Philadelphia: Philadelphia Chamber of Commerce, 1917), G1–G32.

5. United States Census Bureau, *Reports: Thirteenth Census of the United States Taken in the Year 1910*, vol. 9 (Washington, DC: U.S. Census Bureau, 1912), 1052; Miller, Vogel, and Davis, *Still Philadelphia*, 73.

6. George Morgan, *The City of Firsts* (Philadelphia: Historical Publication Society, 1926), 248; Logan I. Ferguson, *Commercial Buildings Related to the Textile Industry in the Kensington Neighborhood of Philadelphia* (Philadelphia: Powers, 2012); Folwell, "The Textile Capital of the World"; Weber, Kosmin, and Kirkpatrick, *Workshop of the World*.

7. Philip Scranton, *Endless Novelty: Specialty Production and American Industrialization, 1865–1925* (Princeton, NJ: Princeton University Press, 1997); Ferguson, *Commercial Buildings Related to the Textile Industry*.

8. Scranton, "Build a Firm, Start Another"; Charles Robson, *The Manufactories and Manufacturers of Pennsylvania of the Nineteenth Century* (Philadelphia: Galaxy Publishing Company, 1875).

9. Scranton, "Build a Firm, Start Another"; Scranton, *Endless Novelty*; Robson, *The Manufactories and Manufacturers of Pennsylvania*.

10. Philip Scranton, *Proprietary Capitalism: The Textile Manufacture at Philadelphia, 1800–1885* (Cambridge: Cambridge University Press, 1983).

11. Scranton, *Proprietary Capitalism*; Philip Scranton, *Figured Tapestry: Production, Markets and Power in Philadelphia Textiles, 1855–1941* (Cambridge: Cambridge University Press, 1989), 46–47; "Understanding After Great Losses on Both Sides Arbitration Prevails," *Philadelphia Inquirer*, April 13, 1835.

12. Scranton, *Figured Tapestry*; Scranton, "Build a Firm, Start Another."

13. Walter Licht, *Getting Work: Philadelphia, 1840–1950* (Cambridge, MA: Harvard University Press, 1992), 11.

14. Daniel Rubin, "Fire Site Once Did Fine Business," *Philadelphia Inquirer*, September 21, 1994; Scranton, "Build a Firm, Start Another"; Weber, Kosmin, and Kirkpatrick, *Workshop of the World*.

15. John D. Kasarda, "Jobs, Migration, and Emerging Urban Mismatches," in *Urban Change and Poverty*, ed. Michael McGeary and Laurence E. Lynn Jr. (Washington, DC: National Academies Press, 1988): 148–98; David Elesh, "Deindustrialization," *The Encyclopedia of Greater Philadelphia*; Carolyn Adams, David Bartelt, David Elesh, Ira Goldstein, Nancy Klenewski, and William Yancey, *Philadelphia: Neighborhoods, Division, and Conflict in a Postindustrial City* (Philadelphia: Temple University Press, 1991); James Wolfinger, *Philadelphia Divided: Race and Politics in the City of Brotherly Love* (Chapel Hill: University of North Carolina Press, 2007); John Bauman et al., "Public Housing, Isolation, and the Urban Underclass: Philadelphia's Richard Allen Homes, 1941–1965," in *African Americans in Pennsylvania: Shifting Historical Perspectives*, ed. Joe W. Trotter and Eric Ledell Smith (University Park: Pennsylvania State University Press, 1997), 443–68.

16. Barry Bluestone and Bennett Harrison, *The Deindustrialization of America: Plant Closings, Community Abandonment, and the Dismantling of Basic Industry* (New York: Basic Books, 1982); Gladys Louise Palmer, *Philadelphia Workers in a Changing Economy* (Philadelphia: University of Pennsylvania Press, 1956); William Julius Wilson, *The Truly Disadvantaged: The Inner City, the Underclass, and Public Policy* (Chicago: University of Chicago Press, 1987); William Julius Wilson, *When Work Disappears: The World of the New Urban Poor* (New York: Knopf, 1996); Steve Fraser, *The Age of Acquiescence: The Life and Death of American Resistance to Organized Wealth and Power* (New York: Little, Brown, 2015).

17. Peter Binzen, *Whitetown, U.S.A.* (New York: Random House, 1970), 81; Murray Friedman, *Overcoming Middle Class Rage* (Philadelphia: Westminster Press, 1971); Jean Seder, *Voices of Kensington: Vanishing Mills, Vanishing Neighborhoods* (Ardmore, PA: Whitmore Publishing, 1982).

18. Seder, *Voices of Kensington*, 3–4.

19. Wolfinger, *Philadelphia Divided*; John F. Bauman, *Public Housing, Race, and*

Renewal: Urban Planning in Philadelphia, 1920–1974 (Philadelphia: Temple University Press, 1987); Binzen, *Whitetown, U.S.A.*

20. Carmen T. Whalen, *From Puerto Rico to Philadelphia: Puerto Rican Workers and Postwar Economies* (Philadelphia: Temple University Press, 2001); Eugene P. Ericksen et al., *The State of Puerto Rican Philadelphia* (Philadelphia: Institute for Public Policy Research, Temple University, 1985).

21. Cesar J. Ayala, "The Decline of the Plantation Economy and the Puerto Rican Migration of the 1950s," *Latino Studies Journal* 7, no. 1 (1996): 61–90; Whalen, *From Puerto Rico to Philadelphia*; Edgardo Meléndez, *Sponsored Migration: The State and Puerto Rican Postwar Migration to the United States* (Columbus: Ohio State University Press, 2017); Ericksen et al., *The State of Puerto Rican Philadelphia.*

22. Whalen, *From Puerto Rico to Philadelphia*; Edwin Maldonado, "Contract Labor and the Origins of Puerto Rican Communities in the United States," *International Migration Review* 13, no. 1 (1979): 103–21; Whalen, *From Puerto Rico to Philadelphia*; Carmen T. Whalen, "Colonialism, Citizenship, and the Making of the Puerto Rican Diaspora: An Introduction," in *Puerto Rican Diaspora: Historical Perspectives*, ed. Carmen T. Whalen and Víctor Vázquez-Hernandez (Philadelphia: Temple University Press, 2005), 1–42; José Ramón Sánchez, *Boricua Power: A Political History of Puerto Ricans in the United States* (New York: New York University Press, 2007); Joan D. Koss, *Puerto Ricans in Philadelphia: Migration and Accommodation* (PhD diss., University of Pennsylvania, 1965); Commission on Human Relations, *Philadelphia's Puerto Rican Population: A Descriptive Summary Including 1960 Census Data* (Philadelphia: Commission on Human Relations, March 1964).

23. Commission on Human Relations Staff, "Incident at 428 Belgrade Street-June 1960," Commission on Human Relations, City of Philadelphia, November 4, 1960.

24. Judith Goode and Jo Anne Schneider, *Reshaping Ethnic and Racial Relations in Philadelphia: Immigrants in a Divided City* (Philadelphia: Temple University Press, 1994); Jamie Catrambone and Harry C. Silcox, eds., *Kensington History: Stories and Memories* (Philadelphia: Brighton Press, 1996); "2 Bombs Hit School Closed in Puerto Rican Boy's Drowning," *Philadelphia Evening Bulletin*, June 20, 1973; Charles F. Thomson and Alfonso D. Brown, "15 Ask O'Neill to Press Probe of Boy's Drowning," *Philadelphia Evening Bulletin*, June 22, 1973.

25. Kasarda, "Jobs, Migration, and Emerging Urban Mismatches"; Elesh, "Deindustrialization"; Adams, Bartelt, Elesh, and Goldstein, *Philadelphia: Neighborhoods, Division, and Conflict in a Postindustrial City*; Wolfinger, *Philadelphia Divided.*

26. Dana Adams Schmidt, "Addiction in Vietnam Spurs Nixon and Congress to Take Drastic New Steps," *New York Times*, June 16, 1971; Richard Nixon, "Remarks About an Intensified Program for Drug Abuse Prevention and Control," June 17, 1971; Michael Massing, *The Fix* (Berkeley: University of California Press, 1998); Johann Hari, *Chasing the Scream: The First and Last Days of the War on Drugs* (New York: Bloomsbury, 2015); Radley Balko, *Rise of the*

Warrior Cop: The Militarization of America's Police Forces (New York: Public-Affairs, 2013); Michelle Alexander, *The New Jim Crow: Mass Incarceration in the Age of Colorblindness* (New York: The New Press, 2010); Dan Baum, *Smoke and Mirrors: The War on Drugs and the Politics of Failure* (New York: Little, Brown, 1996); Mike Davis, *City of Quartz: Excavating the Future in Los Angeles* (New York: Verso, 1990); James Forman Jr., *Locking Up Our Own: Crime and Punishment in Black America* (New York: Farrar, Straus & Giroux, 2017); Naomi Murakawa, *The First Civil Right: How Liberals Built Prison America* (New York: Oxford University Press, 2014); Carl Hart, *High Price: A Neuroscientist's Journey of Self-Discovery That Challenges Everything You Know About Drugs and Society* (New York: Harper, 2013); Elizabeth Hinton, *From the War on Poverty to the War on Crime: The Making of Mass Incarceration in America* (Cambridge, MA: Harvard University Press, 2016); Heather Ann Thompson, "Why Mass Incarceration Matters: Rethinking Crisis, Decline, and Transformation in Postwar American History," *Journal of American History* 97, no. 3 (December 2010): 703–34.

27. German Lopez, "Was Nixon's War on Drugs a Racially Motivated Crusade? It's a Bit More Complicated," *Vox*, March 29, 2016; Balko, *Rise of the Warrior Cop*; Hinton, *From the War on Poverty to the War on Crime*, 156–59, 207–8.

28. Dan Baum, "Legalize It All," *Harper's Magazine*, April 2016.

29. Michael Demarest, "Cocaine: Middle Class High," *Time*, July 6, 1981.

30. Drug Enforcement Administration, "History: 1985–1990."

31. Drug Enforcement Administration, "History: 1985–1990"; Stephanie Watson and Nathan Chandler, "How Crack Cocaine Works," *HowStuffWorks*.

32. Editorial Staff, "What Is Crack? Differences Between Crack and Cocaine?" American Addiction Centers; Roland G. Fryer Jr., Paul S. Heaton, Steven D. Levitt, and Kevin M. Murphy, "Measuring Crack Cocaine and Its Impact," *Economic Inquiry* 51, no. 3 (2013): 1651–81.

33. Ronald Reagan, "Remarks on Signing Executive Order 12368, Concerning Federal Drug Abuse Policy Functions" (speech, Washington, D.C., June 24, 1982).

34. Baum, *Smoke and Mirrors*.

35. Jack McCallum, "'The Cruelest Thing Ever,'" *Sports Illustrated*, June 30, 1986; Michael Weinreb, "The Day Innocence Died," ESPN, June 2008; Associated Press, "Examiner Confirms Cocaine Killed Bias," June 25, 1986.

36. Baum, *Smoke and Mirrors*.

37. Associated Press, "Evidence Indicates Bias Had Smoked Pure Form of Drug," July 10, 1986.

38. Baum, *Smoke and Mirrors*; Weinreb, "The Day Innocence Died."

39. Ronald Reagan and Nancy Reagan, "Address to the Nation on the Campaign Against Drug Abuse" (speech, Washington, D.C., September 14, 1986).

40. Michael Tonry, "Race and the War on Drugs," *University of Chicago Legal Forum* 1994, no. 1 (1994): 25–81; Lloyd D. Johnston, Patrick M. O'Malley, and Jerald G. Bachman, *Illicit Drug Use, Smoking, and Drinking by America's High*

School Students, College Students, and Young Adults, 1975–1987 (Washington, DC: National Institute on Drug Abuse, 1988); National Research Council, *Preventing Drug Abuse: What Do We Know?* (Washington, DC: National Academies Press, 1993); Joseph Gfroerer and Marc Brodsky, "The Incidence of Illicit Drug Use in the United States, 1962–1989," *British Journal of Addiction* 87, no. 9 (September 1992): 1345–51; Craig Reinarman and Harry G. Levine, "The Crack Attack Politics and Media in the Crack Scare," in *Crack in America: Demon Drugs and Social Justice*, eds. Craig Reinarman and Harry G. Levine (Berkeley: University of California Press, 1997): 18–51; Jerome L. Himmelstein, "How the Mass Media Use Numbers to Tell a Story: The Case of the Crack Scare of 1986," *Numeracy* 7, no. 1 (2014); Matthew D. Lassiter, "Impossible Criminals: The Suburban Imperatives of America's War on Drugs," *Journal of American History* 102, no. 1 (June 2015): 126–40; Peter Kerr, "Anatomy of the Drug Issue: How, After Years, It Erupted," *New York Times*, November 17, 1986; James D. Orcutt and J. Blake Turner, "Shocking Numbers and Graphic Accounts: Quantified Images of Drug Problems in the Print Media," *Social Problems* 40, no. 2 (1993): 190–206; Alexander, *The New Jim Crow*.

41. Beverly Xaviera Watkins and Mindy Thompson Fullilove, "Crack Cocaine and Harlem's Health," in *Dispatches from the Ebony Tower: Intellectuals Confront the African American Experience*, ed. Manning Marable (New York: Columbia University Press, 2000): 121–37; Doris Marie Provine, "Creating Racial Disadvantage: The Case of Crack Cocaine," in *The Many Colors of Crime: Inequalities of Race, Ethnicity, and Crime in America*, eds. Ruth Peterson, Lauren Krivo, and John Hagan (New York: New York University Press, 2006), 277–94; Criminal Justice Policy Foundation, "Mandatory Minimums and Sentencing Reform"; Solomon Moore, "Justice Dept. Seeks Equity in Sentences for Cocaine," *New York Times*, April 29, 2009.

42. U.S. Justice Department, Bureau of Justice Statistics Bulletin, "Prisoners 1925–81," December 1982; Tracey L. Snell, *Correctional Populations in the United States, 1993* (Washington, DC: Office of Justice Programs, Bureau of Justice Statistics, U.S. Department of Justice, October 1995).

43. David Zucchino, "In the Badlands of the City, Drugs Still Riding High," *Philadelphia Inquirer*, April 3, 1991; David Zucchino, "Razing the Ruins That Heroin Built," *Philadelphia Inquirer*, March 13, 1992; David Zucchino, "How an Illicit World Flourishes Just Three Miles from City Hall," *Philadelphia Inquirer*, April 5, 1992; David Zucchino, "The Badlands: In the Grip of Drugs," *Philadelphia Inquirer*, April 6, 1992; David Zucchino, "How Small Operators Cash In on the Big Miseries of Drugs," *Philadelphia Inquirer*, April 7, 1992; David Zucchino, *Myth of the Welfare Queen: A Pulitzer Prize–Winning Journalist's Portrait of Women on the Line* (New York: Scribner, 1997).

44. Forman, *Locking Up Our Own*, 12–13; Khalil Gibran Muhammad, *The Condemnation of Blackness: Race, Crime, and the Making of Modern Urban America* (Cambridge, MA: Harvard University Press, 2010).

45. Craig R. McCoy, Nathan Gorenstein, and Amy S. Rosenberg, "Bush's Visit Greeted with Loud Protest," *Philadelphia Inquirer*, May 12, 1992; Mark Wagenveld, "Kensington Rally Decries Drug Use," *Philadelphia Inquirer*, July 31, 1985; Amy Linn, "Residents in Kensington Rally Against Drugs," *Philadelphia Inquirer*, November 3, 1985; David Zucchino, "Off the Street and Into Court," *Philadelphia Inquirer*, October 28, 1990; Mark Wagenveld, "Kensington March and Vigil Fight Street Drug Sales Near North Philadelphia," *Philadelphia Inquirer*, April 13, 1989.

46. McCoy, Gorenstein, and Rosenberg, "Bush's Visit Greeted with Loud Protest."

47. Commonwealth of Pennsylvania, Department of Corrections, *1990 Annual Statistical Report: State Correctional System* (1990); Gary Cohn and David Zucchino, "Drug Dealers' Properties Give New Lease to the Community," *Philadelphia Inquirer*, October 27, 1992; David Zucchino, "Shaking the Grip of Drugs," *Philadelphia Inquirer*, December 20, 1992; Janice A. Roehl, Robert Huitt, Mary Ann Wycoff, Antony Pate, Donald Rebovich, and Ken Coyle, *National Process Evaluation of Operation Weed and Seed* (Washington, DC: National Institute of Justice, U.S. Department of Justice, October 1996); Public Papers, "Statement on Urban Aid Initiatives," George H. W. Bush Presidential Library & Museum, May 12, 1992; "The Right Response to Riots," *New York Times*, May 17, 1992; Christian Parenti, "Weed and Seed: The Fortress Culture," *Prison Legal News*, January 15, 1994; Julie Garfield, "Landscaping Neo-Liberalism: The Weed and Seed Strategy," *Advocates' Forum* (2010); David Havey, *Social Justice and the City* (Baltimore: Johns Hopkins University Press, 1978); David Harvey, *A Brief History of Neoliberalism* (New York: Oxford University Press, 2007); Loïc Wacquant, "Deadly Symbiosis: When Ghetto and Prison Meet and Mesh," *Punishment & Society* 3, no. 1 (2001): 95–133.

48. McCoy, Gorenstein, and Rosenberg, "Bush's Visit Greeted with Loud Protest"; Michael Decourcy Hinds, "Experts Are Critical of Bush Anti-Drug Program," *New York Times*, July 20, 1992; Public Papers, "Remarks in a Roundtable Discussion with the Weed and Seed Revitalization Committee and Community Leaders in Philadelphia, Pennsylvania," George H. W. Bush Presidential Library & Museum, May 11, 1992.

49. E. J. Dionne Jr., "Bush Hears Calls for More Aid to Philadelphia's Inner City," *Washington Post*, May 12, 1992.

50. Craig R. McCoy and Terence Samuel, "In Area on Display, the Mood Was Blase," *Philadelphia Inquirer*, May 12, 1992; McCoy, Gorenstein, and Rosenberg, "Bush's Visit Greeted with Loud Protest."

CHAPTER SIX: MY BABY DADDY

1. Jason DeParle, "The Clinton Welfare Bill: A Long Stormy Journey," *New York Times*, July 15, 1994; William J. Clinton, "Campaign Rally in Detroit" (speech, Cobo Hall, October 29, 1992).

2. Michael B. Katz, *In the Shadow of the Poorhouse: A Social History of Welfare in America* (New York: Basic Books, 1986); William Julius Wilson, *The Truly Disadvantaged: The Inner City, the Underclass, and Public Policy* (Chicago: University of Chicago Press, 1987); Christopher Jencks, *Rethinking Social Policy: Race, Poverty, and the Underclass* (Cambridge, MA: Harvard University Press, 1992); Jill S. Quadagno, *The Color of Welfare: How Racism Undermined the War on Poverty* (New York: Oxford University Press, 1994); William Julius Wilson, *When Work Disappears: The World of the New Urban Poor* (New York: Knopf, 1996); Kathryn J. Edin and H. Luke Shaefer, *$2.00 a Day: Living on Almost Nothing in America* (New York: Houghton Mifflin Harcourt, 2015); Mitchell Duneier, *Ghetto: The Invention of a Place, the History of an Idea* (New York: Farrar, Straus & Giroux, 2016); Josh Levin, *The Queen: The Forgotten Life Behind an American Myth* (New York: Little, Brown, 2019).

3. Mary Jo Bane and David T. Ellwood, "Slipping Into and Out of Poverty: The Dynamics of Spells," *Journal of Human Resources* 21, no. 1 (1986): 1–23; David T. Ellwood and Lawrence H. Summers, *Poverty in America: Is Welfare the Answer or the Problem?* (Cambridge, MA: National Bureau of Economic Research, October 1985); Patricia Ruggles, *Welfare Dependency and Its Causes: Determinants of the Duration of Welfare Spells* (Washington, DC: U.S. Department of Commerce, United States Census Bureau, May 1989).

4. Christopher Jencks, "How Poor Are the Poor?" *New York Review of Books*, May 9, 1985; Jencks, *Rethinking Social Policy*; Mary Jo Bane and David T. Ellwood, "The Impact of AFDC on Family Structure and Living Arrangements," *Research in Labor Economics* 7 (1985): 137–207.

5. Ife Floyd et al., "TANF Policies Reflect Racist Legacy of Cash Assistance: Reimagined Program Should Center Black Mothers," Center on Budget and Policy Priorities, August 4, 2021.

6. U.S. House of Representatives, Committee on Ways and Means, *Section 8. Aid to Families with Dependent Children and Related Programs (Title IV-A)* (Washington, DC: U.S. Government Printing Office, 1996).

7. Carol B. Stack, *All Our Kin: Strategies for Survival in a Black Community* (New York: Harper & Row, 1974); Floyd et al., "TANF Policies Reflect Racist Legacy of Cash Assistance"; Office of Assistant Secretary for Planning and Evaluation, U.S. Department of Health and Human Services, *A Brief History of the AFDC Program*.

8. Congressional Research Service, *The Temporary Assistance for Needy Families (TANF) Block Grant: A Legislative History* (October 6, 2021); U.S. Congress, House, *Personal Responsibility and Work Opportunity Reconciliation Act of 1996*, H.R. 3734, 104th Congress, enacted August 22, 1996; Jason DeParle, *American Dream: Three Women, Ten Kids, and a Nation's Drive to End Welfare* (New York: Viking, 2004).

9. Daniel Patrick Moynihan, *The Negro Family: The Case for National Action*

(Washington, DC: Office of Policy Planning and Research, U.S. Department of Labor, March 1965); Ta-Nehisi Coates, "The Black Family in the Age of Mass Incarceration," *Atlantic*, October 2015; Sam Klug, "The Moynihan Report Resurrected," *Dissent*, Winter 2016; Floyd et al., "TANF Policies Reflect Racist Legacy of Cash Assistance."

10. Robin Toner, "New Senate Push on Welfare Revives Tensions in Both Parties," *New York Times*, September 9, 1995.

11. Peter T. Kilborn and Sam Howe Verhovek, "Clinton's Welfare Shift Ends Tortuous Journey," *New York Times*, August 2, 1996; Daniel Patrick Moynihan, *Miles to Go: A Personal History of Social Policy* (Cambridge, MA: Harvard University Press, 1996).

12. Alison Mitchell, "Two Clinton Aides Resign to Protest New Welfare Law," *New York Times*, September 12, 1996; Peter Edelman, "The Worst Thing Bill Clinton Has Done," *Atlantic*, March 1997.

13. Center on Budget and Policy Priorities, "Pennsylvania | TANF Caseload Factsheet," September 2011.

14. Ali Safawi and Cindy Reyes, "States Must Continue Recent Momentum to Further Improve TANF Benefit Levels," Center on Budget and Policy Priorities, December 2, 2021.

15. Arloc Sherman and Danilo Trisi, "Deep Poverty Among Children Worsened in Welfare Law's First Decade," Center on Budget and Policy Priorities, July 23, 2014; Liana Fox, Christopher Wimer, Irwin Garfinkel, Neeraj Kaushal, and Jane Waldfogel, "Waging War on Poverty: Poverty Trends Using a Historical Supplemental Poverty Measure," *Journal of Policy Analysis and Management* 34, no. 3 (2015): 567–92; Matt Bruenig, "The Evidence Clearly Shows That Deep Poverty Has Worsened," *Demos*, February 23, 2016; Edin and Shaefer, *$2.00 a Day*; Dylan Matthews, "'If the Goal Was to Get Rid of Poverty, We Failed': The Legacy of the 1996 Welfare Reform," *Vox*, June 20, 2016; Jordan Weissmann, "The Failure of Welfare Reform," *Slate*, June 1, 2016.

16. William J. Clinton, "State of the Union Address" (speech, Washington, D.C., February 4, 1997); White House, Office of the Press Secretary, "President Clinton: Opening the Doors to College and Economic Opportunity for All Americans," June 10, 2000.

17. Janet Quint et al., *Big Cities and Welfare Reform: Early Implementation and Ethnographic Findings from the Project on Devolution and Urban Change* (New York: Manpower Demonstration Research Corporation, April 1999); Pennsylvania Department of Human Services, *Temporary Assistance for Needy Families (TANF)*.

18. Coates, "The Black Family in the Age of Mass Incarceration"; Pew Charitable Trusts, *Philadelphia's Crowded, Costly Jails: The Search for Safe Solutions* (2010).

19. Anna Orso, "'Burn It. Demolish It. Close It.': Why Philly Officials Say the 100-Year-Old House of Correction Needs to Go," *Billy Penn*, July 28, 2015.

CHAPTER SEVEN: OUR PYROMANIAC

1. David Hill, "California Dreamer," *Education Week*, November 1, 1993.
2. Jonathan Kozol, *Savage Inequalities: Children in America's Schools* (New York: Crown, 1991).
3. Hill, "California Dreamer"; Pamela R. Aschbacher, "Humanitas: A Thematic Curriculum," *Educational Leadership* 49, no. 2 (1991): 16–19.
4. Nikhil Goyal, "These Politicians Think Your Kids Need High-Stakes Testing— but Not Theirs," *Nation*, March 29, 2016; John Dewey, *The School and Society: Being Three Lectures* (Chicago: University of Chicago Press, 1899).
5. *Life*, "Dropout Tragedies: School Problem, Huge but Ignored," May 2, 1960.
6. Jeanne Ellsworth and Robert B. Stevenson, "The Image of the High School Dropout in the Twentieth Century," in *Schooling in the Light of Popular Culture*, ed. Paul Farber, Eugene F. Provenzo Jr., and Gunilla Holm (Albany: State University of New York Press, 1994), 103–29; Sherman Dorn, "Origins of the 'Dropout Problem,'" *History of Education Quarterly* 33, no. 3 (1993): 353–73; Claudia Goldin, "America's Graduation from High School: The Evolution and Spread of Secondary Schooling in the Twentieth Century," *Journal of Economic History* 58, no. 2 (1998): 345–74; James Bryant Conant, *Slums and Suburbs* (New York: McGraw-Hill, 1961).
7. John F. Kennedy, "Annual Message to the Congress on the State of the Union," speech, Washington, D.C., January 14, 1963; U.S. Department of Health, Education, and Welfare, *The 1963 Dropout Campaign: Summary and Analysis of the Special Summer Program to Combat School Dropout Financed from The President's Emergency Fund* (Washington, DC: U.S. Government Printing Office, 1964); Fred M. Hechinger, "The Year Ahead," *New York Times*, September 1, 1963.
8. Lucius F. Cervantes, *The Dropout: Causes and Cures* (Ann Arbor: University of Michigan Press, 1965).
9. William Ryan, *Blaming the Victim* (New York: Pantheon, 1971); Dorn, "Origins of the 'Dropout Problem'"; Cervantes, *The Dropout*; Thomas Sugrue, "The Impoverished Politics of Poverty," *Yale Journal of Law & the Humanities* 6, no. 1 (1994): 163–79; Daniel Patrick Moynihan, *The Negro Family: The Case for National Action* (Washington, DC: Office of Policy Planning and Research, U.S. Department of Labor, March 1965); Elizabeth Hinton, *From the War on Poverty to the War on Crime: The Making of Mass Incarceration in America* (Cambridge, MA: Harvard University Press, 2016).
10. Nathan Thornburgh, "Dropout Nation," *Time*, April 9, 2006.
11. Robert Balfanz, Jennifer DePaoli, Matthew Atwell, and John Bridgeland, *Great American High School Campaign: Reforming the Nation's Remaining Low-Performing High Schools* (Civic Enterprises and Everyone Graduates Center at Johns Hopkins University, October 2018).

12. Ruth Curran Neild and Robert Balfanz, *Unfulfilled Promise: The Dimensions and Characteristics of Philadelphia's Dropout Crisis, 2000–2005* (Philadelphia Youth Network, Johns Hopkins University, and University of Pennsylvania, 2006).

13. Dale Mezzacappa, "How Philadelphia Kept More Kids in School," *Washington Monthly*, July/August 2010; Michael Norton, Eva Gold, and Renata Peralta, *Year One Report on Philadelphia's Accelerated High Schools* (Philadelphia: Research for Action, August 2012); Public Citizens for Children and Youth, *How Does Access to Childcare Affect High School Completion in Philadelphia's Multiple Pathways to Graduation Programs?* (April 2014).

14. Associated Press, "New Philly Mayor: 'We Are Taking' Back City," January 7, 2008.

15. Hanley Chiang and Brian Gill, *Student Characteristics and Outcomes in Alternative and Neighborhood High Schools in Philadelphia* (Cambridge, MA: Mathematica Policy Research, April 14, 2010).

16. Nikhil Goyal, *Schools on Trial: How Freedom and Creativity Can Fix Our Educational Malpractice* (New York: Doubleday, 2016); Nikhil Goyal, "Noam Chomsky for Secretary of Education: Bernie Sanders Needs to Make This Revolutionary Call for Our Public Schools," *Salon*, February 28, 2016; Ron Miller, *Free Schools, Free People: Education and Democracy After the 1960s* (Albany: State University of New York Press, 2002), 46; A. S. Neill, *Summerhill: A Radical Approach to Child Rearing* (New York: Hart, 1960); Paul Goodman, *Compulsory Mis-Education and the Community of Scholars* (New York: Vintage, 1964); Allen Graubard, *Free the Children: Racial Reform and the Free School Movement* (New York: Pantheon, 1972); Jonathan Kozol, *Free Schools* (Boston: Houghton Mifflin, 1972).

17. Mary Anne Raywid, "The First Decade of Public Alternatives," *Phi Delta Kappa* 62, no. 8 (1981): 551–54.

18. Deirdre M. Kelly, *Last Chance High: How Girls and Boys Drop In and Out of Alternative School* (New Haven, CT: Yale University Press, 1993), 68.

19. National Center for Education Statistics, *Public Elementary/Secondary School Universe Survey, 1990–91 through 2014–15* (Washington, DC: U.S. Department of Education, 2016).

20. Priscilla Rouse Carver, Laurie Lewis, and Peter Tice, *Alternative Schools and Programs for Public School Students at Risk of Educational Failure: 2007–08* (Washington, DC: National Center for Education Statistics, U.S. Department of Education, 2010).

21. Robert Pennick King, *A Digest of the Laws and Ordinances, Relating to the City of Philadelphia, in Force on the Twelfth Day of December, A.D. 1868* (Philadelphia: King & Baird, 1869); J. Thomas Scharf and Thompson Westcott, *History of Philadelphia 1609–1884*, vol. 3 (Philadelphia: L. H. Everts, 1884); Kenneth W. Milano, *Remembering Kensington and Fishtown: Philadelphia's Riverward Neighborhoods* (Charleston, SC: History Press, 2008); Mark Reinberger and Elizabeth McLean, "Isaac Norris's Fairhill: Architecture, Landscape, and Quaker Ideals in a Philadelphia Colonial Country Seat," *Winterthur*

Portfolio 32, no. 4 (1997): 243–74; Jamie Catrambone and Harry C. Silcox, eds, *Kensington History: Stories and Memories* (Philadelphia: Brighton Press, 1996); Library Company of Philadelphia, "The Norris Family and Their Networks"; Natalie Kempner, "Norris Square Becomes Escandalo," Philadelphia Horticultural Society's 1994 Philadelphia Flower Show; Norris Square Neighborhood Project documents: https://ubir.buffalo.edu/xmlui/bitstream /handle/10477/35661/2003-Norris-Square-Neighborhood.pdf?sequence=2 &isAllowed=y.

22. Steven J. Peitzman, "Kensington Hospital for Women," Nomination of Historic Building, Structure, Site, or Object, Philadelphia Register of Historic Places, Philadelphia Historical Commission, June 28, 2019; Inga Saffron, "Once, Every Philly Neighborhood Had a Hospital. Just One Independent Survives," *Philadelphia Inquirer*, March 25, 2020.

23. Milano, *Hidden History of Kensington and Fishtown*.

24. Inga Saffron, "Where the Home Meets the Street," *Philadelphia Inquirer*, February 25, 1994.

25. Neeta Fogg and Paul Harrington, *The Human Capital Deficit of Disconnected Youth in Philadelphia* (Philadelphia: Center for Labor Markets and Policy, Drexel University, 2015).

26. Goyal, "These Politicians Think Your Kids Need High-Stakes Testing—but Not Theirs"; Tom Little and Katherine Ellison, *Loving Learning: How Progressive Education Can Save America's Schools* (New York: W. W. Norton, 2015); Alfie Kohn, "Progressive Education: Why It's Hard to Beat, But Also Hard to Find," *Independent School* (Spring 2008).

27. Chiang and Gill, *Student Characteristics and Outcomes in Alternative and Neighborhood High Schools in Philadelphia*.

CHAPTER EIGHT: NOT MY GOVERNMENT NAME

1. Michelle Fine, *Framing Dropouts: Notes on the Politics of an Urban Public High School* (Albany: State University of New York Press, 1991), 8; Youth United for Change, *Pushed Out: Youth Voices on the Dropout Crisis in Philadelphia* (2011); Wendy Harris, "Dropped Out? No, Pushed Out," *Philadelphia Public School Notebook*, March 31, 2010; Monique W. Morris, *Pushout: The Criminalization of Black Girls in Schools* (New York: The New Press, 2015); Dignity in Schools Campaign, "National Resolution for Ending School Pushout," December 3, 2009.

2. Pierre Bourdieu, *Outline of a Theory of Practice* (Cambridge: Cambridge University Press, 1977).

3. Elijah Anderson, "The White Space," *Sociology of Race and Ethnicity* 1, no. 1 (2015): 10–21.

4. Michael Norton, Eva Gold, and Renata Peralta, *Year One Report on Philadelphia's Accelerated High Schools* (Philadelphia: Research for Action, August 2012); Martha Woodall, "To Save $25 Million, Philly District to Close 13

Schools for At-Risk Students," *Philadelphia Inquirer*, May 21, 2011; Dale Mezzacappa, "District Plans Five Regional Centers in Place of Accelerated Schools," *Philadelphia Public School Notebook*, May 23, 2011.

5. Dale Mezzacappa, "District to Close Accelerated Schools," *Philadelphia Public School Notebook*, May 20, 2011; Martha Woodall, "Council Urged to Increase District's Funding," *Philadelphia Inquirer*, May 25, 2011; West Philly Local, "Proposed Budget Eliminates Full-Day Kindergarten, Thousands of Jobs, Dozens of Programs," April 28, 2011; Kristen A. Graham, "Accelerated Schools' Future Still a Hot Philly Topic," *Philadelphia Inquirer*, June 16, 2011.

6. JoAnn Loviglio, "Air Conditioner Leak Floods Philadelphia's City Hall," Associated Press, April 1, 2002; Carl E. Doebley, "Philadelphia City Council Chamber," Nomination of Public Interior Portion of Building or Structure, Philadelphia Register of Historic Places, Philadelphia Historical Society, 2010; Materials Conservation, "Council Chambers: Philadelphia City Hall, Philadelphia, PA."

7. Alia Conley, "Students Rally to Save Accelerated Schools," *Philadelphia Inquirer*, June 15, 2011; Jeniffer Valdez, "Rally to Save Accelerated Schools," *Philadelphia Public School Notebook*, June 16, 2011.

8. WHYY, "Soda Tax Dies Again, but City Hall Delivers $53 Million for Schools," June 17, 2011; Dale Mezzacappa, "Students Key in Saving Accelerated Schools, Officials Say," *Philadelphia Public School Notebook*, June 22, 2011; Kristen A. Graham, "Schools Still $35 Million Short," *Philadelphia Inquirer*, June 30, 2011.

CHAPTER NINE: PRAY THE GAY AWAY

1. United States Department of the Interior, "Philadelphia Public Schools Thematic Resources," National Register of Historic Places Inventory—Nomination Form, December 4, 1986; J. M. Moak, "Russell H. Conwell School," Pennsylvania Historic Resource Survey Form, Office of Historic Preservation, June 19, 1987.

2. Food Research and Action Center, *Food Hardship in America 2010: Households With and Without Children* (August 2011); Alfred Lubrano, "Phila.-Area District 2d-Hungriest in U.S., Study Says," *Philadelphia Inquirer*, January 26, 2010.

3. Michael Harrington, *The Other America: Poverty in the United States* (New York: Macmillan, 1962).

CHAPTER TEN: HOW DO YOU FEEL BOUT ME BEING PREGO?

1. School District of Philadelphia, *S569001; Hunter (Old): Final Site Assessment Report* (February 1, 2017).

2. School District of Philadelphia, *Three-Year Re-Inspection 2015–2016 and Asbestos Management Plan for the Big Picture High School: El Centro de Estudiantes* (November 2015).

3. Nicolas Esposito, "A Neighborhood Son Takes on the 'White Elephant,'" *Hidden City Philadelphia*, January 15, 2013; Michael Bixler, "Breathing Life Back into Bromley," *Hidden City Philadelphia*, September 5, 2014.

CHAPTER ELEVEN: SAVE OUR SCHOOLS

1. Philadelphia Student Union, "Student Apocalypse: A Brainless Future," January 2013; Charlotte Pope, "Students Protest School Closings as Zombie Flash Mob," *Philadelphia Public School Notebook*, January 16, 2013; Kristen Graham, "Zombies Dance to Protest School Closings," *Philadelphia Inquirer*, January 15, 2013; Media Mobilizing Project, "School Closings—A 'Zombie Apocalypse' in the Making," YouTube, February 13, 2013.

2. Boston Consulting Group, *Transforming Philadelphia's Public Schools* (2012); "Hite Releases School-Closing Plan," *Philadelphia Public School Notebook*, December 13, 2012; Kristen A. Graham, "Philadelphia Superintendent Identifies Schools He Intends to Close," *Philadelphia Inquirer*, December 14, 2012; Jon Hurdle, "Philadelphia School District Plans to Close Dozens of Schools," *New York Times*, December 30, 2012.

3. Philadelphia Coalition Advocating for Public Schools, *The Philadelphia Community Education Plan: Excellent Schools for All Children* (2012); Jake Blumgart, "In the Schools of Philadelphia," *American Prospect*, January 29, 2013.

4. Philadelphia Student Union, "Student Apocalypse."

5. Boston Consulting Group, *Transforming Philadelphia's Public Schools*; Benjamin Herold, "Behind the Scenes, Boston Consulting Group Has Been a Driving Force on Labor Talks, School Closings, and Charters," *Philadelphia Public School Notebook*, July 9, 2012; J. Puckett and Allison Bailey, "Statement of Work: Phase III of School District of Philadelphia Transformation," Letter to Jeremy Nowak, April 30, 2012; Dale Mezzacappa, "Foundation Still Raising Funds," *Philadelphia Public School Notebook*, June 6, 2012; Editorial Board, "Schools Study Shouldn't Collect Dust," *Philadelphia Inquirer*, August 8, 2012.

6. Daniel Denvir, "Money Talks," *Philadelphia City Paper*, July 5, 2012; Dale Mezzacappa, "Community Implores SRC to Fight for More Money," *Philadelphia Public School Notebook*, February 16, 2012; Dale Mezzacappa, "Churches Criticize Transformation Plan," *Philadelphia Public School Notebook*, April 30, 2012; Dale Mezzacappa, "Q+A with William Penn's Jeremy Nowak on Transformation Plan," *Philadelphia Public School Notebook*, May 31, 2012; Benjamin Herold, "From Community and Labor Leaders, Skepticism over BCG," *Philadelphia Public School Notebook*, June 6, 2012; Benjamin Herold, "BCG Documents Show Far-Reaching Proposal to Overhaul District," *Philadelphia Public School Notebook*, June 7, 2012; Herold, "Behind the Scenes, Boston Consulting Group Has Been a Driving Force on Labor Talks, School Closings, and Charters"; Benjamin Herold, "$139 Million: Cost of Charter Expansion So Far," *Philadelphia Public School Notebook*, July 13, 2012; Benjamin Herold, "William

Penn Foundation Bankrolling $160,000 Communications Campaign for District," *Philadelphia Public School Notebook*, July 24, 2012; Christina A. Samuels, "Critics Target Growing Army of Broad Leaders," *Education Week*, June 7, 2011.

7. Kristina Rizga, "Black Teachers Matter," *Mother Jones*, September/October 2016; Jon Hurdle, "Art Show Captures the Wrenching Effects of Closing a School," *New York Times*, August 28, 2015.

8. School District of Philadelphia, "PSSA & Keystone Performance: SY 2011–2012" (2012).

9. Kenneth W. Milano, *Remembering Kensington and Fishtown: Philadelphia's Riverward Neighborhoods* (Charleston, SC: History Press, 2008).

10. 6abc Action News, "Changes Announced to Philadelphia School Closures List," February 19, 2013.

11. Broad Foundation, *School Closure Guide: Closing Schools as a Means for Addressing Budgetary Challenges* (2009).

12. Julie Mazziotta, "Most Students from Closing Schools Would Move to Schools of Similar Caliber," *Philadelphia Public School Notebook*, February 26, 2013.

13. School District of Philadelphia, "PSSA & Keystone Performance."

14. AFTHQ, "Philadelphia SRC Shutters Schools amid Public Outcry," YouTube, March 8, 2013.

15. Tom MacDonald, "Philadelphia Council Calls for Moratorium on School Closings," *Philadelphia Public School Notebook*, January 25, 2013.

16. Benjamin Herold, "SRC Votes to Close 23 Schools, Spares 4," *Philadelphia Public School Notebook*, March 8, 2013; Bill Hangley Jr., "Protesting . . . Mostly in Vain," *Philadelphia Public School Notebook*, March 8, 2013; Jon Hurdle, "Philadelphia Officials Vote to Close 23 Schools," *New York Times*, March 7, 2013; Kristen A. Graham and Martha Woodall, "SRC Votes to Close 23 Schools, Spare Four," *Philadelphia Inquirer*, March 8, 2013; Motoko Rich and Jon Hurdle, "Rational Decisions and Heartbreak on School Closings," *New York Times*, March 8, 2013.

17. Bill Hangley Jr., "Beeber Taken off Closing List; District to Study Alternative Proposal," *Philadelphia Public School Notebook*, April 16, 2013; Bill Hangley Jr., "SRC Votes to Close M. H. Stanton, Create Cyber School," *Philadelphia Public School Notebook*, April 19, 2013.

18. "Thousands of Students Are Marching on City Hall Protesting Budget Cuts," *Philadelphia Public School Notebook*, May 17, 2013.

19. Christopher Moraff, "'Tranq Dope'—The Heroin Combo That's Been Putting Philly to Sleep," *Filter*, April 2, 2019.

20. Dale Mezzacappa, "SRC Listens to Pleas from Students, but Approves Stripped-Down Budget," *Philadelphia Public School Notebook*, May 30, 2013; Martha Woodall and Melissa Chea-Annan, "Phila. SRC Approves Doomsday School Budget," *Philadelphia Inquirer*, May 30, 2013; Martha Woodall, "More than

3,700 School Employees Are Being Laid Off," *Philadelphia Inquirer*, June 7, 2013; Trip Gabriel, "Budget Cuts Reach Bone for Philadelphia Schools," *New York Times*, June 16, 2013; Jesse Montgomery, "On Philly Schools," *n+1*, September 11, 2013.

21. "More Parents Join Hunger Strike for Philly Schools," NBC10 Philadelphia, June 21, 2013; Dale Mezzacappa and Holly Otterbein, "Corbett Plan for Philly Schools Falls Short of $180 Million, Relies Mostly on City Dollars," *Philadelphia Public School Notebook*, June 30, 2013; "Corbett Plan Finds Philly Schools Roughly $127M in New Funding," WHYY, July 1, 2013; NBC10 Philadelphia, "Corbett Says $140M Deal Will Bail Out Philly Schools," July 3, 2013.

22. Frank Griffiths, "Puerto Rican Town Faces Economic Downturn," *Washington Post*, September 5, 2004.

23. Amy Yeboah, *Goodbye to City Schools: Fairhill Elementary School*, 2016; Rizga, "Black Teachers Matter."

24. Mark McHugh, "Fairhill Graduates Its Final Class," *Philadelphia Public School Notebook*, June 22, 2013.

CHAPTER THIRTEEN: *ABOMBAO*

1. GLSEN, *Educational Exclusion: Drop Out, Push Out, and the School-to-Prison Pipeline among LGBTQ Youth* (2016).

2. Youth United for Change, "YUC Leader Giancarlos Speaks at City Council President Clark Office for Full & Fair Funding," YouTube, September 6, 2013; Daniel Denvir, "Welcome to Comcast Country," *New York Times*, April 23, 2014.

3. Regina Medina, "Philly Schools Open Today with Less Staff," *Philadelphia Inquirer*, September 9, 2013; Rick Lyman and Mary Williams Walsh, "Philadelphia Borrows So Its Schools Open on Time," *New York Times*, August 15, 2013; Hilary Russ, "Philadelphia to Borrow $50 Mln for On-Time School Opening," Reuters, August 15, 2013.

4. Jane Rath and Travis Alderson, "Champion for Change," *High Performing Buildings*, Winter 2013, 6–18; Inga Saffron, "Changing Skyline: Philadelphia Learns a Lesson in School Design," *Philadelphia Inquirer*, September 17, 2010.

5. Daniel Denvir, "He Says His Daughter Might be Alive if Not for School-Nurse Cuts," *Philadelphia City Paper*, October 10, 2013; Denisa R. Superville and Evie Blad, "Philadelphia Tragedy Highlights Role of School Nurses," *Education Week*, June 2, 2014; Pew Charitable Trusts, *Philadelphia 2013: The State of the City* (2013); Valerie Strauss, "Girl Dies After Getting Sick at School Without Nurse," *Washington Post*, October 12, 2013; Rebecca Klein, "Philadelphia School Nurse Shortage Causing 'Crisis,' Says Documentarian," *Huffington Post*, January 17, 2014.

6. Vince Lattanzio, "Gov. Corbett to Release $45M in Funding for Philadelphia Schools," NBC10 Philadelphia, October 16, 2013; "Philly State Lawmakers to Corbett: Give Extra Money to Schools Now," WHYY, August 9, 2013; Trymaine Lee, "Gov. Tom Corbett to Release $45 Million to Philly Schools," MSNBC, October 16, 2013.

7. Matthew Albasi and Max Pulcini, *Rise of the Tigers*, Downhill Productions, 2013; see the following *Philadelphia Neighborhoods* articles: "Kensington: A Football Team Inspires the Players and the Community," "Kensington: Rise of the Kensington Tigers Football Team," "Kensington: Football and Dreams of Friday Night Lights Under the El," "Kensington: The Kensington Multiplex of High Schools Grapple with Budget Cuts," "Kensington: The Families of Kensington Football," "Kensington: Members of the Team Look Toward Their Futures."

8. Kathleen Cotton, "School Size, School Climate, and Student Performance," *School Improvement Research Series*, May 1996; Research for Action, *Going Small: Progress & Challenges of Philadelphia's Small High Schools* (July 2009).

9. "Two Student Groups Formulate Vision of Small Schools," *Philadelphia Public School Notebook*, March 10, 2004; Joanna Klonsky, "Youth United for Change Takes on Philadelphia's Public Schools," *What Kids Can Do*, April 1, 2007; Beandra Davis, "Photo Essay: Student Group Impressed by Visit to Small Schools in New York," *Philadelphia Public School Notebook*, December 10, 2004.

10. "Win for Student Group in Small-Schools Effort," *Philadelphia Public School Notebook*, November 24, 2005.

11. Sara McAlister, Kavitha Mediratta, and Seema Shah, *Keeping Parent and Student Voices at the Forefront of Change* (Providence, RI: Annenberg Institute for School Reform at Brown University, September 2009).

12. Kristen A. Graham, "Teacher-Prep High School to Open in Kensington," *Philadelphia Inquirer*, November 19, 2009; Laura Benshoff, "In Kensington, Concerns and 'Nuanced' Case for Merging Two Low-Performing Public Schools," WHYY, July 21, 2015.

13. Ron Whitehorne, "The Case Against Closing Kensington Urban Education Academy," *Philadelphia Public School Notebook*, April 15, 2015.

14. William Crosby, Antonia George, Ashley Hatch, Rahdia Robinson, and Terrese Thomas, *Writing to Be Heard: Building Respectful Communities: Kensington Students Examine Adult-Student Relationships in Their New Small Schools* (Philadelphia: Research for Action, November 2006).

15. Youth United for Change and Advancement Project, *Zero Tolerance in Philadelphia: Denying Educational Opportunities and Creating a Pathway to Prison* (2011); Amanda Scanlon, *School Discipline, Law Enforcement, and Student Outcomes* (PhD diss., University of Pennsylvania, 2016).

16. Philadelphia Student Union, "Campaign for Nonviolent Schools"; Michele Aweeky, "Campaign for Nonviolent Schools Mobilizes Support for New Platform," *Philadelphia Public School Notebook*, April 1, 2011.

17. Philebrity, "Students, Parents, Teachers to Protest School District's Strict Discipline Code," July 18, 2012.

18. Scanlon, *School Discipline, Law Enforcement, and Student Outcomes*; Philadelphia Student Union, "Campaign for Nonviolent Schools"; Kristen A. Graham, "New Code of Conduct in Philadelphia Schools Gives Principals More Leeway," *Philadelphia Inquirer*, August 17, 2012; Dale Mezzacappa, "SRC Adopts Revised Student Code of Conduct," *Philadelphia Public School Notebook*, August 17, 2012.

19. Jonathan Simon, *Governing Through Crime: How the War on Crime Transformed American Democracy and Created a Culture of Fear* (New York: Oxford University Press, 2007); Victor M. Rios, *Punished: Policing the Lives of Black and Latino Boys* (New York: New York University Press, 2011).

CHAPTER FOURTEEN: THIS IS SOME GROWN MAN SHIT

1. Drug Enforcement Administration, *The Heroin Signature Program and Heroin Domestic Monitor Program 2014 Reports* (September 2016).

2. Jennifer Percy, "Trapped by the 'Walmart of Heroin,'" *New York Times Magazine*, October 10, 2018.

3. Elliot Liebow, *Tally's Corner: A Study of Negro Streetcorner Men* (Boston: Little, Brown, 1967); Stephen Steinberg, "Poor Reason: Culture Still Doesn't Explain Poverty," *Boston Review*, January 13, 2011.

4. Pew Charitable Trusts, *Philadelphia's Crowded, Costly Jails*; Justin Wolfers, David Leonhardt, and Kevin Quealy, "1.5 Million Missing Black Men," *New York Times*, April 20, 2015; Maura Ewing, "A Reckoning in Philadelphia," *Atlantic*, March 3, 2016.

5. Loïc Wacquant, "From Slavery to Mass Incarceration: Rethinking the 'Race Question' in the US," *New Left Review* 13 (January–February 2002): 41–60.

CHAPTER FIFTEEN: SUNBEAM, FLU-FLU, JU-JU

1. Mehmet Oz, "Inside Ground Zero of the Heroin Epidemic in Philadelphia," *The Dr. Oz Show*, April 18, 2017; George Karandinos, Laurie Kain Hart, Fernando Montero Castrillo, and Philippe Bourgois, "The Moral Economy of Violence in the US Inner City," *Current Anthropology* 55, no. 1 (2014): 1–22; Alfred Lubrano, "The Drugs Dilemma," *Philadelphia Inquirer*, December 11, 2010; Alfred Lubrano, "A Struggle to Make an Honest Living," *Philadelphia Inquirer*, December 29, 2010; Kate Kilpatrick, "On Drug-Infested North Philly Corners, Hope and Good Luck Come in Bags," *Al Jazeera*, February 17, 2016; Sharon Christner and Jack Hostager, "Philadelphia's Opioid Crisis," *Penn Political Review*, August 30, 2017; Jennifer Percy, "Trapped by the 'Walmart of Heroin,'" *New York Times Magazine*, October 10, 2018; Courtenay Harris Bond, "Another Day in

Kensington," *Medium*, December 20, 2017; Alfred Lubrano, "How Kensington Got to Be the Center of Philly's Opioid Crisis," *Philadelphia Inquirer*, January 23, 2018; Alfred Lubrano, "Camp Heroin: Fairhill's 'El Campamento,' Where the Drugs Make the Rules," *Philadelphia Inquirer*, November 12, 2016.

2. Stephanie Farr and Sam Wood, "A Hidden Hellscape," *Philadelphia Inquirer*, February 19, 2017.

3. Farr and Wood, "A Hidden Hellscape."

4. Mike Newall, "At Heroin Encampment, Time to Stop Talking and Start Cleaning," *Philadelphia Inquirer*, April 7, 2017; Chris Palmer and Don Sapatkin, "'A Big Step': Cleanup of Gurney Street Heroin Camp Begins," *Philadelphia Inquirer*, July 31, 2017.

5. Larry Eichel and Meagan Pharis, "Philadelphia's Drug Overdose Death Rate Among Highest in Nation," Pew Charitable Trusts, February 15, 2018.

6. Centers for Disease Control and Prevention, "Synthetic Opioid Overdose Data"; Philadelphia Department of Public Health, "Fatal Drug Overdoses in Philadelphia, 2017," *CHART* 3, no. 1 (April 2018): 1–4.

7. Marianne Rose Spencer et al., "Drug Overdose Deaths Involving Fentanyl, 2011–2016," *National Vital Statistics Reports* 68, no. 3 (2019): 1–18.

8. Alex W. Palmer, "The China Connection: How One D.E.A. Agent Cracked a Global Fentanyl Ring," *New York Times Magazine*, October 16, 2019.

9. Marco Werman, "How the Deadly Drug Fentanyl Is Making Its Way to the US," *World*, July 19, 2019; Scott Higham, "The Flow of Fentanyl: In the Mail, Over the Border," *Washington Post*, August 23, 2019.

10. Isaiah Thompson and Anthony Campisi, "The Wasteland: A Neglected Railroad Has Become a Neighborhood Nightmare," *Philadelphia City Paper*, March 10, 2011.

11. Joel Gunter, "As an Open-Air Heroin Camp Is Closed, Options Narrow," *BBC News*, July 21, 2017; Palmer and Sapatkin, "'A Big Step'"; Vince Lattanzio, "Cleanup of 'The Tracks,' Infamous Philly Heroin Hotbed, Begins," NBC10 Philadelphia, July 31, 2017; Chris Palmer, "'It's Gone Now': Gurney Street Heroin Camps Mostly Cleaned Up," *Philadelphia Inquirer*, September 1, 2017; City of Philadelphia, "City Completes Kensington Avenue Cleanup, Announces Next Cleanup," November 2, 2018.

12. Stephen Metraux et al., *An Evaluation of the City of Philadelphia's Kensington Encampment Resolution Pilot* (Philadelphia: University of Pennsylvania, March 5, 2019); Percy, "Trapped by the 'Walmart of Heroin.'"

13. Philadelphia Police Department, "Crime Maps & Stats."

14. Larry Eichel and Octavia Howell, "Philadelphia's Drug-Related Homicides Continue to Rise," Pew Charitable Trusts, September 28, 2017.

15. Philadelphia Police Department, *Annual Murder and Shooting Victim Report: 2016*.

16. Dan Werb et al., "Effect of Drug Law Enforcement on Drug Market Violence: A Systematic Review," *International Journal for Drug Policy* 22, no. 2 (2011):

87–94; Johann Hari, *Chasing the Scream: The First and Last Days of the War on Drugs* (New York: Bloomsbury, 2015), chapters 5 and 6; Dan McQuade, "How Drug Busts in Kensington Could Make Things Even Worse," *Philadelphia Magazine*, December 21, 2016.

17. Leo Beletsky and Jeremiah Goulka, "The Federal Agency That Fuels the Opioid Crisis," *New York Times*, September 17, 2018.
18. Chris Palmer, "How One Man's Case Shines a Light on Kensington Drug Trade," *Philadelphia Inquirer*, July 21, 2017.
19. Jill Leovy, *Ghettoside: A True Story of Murder in America* (New York: Spiegel & Grau, 2015).
20. CBS Philadelphia, "Crime Without Punishment: Homicide Clearance Rates Are Dropping in Philadelphia as Murder Rates Skyrocket," June 29, 2022; Joshua Vaughn, "Philly Cops Are Solving Fewer Homicides. The City Keeps Paying Them Millions," *Appeal*, March 1, 2021.
21. Vincent Schiraldi, *The Pennsylvania Community Corrections Story* (New York: Columbia University Justice Lab, April 25, 2018); Samantha Melamed and Dylan Purcell, "The Probation Trap: Lenient Sentences in Pennsylvania Often Have Harsh Consequences," *Philadelphia Inquirer*, October 24, 2019; Samantha Melamed, "How Philly, the Nation's Most Supervised Big City, Cut Its Probation Numbers by a Third," *Philadelphia Inquirer*, April 19, 2021.
22. Kur, "Heaven or Hell," YouTube, January 11, 2014.

CHAPTER SIXTEEN: I AM NOT A NUMBER

1. School District of Philadelphia, "2016–2017 Code of Student Conduct."
2. Pennsylvania Department of Education, "Keystone Project Based Assessments."
3. Kathy Boccella, "Some Phila. Students Opt Out of Keystone Exams," *Philadelphia Inquirer*, May 13, 2015.
4. Caucus of Working Educators, "KCAPA Keystone Walk Out," May 13, 2015.
5. Stephanie Simon, "'White Moms' Remark Fuels Clash," *Politico*, November 18, 2013; Casey Quinlan, "The Whitewashing of the Opt-Out Movement," *ThinkProgress*, April 11, 2016.
6. Caucus of Working Educators, "KCAPA Keystone Walk Out."
7. Rick Smith Show, "#OptOut Walkout: Philadelphia Student Organizer Explains Why He and His Classmates Walked Out of High Stakes Keystone Exams," May 13, 2015.
8. Rick Smith Show, "#OptOut Walkout."
9. Lara Akinbami, "Asthma Prevalence, Health Care Use and Mortality: United States, 2003–05," Centers for Disease Control and Prevention.
10. Child Welfare Policy and Practice Group, *Evaluation of the Improving Outcomes for Children Transformation in the Child Welfare System in Philadelphia* (2017); Education Law Center, "Improving Outcomes for Children (IOC) Evaluation Comments," September 13, 2017.

11. "Woman Jailed over Truancy Fines Found Dead in Cell," CBS News, June 13, 2014; Education Law Center, "Education Law Center Statement on Truancy Legislation: HB1907," October 28, 2016; Pennsylvania General Assembly, "Act 138," 2016; Kathy Boccella, "Under Improved Truancy Law, Pa. Parents Still Face Jail and Even Higher Fines," *Philadelphia Inquirer*, November 13, 2016; Greg Windle, "State Truancy Law Amended to Improve Attendance, Prevent Jail Time for Parents," *Philadelphia Public School Notebook*, October 7, 2017; Education Law Center, "When Must a Child Attend School? Compulsory School Age and Pennsylvania Truancy Laws," August 2019; Dana Goldstein, "Inexcusable Absences," *New Republic*, March 6, 2015.

12. Joanne W. Golann, "The Paradox of Success at a No-Excuses School," *Sociology of Education* 88, no. 2 (2015): 103–19; Joanne W. Golann, *Scripting the Moves: Culture and Control in a "No-Excuses" Charter School* (Princeton, NJ: Princeton University Press, 2021).

13. Kathleen Nolan, *Police in the Hallways: Discipline in an Urban High School* (Minneapolis: University of Minnesota Press, 2011), 157; Michel Foucault, *Discipline and Punish: The Birth of the Prison* (New York: Vintage, 1995); Tina (A.C.) Besley, "Governmentality of Youth: Managing Risky Subjects," *Policy Futures in Education* 8, no. 5 (2010): 528–47.

14. United States Census Bureau, "American Housing Survey," 2019; Michael Sellner and Jordan Wicht, "Residents of 14 Million Housing Units Reported Seeing Roaches, 14.8 Million Saw Rodents in Last 12 Months," United States Census Bureau, April 21, 2021.

CHAPTER SEVENTEEN: OG BOBBY JOHNSON

1. United States Department of Education, *The State of Racial Diversity in the Educator Workforce* (Washington, DC: Department of Education, 2016).

2. Seth Gershenson, Cassandra M. D. Hart, Joshua Hyman, Constance Lindsay, and Nicholas W. Papageorge, *The Long-Run Impacts of Same-Race Teachers* (Bonn, Germany: IZA–Institute of Labor Economics, March 2017).

3. Chris Palmer, "Two Shot in Kensington—One Fatally," *Philadelphia Inquirer*, February 4, 2016.

CHAPTER EIGHTEEN: HE IS A MIRACLE

1. Philadelphia Neighborhoods, "Fairhill: Hannah House Helps Incarcerated Women Back onto Their Feet," February 17, 2011; Dana DiFilippo, "LGBTQ Home for Hope Riding 'Wall of Love' Momentum Toward Funding Goals," WHYY, September 15, 2016; Natalie Hope McDonald, "Gay, Trans and Homeless: Inside Philly's LGBTQ Home for Hope," *PhillyVoice*, March 16, 2017; Thomas H. Keels, *Philadelphia Graveyards and Cemeteries* (Mount Pleasant, SC: Arcadia Publishing, 2003).

2. Some names have been changed to account for pseudonyms.

CHAPTER NINETEEN: ANOTHER BOY IN A BOX

1. Ricki Sablove, "St. Michael's Lutheran Church, 2139 East Cumberland Street, Philadelphia, Philadelphia County, PA," *Historic American Buildings Survey* (Washington, DC: National Park Service, U.S. Department of the Interior).

2. "Teen Found Shot in the Head, Police Investigate Shooting," CBS Philadelphia, November 7, 2016; Julie Shaw, "Police: Man Who Intervenes in Kensington Fight Gets Assaulted, Then Shoots Teen," *Philadelphia Inquirer*, November 8, 2016; Jason Fagone, "What Bullets Do to Bodies," *Huffington Post*, April 26, 2017; Elizabeth Van Brocklin, "Philly Police Are Saving Lives by Taking Shooting Victims to the Hospital Without Waiting for Paramedics," *Slate*, November 14, 2018.

3. *New York Times* Editorial Board, "Cory Booker," January 13, 2020.

4. Philadelphia Police Department, "Crime Maps & Stats."

5. Henry George, "The Crime of Poverty: An Address Delivered in the Opera House" (speech, Burlington, Iowa, April 1, 1885).

6. Philadelphia Police Department, *Annual Murder and Shooting Victim Report: 2016* (July 20, 2017).

7. Douglas S. Massey, "Getting Away with Murder: Segregation and Violent Crime in Urban America," *University of Pennsylvania Law Review* 143, no. 5 (1995): 1203–32; Douglas S. Massey and Jonathan Tannen, "A Research Note on Trends in Black Hypersegregation," *Demography* 52, no. 3 (2015): 1025–34.

8. Christopher Dornblaser, "Woman Gets Prison in Bensalem Robbery, Killing," *Bucks County Courier Times*, December 20, 2019.

9. "Police ID Germantown Homicide Victim," 6abc Action News, July 6, 2017.

10. Jenice Armstrong, "Almost out of Harm's Way, Philly Streets Got Him," *Philadelphia Inquirer*, August 5, 2017.

11. Chris Palmer, "'Half of Me Is Gone': A Month On, a Mother Mourns Two Sons Murdered in East Mount Airy," *Philadelphia Inquirer*, March 16, 2017.

12. Paul Dix and Pamela Fitzpatrick, *Nicaragua: Surviving the Legacy of U.S. Policy* (Eugene, OR: Just Sharing Press, 2011), 50–57; Goshen College, "Field Trip to Matagalpa and Esteli: Saturday, June 1," June 10, 2013.

CHAPTER TWENTY: MARCH FOR OUR LIVES

1. Larry Krasner, "On the Issues," Krasner for District Attorney; Alan Feuer, "He Sued Police 75 Times. Democrats Want Him as Philadelphia's Top Prosecutor," *New York Times*, June 17, 2017.

2. Larry Krasner, "New Policies Announced February 15, 2018," Philadelphia District Attorney's Office, March 13, 2018.

3. Claire Sasko, "DA Krasner Will Drop Cash Bail for Most Non-Violent Crimes," *Philadelphia Magazine*, February 21, 2018.

4. Joe Trinacria, "Krasner's First 100 Days: DA Says Social Reform More Effective than Prison in Preventing Crime," *Philadelphia Magazine*, April 16, 2018.

5. Jake Blumgart, "The Brutal Legacy of Frank Rizzo, the Most Notorious Cop in Philadelphia History," *VICE*, October 22, 2015; Tina Rosenberg, "The Deadliest D.A.," *New York Times Magazine*, July 16, 1995; Ed Pilkington, "America's Deadliest Prosecutors: Five Lawyers, 440 Death Sentences," *Guardian*, June 30, 2016; Jennifer Gonnerman, "Larry Krasner's Campaign to End Mass Incarceration," *New Yorker*, October 22, 2018; Ben Austen, "In Philadelphia, a Progressive D.A. Tests the Power—and Learns the Limits—of His Office," *New York Times Magazine*, October 30, 2018.

6. Lincoln Anthony Blades, "Black Teens Have Been Fighting for Gun Reform for Years," *Teen Vogue*, February 23, 2018.

7. John Wagner and Jenna Johnson, "'We Have to Harden Our Schools': Trump Makes Arming Teachers His Top Safety Goal," *Washington Post*, February 22, 2018; United States Department of Justice, "Attorney General Sessions Announces New Actions to Improve School Safety and Better Enforce Existing Gun Laws," March 12, 2018; Evie Blad, "Trump, Biden Both Have Backed School Police. Will Protests Make That a Campaign Issue?" *Education Week*, June 14, 2020.

8. William R. Hite, "Letter to Families on March 14 Nationwide Walkout," School District of Philadelphia, March 8, 2018; Joseph A. Gambardello, "National School Walkout Recap: Scenes from Student Protests in and around Philadelphia," *Philadelphia Inquirer*, March 14, 2018.

9. Natalie Kempner, "Norris Square Becomes Escandalo," Pennsylvania Horticultural Society's 1994 Philadelphia Flower Show; Catalina Jaramillo, "As Norris Square Changes, Las Parcelas Puts Down New Roots," WHYY, June 2, 2017; Laura Lawson, *City Bountiful: A Century of Community Gardening in America* (Berkeley: University of California Press: 2005), 253–57; Sharon P. Simson and Martha C. Straus, *Horticulture as Therapy: Principles and Practice* (Binghamton, NY: Food Products Press, 1998), 389–93; Norris Square Neighborhood Project, "Our Gardens"; Norris Square Neighborhood Project, "Map of Greene Countrie Towne."

10. Mike Kuetemeyer and Anula Shetty, *Las Parcelas* (Philadelphia: Norris Square Neighborhood Project with Scribe Video Center, 2005); Mike Kuetemeyer and Anula Shetty, *Villa African Colobó* (Philadelphia: Norris Square Neighborhood Project with Scribe Video Center, 2006); Norris Square Neighborhood Project, "Our Gardens"; Michael Nairn and Dominec Vitiello, "Lush Lots: Everyday Urban Agriculture," *Harvard Design Magazine* 2, no. 31 (Fall/Winter 2009/2010); Hilary Jay, "Mi Casita: A Vibrant Playhouse Tells a Story of Puerto Rico," *Philadelphia Inquirer*, April 26, 1998; Kempner, "Norris Square Becomes Escandalo."

CONCLUSION

1. Alux, "15 Things Poor People Do That the Rich Don't," YouTube, June 18, 2017.

2. Henry George, "The Crime of Poverty: An Address Delivered in the Opera House" (speech, Burlington, Iowa, April 1, 1885).

3. Johan Galtung, "Violence, Peace, and Peace Research," *Journal of Peace Research* 6, no. 3 (1969): 167–91; Paul Farmer, "On Suffering and Structural Violence: A View from Below," *Race/Ethnicity: Multidisciplinary Global Contexts* 3, no. 1 (2009): 11–28; Paul Farmer, *Pathologies of Power: Health, Human Rights, and the New War on the Poor* (Berkeley: University of California Press, 2003), 50.

4. Raj Chetty, Nathaniel Hendren, Patrick Kline, and Emmanuel Saez, "Where Is the Land of Opportunity: The Geography of Intergenerational Mobility in the United States," *Quarterly Journal of Economics* 129, no. 4 (2014): 1553–1623.

5. Paul Willis, *Learning to Labour: How Working Class Kids Get Working Class Jobs* (Farnborough, UK: Saxon House, 1977).

6. Orlando Patterson, *Slavery and Social Death: A Comparative Study* (Cambridge, MA: Harvard University Press, 1982); Ta-Nehisi Coates, *Between the World and Me* (New York: Spiegel & Grau, 2015); Édouard Louis, *The End of Eddy: A Novel*, trans. Michael Lucey (New York: Farrar, Straus & Giroux, 2017); Édouard Louis, *Who Killed My Father*, trans. Lorin Stein (New York: New Directions, 2019); Pauline Bock, "'Macron Should Be Punished': Edouard Louis on Poverty, Violence, and the Gilets Jaunes," *New Statesman*, February 20, 2019; Erving Goffman, *Stigma: Notes on the Management of Spoiled Identity* (New York: Simon & Schuster, 1963); W. E. B. Du Bois, *The Souls of Black Folk* (Chicago: A. C. McClurg, 1903); Giorgio Agamben, *Homo Sacer: Sovereign Power and Bare Life* (Stanford, CA: Stanford University Press, 1998); Loïc Wacquant, *Urban Outcasts: A Comparative Sociology of Advanced Marginality* (Cambridge: Polity, 2008).

7. Nikhil Pal Singh, *Race and America's Long War* (Oakland: University of California Press, 2017), 109; Achille Mbembe, *Necropolitics* (Durham, NC: Duke University Press, 2019); Michel Foucault, *"Society Must Be Defended": Lectures at the Collège de France, 1975–1976*, eds. Mauro Bertani and Alessandro Fontana (New York: Picador, 2003); Ruth Wilson Gilmore, *Golden Gulag: Prisons, Surplus, Crisis, and Opposition in Globalizing California* (Berkeley: University of California Press, 2007); João Biehl, *Vita: Life in a Zone of Social Abandonment* (Berkeley: University of California Press, 2005); Gøsta Esping-Andersen, *The Three Worlds of Welfare Capitalism* (Princeton, NJ: Princeton University Press, 1990); Jedediah Purdy, *This Land Is Our Land: The Struggle for a New Commonwealth* (Princeton, NJ: Princeton University Press, 2019); Chris Hedges, *Death of the Liberal Class* (New York: Nation Books, 2010).

8. Karl Polanyi, *The Great Transformation: Economic and Political Origins of Our Time* (New York: Farrar and Rinehart, 1944).

9. Keeanga-Yamahtta Taylor, "Reality Has Endorsed Bernie Sanders," *New Yorker*,

March 30, 2020; Keeanga-Yamahtta Taylor, "The Black Plague," *New Yorker*, April 16, 2020; Keeanga-Yamahtta Taylor, "How Do We Change America?" *New Yorker*, June 8, 2020; Zadie Smith, "The American Exception," *New Yorker*, April 10, 2020; Pankaj Mishra, "Flailing States," *London Review of Books* 42, no. 14 (July 16, 2020).

10. Sophie Collyer, David Harris, and Christopher Wimer, "Left Behind: The One-Third of Children," *Poverty and Social Policy Brief* 3, no. 6 (May 13, 2019); Jason DeParle, "The Tax Break for Children, Except the Ones Who Need It Most," *New York Times*, December 16, 2019; Nikhil Goyal, "How Biden Can Transform Kids' Lives: A Child Allowance Would Lift Children Out of Poverty by the Millions," *New York Daily News*, February 12, 2021.

11. Daniel J. Perez-Lopez, "Household Pulse Survey Collected Responses Just Before and Just After the Arrival of the First CTC Checks," United States Census Bureau, August 11, 2021; Claire Zippel, "After Child Tax Credit Payments Begin, Many More Families Have Enough to Eat," Center on Budget and Policy Priorities, August 30, 2021; Zachary Parolin, Sophie Collyer, and Megan A. Curran, "Sixth Child Tax Credit Payment Kept 3.7 Million Children out of Poverty in December," *Poverty and Social Policy Brief* 6, no. 1 (January 18, 2022); Tara Golshan and Arthur Delaney, "Joe Manchin Privately Told Colleagues Parents Use Child Tax Credit Money on Drugs," *Huffington Post*, December 20, 2021.

12. Zachary Parolin, Sophie Collyer, and Megan A. Curran, "Absence of Monthly Child Tax Credit Leads to 3.7 Million More Children in Poverty in January 2022," *Poverty and Social Policy Brief* 6, no. 2 (February 17, 2022); Katherine G. Giefer, "Households with Children That Struggled to Cover Household Expenses Were at Least Twice as Likely to Rely on CTC," United States Census Bureau, February 28, 2022.

13. Greg Duncan and Suzanne Le Menestrel, eds., *A Roadmap to Reducing Child Poverty* (Washington, DC: National Academies of Sciences, Engineering, and Medicine, 2019).

14. Clio Chang, "Why Democrats Must Embrace a Universal Child Allowance," *New Republic*, March 21, 2016; Dylan Matthews, "Child Poverty in the US Is a Disgrace. Experts Are Embracing This Simple Plan to Cut It," *Vox*, April 27, 2017; H. Luke Shaefer et al., "A Universal Child Allowance: A Plan to Reduce Poverty and Income Instability Among Children in the United States," *RSF: The Russell Sage Foundation Journal of the Social Sciences* 4, no. 2 (2018): 22–42; Duncan and Le Menestrel, *A Roadmap to Reducing Child Poverty*; Jeff Madrick, *Invisible Americans: The Tragic Cost of Child Poverty* (New York: Knopf, 2020); Jason DeParle, "How to Fix Child Poverty," *New York Review of Books*, July 23, 2020; Jason DeParle, "The Coronavirus Generation," *New York Times*, August 22, 2020; People's Policy Project, "Family Fun Pack."

15. Randall K. Q. Akee et al., "Parents' Incomes and Children's Outcomes: A Quasi-Experiment," *American Economic Journal: Applied Economics* 2, no. 1 (2010):

86–115; Anna Aizer et al., "The Long-Run Impact of Cash Transfers to Poor Families," *American Economic Review* 106, no. 4 (2016): 935–71; E. Jane Costello et al., "Relationships between Poverty and Psychopathology: A Natural Experiment," *JAMA* 290, no. 15 (2003): 2023–29.

16. Amartya Sen, *Development as Freedom* (New York: Knopf, 1999), 87–90; Martha Nussbaum, *Creating Capabilities: The Human Development Approach* (Cambridge, MA: Harvard University Press, 2011).

17. Michael B. Katz, *Class, Bureaucracy, and Schools: The Illusion of Educational Change in America* (New York: Praeger, 1971); Christopher Jencks et al., *Inequality: A Reassessment of the Effect of Family and Schooling in America* (New York: Basic Books, 1972); Samuel Bowles and Herbert Gintis, *Schooling in Capitalist America: Educational Reform and the Contradictions of Economic Life* (London: Routledge & Kegan Paul, 1976); Paul Willis, *Learning to Labour: How Working Class Kids Get Working Class Jobs* (Farnborough, UK: Saxon House, 1977); Harold Silver and Pamela Silver, *An Educational War on Poverty: American and British Policy-making 1960–1980* (Cambridge: Cambridge University Press, 1991); John Marsh, *Class Dismissed: Why We Cannot Teach or Learn Our Way out of Inequality* (New York: New York University Press, 2011).

18. Franklin Delano Roosevelt, "State of the Union Address" (speech, Washington, D.C., January 11, 1944); Bernie Sanders, "Speech at George Washington University" (speech, Washington, D.C., June 12, 2019); Tony Judt, *Ill Fares the Land* (New York: Penguin Press, 2010); William H. B. Beveridge, *Social Insurance and Allied Services: Report by Sir William Beveridge* (London: Her Majesty's Stationery Office, 1942); T. H. Marshall, *Citizenship and Social Class and Other Essays* (Cambridge: Cambridge University Press, 1950); Esping-Andersen, *The Three Worlds of Welfare Capitalism*; A. Philip Randolph and Bayard Rustin, *A "Freedom Budget" for All Americans: A Summary* (New York: A. Philip Randolph Institute, 1967); Lane Kenworthy, *Social Democratic America* (New York: Oxford University Press, 2014); Sylvie Laurent, *King and the Other America: The Poor People's Campaign and the Quest for Economic Equality* (Oakland: University of California Press, 2018); Thomas Piketty, *Capital and Ideology*, trans. Arthur Goldhammer (Cambridge, MA: Belknap Press of Harvard University Press, 2020).

19. White House, "The Build Back Better Framework: President Biden's Plan to Rebuild the Middle Class," October 28, 2021; Jonathan Weisman, "From Cradle to Grave, Democrats Move to Expand Social Safety Net," *New York Times*, September 6, 2021.

20. U.S. Congress, House, Inflation Reduction Act of 2022, H.R. 5376, 117th Congress, 2nd session, introduced in the House on August 12, 2022; Emily Cochrane and Lisa Friedman, "What's in the Climate, Tax and Health Care Package," *New York Times*, August 7, 2022.

21. Paul Krugman, Twitter post, August 7, 2022.

22. Polanyi, *The Great Transformation: Economic and Political Origins of Our Time.*
23. Franklin Delano Roosevelt, "Fireside Chat" (speech, Washington, D.C., April 14, 1938); Bernie Sanders, "Speech at George Washington University" (speech, Washington, D.C., June 12, 2019); Zachary D. Carter, *The Price of Peace: Money, Democracy, and the Life of John Maynard Keynes* (New York: Random House, 2020), 296; Gene Sperling, *Economic Dignity* (New York: Penguin Press, 2020); Robert Kuttner, *Going Big: FDR's Legacy, Biden's New Deal, and the Struggle to Save Democracy* (New York: The New Press, 2022); Josh Zeitz, "The Speech That Set Off the Debate About America's Role in the World," *Politico*, December 29, 2015.
24. Langston Hughes, "Let America Be America Again," *Esquire*, July 1936.

INDEX

ABOUT THE AUTHOR

NIKHIL GOYAL is a sociologist and policymaker who served as senior policy advisor on education and children for Chairman Senator Bernie Sanders on the U.S. Senate Committee on Health, Education, Labor and Pensions and on the Committee on the Budget. He developed education, child care, and child tax credit federal legislation as well as a tuition-free college program for incarcerated people and correctional workers in Vermont. He has appeared on CNN, Fox, and MSNBC and written for the *New York Times*, the *Washington Post*, the *Wall Street Journal*, *Time,* the *Nation*, and other publications. Goyal earned his BA at Goddard College and his MPhil and PhD at the University of Cambridge. He lives in Vermont.